ORTE UNTER EINFLUSS
AFFECTED PLACES

CLEMENS VON WEDEMEYER

HAMBURGER
KUNSTHALLE

SPECTOR BOOKS
LEIPZIG

SCREEN 9

DATA BANK 53

CHURCH, PRISON, MUSEUM 93

BACKSTAGE 141

ORTE UNTER EINFLUSS
VORWORT

Clemens von Wedemeyer zählt zu den herausragenden Film- und Videokünstlern der Gegenwart. In seinen experimentellen Filmen befragt er das Kino als Institution, beschäftigt sich mit der Wahrnehmung des Betrachters und seinem Verhältnis zum konstruierten wie dekonstruierten Raum im Film. Seine Arbeiten bewegen sich zwischen Dokumentation und Spielfilm, Realität und Fiktion. Dabei reflektiert der Berliner Filmemacher vor allem die verschiedenen Ebenen des Kinos als Denk-, Projektions- und Produktionsraum und ihre Verflechtungen. Von Wedemeyers Geschichten entwickeln sich um vorgefundene Situationen und Orte, Strukturen und Systeme, die mit diesen verbunden sind. So impliziert der Titel der vorliegenden Publikation bewusst auch die Facette von Macht und Einflussnahme auf bestimmte Orte und ihre Geschichte. Es sind Orte, die, wie der Literaturwissenschaftler Michail Bachtin es formuliert hat, immer auch „chronotopisch", das heißt raumzeitlich geprägt sind. Schauplätze, die räumlich, zeitlich oder inhaltlich weit voneinander entfernt scheinen, werden in von Wedemeyers Arbeiten verwoben und gehen ineinander über. Damit einher geht die Frage nach der Verortung des Betrachters. Sind wir nur Zuschauer oder Teil der Aufführung? Kinoleinwand wie Theaterbühne bilden eine „Vierte Wand", die von Wedemeyer zum Teil aufbricht und einen Zwischenraum öffnet. Die Leinwand ist in seinen Installationen daher nicht nur eine Projektionsfläche, sie wird auch zur Membran – der Naht zwischen Aufführung und den Orten der Produktion. Beispielhaft dafür ist sein Beitrag zur dOCUMENTA (13), die 3-Kanal-Videoinstallation *Muster* (2012), mit der Clemens von Wedemeyer international bekannt wurde. Darin wird die wechselhafte Geschichte des bei Kassel gelegenen Benediktinerklosters Breitenau aufgegriffen. In der Arbeit hat der Künstler die verschiedenen historischen Nutzungen des Gebäudes als Kloster, Gefängnis, Konzentrationslager und schließlich Erziehungsheim für Mädchen auf drei Projektionsflächen im Dreieck angeordnet. Die Zeitreise verläuft nicht linear, sondern ineinander verschränkt als Parallelisierung unterschiedlicher Zeitebenen.

Die Ausstellung sowie das Buch konzentrieren sich auf diese *Orte unter Einfluss* und bieten, aufgeteilt in vier Themenbereiche, erstmals einen tieferen Einblick in das weit gefasste Werk des Künstlers. In diesen vier Kapiteln (1. *Screen*, 2. *Data Bank*, 3. *Church, Prison, Museum* und 4. *Backstage*) hinterfragt von Wedemeyer zeitliche Bedingungen, räumliche Konstruktionen und gesellschaftliche Bedeutungen von Orten und ihren Heterotopien und stellt, wie etwa in *Sun Cinema* (2010), grundsätzliche Fragen an das Kino. In Anspielung an die klassische Filmeinstellung des Point-of-View-Shot, durch den der Zuschauer unmittelbar in die Handlung eingebunden wird, lotet er dagegen in seiner neuesten Arbeit *Against the Point of View* (2016) alternative Lösungen zur subjektiven Kamera durch Simulation im digitalen Computerspiel aus. Sein Spiel mit Ort und Zeit zieht sich bis in die Ausstellungsräume hinein, in denen Making-ofs, Entwürfe und Dokumentationen wie Interventionen in die Präsentationen eingefügt sind. Die vorliegende Publikation nimmt das Prinzip des Making-of auf und vereint im Stil eines Filmskripts neben neuen Essays und unveröffentlichten Texten, Interviews, Installationsansichten sowie Filme des Künstlers aus den letzten fünfzehn Jahren. Die umfangreichen, den vier Kapiteln thematisch zugeordneten Bildstrecken erschließen mithilfe von Assoziationsketten Beziehungen zwischen einzelnen Arbeiten. Analytisch legt von Wedemeyer in diesen Bildessays wiederkehrende Motive in seinem Werk frei. Trotz der heterogenen Ästhetiken macht er damit auf genuine Weise sein beständiges Interesse für Zustände zwischen Orten, Dingen und Zeiten sichtbar. Das Kino als selbstreflexive Blickmaschine wird so als dieses instruktive Dazwischen vorgeführt.

Die Ausstellung *Clemens von Wedemeyer. Orte unter Einfluss / Affected Places* ist die erste Einzelausstellung des Künstlers in einem deutschen Museum. Unser ganz besonderer Dank gilt Clemens von Wedemeyer, der unserer Einladung zur Ausstellung mit großem Enthusiasmus gefolgt ist. Die Ausstellung schließt damit zugleich an eine Reihe von Ausstellungen in der Hamburger Kunsthalle an, die auf unterschiedliche Weise Orte und ihre Geschichte thematisieren, wie die

Ausstellung *Thomas Demand. Camera* (2008)
oder *Lost Places. Orte der Photographie* (2012).
Für die Unterstützung bei der umfangreichen
Planung und Vorbereitung der Ausstellung danken wir besonders Lukas Hoffmann und Marisa
Baptista vom Atelier Clemens von Wedemeyer
sowie Mechthild Achelwilm und Tobias Boner für
ihren großartigen Einsatz bei der Planung des
Projekts in der Hamburger Kunsthalle. Dem Team
um Gunther Maria Kolck sowie den Kolleginnen
und Kollegen sei für ihre Hilfe bei Aufbau und
Realisierung der Ausstellung gedankt. Gefördert
wurde die Ausstellung durch die Stiftung Kunstfonds und aus dem Ausstellungsfonds der Freien
und Hansestadt Hamburg. Beiden danken wir
herzlich für ihre Unterstützung. Den Galerien
Jocelyn Wolff in Paris und KOW in Berlin danken
wir für die gute und inspirierende Zusammenarbeit bei den Vorbereitungen zur Ausstellung,
ebenso der Collection Antoine de Galbert, Paris,
für ihre großzügige Leihgabe. Nicht zuletzt gilt
unser großer Dank den Autoren des Katalogs sowie dem Verlag Spector Books in Leipzig für
die engagierte Mitarbeit an diesem außergewöhn-
lichen Ausstellungsprojekt.

Hubertus Gaßner
Direktor

Petra Roettig
Leitung Sammlung Kunst der Gegenwart

AFFECTED PLACES FOREWORD

Clemens von Wedemeyer is considered one of the most outstanding film and video artists of his time. In his experimental films he explores the cinema as an institution, focusing on the viewers' perception and their relationship to both constructed and deconstructed space in films. His work ranges between documentaries and feature films, reality and fiction. The Berlin filmmaker primarily views the various cinematic levels as a space for thought, projection and production and as an interface of those elements. Von Wedemeyer's stories evolve around existing interconnected situations and places, structures and systems. In that sense, the title of the present publication consciously implies the aspect of power and the exertion of influence on diverse locations and their particular history. As the literary scholar Mikhail Bakhtin put it, the places are always "chronotopical", locations defined by space and time. Settings which seem to be far apart in terms of space, time and content are interwoven in von Wedemeyer's works and linked, a process which goes hand-in-hand with the viewers' context. Are we only viewers, or are we part of the performance? Von Wedemeyer pries open the "fourth wall" created by the projection screen or the stage, revealing an interspace. So the screen in his works is not only a projection screen, it is also a membrane—the seam between the performance and the places of production. This is perfectly exemplified in his contribution to the dOCUMENTA (13), the 3-channel video installation *Rushes* (2012) which paved the way for Clemens von Wedemeyer's international renown. In it, von Wedemeyer seizes on the unsettling history of Breitenau, the Benedictine monastery near Kassel, Germany, arranging the building's various functions (as a prison, a concentration camp and, finally, a reformatory for girls) on three projection screens in the form of a triangle. However this journey through time does not run in a straight line, it is intertwined as a parallelisation of contradicting levels of time.

Both the exhibition and the book devote themselves to these *Affected Places* and, for the first time, offer an in-depth look at the artist's extensive work—divided into four topics. In those four chapters (1. *Screen*, 2. *Data Bank*, 3. *Church, Prison, Museum* and 4. *Backstage*) von Wedemeyer scrutinises the time-related conditions, the spatial constructions and the social significance of places and their heterotopias and raises fundamental questions about the cinema, for instance with *Sun Cinema* (2010). In reference to the classical POV shot, that instantly draws viewers into the action, von Wedemeyer explores alternatives for a subjective camera in his latest artwork *Against the Point of View* (2016) by using computer game-like simulations. His technique of playing with place and time is extended into the exhibition rooms where the making-ofs, the concepts and the documentations intervene in the presentations. The present publication picks up the principle of a making-of and combines it in the fashion of a screenplay with new essays and unpublished texts, interviews and reviews of installations, as well as the artist's films from the past 15 years. The comprehensive pictorial essays, which are thematically arranged according to the four chapters, access the relationships between individual images by relying on the power of association. Von Wedemeyer analytically exposes recurring motifs in his pictorial essays. And despite the heterogenic aesthetics, he genuinely reveals his never-ending interest in the conditions linking places, things and time. The cinema, this self-reflexive viewing machine, is presented as an instructive intermediate realm.

The exhibition *Clemens von Wedemeyer. Orte unter Einfluss / Affected Places* is the first solo exhibition of the artist in a German museum, so we would particularly like to thank Clemens von Wedemeyer who accepted our invitation to exhibit his works with the utmost enthusiasm. At the same time, the exhibition is part of a series of exhibitions at the Hamburger Kunsthalle which deals with places and their history, such as the exhibition *Thomas Demand. Camera* (2008) or *Lost Places. Sites of Photography* (2012).

We are especially grateful to Lukas Hoffmann and Marisa Baptista from the atelier of Clemens von Wedemeyer as well as Mechthild Achelwilm and Tobias Boner for the extraordinary commitment they showed while planning the project

in the Hamburger Kunsthalle. We also wish to
thank Gunther Maria Kolck and his team as well
as the colleagues of the Hamburger Kunsthalle
for their assistance in helping to organise this
exhibition and realise it. The exhibition was kindly
supported by the Stiftung Kunstfonds and the
Exhibition Fund of Ministry of Culture, Hamburg.
We are extremely grateful to both institutions
for their support. Furthermore, we wish to thank
the Jocelyn Wolff Gallery in Paris and KOW in
Berlin for their inspirational cooperation. We also
extend our thanks to the Antoine de Galbert
Collection, Paris, for generously sending works
on loan. And, last but not least, we wish to
thank the authors of the catalogue as well as the
publishing house Spector Books in Leipzig
for their dedication to this remarkable project.

Hubertus Gaßner
Director

Petra Roettig
Head of Collection Contemporary Art

SCREEN

INDEX

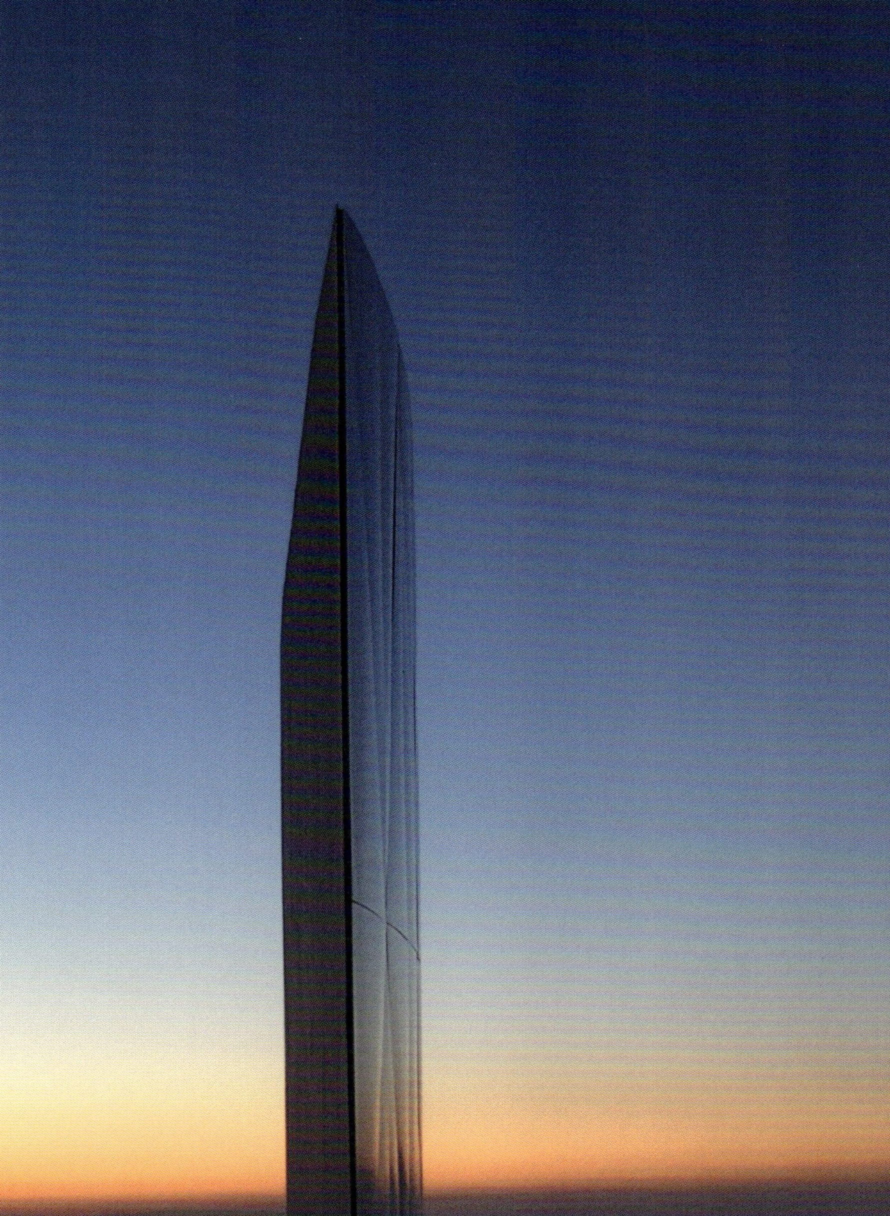

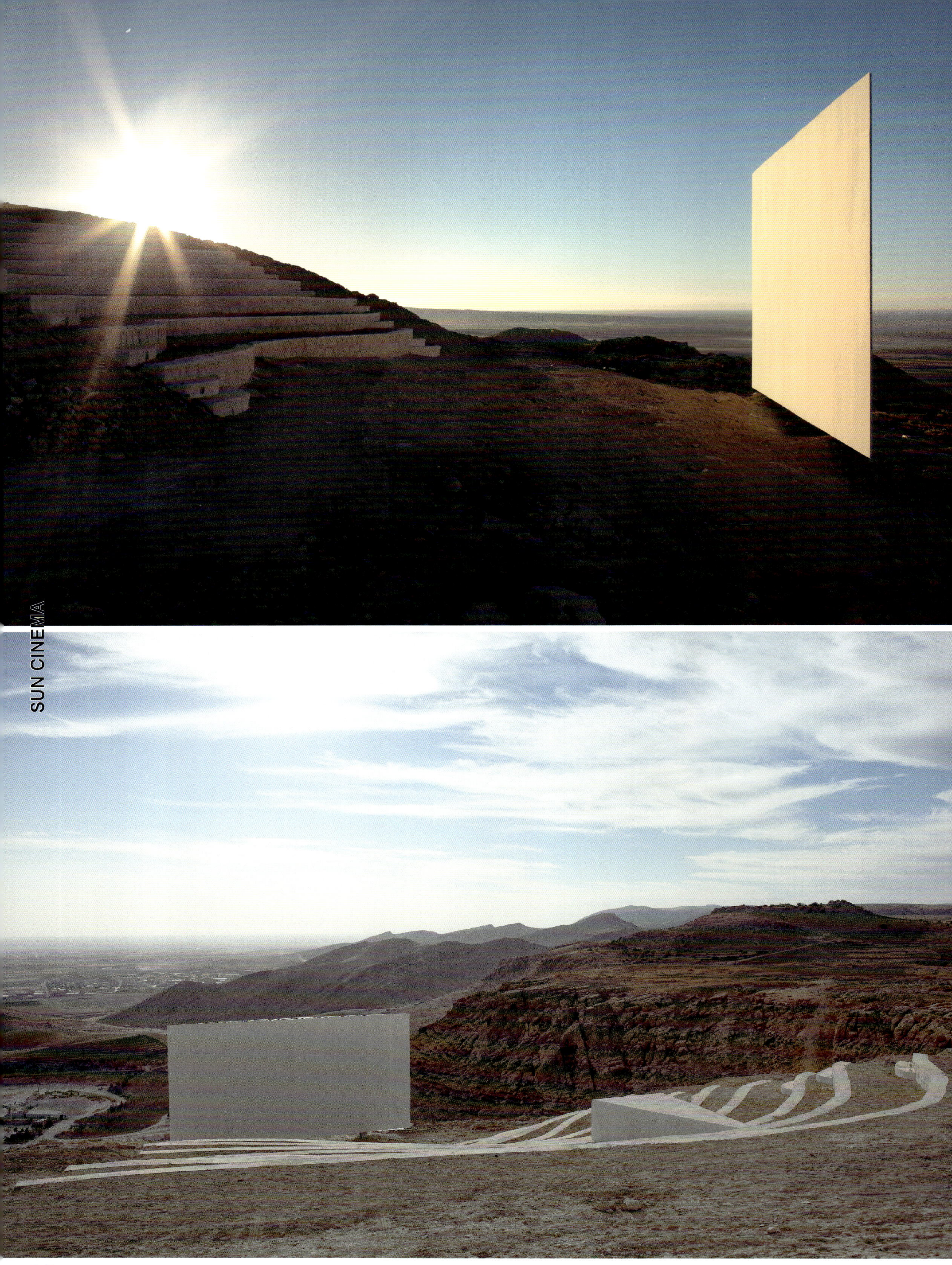
SUN CINEMA

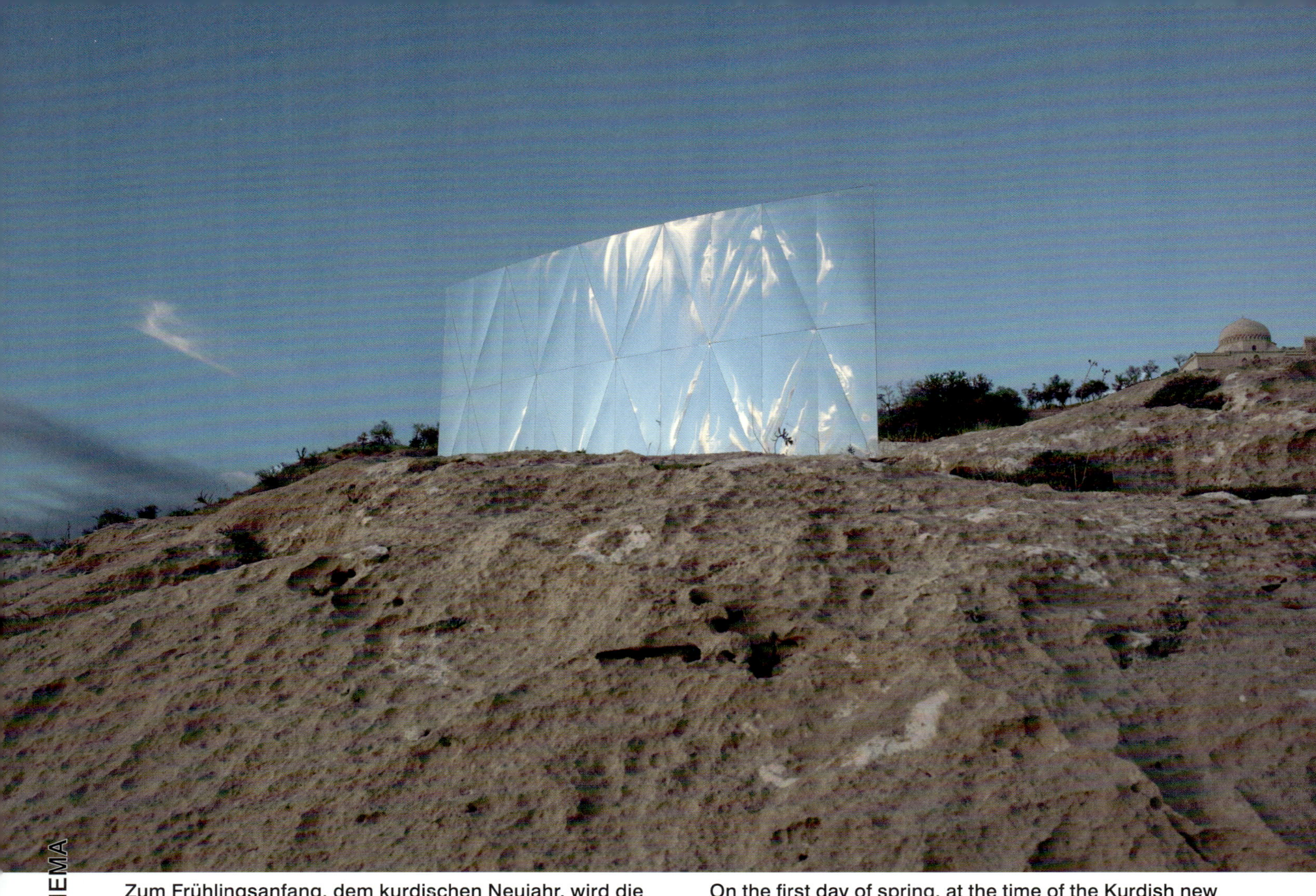

Zum Frühlingsanfang, dem kurdischen Neujahr, wird die Sonne bei Sonnenuntergang nach Süden in die mesopotamische Ebene reflektiert. Im Spiegel auf der Rückseite kann man sich selbst in der Landschaft betrachten.

On the first day of spring, at the time of the Kurdish new year, the sunset is reflected south onto the Mesopotamian plain. The mirror on the backside also allows the viewers to see themselves in the landscape.

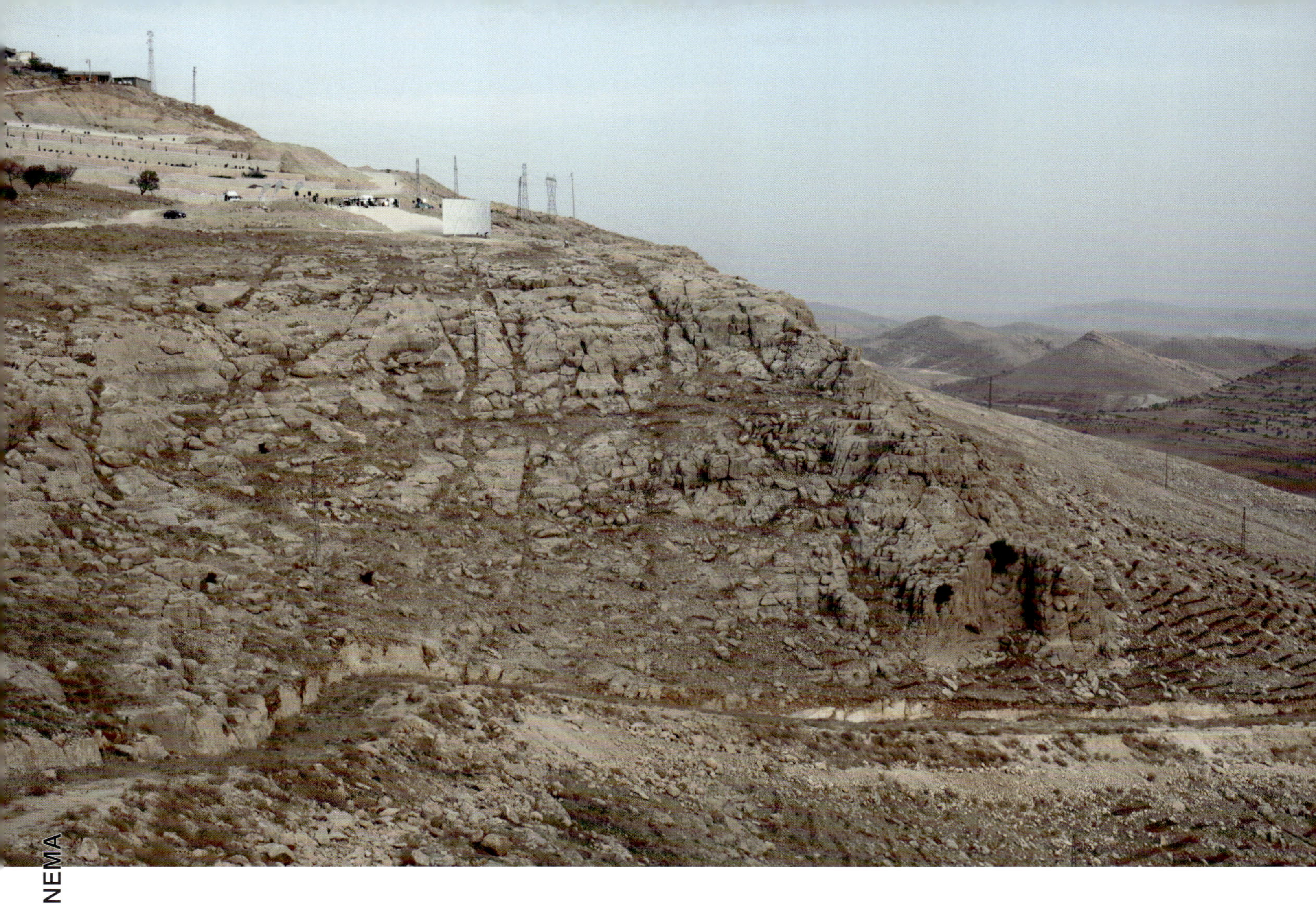
SUN CINEMA

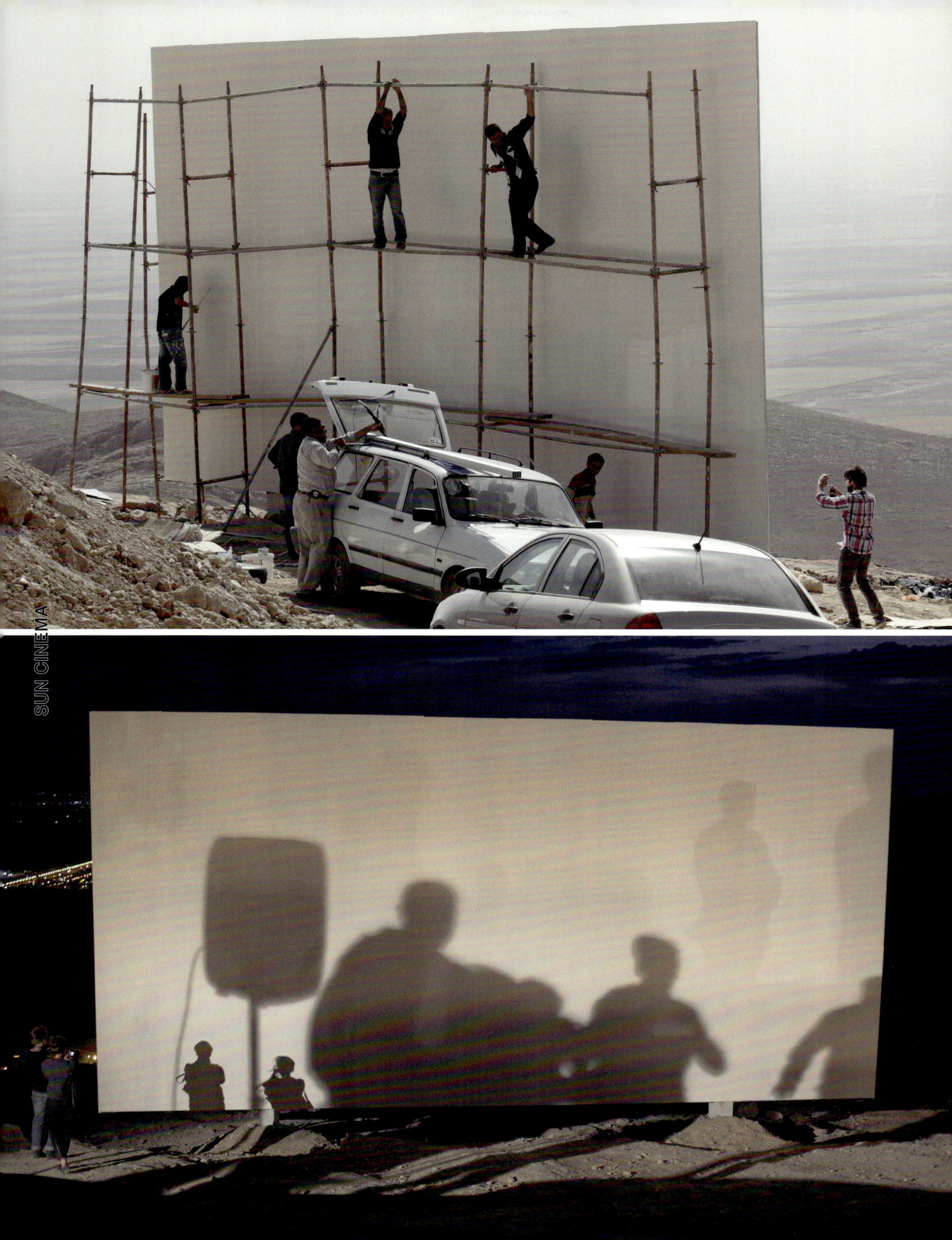
SUN CINEMA

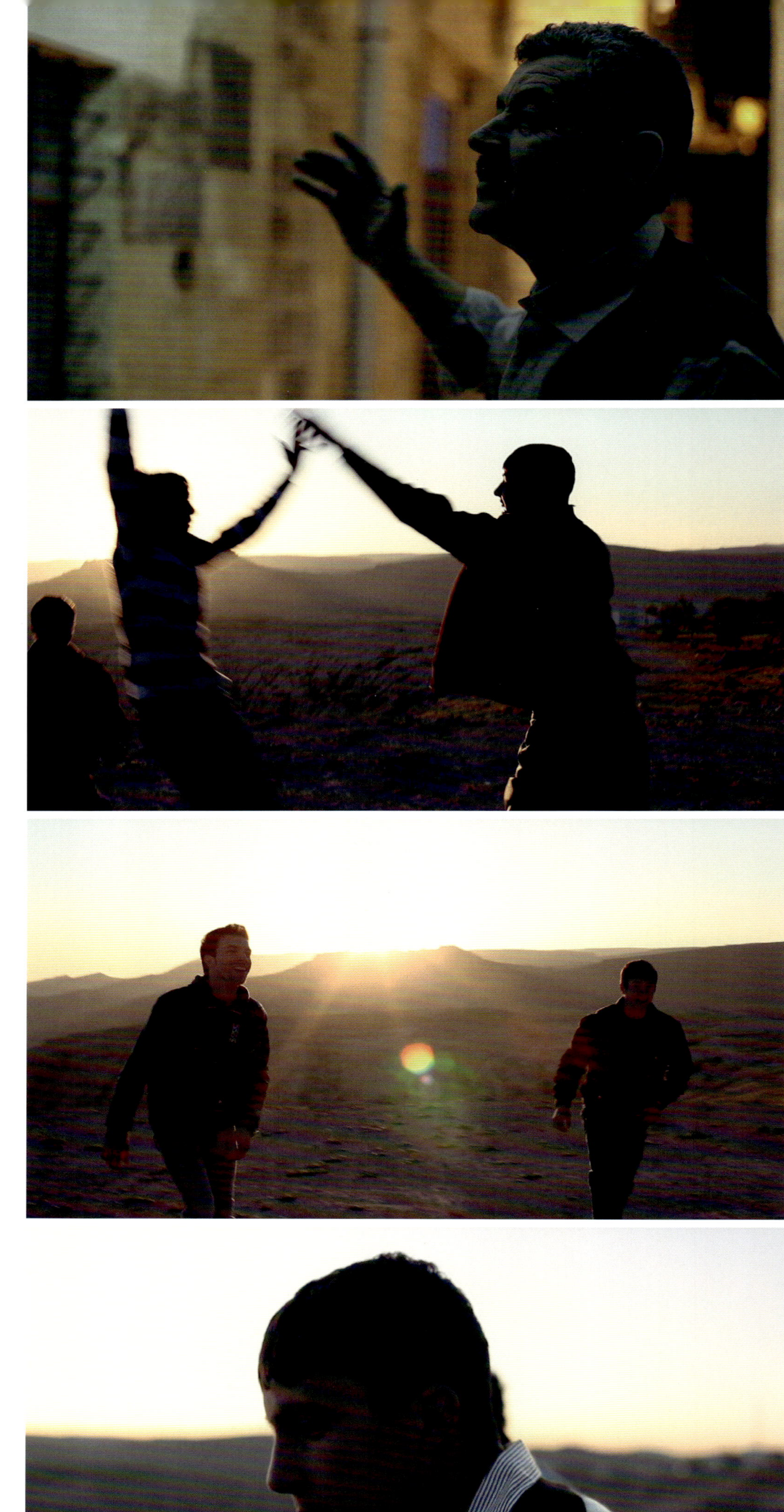

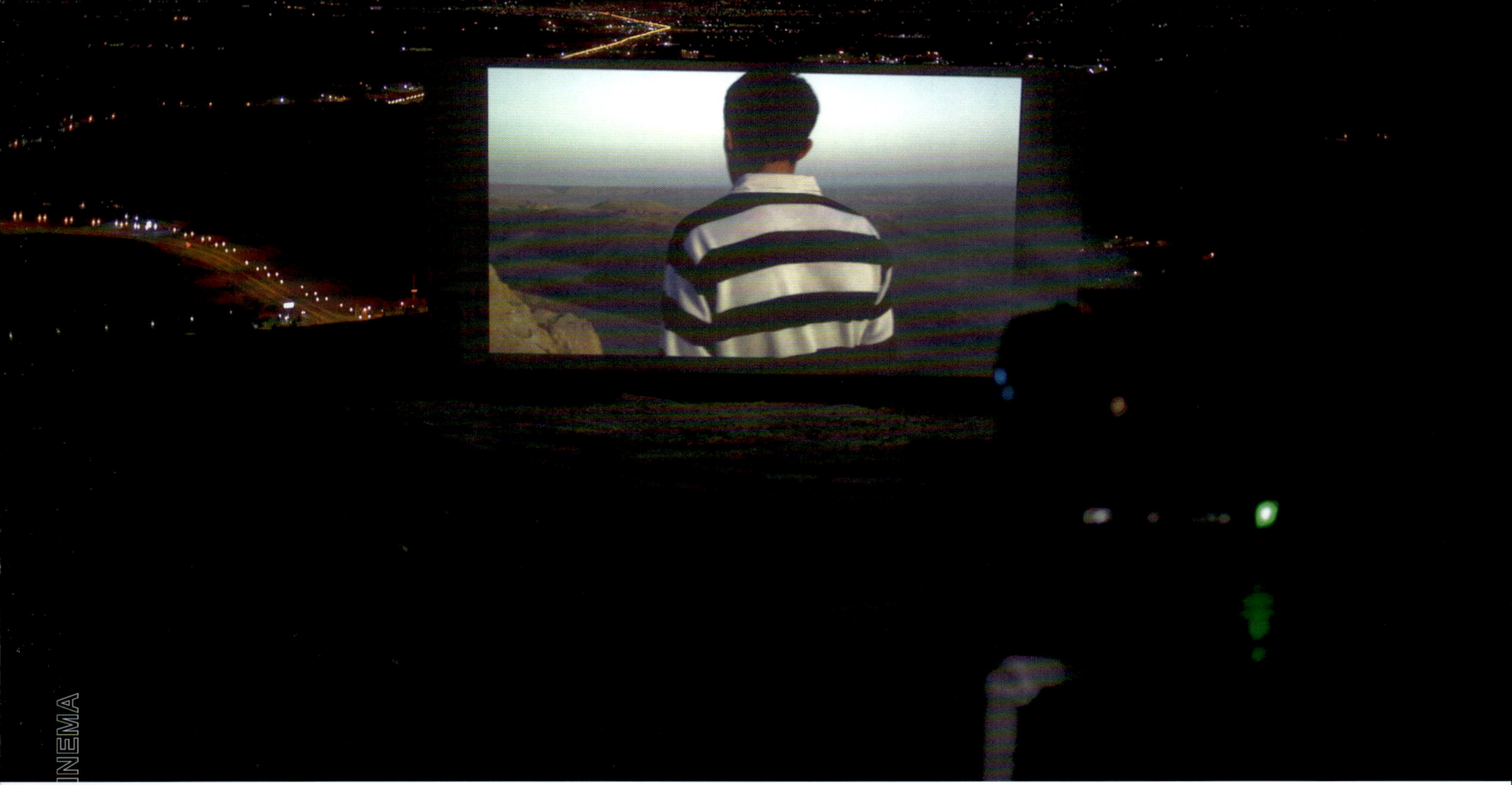

SUN CINEMA

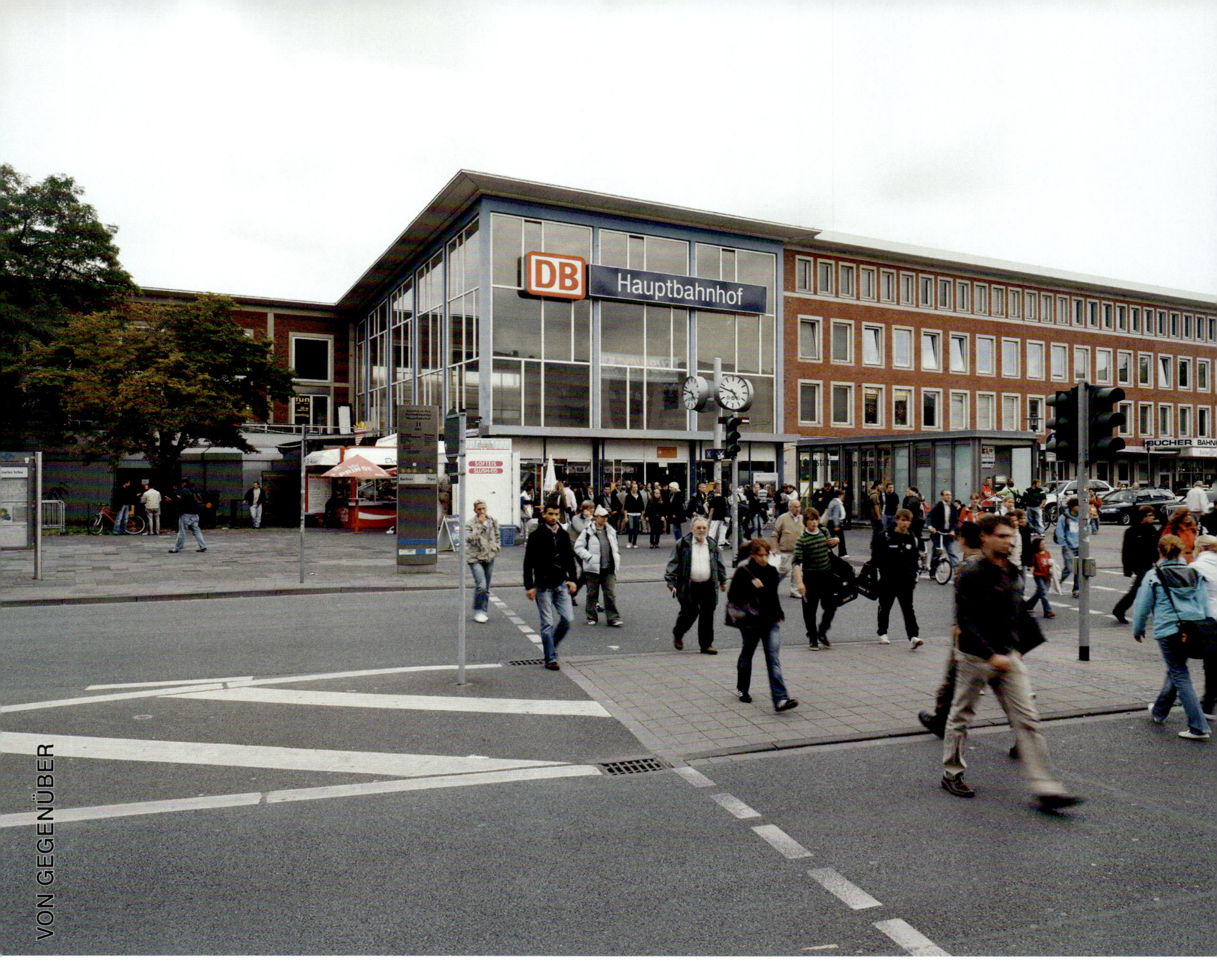

VON GEGENÜBER

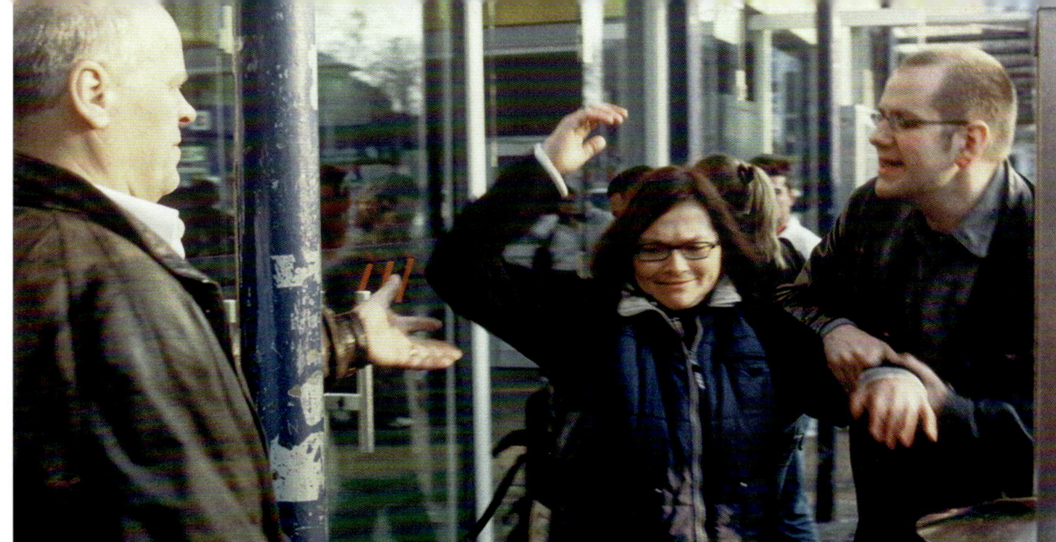
Leave me alone!
I won't come back …
Come along, it's pointless.
I'm not coming back!

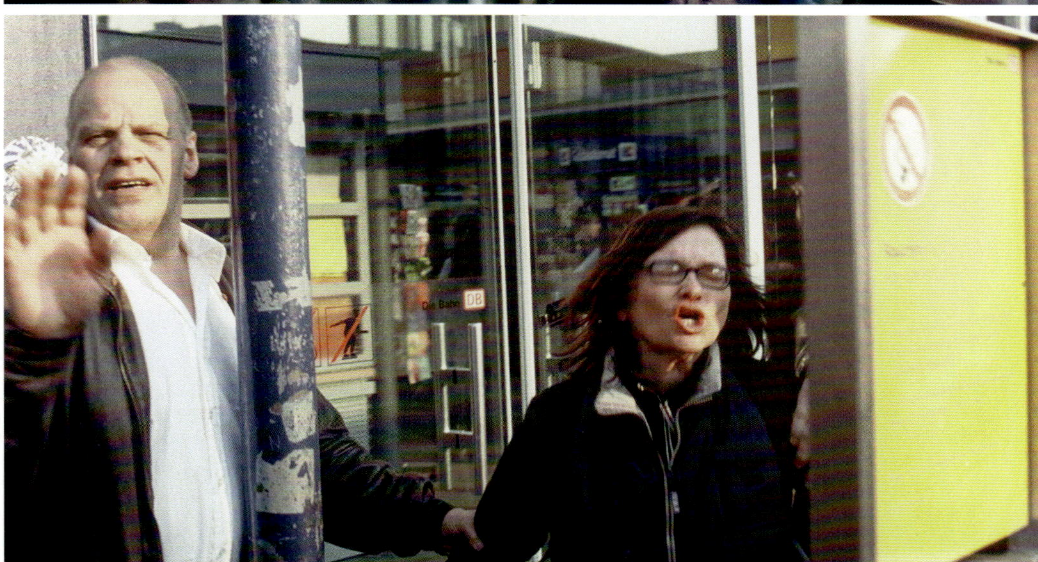
But he apologised!
Let me go! Help, police!
They aren't police!

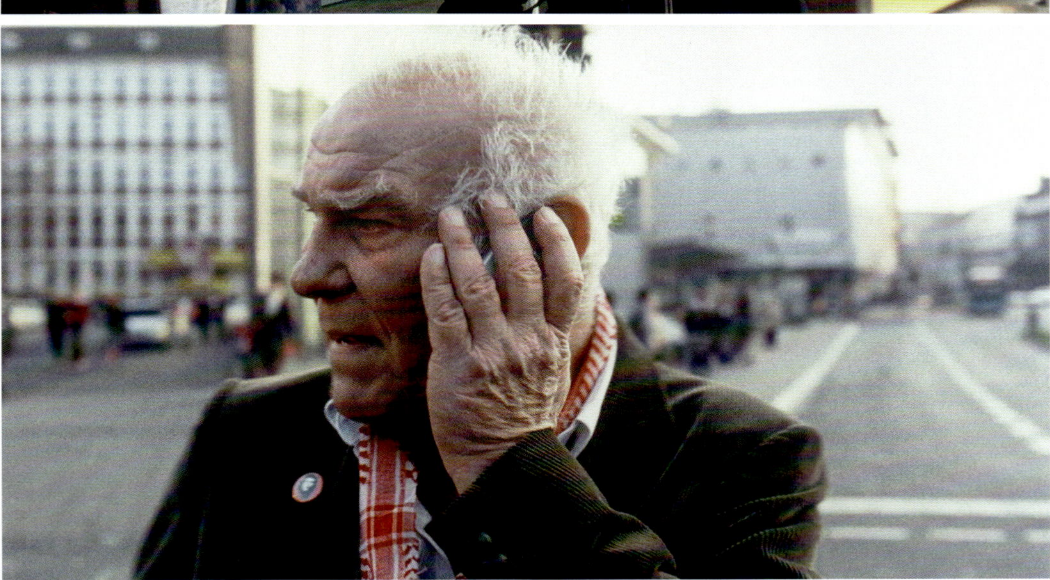

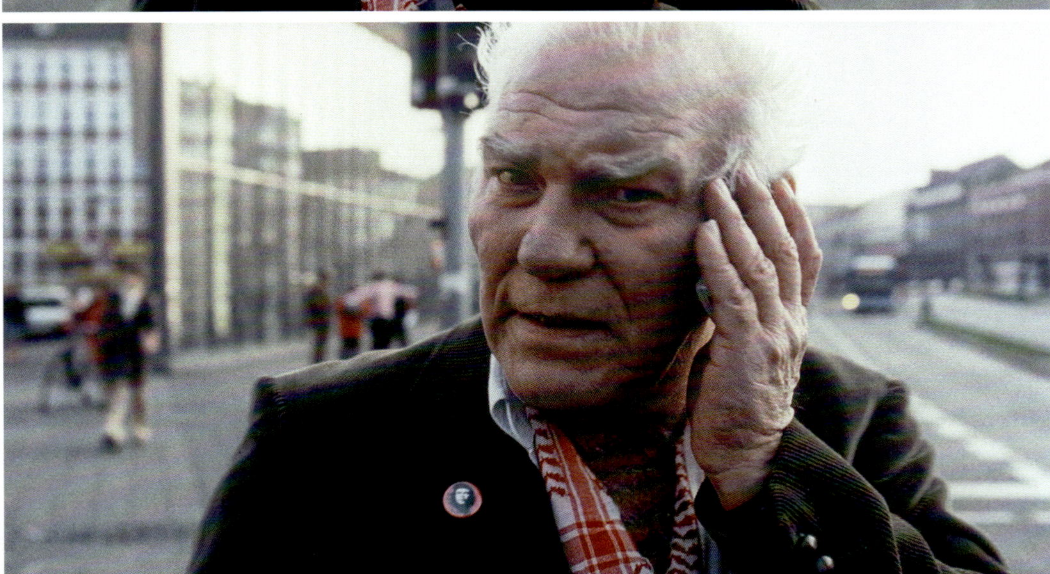

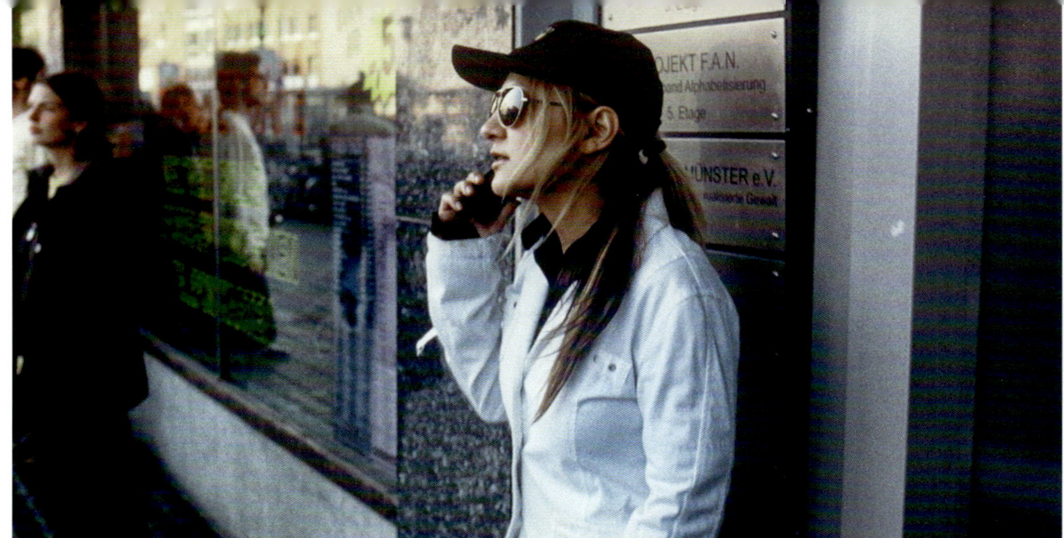

…I'll call you back later,
something's just happened.
Over in the train station.

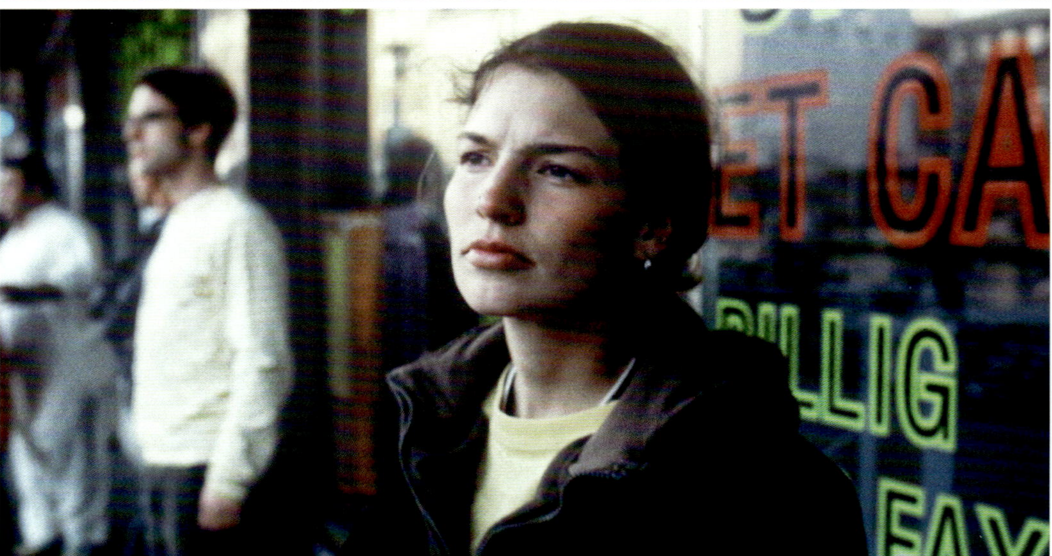

I saw somebody run out
of the train station and
the police were following,
and then back again,
and then…

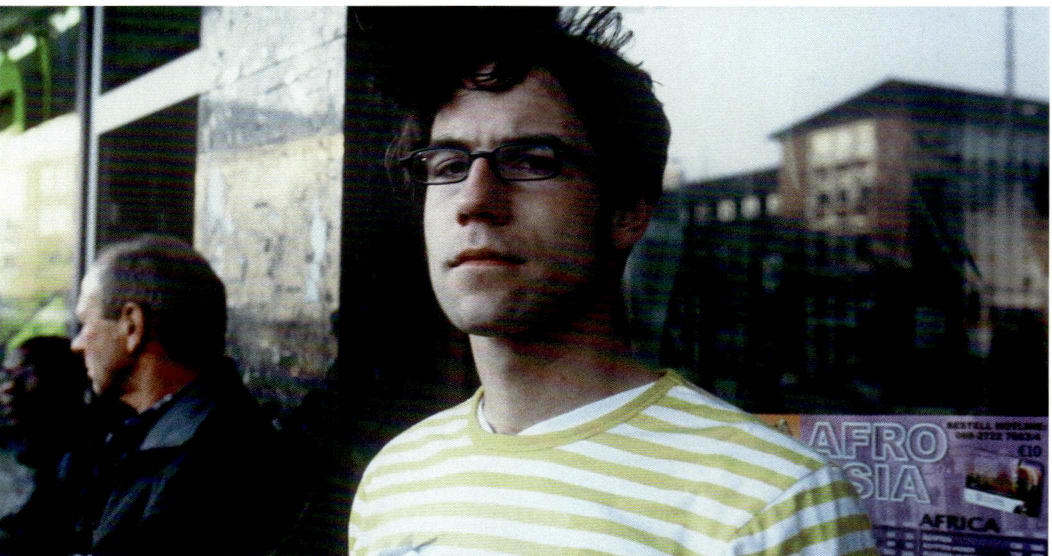

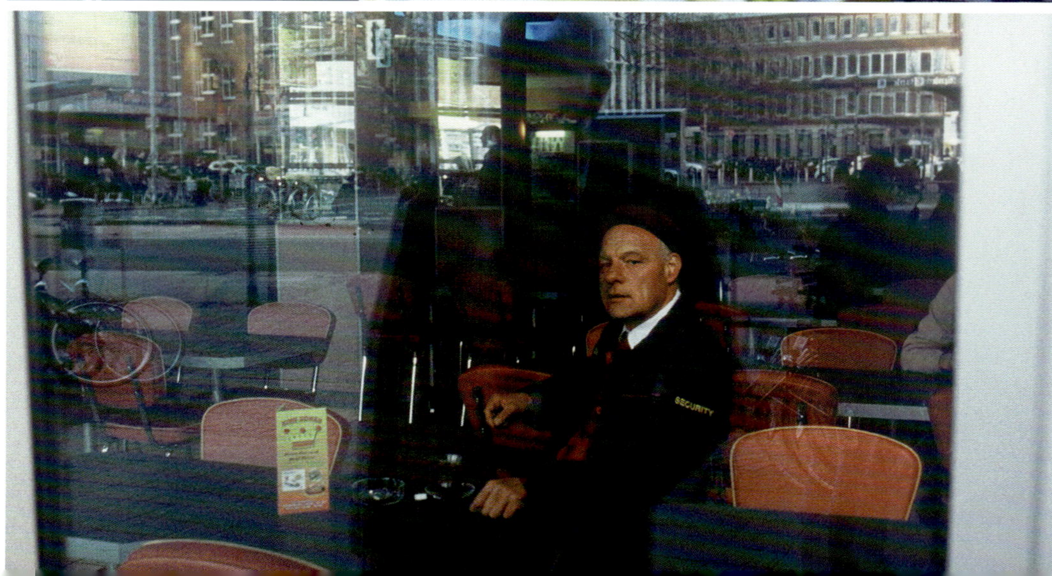

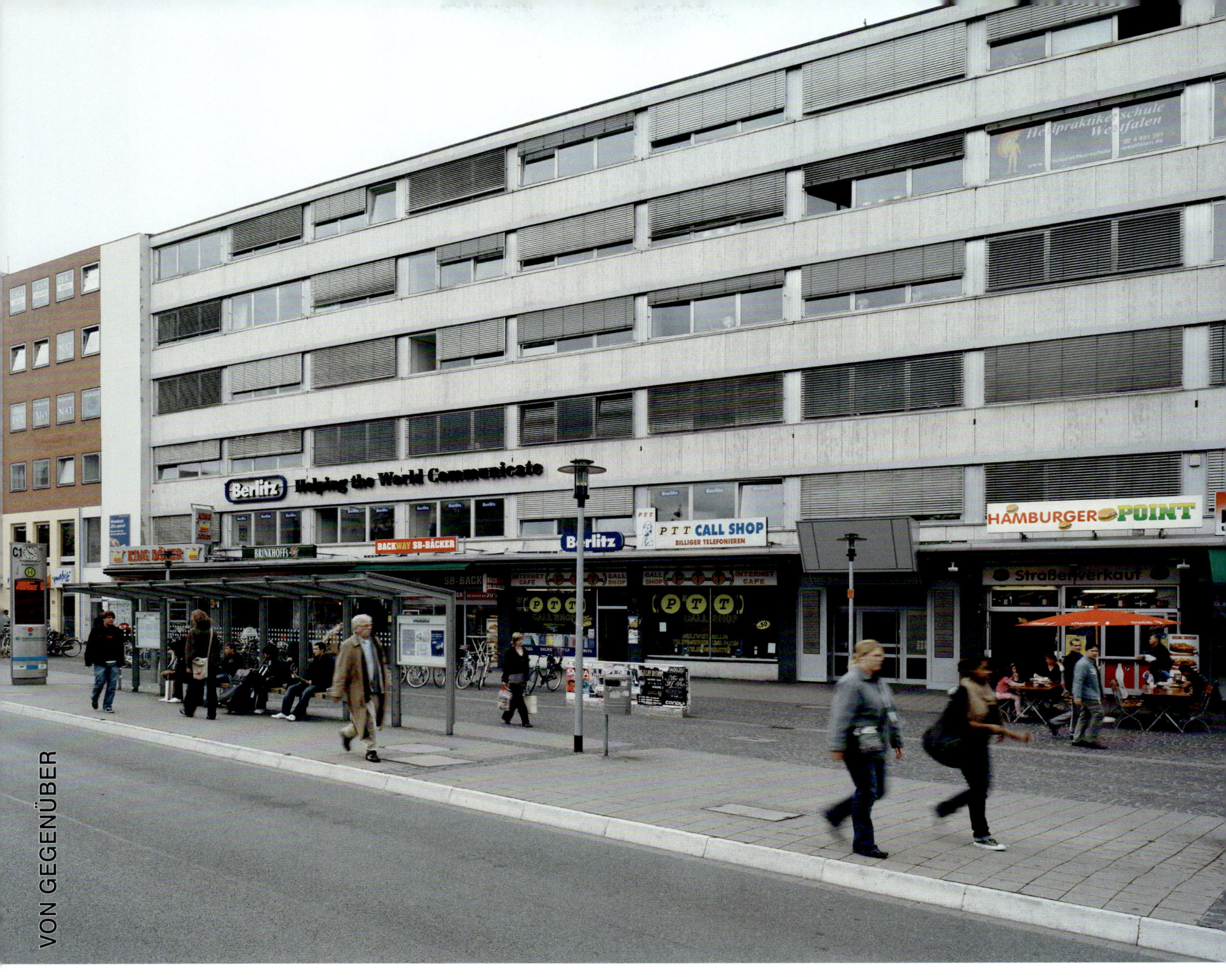

Berlitz
Helping the World Communicate
KING DÖNER
BRINKHOFFS
BACKWAY SB-BÄCKER
Berlitz
PTT CALL SHOP
BILLIGER TELEFONIEREN
HAMBURGER POINT
Straßenverkauf
Heilpraktikerschule Westfalen

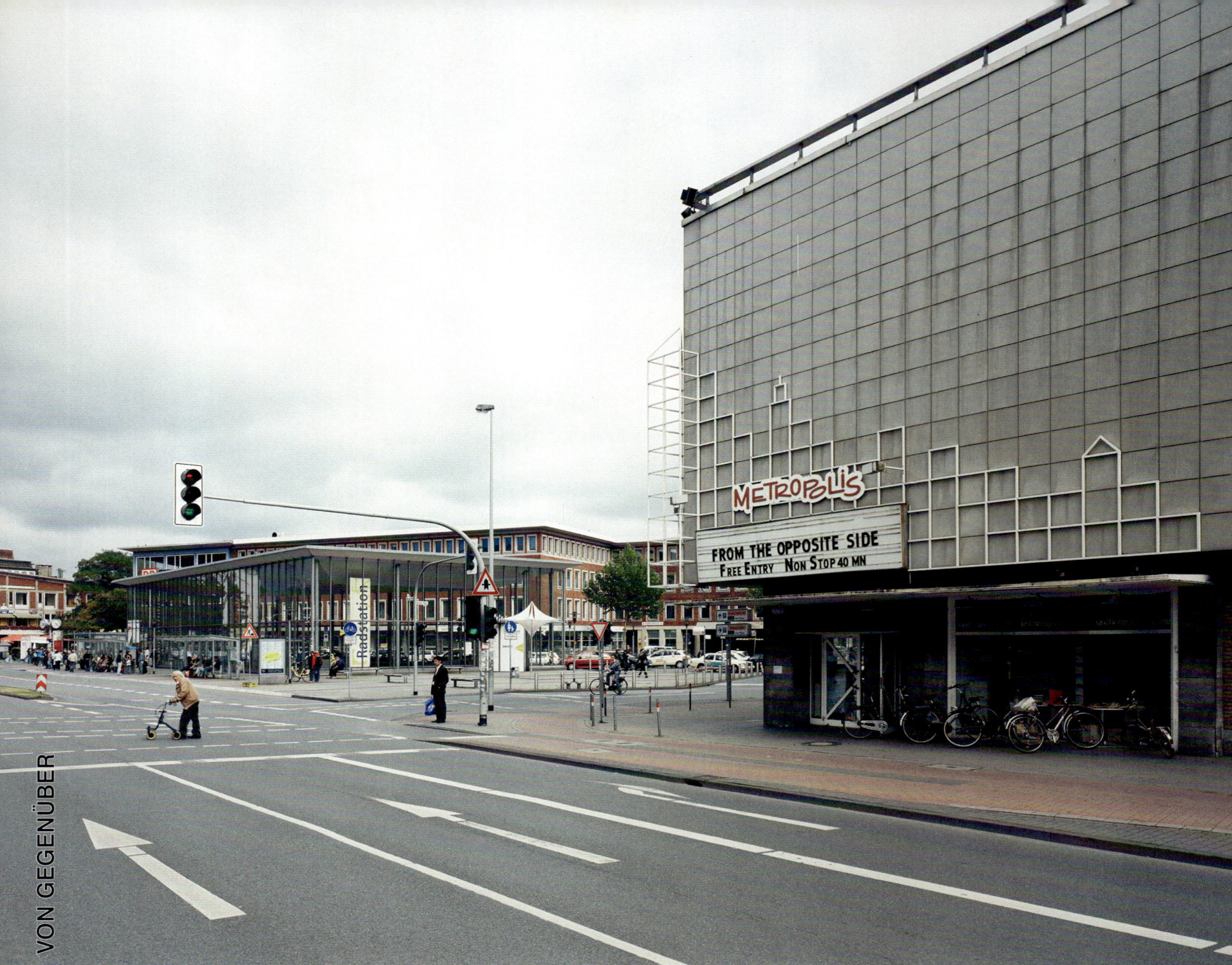

Das Kino Metropolis liegt in der Nähe des Hauptbahnhofs. Ein Film, der vor dessen Türen gedreht wurde, wird hier gezeigt: Passanten laufen darin durch den Bahnhof, Polizisten drehen ihre Runden. Man hört Atem und Schritte: Jemand schaut in die Kamera, als ob er den, der ihn filmt, kennen würde.

The Metropolis cinema lies near the main railway station. Here a film is being screened that was shot in front of its very doors: Passers-by walk through the station, police officers do their rounds. One hears breathing and footsteps: Someone looks into the camera as if they know the person filming them.

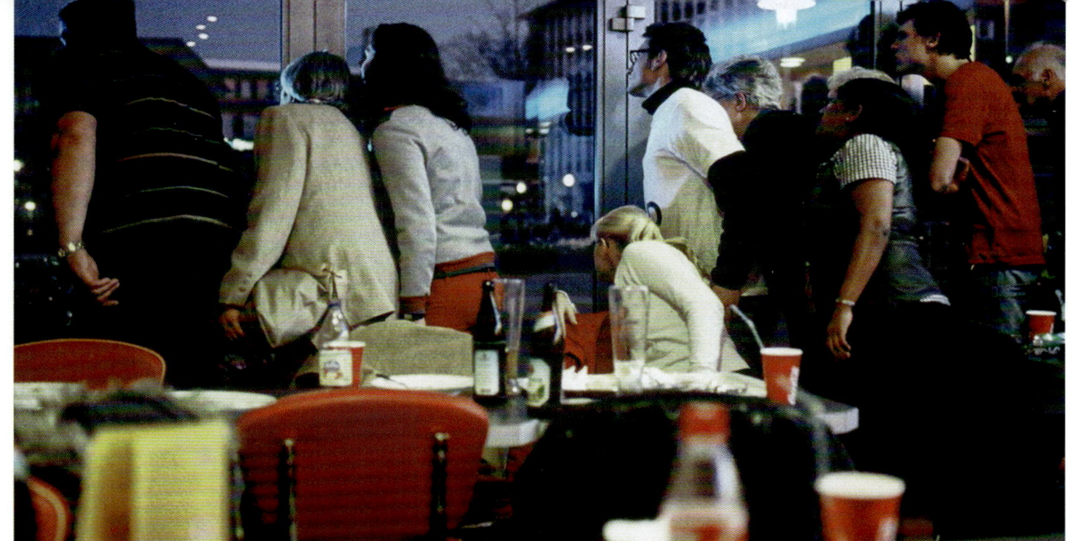

Follow the instructions of the police and the aid workers. Attention, please, this is not a false alarm.

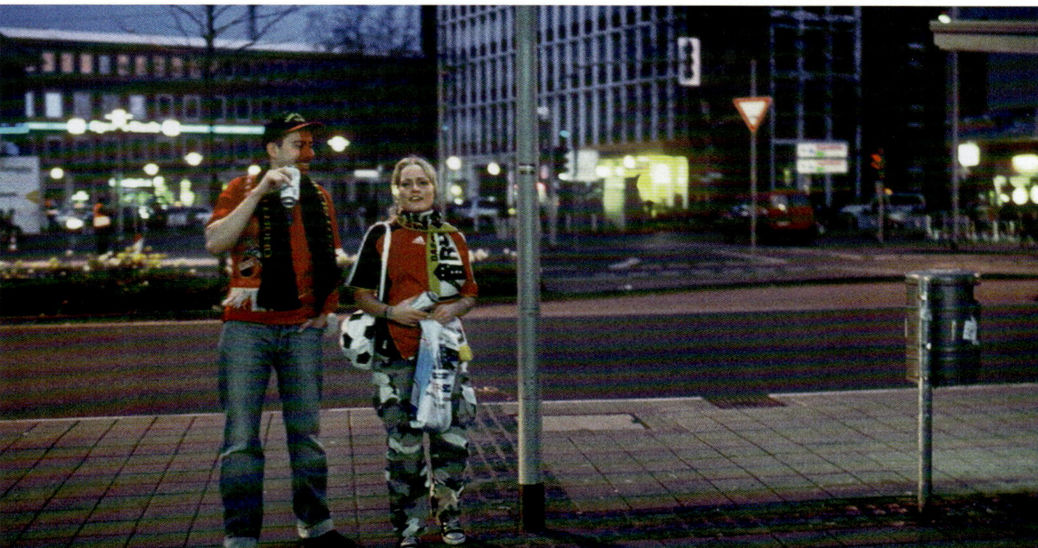

Hey old lady, you wanna get us a doner kebab?

A beer would be better.

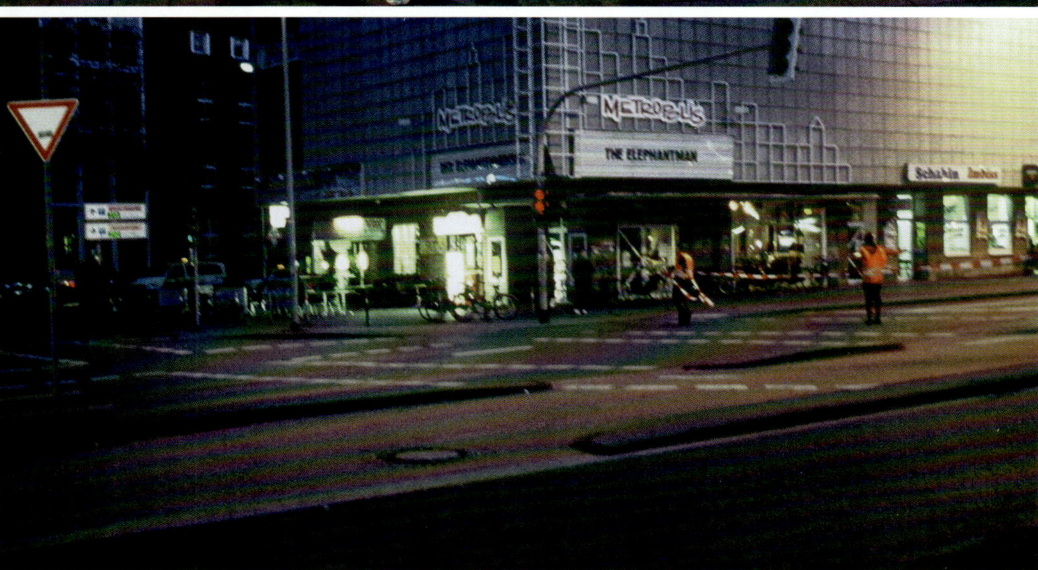

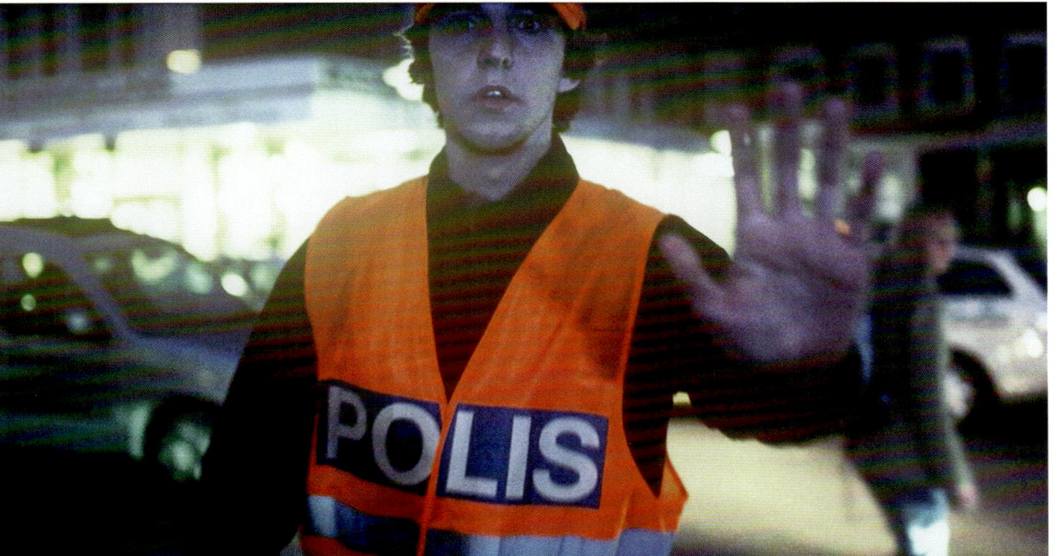

You can't come through here!

23

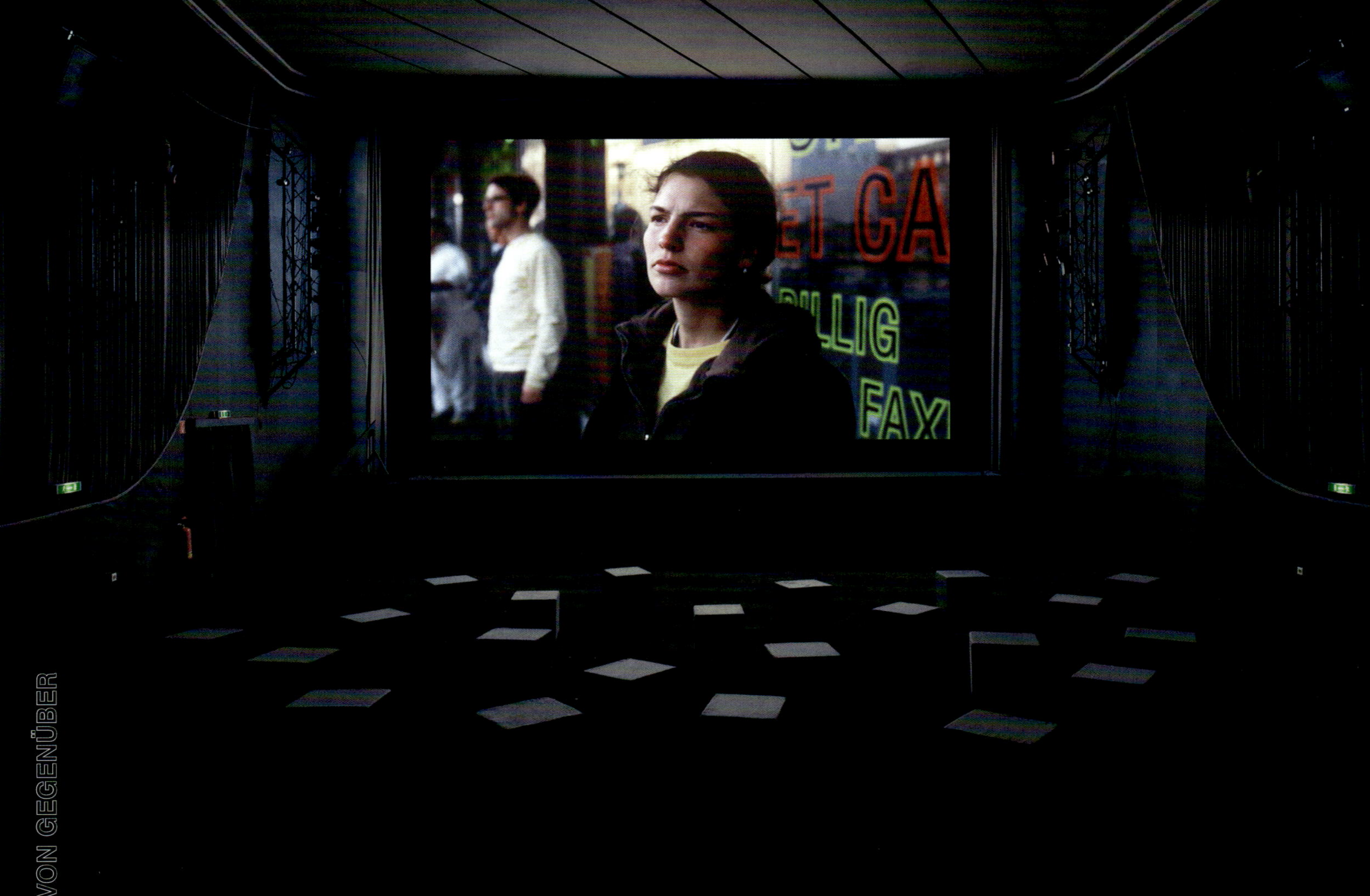

Kinoräume sind halböffentliche Orte. Man begegnet dort Bildern, mit denen man sich auseinandersetzen muss: Beim Verlassen des Kinos tritt man in die gefilmte Welt, die jetzt eine andere ist. Ein Déjà-vu, ein Taumel – in jedem Fall gibt es einen fließenden Übergang vom Kinosaal zur Außenwelt.

Cinemas are semi-public places. Here we encounter images we are forced to deal with: When we leave the cinema, we enter the filmed world which is now different. A déjà vu, we stagger—in every sense, it is a smooth transition from the cinema to the outside world.

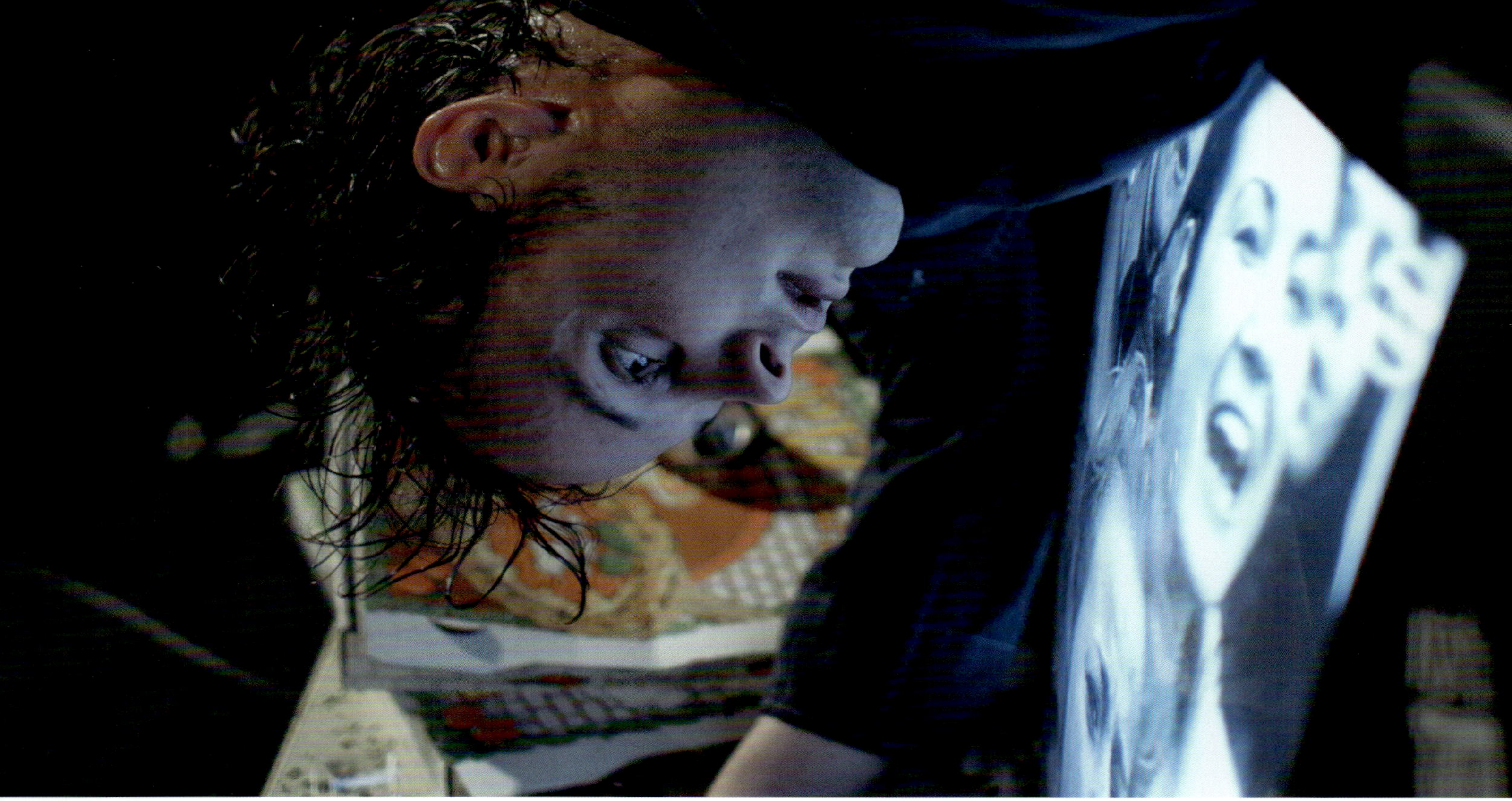

1994. Einige sitzen auf Bierkisten und Sofas vor einem Fernseher. Andere liegen müde herum. Heute wird *Bambule* gezeigt, zum ersten Mal seit 24 Jahren.

1994. Backstage some people are sitting on beer crates and sofas in front of a TV. Others are just lying around. Today they are showing *Bambule* for the first time in 24 years.

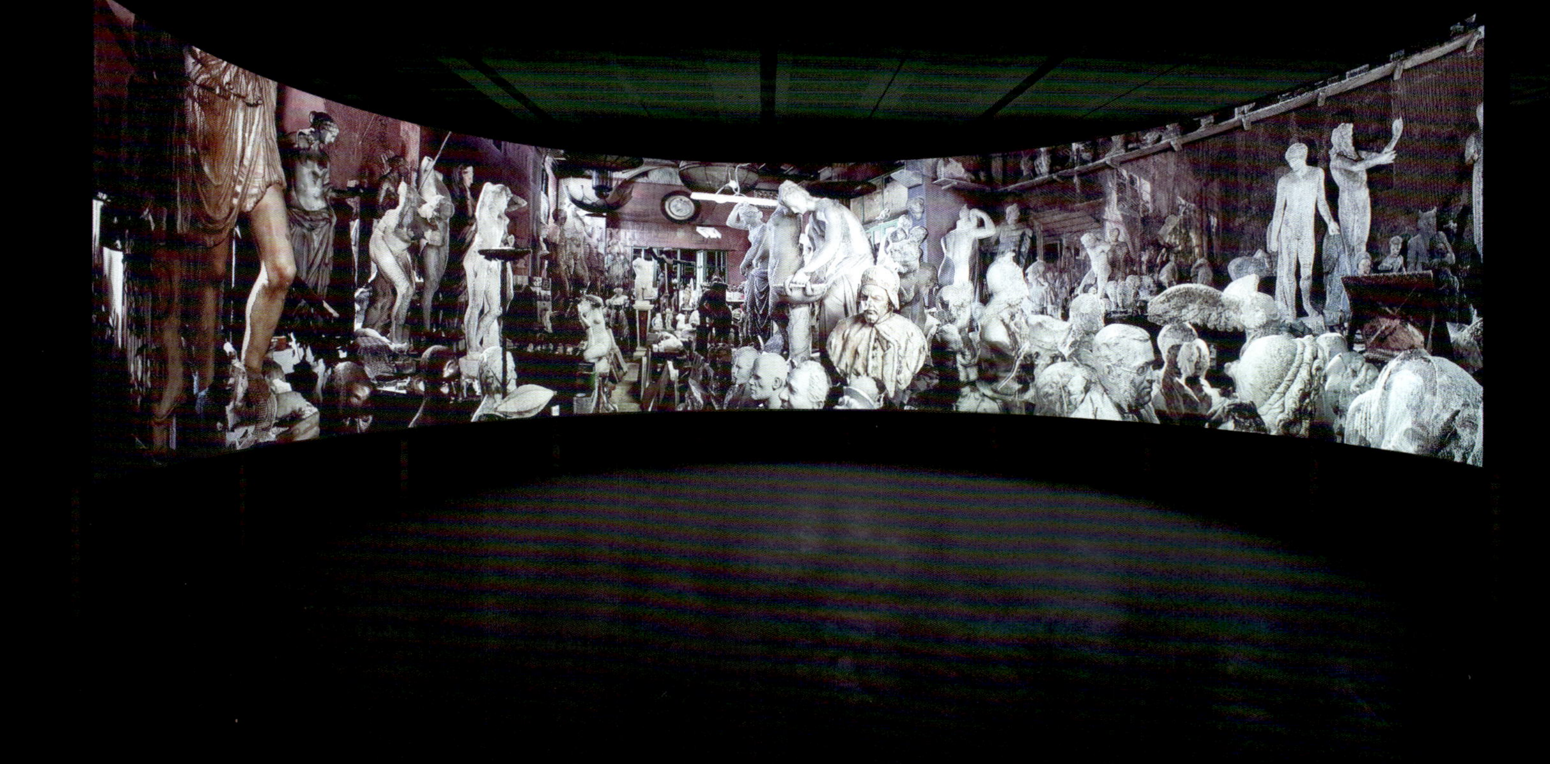

Die Lagerräume des Skulpturenateliers in den römischen Filmstudios von Cinecittà wurden 3D gescannt, um die Betrachter durch den visuellen Datensatz zu navigieren.

The storerooms of the sculpture studios at the Roman film studios of Cinecittà were 3D scanned to navigate viewers through the visual dataset.

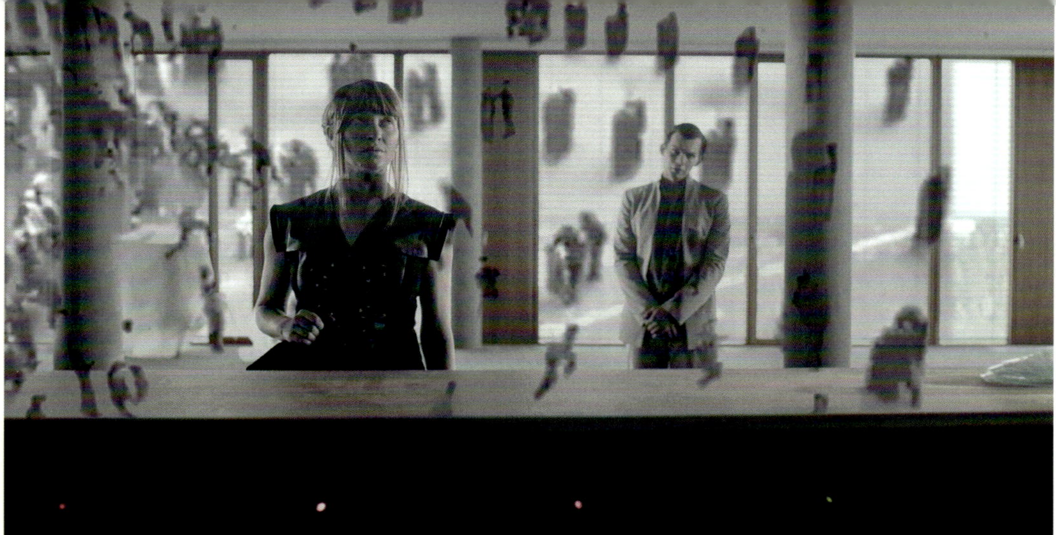

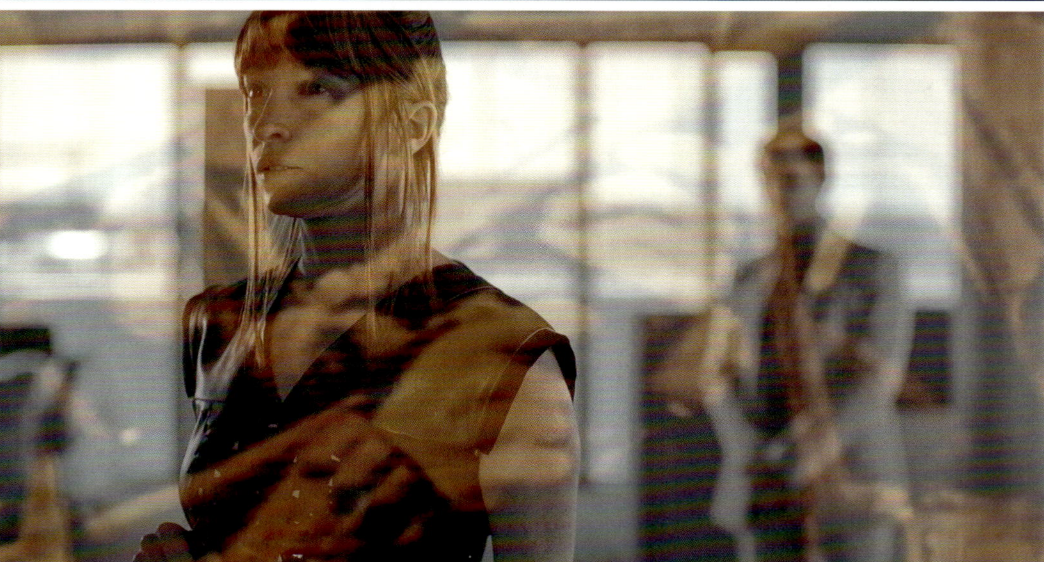

But I feel like I'm seeing these memories for the first time.

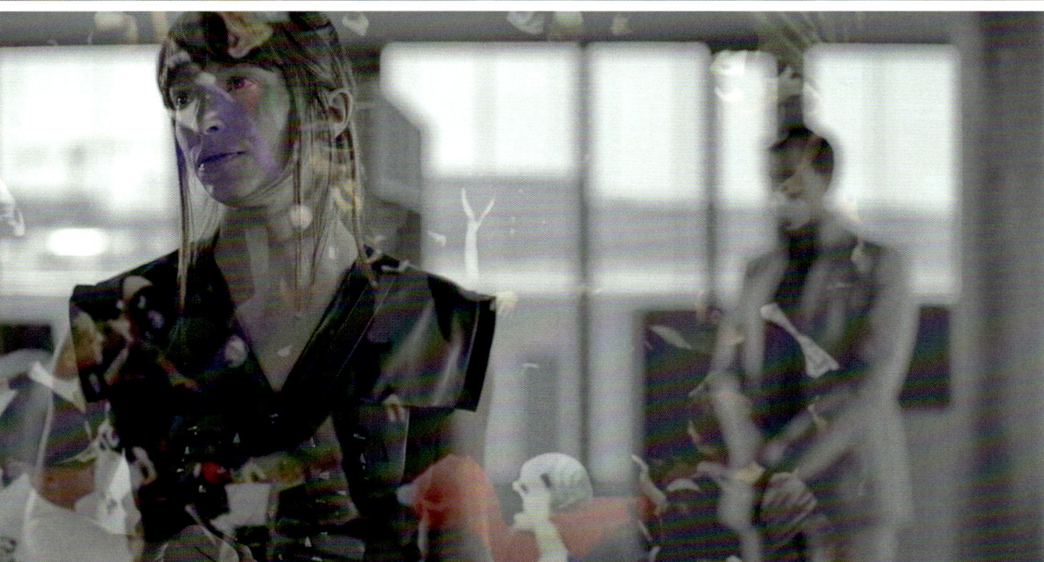

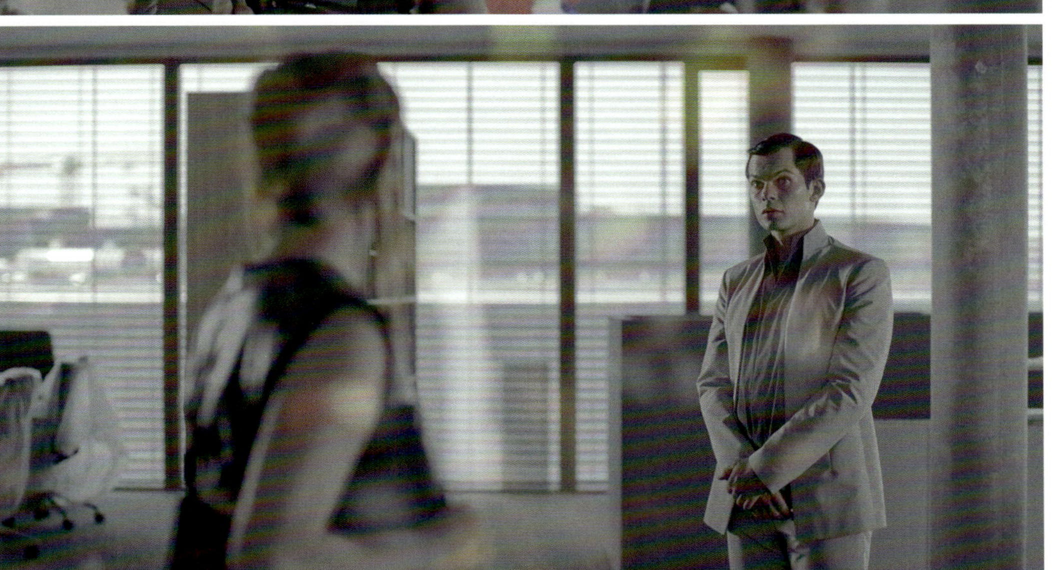

Correct. These events are no longer accessible in the shared history archive.

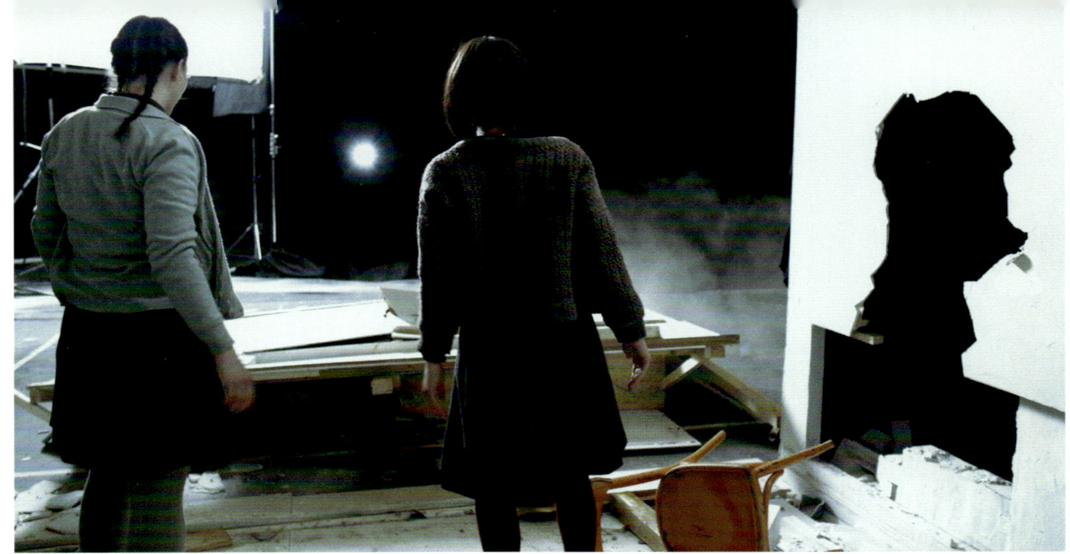

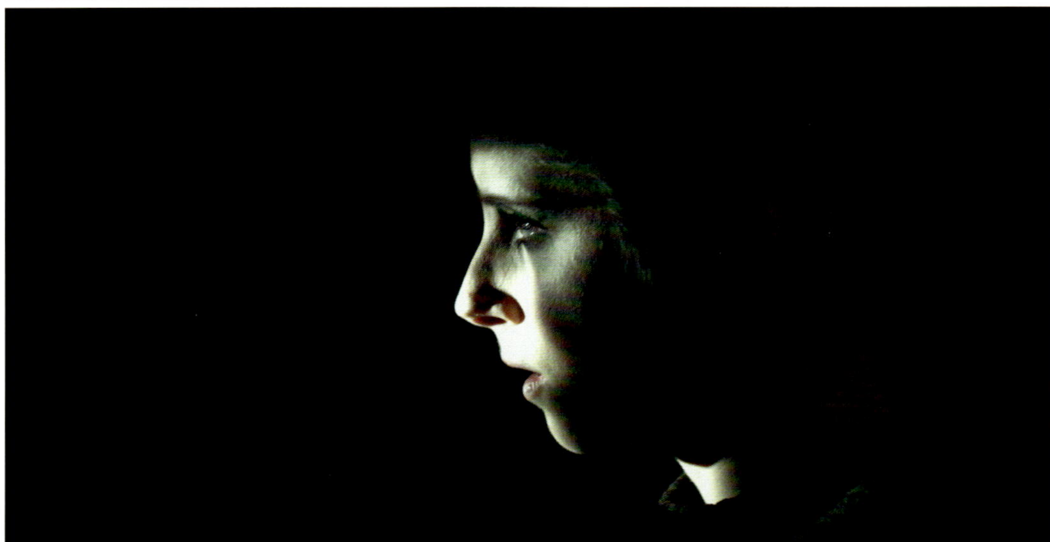

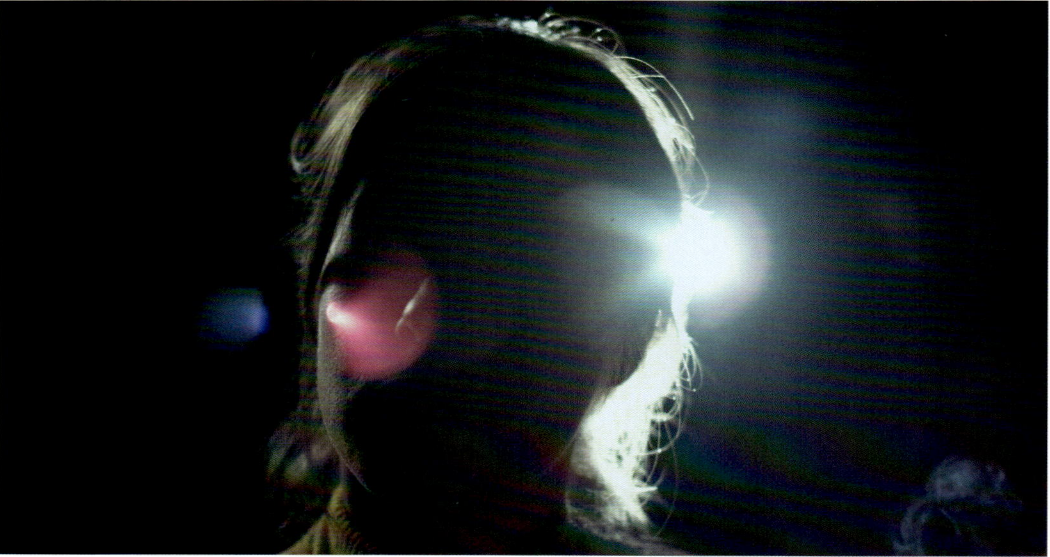

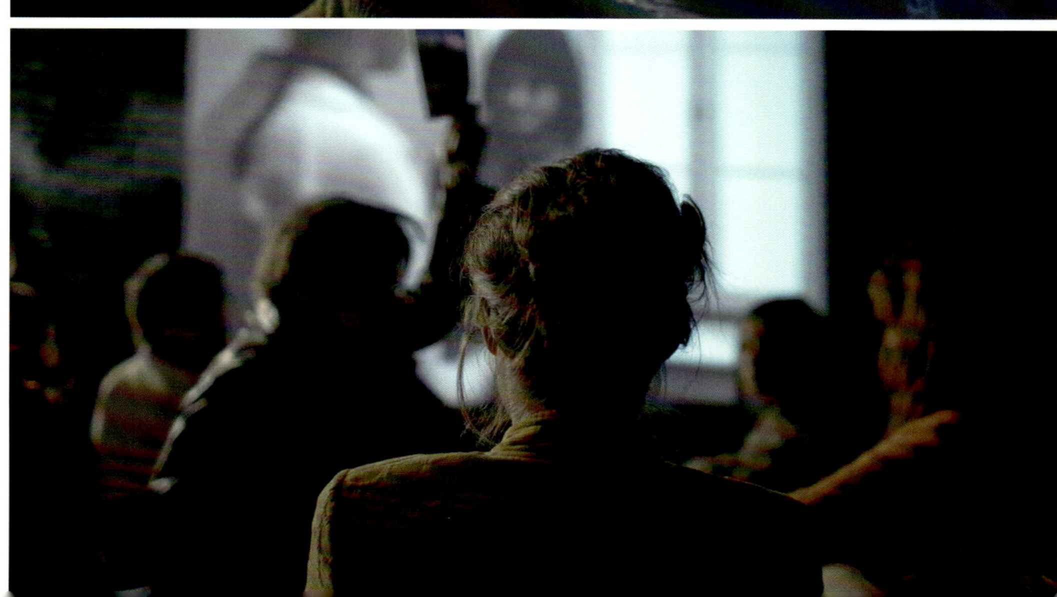

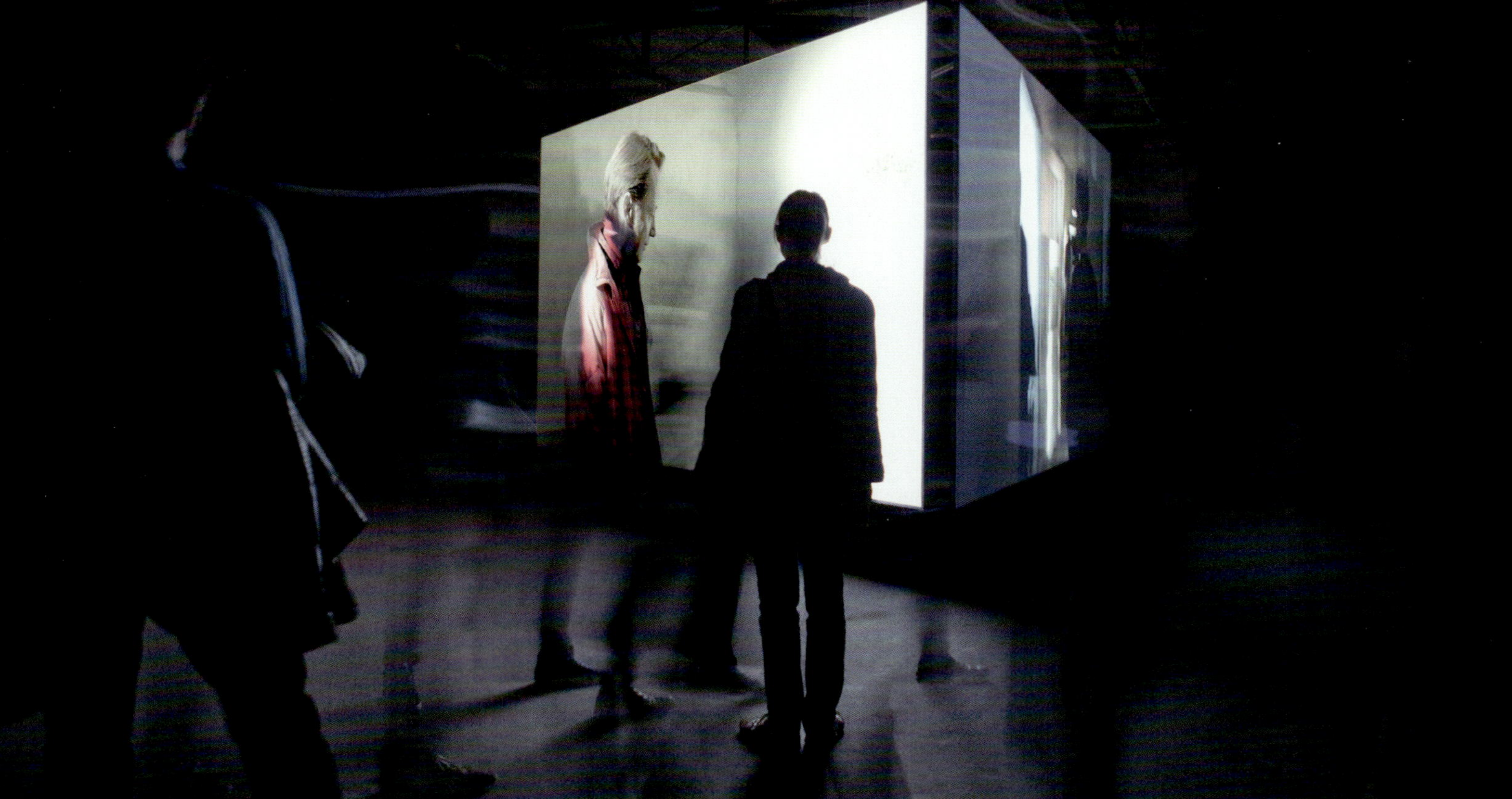

Auf der dritten Leinwand erscheint Amelie sowohl als Insassin des Mädchenerziehungsheims und zugleich als Hauptdarstellerin bei den Dreharbeiten für einen Film, der frei an Ulrike Meinhofs *Bambule* angelehnt ist. Die drei unterschiedlichen Filmschleifen greifen immer wieder ineinander und die Zeitebenen werden aufgehoben. Verfremdungseffekte des Kinos – Schatten, Rückprojektionen und Doppelbelichtungen – werden genutzt, um eine Zeit in die andere zu blenden.

On the third screen, Amelie appears both as a reformatory girl and as the leading actress in the making of a film based in part on Ulrike Meinhof's *Bambule*. The three separate film loops keep intertwining and time levels are suspended. Cinematic alienation effects—shadows, projections, and double exposures—are employed to superimpose one time level onto the other.

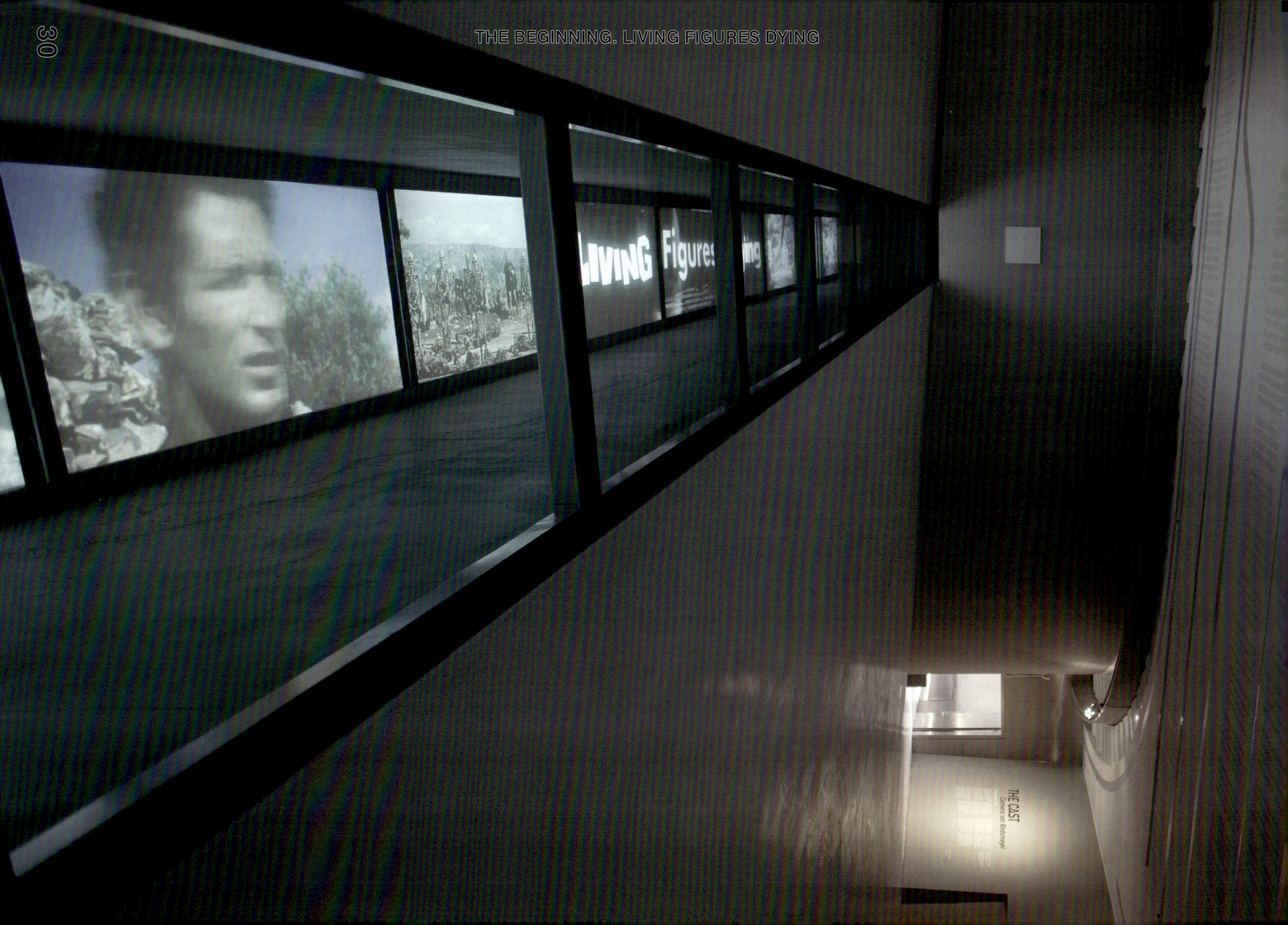

LIVING Figures
THE CAST
Clemens von Wedemeyer

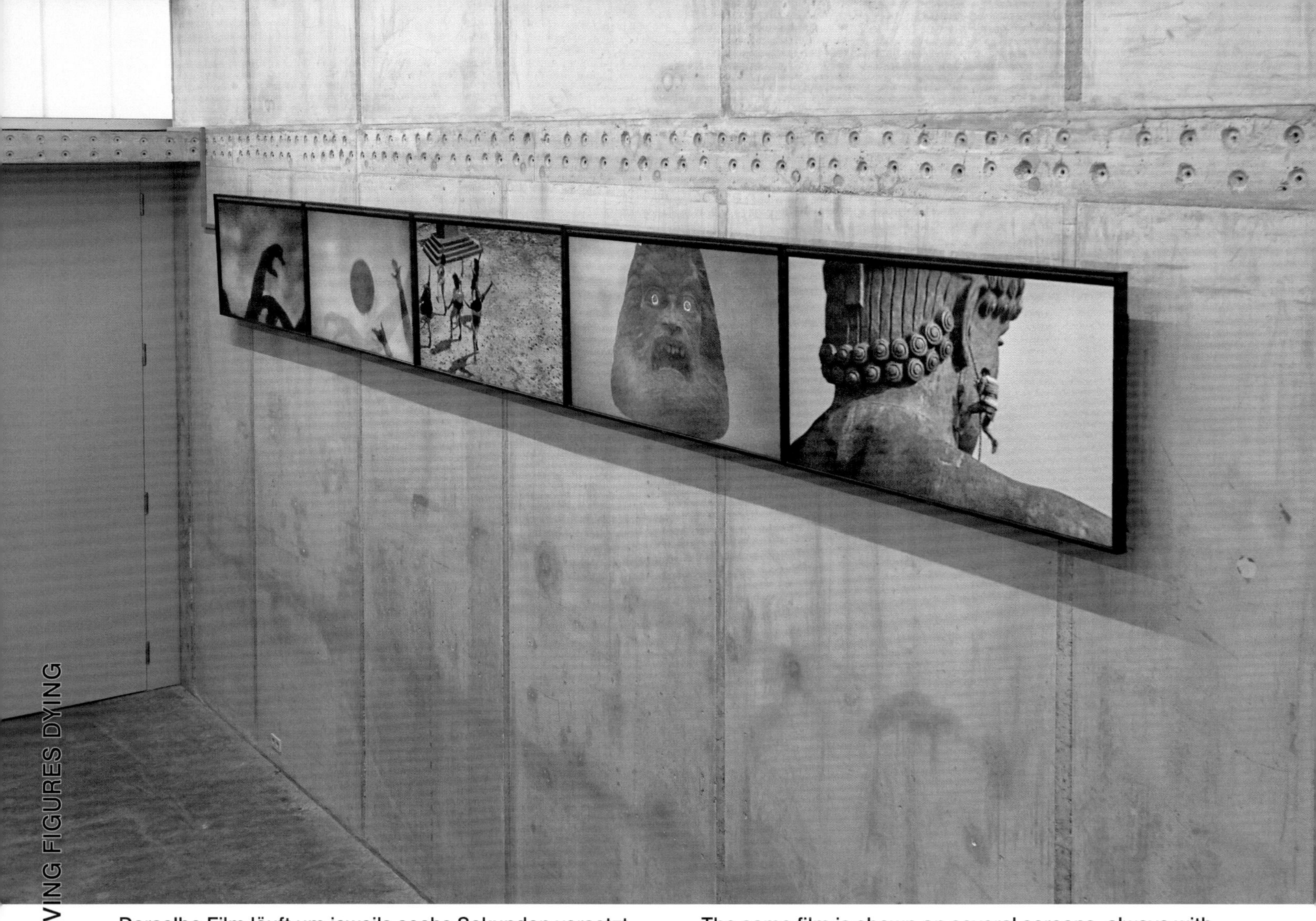

Derselbe Film läuft um jeweils sechs Sekunden versetzt auf mehreren Bildschirmen. Die Bilder bewegen sich durch den Raum und können wiederholt betrachtet werden. Das Video besteht aus Filmfragmenten über die Produktion, Anbetung und Zerstörung menschlicher Skulpturen in der Kinogeschichte.

The same film is shown on several screens, always with a time delay of six seconds. The pictures move through the room and can be viewed repeatedly. The video consists of film fragments about the production, adoration and destruction of human sculptures in the course of cinematic history.

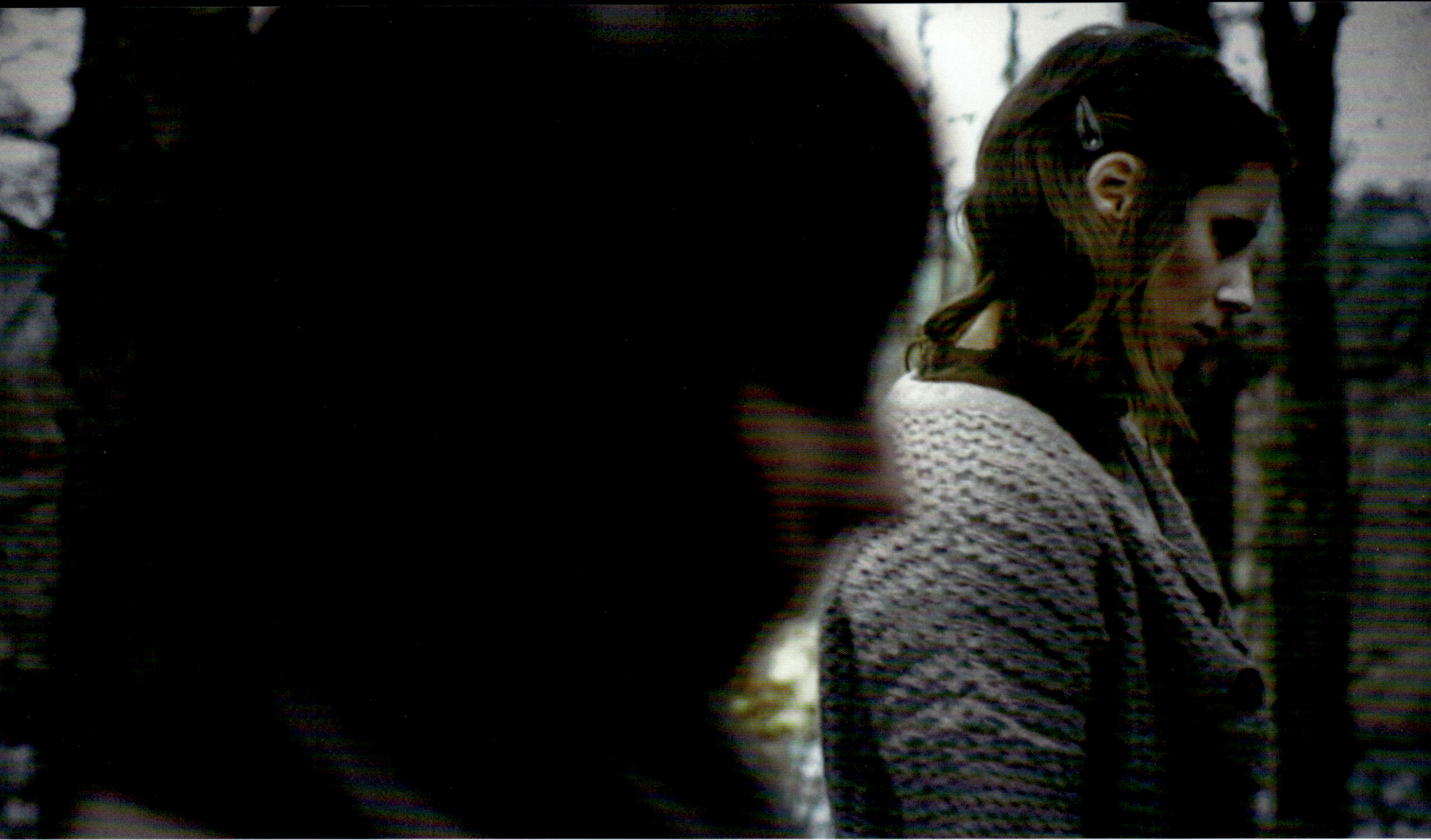

In der Rückprojektion begegnen sich die Schauspielerin Amelie Kiefer und das von ihr gespielte Heimmädchen.

In the rear projection, the actress Amelie Kiefer meets the reformatory girl she plays.

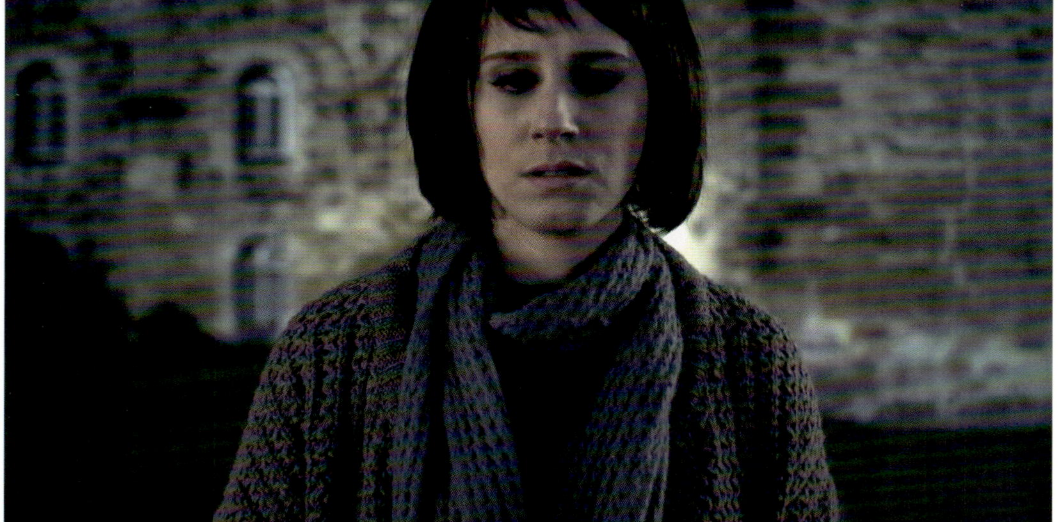

You can't speak the way we do in detention.

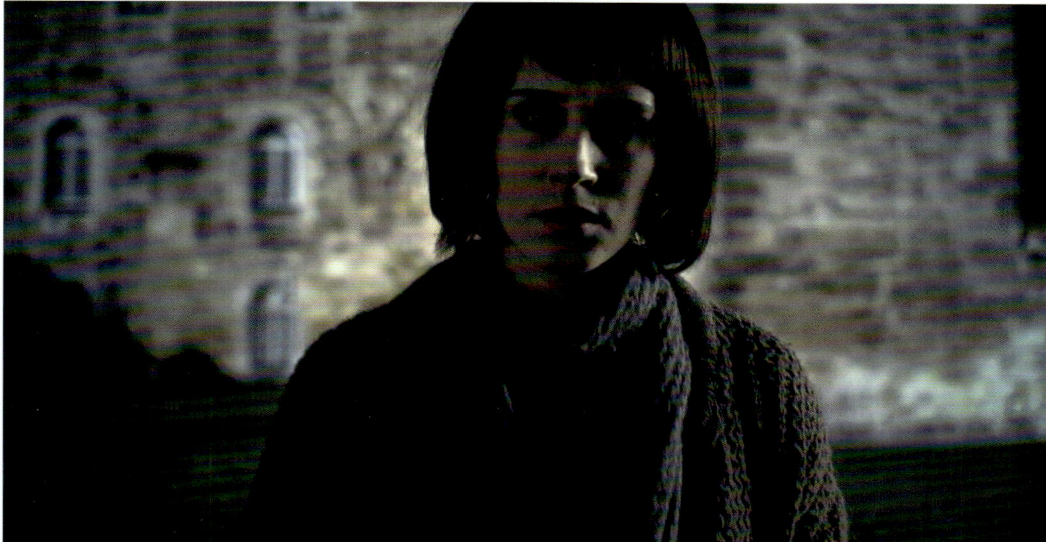

Or vice versa.

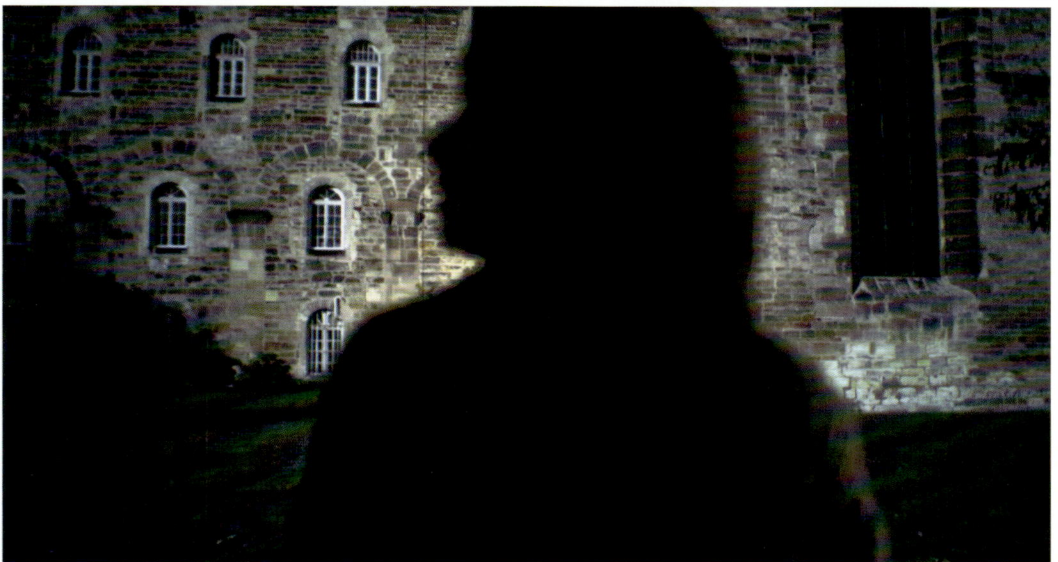

So it sounds wrong.

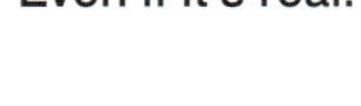

Even if it's real.

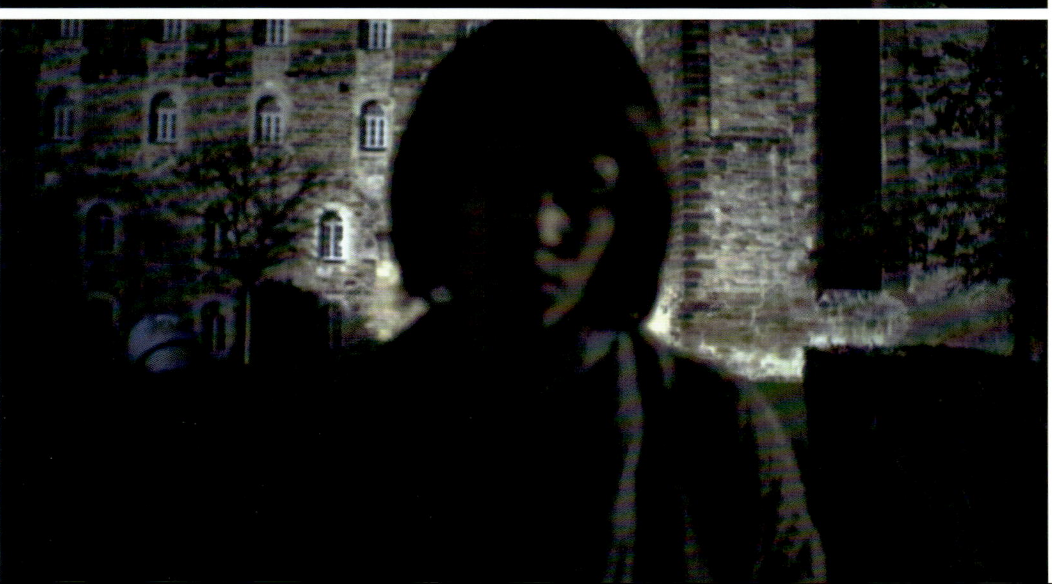

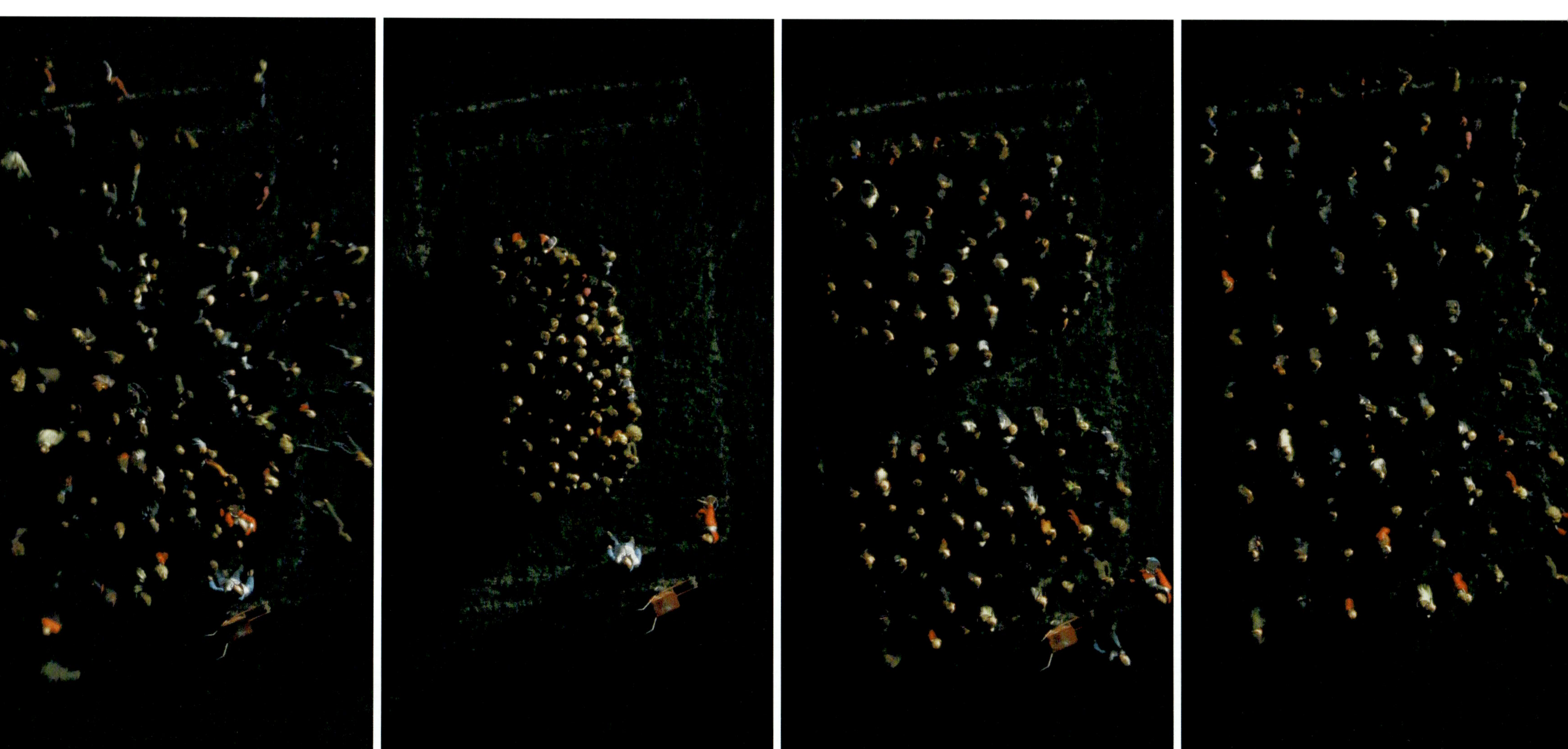

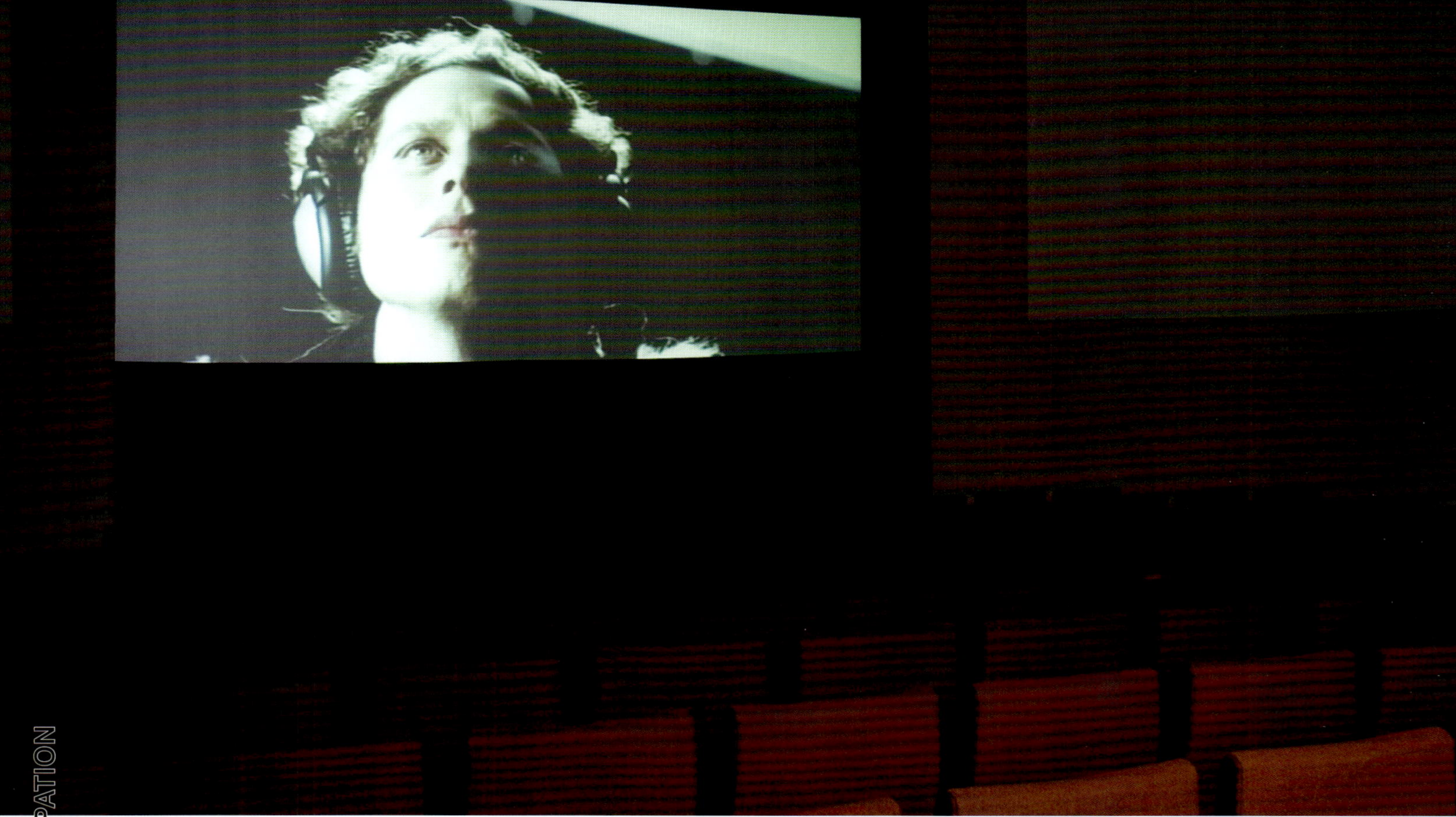

200 Statisten stehen nachts auf einem markierten Rechteck und folgen den Anweisungen des Filmteams. Im Idealfall sind sie bei der Premiere des Films auch die Zuschauer im Kinosaal.

200 extras stand at night on a marked-off rectangle, obeying the film crew's instructions. At best, they will be allowed to attend the film premiere.

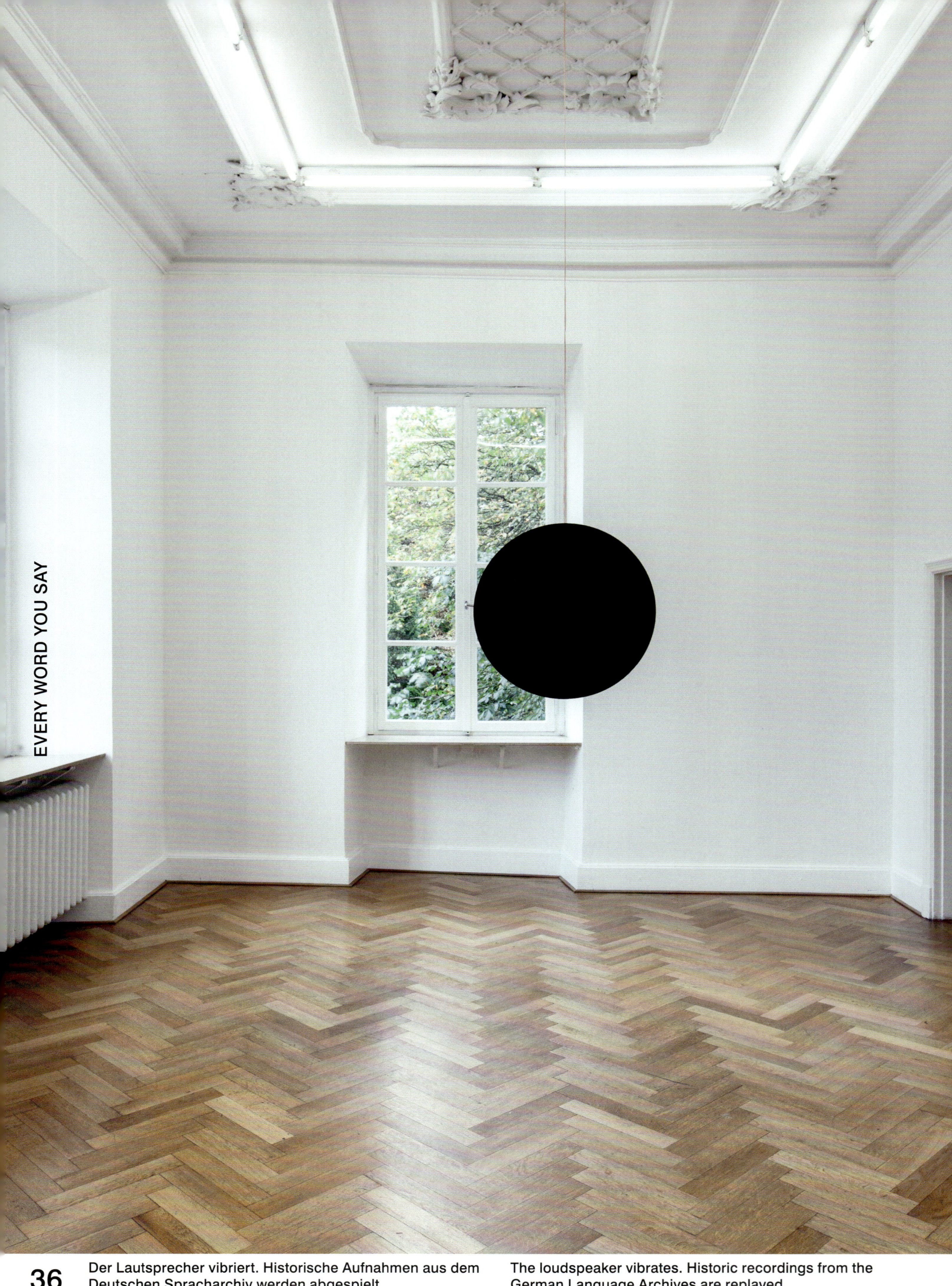

Der Lautsprecher vibriert. Historische Aufnahmen aus dem Deutschen Spracharchiv werden abgespielt.

The loudspeaker vibrates. Historic recordings from the German Language Archives are replayed.

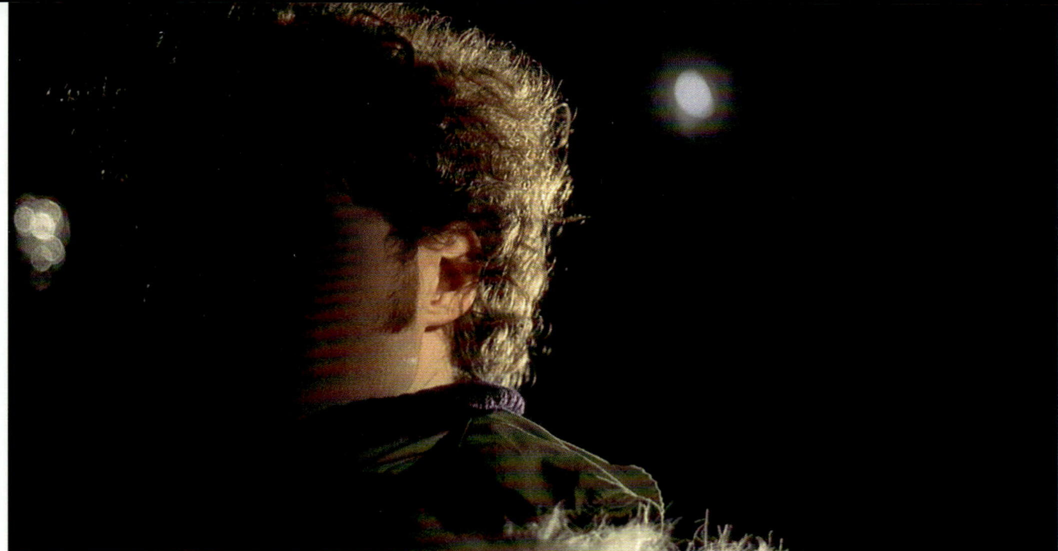

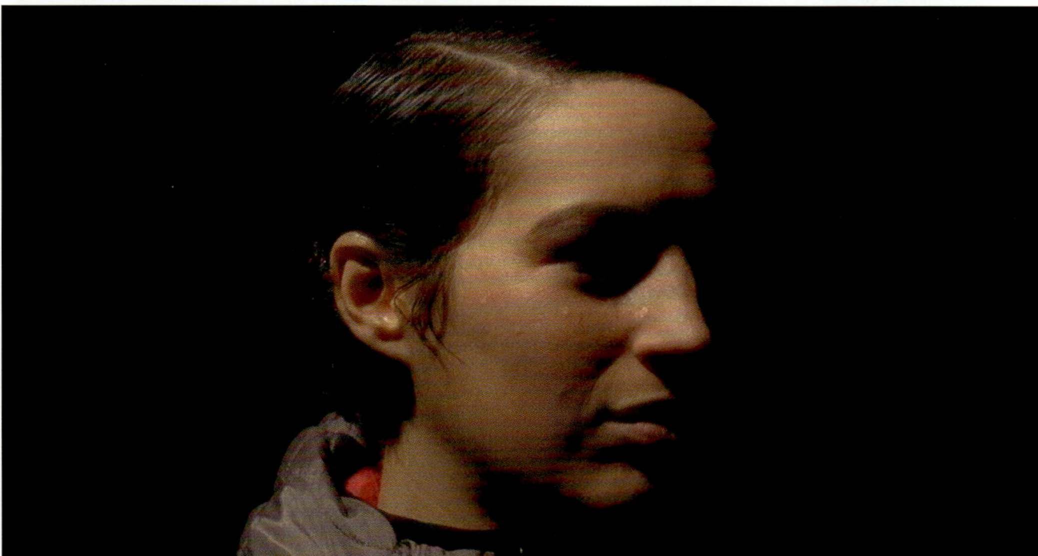

Everything's okay,
we may start.

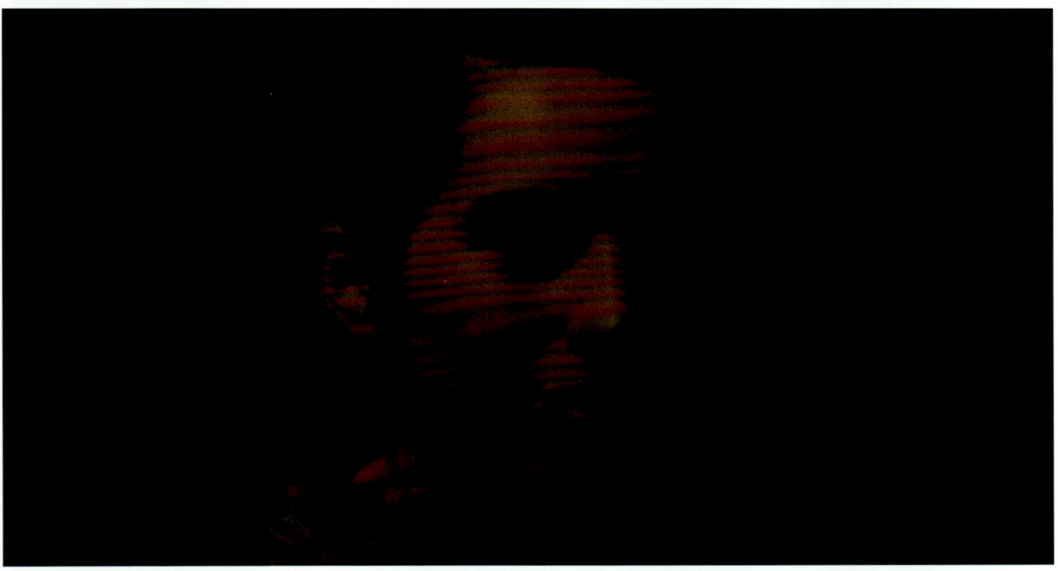

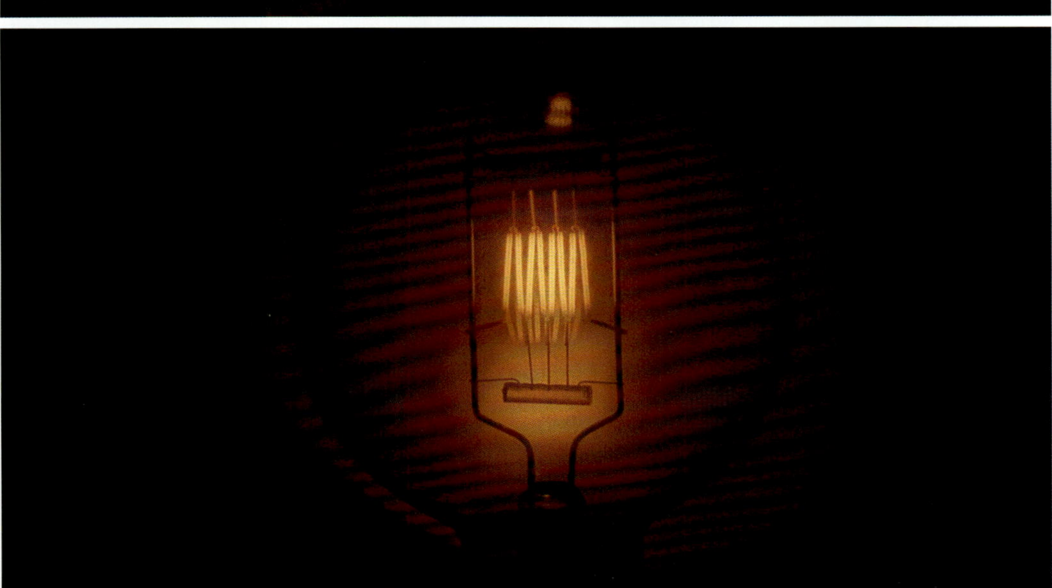

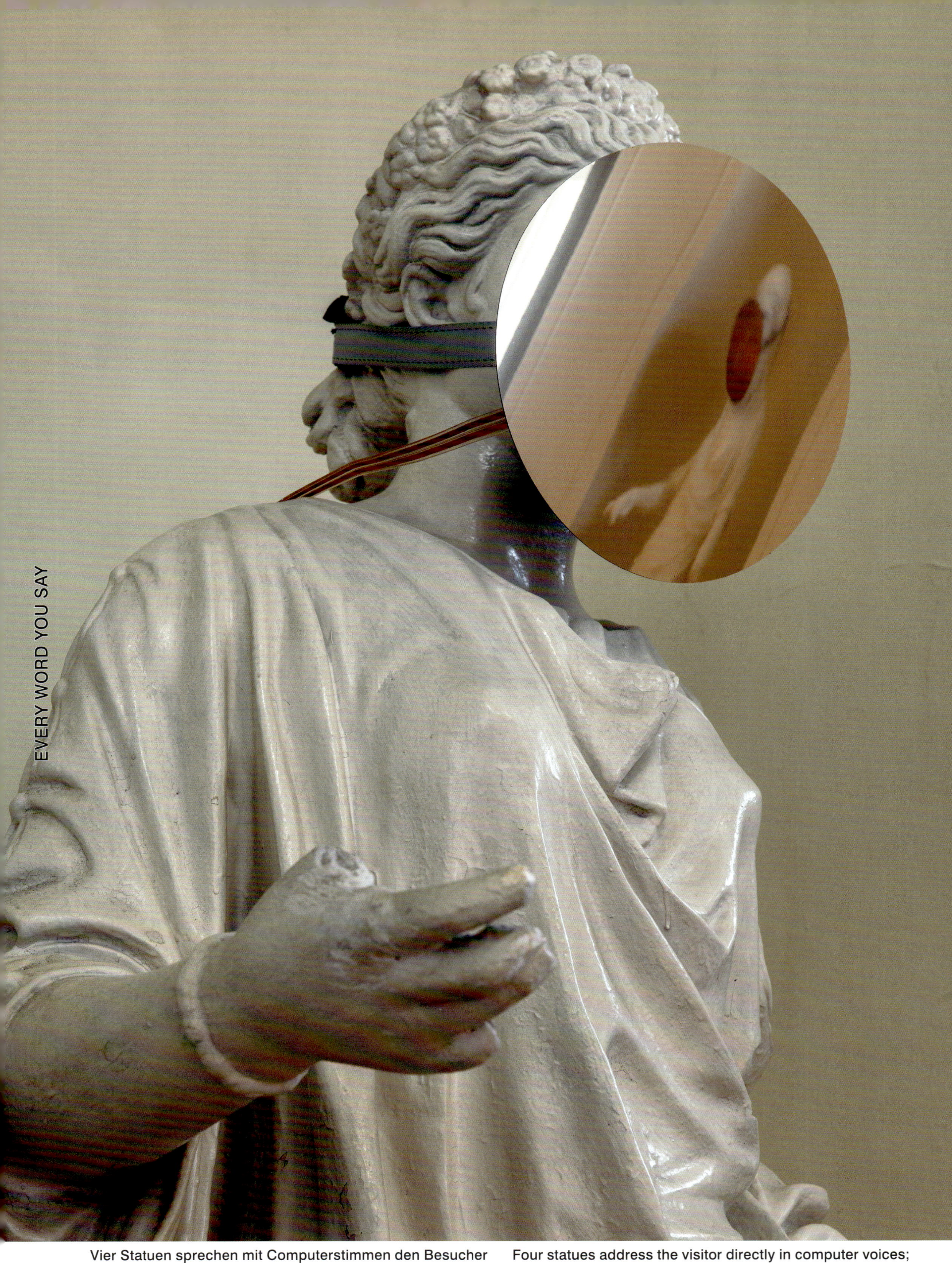

Vier Statuen sprechen mit Computerstimmen den Besucher direkt an, geben ihm Hinweise und eine kurze Einführung in das Thema der Ausstellung.

Four statues address the visitor directly in computer voices; they provide information and a brief introduction to the exhibition.

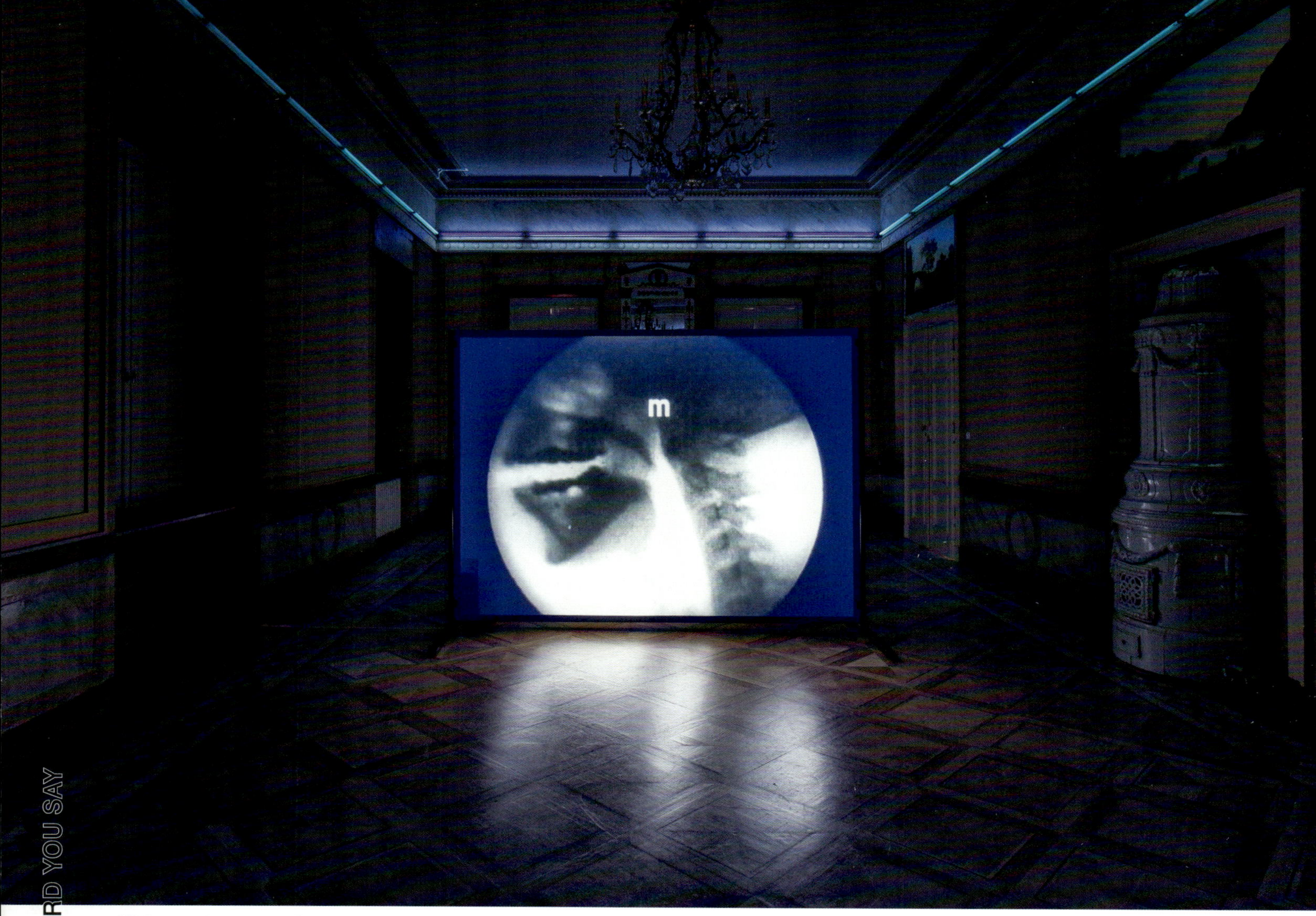

Videoprojektion: *Röntgentonfilm der Sprache*, Robert Janker, Deutschland, 1937. Neu synchronisiert mit der Sprecherin Heike Hagen, deren Stimme aus modernen Sprachanwendungen wie Navigations- und Sprachsteuerungssystemen bekannt ist.

Video projection: *Röntgentonfilm der Sprache* (X-ray sound film of speech), Robert Janker, Germany, 1937. Resynchronised with the German presenter Heike Hagen, whose voice is well known from such modern speech applications as navigation and voice command systems.

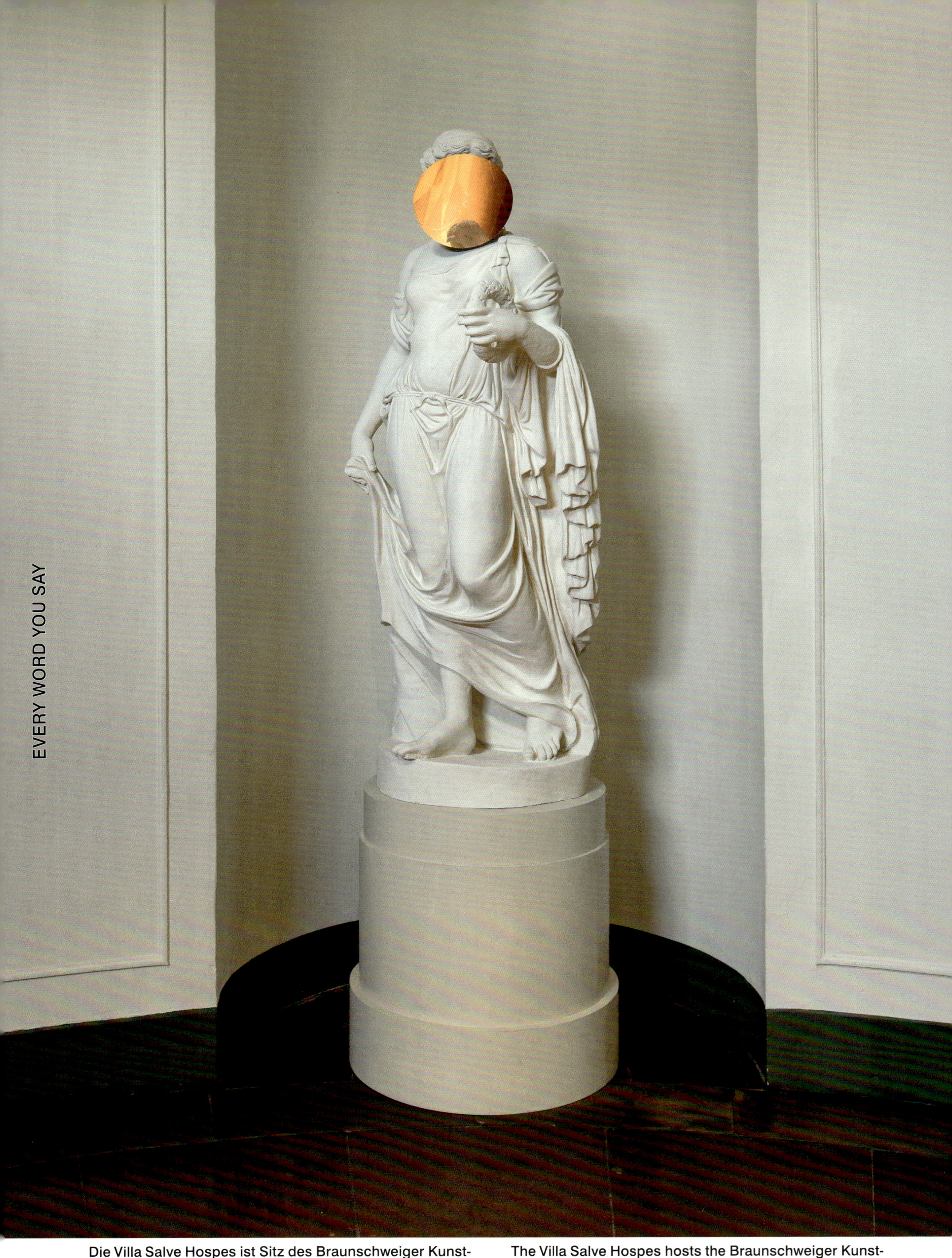

40 Die Villa Salve Hospes ist Sitz des Braunschweiger Kunstvereins. Das Deutsche Spracharchiv nutzte das Gebäude von 1940 bis 1942.

The Villa Salve Hospes hosts the Braunschweiger Kunstverein. The German Language Archives used the building from 1940 – 1942.

SCREENS IN TRANSITION: ZUR DIFFUSION IM KINORAUM

Lilian Haberer

„Der Film hat die Frage selbst nach dem Bühnenraum, nach seiner Immobilität und der Distanz zwischen ihm und der Distanz zwischen dem Zuschauer ad absurdum geführt. Die Leinwand ist ein imaginärer Punkt und ihre Immobilität ist ebenfalls nur eine imaginäre. Die Distanz zwischen Zuschauer und Schauspieler verändert sich ununterbrochen, sie existiert im Grunde gar nicht. Es gibt lediglich Maßstäbe, Aufnahmedistanzen."[1]

Der Kinoraum wird historisch und kulturell nicht nur als ein Ort der Entgrenzung wahrgenommen. Vielmehr zeigen sich in ihm und seinen Vorgängermodellen der Licht- und Schattenspiele[2] verschiedene Formen gemeinschaftlicher Teilhabe an einem gleichsam filmischen wie sozialen Ereignis. Dabei umfasst der Projektionsvorgang diaphaner Bilder auf eine Leinwand bereits die zeitliche Durchquerung eines gegebenen Raums und das Eröffnen eines anderen Bild- und Imaginationsfeldes. Der französische Filmtheoretiker Dominique Païni hat auf die semantische Vielfalt des Projektionsbegriffs hingewiesen, die sowohl die Vorstellungskraft und Vergegenwärtigung als auch die Wucht des Nach-vorne-Schleuderns eines Bildes beinhaltet.[3] An dem Schauplatz eines Screenings findet demnach auch ein Transfer sowie eine Transformation der Bilder statt: von gezeigten und filmisch vergegenwärtigten Orten sowie ein kultureller Übersetzungsprozess.

Es ist dieser Raum des Übergangs filmischer und imaginierter Bilder, sozialer und kultureller Schauplätze, der im Werk von Clemens von Wedemeyer zum zentralen Motiv und zur Reflexionsfigur wird. Dabei fungiert der Screen gleichsam als Grenze und als Schnittstelle zwischen verschiedenen sozialen Gruppen, aber auch zu den damit verbundenen Machtkonstellationen. Der Screen wird in seinen Film- und Videoinstallationen durchlässig und bringt damit Sicht- und Wertordnungen ins Wanken, wie es bereits in seiner Abschlussarbeit *Drehbuch* an der Hochschule für Grafik und Buchkunst Leipzig deutlich wird. Die eingangs zitierte Textstelle des russischen Formalisten Boris Eichenbaum

verwendete der Künstler 2001 in seinem *Drehbuch*, das in sieben Kapiteln eine Kinoerfahrung sowie die Produktion eines Films skizziert, indem es Zitate von maßgeblichen Film- und Gesellschaftstheorien mit Regieanweisungen zusammenführt. Das Zitat deutet an, dass der Film sich aufgrund der verstärkten Wahrnehmung einzelner Gesten und filmischer Techniken der Erzählung als „synkretistischer Form" gegenüber dem Theater und der Literatur behaupten könne. Das Kinopublikum geht dabei ebenfalls aus der Filmerfahrung verändert hervor, wie Eichenbaum in seinem programmatischen Text *Probleme der Filmstilistik* (1927) in Abgrenzung zum Theaterraum betonte.[4]

Clemens von Wedemeyers Text entstand als Theorieteil seiner Diplomarbeit aus der Idee heraus, dass Protagonisten der Filmkultur die Zitate vor der Kamera rezitieren.[5] Das Drehbuch, das der Künstler parallel zu seinem 35 mm Diplomfilm *Occupation* (2001–2002) konzipiert hatte und das den institutionellen wie sozialen Raum des Kinos untersucht, wurde jedoch nie verfilmt, sondern erschien 2009 in Buchversion. 2010 folgte eine Inszenierung als „Live-Hörspiel".

Adressierte Clemens von Wedemeyer in *Occupation* Statisten als agierende Masse während eines nächtlichen Außendrehs, wechselweise im Close-up und aus dem high-angle shot, die gemäß den Anweisungen der Regieführenden sich auf einem immer kleineren Feld zusammendrängen und zum Schluss ein explosives Eigenleben entwickeln, so variiert bei der Präsentation des Films die individuelle Projektionserfahrung: Wurde die Arbeit 2006 im Kölnischen Kunstverein im Kinosaal gezeigt, war sie in Santiago de Compostela für eine ca. vier mal sechs Meter große Leinwand vorgesehen, welche das sich frei bewegende Publikum in die Gruppe der lebensgroß und oftmals in Rückenansicht projizierten Personen einbezog. Darüber hinaus diffundierten die Darstellenden durch Anschnitte, Großaufnahmen, Suspense und die Inszenierung von Licht und Schatten in den Installationsraum. Ebenso trugen mehrfache Wiederholungen gezeigter

Einstellungen, ähnlich wie kurze Loops, zur Modellhaftigkeit und Skulpturalität der filmischen Versuchsanordnung bei, als könnten die Szenen und ihre filmischen Kunstgriffe extrahiert und erneut für sich betrachtet werden: etwa bei der Kamerabewegung durch eine Statistenreihe und ihre teilweise Untermalung durch ein filmisches Zitat mit einem Dialog aus Jean-Luc Godards *Le Mépris* (1963). Der Screen wird hier zu einer durchlässigen Membran und ermöglicht eine kinästhetische Einbeziehung, anders als die illusionäre und identifikatorische des Publikums als „Vierte Wand"[6]. Andererseits lässt er auch die verschiedenen Kollektive – Regieteam, Statisten und Zuschauende – und ihre Einflussnahme auf die jeweils andere Gruppe in ihrer Dynamik hervortreten. Clemens von Wedemeyer erzeugt diese Öffnung des Screens jedoch auch über Irritationsmomente, bestimmte Handlungen und Gesten, die nicht oder anders als erwartet in dem für sie vorgesehenen Kontext der Filmproduktion ausgeführt werden. Diese wirken disloziert, wie das stumme Ziehen einer Linie mit Farbe auf dem Gras als Grenze für die Statistengruppe, die bereits über die strenge Begrenzung quillt, oder die Bewegung der Masse als zum Selbstzweck erhobene Choreografie.

Saskia Vermeulen hat in ihrer luziden Analyse von *Occupation* nicht nur auf die Verbindung dieser den Statisten im Film aufgezeigten Begrenzung analog zur cinematischen Kadrierung hingewiesen und auf das Spiegelungsmoment der Filmproduktion im real produzierten Film, sondern auch auf das Gebanntsein von und vor der Leinwand („to become glued to the screen").[7] Der Klebstoff zwischen Betrachterschaft und Screen bei gleichzeitiger Durchlässigkeit desselben besteht somit in der losen Verbindung schauspielerisch ausagierter Szenen, effektvoll eingesetzter filmischer Techniken und dislozierter Gesten. Ebenso ist das Skript in *Drehbuch* durch ein heterogenes Montageprinzip geprägt: Die modellhaft betitelten Kapitel (beispielsweise „Trennung"), ihre Szenen und die von Protagonisten in den Mund gelegten Filmtheorien variieren mit den Beschreibungen ritualisierter Handlungen im Kino und Begriffen der Prä- und Postproduktion.

Diese Kinoräume als Projektionsflächen des Übergangs werden in den filmischen Arbeiten und Ausstellungsprojekten Clemens von Wedemeyers subtil und mit den diversen Begleiterscheinungen, die Übersetzungsprozesse wie auch Grenz- und Entgrenzungserfahrungen mit sich bringen, in Szene gesetzt.

Dabei ist der Kinoraum einerseits ein gewählter Rahmen seiner Screenings, wie bei dem 35 mm Film *Von Gegenüber*, den der Künstler 2007 im Rahmen der skulptur projekte münster 07 in dem leerstehenden Metropolis Kino neben dem Hauptbahnhof zeigte. Andererseits wird der Filmdreh bei *Occupation* selbst Gegen-

stand der Mise en Scène, oder in zahlreichen Making-ofs, die Clemens von Wedemeyer jeweils von seinen künstlerischen Projekten realisierte. Diese, den Modus der Produktion dokumentierenden und reflektierenden Videoarbeiten (*The Making of Occupation*, *The Making of Big Business*, *The Making of Otjesd*) etablieren, wie Manuel Segade konstatierte, eine alternative Perspektive, einen anderen dekonstruierenden Blick[8] oder ermöglichen eine Distanznahme zum kinematografischen Dispositiv mit filmischen Mitteln. Dient das Genre des Making-of von Spielfilmen vielfach auch der Authentifizierung oder Identifikation mit einem filmischen Projekt, so erweitert Clemens von Wedemeyer die filmische Kadrierung der Ausgangsarbeit jenseits einer selbstreferenziellen Struktur um den Blick auf die Abläufe und Mechanismen des Drehs.

Aber auch das Screening im Kinoraum oder in der Black Box der Ausstellung in ihren dispositiven Anordnungen von Projektor, Leinwand, Licht, Raum und Zuschauer erfahren eine Erweiterung mittels ihrer sozialen Situierung, auf die der Künstler fokussiert, und der von ihm thematisierten Verflechtung vom Kino- mit dem städtischen Raum, wie in seiner Arbeit *Von Gegenüber*. Der rund neununddreißigminütige 35 mm Film dokumentiert im Point-of-View-Shot einen Tag von der Morgen- in die Abenddämmerung rund um den Hauptbahnhof Münster. Die Aneignung des öffentlichen Raums fand in unmittelbarer Nachbarschaft desjenigen leerstehenden Metropolis Kinos statt, in dem der Film während der skulptur projekte münster 07 gezeigt wurde. *Von Gegenüber* beginnt mit Schwarzfilm, bevor die subjektive Kamera ihre Bewegung im Schritttempo aus einem Park heraus in den Hauptbahnhof Münster hinein, auf den Gleisen in die Bahnhofsmission und durch die Gänge hindurch aufnimmt. Dabei erfasst sie Reisende, Personengruppen, Flanierende und Versatzstücke ihrer Gespräche, die dann aus der allgemeinen Geräuschkulisse herausgefiltert hervorgehoben werden. Mitunter nimmt die Umgebung auch von der Kamera Notiz, indem sich ein Passant umdreht oder eine Person ausweicht. Wie bei der selektiven Wahrnehmung eines Reisenden werden filmisch einzelne Szenen herausgestellt, die ein Narrativ erzeugen. Dieses funktioniert analog zum literarischen Erzählen mit der Technik eines stream of consciousness in den verschiedene Figuren, Kollektive und Irritationsmomente, Haupt- und Nebenstränge wie beiläufig eingeflochten werden: sei es die fein gekleidete Dame, die als Flaneurin innehält und ihren eigenen Beobachtungen nachhängt oder eine Gruppe von Demonstranten für mehr Konsum, aber auch drei Geschäftsleute, die sich über die Stadtentwicklung des Bahnhofsgrundstücks austauschen. Dabei variieren die Szenen zwischen der Aufzeichnung des alltäglichen Betriebs am Bahnhof und inszenierten Szenen, die mitunter ununterscheidbar werden. Wie Tessa Giblin analysierte, werden wir Zeugen dieser Dichotomie von Innen- und Außenleben des Bahnhofs, der Geschichten und seiner bedingt öffentlichen Räume, von Ein- wie Ausgrenzungsprozessen.[9] Die Kamera wird hier zur Flaneurin. Clemens von Wedemeyer relativiert jedoch den Bahnhof als transitorischen „Nicht-Ort"[10], da er dort andere Aktivitäten und Handlungen als nur diejenigen der Reisenden in den Blick nimmt. Die Bewegung durch den Außenraum von Münster während der skulptur projekte im und um das Metropolis Kino ermöglicht darüber hinaus eine Überblendung der filmischen mit der eigenen Erfahrung, wie bei dem Spiegelungsmoment der Filmproduktion in *Occupation*. Sie lässt „das Filmtheater zu einer Skulptur werden, zu einer negativen Skulptur", wie der Künstler betonte,[11] da sie keine Übersicht bietet, sondern sein Innenleben in Bewegung nachvollzieht. Eine skulpturale Setzung hingegen nimmt die hier nur beispielhaft erwähnte 3-Kanal-Videoinstallation *Muster* (2012) vor, die aus drei großformatigen, zum Trapez mit schmalen Zwischenräumen mittig im Raum installierten Leinwänden besteht und so in der großen Halle des Kulturbahnhofs der dOCUMENTA (13) in Kassel gezeigt wurde: Auf drei Screens entfaltet sich das Reenactment dreier Zeiten und Begebenheiten (1945, 1970 und 1994) des als Konzentrations- und Arbeitslager, aber auch als Mädchenerziehungsheim genutzten Benediktinerklosters Breitenau bei Kassel. Erst im Umrunden des Dreiecksscreens und der sich mitunter überlagernden Tonspur werden die Schnittstellen, filmischen Anschlüsse des Ortes und seiner inszenierten Begebenheiten vergegenwärtigt. Einzig die Bewegung und die auf den Screens unterschiedlich aktivierten (Psycho-)Topografien des Klosters ermöglichen sowohl eine affektive Einbeziehung in das sichtbar reinszenierte Geschehen als auch einen Blick durch die Zeit hindurch und seine kaleidoskopische Brechung.

Wie Giuliana Bruno in ihrer Studie zu filmischen und architektonischen Reisen beschreibt, wird das mit Bewegung übersetzte altgriechische Wort „kinema" zudem affektiv aufgefasst. Sie analysiert verschiedene Formen des Transports, derjenigen der Filmspule, aber auch der Emotion, und verweist ähnlich wie die Situationisten der 1960er Jahre auf eine Psychogeografie der Bilder, Orte und Kartografien, die in andere Räume diffundieren.[12] Fragen der Diffusion, Migration und des Transits von Menschen an territorialen Grenzen, die dort verhandelten Machtpolitiken bearbeitet der Künstler ebenfalls in seinen Filmarbeiten *Otjesd* und *The Making of Otjesd* (beide 2005) anhand von modellhaft inszenierten Nicht-Orten des Wartens und des Schlangestehens vor der Deutschen Botschaft in Moskau zur Ausreise in den Westen. Im Rahmen der Ausstellung *When there is hope* in der Hamburger Kunsthalle 2015 wurde *Otjesd* projiziert und das Making-of auf dem gegenüberliegenden

Monitor so installiert, dass die Besucher ähnlich wie bei einer Grenzkontrolle durch die Ausstellungsarchitektur gelenkt wurden. Eine Übertragung des psychischen Apparats auf den kinematografischen findet dennoch in dieser Zeit statt, etwa mit Thierry Kuntzels Metapher des Projektionsstrahls als Element der Einschreibung in den Filmtext.[13] Inwiefern verändert sich die Wahrnehmung der in einem Kino sowohl kinästhetisch wahrgenommenen wie auch affizierenden Sequenzen, wenn ein öffentlicher Ort ohne spezifische Zugangsbedingungen für die Screenings fungiert, wie bei Clemens von Wedemeyers nachfolgend analysiertem *Sun Cinema* (2010) oder auch bei *Von Gegenüber* mit dem semiöffentlichen Raum des Kinos der skulptur projekte münster 07? Welche Projektionen brechen sich im Kinoraum als einem Ort kultureller Praxis, Schauplatz utopischer, fiktionaler wie auch realistischer Aushandlung? Anhand der diskutierten Filmarbeiten, beispielhaft erwähnter Werke und ihrer installativen Kontexte wird deutlich, dass Film und Screen die Folie der zwischenmenschlich ausgehandelten Grenz- und Übergangssituationen bilden. Selbst in *Muster* wird ein Filmdreh reinszeniert, derjenige zu Ulrike Meinhofs *Bambule* (1970). Bei *Otjesd* ist es das nur aus wenigen Requisiten wie Absperrgittern und Metalldetektoren bestehende Filmset, das als Grenzzone in einem Waldstück mit Einwanderern als Akteure und ihren Dialogen gleichsam zeichenhaft wie überzeichnet vergegenwärtigt wird und die prekäre Realität dieser Transitzonen hervortreten lässt. Der Film, sein kultureller Raum wie auch der Screen als Übergangszone sind für die künstlerische Arbeit ein notwendiger Rahmen, um in der Inszenierung real vorhandene und fragile Bruchstellen menschlicher Interaktion aufzuspüren wie auch begreifbar werden zu lassen.

Die Frage sowohl nach einer kulturellen Verortung der Projektionen als auch ihrer Entgrenzung in andere Orte und Kontexte wird anhand von Clemens von Wedemeyers jüngster Arbeit *Sun Cinema* aufgeworfen: Sie besteht aus einem großformatigen Screen an einem markanten Abhang, einen Kilometer westlich von der ca. siebentausend Jahre alten, hoch gelegenen Stadt Mardin in der südöstlichen Türkei, nahe der Grenze zu Syrien und zum Irak. Zur Altstadt hin weist das Projekt eine flache, helle Seite, zur Ebene eine Fläche aus leicht konvex gewölbten, spiegelnd polierten Stahlplatten auf. Vor dem freistehenden Projektionsschirm sind weiße Stufen in den Hügel eingelassen, den Höhenlinien nachempfunden, die abgetreppt ein Amphitheater formen. Auf Einladung des British Council im Rahmen von „My City" hat Clemens von Wedemeyer die Gestaltung und Architektur des *Sun Cinema* während eines Workshops mit Studierenden der Technischen Hochschule Istanbul und mit dem Architekten Gürden Gür realisiert. Signifikant ist ein konischer Steinquader in den hinteren Zuschauerreihen, auf dem der Projektor platziert wird und der dem Projektionsstrahl nachempfunden wurde.[14]

Der Kinoraum als Referenzgröße, Rahmen und Gegenstand erfährt ohne Wände in diesem Projekt eine reale und kulturelle Entgrenzung. Er ist frei zugänglich und von allen Seiten sichtbar. Als Freiluftlichtspiel weist er einzig die dispositive Grundanordnung von Projektor, Auditorium und Leinwand auf. Je nach Jahreszeit und Frequentierung der Gegend ändert sich der Rahmen. Jedoch zeigt dieses nur eine Seite des Projekts: den Wunsch, einen kulturellen Raum für Screenings als Versammlungsort und als Blickdispositiv auf die Landschaft zu realisieren. Die andere entsteht mit dem großformatigen, fragmentierten Spiegel, der eine Projektion und Reflexion des Sonnenlichts ermöglicht, das sich tagsüber auf der Fläche bricht und ein anderes, natürliches Lichtschauspiel erzeugt. Die Geschichte der Projektion des Lichts wie des Blicks, eine Typologie von Amphitheatern und historischen Sonnenuhren, Sonnensymboliken und -kulten stellen demnach wesentliche Referenzen für dieses Kinoprojekt dar, das der Künstler in seinem programmatischen Text als „Sonnenskulptur" bezeichnete.[15] Es liegt zwischen Stadt und Land und bewegt sich ebenfalls kulturell in einem Zwischenraum –, da es dort zwar ein Filmfestival, aber fünfundzwanzig Jahre lang kein Kino gab: ein Raum, den der Künstler mit seiner Skulptur für die Stadt und die lokale Filmgesellschaft kooperativ entwickelt und zur Verfügung gestellt hat. Das Kino findet hier als Kulturtechnik und sozialer, kommunaler Raum seine Wiederbelebung.[16]

Die Platzierung dieses neuen Open-Air-Kinoraums für die aus vielen Kulturen gewachsene Stadt Mardin, die wegen ihres städtebaulichen Bestands nicht nur als Kulturerbe-Anwärter, sondern auch durch die jüngst aufgeflammten Konflikte der türkischen Regierung mit der PKK wieder in den Fokus rückte, ist demnach von Kontroversen begleitet, wie der rund fünfzigminütige Film *Sun Cinema Location* (2010) nahelegt. Dieser wirft einen Blick auf die Geschichte der Suche nach dem richtigen Ort und die Debatte über das Kino in der Bevölkerung. Er situiert auch den Künstler, der mitunter aus dem Off Stellung bezieht und die kritischen Fragen des Plenums filmisch integriert. Der Film umschreibt wie bei früheren Arbeiten ein Making-of des künstlerischen Projekts, lässt jedoch weniger seine filmische Entstehung als den Prozess einer kulturellen und lokalen Situierung des Kinoraums nachvollziehbar werden. Die eingangs im Eichenbaum-Zitat erwähnte Aufhebung zwischen Film- und Betrachterfigur erfährt durch das Making-of, das den eigenen Entstehungsprozess mit allen seinen lokalen Akteuren inszeniert, eine Spiegelung: Agierende werden zu Rezipierenden und umgekehrt. Damit eröffnet *Sun Cinema Location* neben dem transitorischen Ort des Kinos zwischen

Natur- und filmischer Projektion einen parallelen Diskurs, der mit der Nutzung dieses neuen Kinoraums von den Bewohnern und Reisenden jeweils neu ausgehandelt wird.

1 Zitat eines Beobachters aus: Clemens von Wedemeyer: *Drehbuch*, Leipzig: Spector Books, 2009. Ohne Seitenangabe. Zitiert nach Boris M. Eichenbaum: „Probleme der Filmstilistik" (1927), in: Franz-Josef Albersmeier (Hg.): *Texte zur Theorie des Films*, Stuttgart: Reclam, 1984, S.116.
2 Vgl. Tom Gunning: „The Long and Short of it: Centuries of Projecting Shadows From Natural Magic to the Avant-Garde", in: Stan Douglas, Christopher Eamon (Hg.): *The Art of Projection*, Ostfildern: Hatje Cantz, 2009, S.23–35.
3 Vgl. Dominique Païni: „Should we Put an End to Projection?" (übersetzt von Rosalind Krauss), *October*, H.110 (2004), S.23.
4 Eichenbaum: „Probleme der Filmstilistik", S.116 f.
5 Manuel Segade: „On Cinema as Public Space", Interview, in: Quinn Latimer: „Mono: Clemens von Wedemeyer", *Kaleidoscope*, H.7 (2010), S.125.
6 Vgl. zu Denis Diderots Konzept der „Vierten Wand" im Theater und Bertolt Brechts Verfremdungseffekt bis hin zu den Filmtheoretikern Sergej Eisenstein u.a., Ilse Lafer: „Hinter der Vierten Wand. Einführung", in: dies. (Hg.): *Hinter der Vierten Wand. Fiktive Leben – Gelebte Fiktionen*, Ausstellungskatalog Generali Foundation Wien, Nürnberg: Verlag für Moderne Kunst, 2010, S.15–29.
7 Saskia Vermeulen: „Occupation. The Making of Occupation", in: *Clemens von Wedemeyer. The Repetition Festival Show*, Ausstellungskatalog, Trento/Dublin: Projects Arts Center Dublin/Fondazione Galleria Civica Trento, 2010, S.6.
8 Manuel Segade: „Screen Affections", in: Clemens von Wedemeyer: *Seven Films*, Santiago de Compostela/Leipzig: Xunta de Galicia/Spector Books, 2009, S.118 f.
9 Tessa Giblin: „From the Opposite Side", in: *Clemens von Wedemeyer. The Repetition Festival Show*, 2010, S.25.
10 Marc Augé: *Orte und Nicht-Orte. Vorüberlegung zu einer Ethnologie der Einsamkeit*, Frankfurt am Main: Fischer, 1994.
11 Manuel Segade: „On Cinema as Public Space", S.127.
12 Vgl. Giuliana Bruno: „Bewegung und Emotion: Reisen in Kunst, Architektur und Film", in: Gertrud Koch (Hg.): *Umwidmungen – architektonische und kinematographische Räume*, Berlin: Vorwerk 8, 2005, S.120. Vgl. auch dies.: *Atlas of Emotion. Journeys in Art Architecture and Film*, London: Verso, 2002.
13 Vgl. Thierry Kuntzel: „A note Upon the Filmic Apparatus", *Quarterly Review of Film Studies*, H.3 (1976), S.266–275.
14 Clemens von Wedemeyer: „Sun Cinema", in: *Slash*, www.slash.fr/en/evenements/clemens-von-wedemeyer (letzte Sichtung 18.8.2016).
15 Clemens von Wedemeyer: „Sun Cinema, Mardin, Türkei, 2010", in: Clemens von Wedemeyer: *Orte unter Einfluss / Affected Places*, Leipzig: Spector Books, 2016, S.50.
16 Gertrud Koch, Volker Pantenburg, Simon Rothöhler (Hg.): *Screen Dynamics. Mapping the Borders of Cinema*, Wien: Synema, 2002, S.5.

SCREENS IN TRANSITION: ON DIFFUSION IN THE CINEMA

Lilian Haberer

"Film has rendered absurd any questions about the immobility of the stage and the distance between stage and spectator. The screen is an imaginary point, and its immobility is also only imaginary. The distance between spectator and actor changes continuously—basically, it does not exist at all. There are merely different scales and camera distances."[1]

Historically and culturally, the cinema is not only seen as a boundless site. Instead, the cinema and its predecessors of light and shadow play[2] reveal various forms of social participation in an event that, as it were, is cinematic and social. In the process, the act of projecting diaphanous images on the screen includes the temporal transition through a given space and the opening of a different space of image and imagination. French film theorist Dominique Païni referred to the semantic diversity of the concept of projection, which includes both imagination and presentation as well as the power of hurling an image forward in space.[3] Accordingly, when a film is screened, a transfer of images takes place: from sites that are shown in and imagined during the film, combined with a cultural process of translation.

It is this space between the transition of filmed and imagined images, the social and cultural settings that becomes a central motif and figure of reflection in the work of Clemens von Wedemeyer. Here, the screen serves as a limit and point of intersection between various social groups, but also a limit to linked constellations of power. This limit becomes permeable in his film and video installations, and destabilises orders of vision and value, as already shown in his thesis project *Screenplay* at Leipzig's Academy of Fine Arts. The text quoted at the opening of this text by the Russian formalist Boris Eikhenbaum was used by the artist in 2001 in *Screenplay*, which sketches a cinema experience and the production of a film in seven chapters, bringing together quotations from important film and social theories with stage directions. The quotation indicates that film due to the amplified perception of individual gestures and film techniques of narrative can assert itself as a "syncretic form" vis-à-vis theatre and literature. The cinema audience, unlike the theatre audience, leaves the film experience altered, as Eikhenbaum emphasised in his programmatic text "Problems of Cine-Stylistics" (1927).[4]

Clemens von Wedemeyer's text was written as the theoretical part of his thesis, with the idea that major figures from the film culture would recite the quotations in front of the camera.[5] Nevertheless, the screenplay, which the artist conceived parallel to his 35mm thesis film *Occupation* (2001–2002) and which examines the institutional and social space of the cinema, was never filmed, but appeared in book form in 2009. In 2010, a "live audio play" version followed.

While in *Occupation*, Clemens von Wedemeyer looked at extras as an acting mass of people during a nocturnal film shooting, alternately in close-up and from a high angle shot that according to the director is to become ever smaller and finally take on an explosive life of its own, the presentation of the film varies the individual projection experience: The work was shown in the cinema of the Kölnischer Kunstverein in 2006, but it was intended for a screen of four by six meters in Santiago de Compostela, including the freely-moving audience among the group of persons that were life-sized and often projected from the rear. Furthermore, the performers diffused by way of partial views, close-ups, suspense and the staging of light and shadows within the space of installation. In addition, several repetitions of shots, like short loops, also contributed to the model-like, sculptural quality of the shots, as if the scenes and their cinematic devices could be extracted from the film and examined on their own: for example, in the camera movement through a series of extras and their projection against the background of a film clip with dialogue from Jean-Luc Godard's *Le Mépris* (1963). The screen here becomes a permeable membrane and allows for inclusion in the kinaesthetic experience, unlike the illusionary and identificatory aspect of the audience as a fourth wall in the film theatre.[6]

Beside that, the various collectives—director team, extras and spectators—and their influence on the respective other groups appear in their dynamics. Nonetheless, Clemens von Wedemeyer also generates this opening of the screen by way of irritations, with actions and gestures that do not take place or are used in a way that is unlike the context intended for them in the film production. These seem dislocated, like the silent marking of a line on the grass as a border for the group of extras that already swells over the strict boundary, or the movement of the mass of extras as a choreography which is an end in itself.

In her lucid analysis of *Occupation*, Saskia Vermeulen not only pointed to the analogy between the line drawn for the extras in the film and cinematic framing and the way the film production itself is mirrored in the actually produced film, but also to the fact that one is "glued to the screen."[7] The glue between the viewers and the screen with simultaneous permeability of the latter thus consists in the loose linkage of acted-out scenes, effectively used film techniques and dislocated gestures. At the same time, the script in *Screenplay* is shaped by a heterogeneous montage principle: the chapters used, with model-like titles, for example "Trennung" (Separation), their scenes and the film theories placed in the mouths of the actors alternate with descriptions of ritualised acts in the cinema and concepts of pre- and post-production.

These cinematic spaces as projection surfaces of transition are subtly staged in the films and exhibition projects of Clemens von Wedemeyer, with diverse side-effects that involve processes of translation as well as experiences of limits and liberation from limitation.

In the process, the cinematic space is, on the one hand, a selected framework for his screenings, as in the 35 mm film *From the Opposite Side*, which the artist showed in 2007 as part of skulptur projekte münster 07 at the vacant Metropolis cinema next to the city's main railway station. At the same time, the act of filmmaking itself becomes a subject of the mise en scène in *Occupation*, or in the numerous making-ofs that Clemens von Wedemeyer realised as part of his artistic projects. These video works (*The Making of Occupation*, *The Making of Big Business*, *The Making of Otjesd*), which document and reflect on the production of video works, establish, as Manuel Segade confirmed, an alternative perspective, a different de-constructing gaze[8] or enable a taking distance from the cinematographic apparatus with film devices. If the genre of the making-of often leads to the authentification of or identification with a film project, Clemens von Wedemeyer expands the cinematic framing of the work in question beyond its self-referential structure by examining the processes and mechanisms of shooting.

But screenings in the cinema or in the black box of the exhibition with their arrangements of projector, screen, light, space, and spectators undergo an expansion by way of their social situation, which the artist focuses on, and the interweaving of the cinema with the urban space as thematised by the artist, as in his work *From the Opposite Side*. The ca. 39 minute, 35 mm film documents a day in the life from morning until evening around Munster's main station in a point-of-view shot. The appropriation of public space took place directly near the vacant Metropolis cinema, where the film was shown during skulptur projekte münster 07. *From the Opposite Side* begins with black film, before the subjective camera initiates its movement at a walking pace out of a park into Munster Main Station past the tracks to the railway mission (Bahnhofsmission) and through the corridors. In the process, it captures travellers, groups of people, flâneurs, and bits of their conversations, which then are filtered out of the general backdrop of sound. Sometimes, the people take notice of the camera, when a passer-by turns around or a person avoids the camera. As in the selective perception of a traveller, individual scenes are selected for their cinematic value, as they generate a narrative. This operates analogously to literary narration with the technique of stream of consciousness in which various figures, collectives, and moments of disturbance, main and auxiliary plot lines are interwoven with one another in a virtually coincidental way: be it the finely dressed woman, who takes pause as a flâneur lost in her own observations, or a group demonstrating for more consumption, or three businessmen exchanging ideas about the urban development of the railroad property. In so doing, the scenes vary between the recording of everyday activity at the train station and staged scenes that become distinguishable from one another. As Tessa Giblin has analysed, we become witnesses of the dichotomy of the inner and outer life of the train station, its stories, and its partially public spaces, processes of inclusion and exclusion.[9] The camera here becomes a flâneur. Clemens von Wedemeyer, however, relativises the train station as a transitory "non-place,"[10] since he looks at other activities and actions as just those of the travellers. Outdoor movement in Munster during skulptur projekte in and around the Metropolis cinema also enables an overlapping of cinematic experience with one's own, as in the moment of mirroring film production in *Occupation*. In this way, "the film theatre can become a sculpture, a negative sculpture," as the artist emphasised,[11] since it doesn't offer an overview, but only traces inner life in movement. A sculptural statement in contrast is made by the 3-channel video installation *Rushes* (2012), here only mentioned by way of example, which consists of three large-format screens installed in the middle of the space as a trapezoid with a narrow intervening space, and was shown in the large hall of the Kulturbahnhof at dOCUMENTA (13) in Kassel in this way. On three screens, the re-enactment of three times and events are unfolded (1945, 1970, and 1994) in the history of the former Benedictine monastery Breitenau near Kassel, which was used as a concentration and labour camp, later as a girls reformatory. Only by walking around the triangular screen and the overlying sound track are the intersections, cinematic references to the location and its staged occurrences presented. Movement and the psycho-topographies of the monastery differently activated on screen allow for both an affective inclusion in the visibly re-staged events, as well as a view through time and its kaleidoscopic refraction.

As Guiliana Bruno describes in her study on cinematic and architectural travel, the ancient Greek word kinema, which can be translated as movement, is understood affectively. She analyses various forms of transportation, that of the film reel, but also emotion, and refers, like the Situationists during the 1960s, to a psycho-geography of images, sites, and cartographies that diffuse to other spaces.[12] Questions of the diffusion, migration, and displacement of people to territorial borders, and the power politics negotiated there, are treated by the artist in his film works *Otjesd* and *The Making of Otjesd* (both 2005) using exemplarily staged non-places of waiting as well as footage of people standing in line at the German Embassy in Moscow for visas to the West. In 2015, within the context of the exhibition *When there is hope* at the Hamburger Kunsthalle, *Otjesd* was projected onto a screen, and the monitor with the making-of was installed opposite the projection, so the visitors were guided through the architecture of the exhibition as if they were being led through a border checkpoint. A transfer of the psychological apparatus to the cinematographic apparatus takes place during this period, for example with Thierry Kuntzel's metaphor of the "beam of projection" as an element of inscription in the film text.[13] To what extent does the perception of sequences perceived in a cinema change both cinematically and affectively when a public site without specific conditions of access is used for the screening, as in Clemens von Wedemeyer's *Sun Cinema*, analysed in the following, or in *From the Opposite Side* with the semi-public space of the cinema of skulptur projekte münster 07? What projections break in the cinematic space as a site of cultural practice, a site of utopian, fictional, and realistic negotiation? Using the films discussed, works mentioned by way of example and their installation contexts, it becomes clear that together film and screen form the backdrop against which interpersonally negotiated situations of limitation and transition play out. Even in *Rushes*, a film shooting is restaged, that of Ulrike Meinhof's *Bambule*. For *Otjesd*, the film set, consisting of only a few props like protective gates and metal detectors, which depict a border zone in a forest, allows the precarious reality of these transit zones to stand out with immigrants as actors together with their sketchy yet overacted dialogues. Film, its cultural space and the screen as a zone of transition, are the necessary frame for the artistic work to reveal actually existing and fragile fissures of human interaction and to make them palpable in the mise en scène.

The question both of the cultural location of projections and their liberation in other sites and contexts is raised using a recent work by Clemens von Wedemeyer, *Sun Cinema* (2010). This work consists of a large-format screen located on a striking cliff, one kilometre west of the ca. 7000 year old city of Mardin in southeastern Turkey, near the border to Syria and Iraq, located high in the mountains. Towards the old city, the project shows a flat, bright side, down towards the valley a series of slightly convex reflecting polished steel plates. Placed in front of the freestanding projection screen are white steps inserted into the hill, recalling the contours that form a terraced amphitheatre. At the invitation of the British Council in the framework of "My City", Clemens von Wedemeyer realised the design and architecture of *Sun Cinema* during a workshop with students from Istanbul's Technical University and with the architect Gürden Gür. Significant here is that a tapered stone block with a projector on top was placed in the back rows to emulate the light beam of the film projector.[14]

In this project, the cinematic space as a referential variable, frame and object undergoes a real and cultural liberation, without walls. It is freely accessible and visible from all sides. As an outdoor project, it only reveals the basic arrangement of projector, auditorium, and screen. Depending on the season and number of visitors, the framework changes. And yet this only shows one side of the project: realising the desire for a cultural space of screening, as a place of assembly and a gaze apparatus onto the landscape. The other emerges with the large-format fragmented mirror that allows for the projection and reflection of the sunlight, which breaks onto the surface during the day generating a different display of natural light. The history of the projection of light and the gaze, a typology of amphitheatres and historical sundials, sun symbolism and sun cultures accordingly represent key references for this cinema project, which the artist refers to in his programmatic text as "solar sculpture".[15] It lies between the city and countryside and thus moves culturally as well in an intermediate space, where a film festival is held, but where there hasn't been a cinema for twenty five years now, a space that the artist developed with his sculpture for the city and the local film society in a cooperative process and placed at their disposal. Cinema here is reanimated as a cultural technology and a social, communal space.[16]

By placing this new open-air cinema in Mardin with its multi-cultured history, it has drawn attention to the town, not only because of its architecture which was the decisive factor for its nomination as a World Cultural Heritage Site, but also due to the conflicts which have recently flared up between the Turkish government and the PKK. So the controversial discussion which accompanies this site is shown accordingly by the ca. 50 minute film *Sun Cinema Location* (2010). This presents a historical view of the search for the right place and the debate about public cinema. It also places the artist, who occasionally takes a position from off screen and integrates the critical questions of the plenum in a cinematic way. Similar to earlier works, the film presents the making-of behind the artistic project, yet explains not so much its emergence as a film, but rather the process of a cultural and local cinematic space. The abolition of the line separating the film and the spectator mentioned in the Eikhenbaum quotation at the opening of this essay undergoes a reflection by way of the making-of that stages the film's own process of emergence with all its local actors: actors become recipients and vice versa. In so doing, *Sun Cinema Location* opens a parallel discourse alongside the transitory site of the cinema between nature and film projection that is renegotiated with the use of this new cinematic space by residents and travellers in new ways.

1   Quotation from a spectator: Clemens von Wedemeyer: *Screenplay*, Leipzig: Spector Books, 2009. See Boris M. Eikhenbaum: "Probleme der Filmstilistik" (1927), in: *Texte zur Theorie des Films*, (translated by Lisa Schmidt).
2   See Tom Gunning: "The Long and Short of It: Centuries of Projecting Shadows From Natural Magic to the Avant-Garde", in: Stan Douglas, Christopher Eamon (eds.): *The Art of Projection*, Ostfildern: Hatje Cantz, 2009, pp. 23–35.
3   See Dominique Païni: "Should We Put an End to Projection?" (translated by Rosalind Krauss), *October*, No. 110 (2004), p. 23.
4   Boris M. Eikhenbaum: "Problems of Cine-Stylistics" (trans. Richard Sherwood), in: Ann Shukman (ed.): *Russian Poetics in Translation, Vol. 9, The Poetics of Cinema*, Oxford: Old School House, 2013.
5   Manuel Segade: "On Cinema as Public Space", interview, in: Quinn Latimer: "Mono: Clemens von Wedemeyer", *Kaleidoscope*, No. 7 (2010), p. 125.
6   From Denis Diderot's concept of the fourth wall in the theatre and Bertolt Brecht's so-called alienation effect to the film theorists Sergei Eisenstein etc., see Ilse Lafer: "Hinter der Vierten Wand. Einführung", in: idem: *Hinter der Vierten Wand. Fiktive Leben – Gelebte Fiktionen*, Nuremberg: Verlag für Moderne Kunst, 2010, pp. 15–29.
7   Saskia Vermeulen: "Occupation. The Making of Occupation", in: *Clemens von Wedemeyer. The Repetition Festival Show*, Trent / Dublin: Projects Arts Center Dublin / Fondazione Galleria Civica Trento, 2010, p. 6.
8   Manuel Segade: "Screen Affections", in: Clemens von Wedemeyer: *Seven Films*, Santiago de Compostela / Leipzig: Xunta de Galicia / Spector Books, 2009, pp. 118.
9   Tessa Giblin: "From the Opposite Side", in: *Clemens von Wedemeyer. The Repetition Festival Show*, 2010, p. 25.
10 Marc Augé: *Non-Places: An Introduction to Supermodernity*, (trans. John Howe), London: Verso, 1995.
11 Manuel Segade: "On Cinema as Public Space", p. 127.
12 See Giuliana Bruno: "Bewegung und Emotion: Reisen in Kunst, Architektur und Film", in: Gertrud Koch (ed.): *Umwidmungen – architektonische und kinematographische Räume*, Berlin: Vorwerk 8, 2005, p. 120. See also idem: *Atlas of Emotion: Journeys in Art Architecture and Film*, London: Verso, 2002.
13 See Thierry Kuntzel: "A Note Upon the Filmic Apparatus", *Quarterly Review of Film Studies*, No. 3 (1976), pp. 266–275.
14 Clemens von Wedemeyer: "Sun Cinema", in: *Slash*, www.slash.fr/en/evenements/clemens-von-wedemeyer (last accessed: Aug. 18, 2016).
15 Clemens von Wedemeyer: "Sun Cinema, Mardin, Turkey, 2010", in: Clemens von Wedemeyer: *Orte unter Einfluss / Affected Places*, Leipzig: Spector Books, 2016, p. 52.
16 Gertrud Koch, Volker Pantenburg, Simon Rothöhler (eds.): *Screen Dynamics. Mapping the Borders of Cinema*, Vienna: Synema, 2002, p. 5.

SUN CINEMA, MARDIN, TÜRKEI, 2010

Clemens von Wedemeyer

„Auch wenn die Kinoprojektoren einmal nicht mehr rattern, wird es, das glaube ich fest, etwas geben, ‚das wie Kino funktioniert'."[1]

Seit längerer Zeit bereitet mir der Kinoraum schlaflose Nächte. 2001 habe ich den kurzen Film *Occupation* gedreht – als Versuch, die Wirkung des Kinosaals auf die in ihm eingesperrten Zuschauer sichtbar zu machen. Wenn die Zuschauer doch nicht nur passive Konsumenten von Licht und Ton wären, sondern selbst Einfluss auf das Gezeigte hätten, selbst auf der Leinwand zu sehen wären! Oder wenn die Wände in einem Multiplex-Kino verschwunden wären und man frei die Blickrichtungen wechseln könnte, nicht nur Auge und Ohr, sondern der ganze Körper zum Teil der Kinoerfahrung würde, wenn man zur nächsten Leinwand wanderte. Oder wenn das Außen zum Innen wird, die Mauern des Kinos verschwinden, aufgelöst aus Zweifel am Machtinstrument Film – so in meinem Projekt *Von Gegenüber* (2007), als ein Film in dem Kino gezeigt wurde, vor dessen Tür er produziert worden ist; und so nachprüfbar für jeden Einzelnen wurde.

Solche Gedanken habe ich unter anderem in der Publikation *Drehbuch*[2] (*Screenplay*) und in einem Artikel für die Reihe *Transversale* als „Notizen zum Kinokomplex" 2005 versucht zu skizzieren.

„Das Kino, wie wir es kennen – es ist schon tot. Kehren wir die Scherben zusammen und suchen wir ein Neues. Besetzen Sie die Räume, die Säle der Multiplex-Theater. Über den roten Teppich, über die Treppen und an den Mauern vorbei, schneiden wir die Leinwand entzwei, rollen sie ein oder nähen sie zusammen mit der Leinwand aus dem Nebensaal."[3]

In diesem Sinne hatte ich immer Interesse, in Zusammenarbeit mit Architekten andere Formen des Kinos auszuprobieren. Über einen großen Umweg kam ich nun 2010 auch dazu, und zwar in der Stadt Mardin in der Türkei, an der Grenze zu Syrien, wo man auf die mesopotamische Ebene schaut. Aufgrund der früher lebhaften multireligiösen und mehrsprachigen Bevölkerung (Arabisch, Kurdisch, Türkisch, Aramäisch und

andere) nennen einige die Stadt Mardin auch Klein-Jerusalem. In den letzten Jahrzehnten litt die Region allerdings unter dem türkisch-kurdischen Konflikt. Erst im Jahr 2009 wurde nach 25 Jahren hier ein Kino wieder eröffnet, das von einem Kinoverein betrieben wird. Auch ein Filmfestival findet seitdem jedes Jahr im September statt. Zu den Vorführungen kommen am meisten Besucher, wenn man unter freiem Himmel sitzt. Es gibt hier also schon Kino, zwischen all den anderen religiösen Festen, mit unerfüllten Erwartungen in einer konfliktreichen Geschichte. In einem vom British Council initiierten Kunstprojekt habe ich hier ein Freiluftkino konzipiert. Dies wird nun auch vom örtlichen Kinoverein betrieben. Ich hätte auch einen Film machen können, doch schien mir dies in der gegebenen Situation zu kompliziert und egoistisch. Wichtiger war mir ein weiteres Kino als neuer, alternativer, öffentlicher Platz. Lange habe ich nach einem Ort für solch ein Freiluftkino gesucht. Es sollte ein neuer Ort werden, ein eigener und dauernder Platz für ein Kino.

A

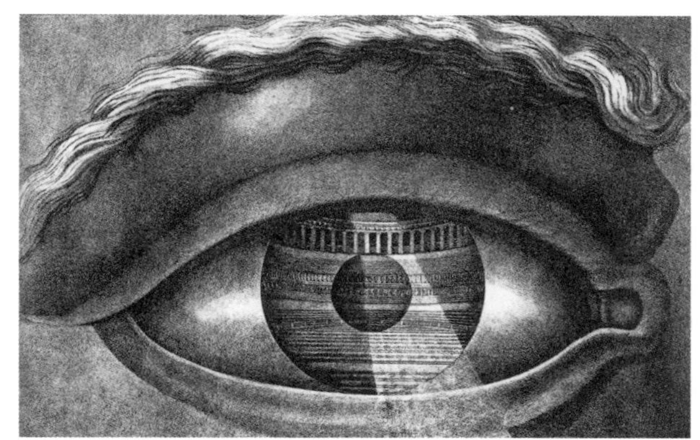

Ich wollte, dass es zwischen der Stadt und der darunter liegenden mesopotamischen Ebene liegt. Unterhalb der Koranschule Kasımiye Medrese aus dem 16. Jahrhundert, am Westrand der Altstadt und direkt über einem Felsen, hatten wir endlich einen fantastischen Ort gefunden. Er liegt etwa einen Kilometer Luftlinie vom Zentrum der Altstadt entfernt; doch direkt hinter der Leinwand beginnt die weite Landschaft. Gleichzeitig fand ein Workshop mit Architekturstudenten aus Istanbul statt, mit denen ich über mögliche

Formen eines Kinos diskutierte, das mit der Sonne in Beziehung steht, oder ein Kino, das sich auf Land-Art bezieht.[4] Es ging mir darum, ein offenes (geöffnetes) Kino zu entwickeln, eines, das von vielen erfahrbar ist und in dem gleichzeitig formale Prinzipien des Kinos sichtbar werden.

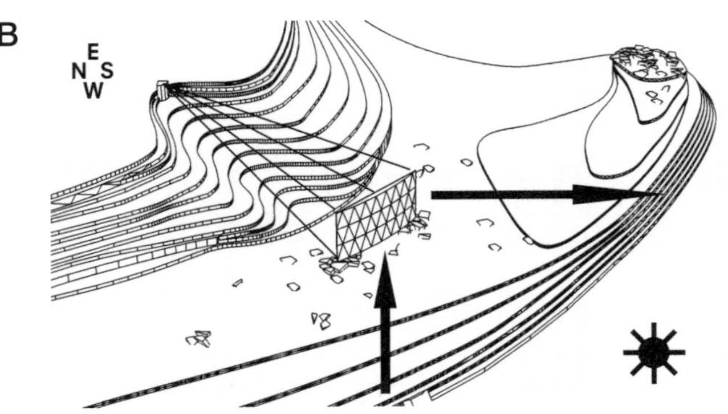

Sun Cinema besteht aus mehreren Teilen: einer frei stehenden Leinwand, einem Amphitheater und einem dreieckigen Sockel für den Projektor. Das Dreieck symbolisiert die Lichtstrahlen des Projektors. Was ist die Beziehung dieses Kinos zur Sonne? Auf die Leinwand fallen morgens die ersten Sonnenstrahlen und man könnte zu dieser Zeit mit dem eigenen Körper Schattenspiele veranstalten. Die untergehende Sonne hingegen wird von der Rückseite, die aus metallenen Spiegelplatten besteht, gen Süden reflektiert. Dazu ist die Leinwand in einem Winkel von 45 Grad zur untergehenden Sonne im Westen aufgebaut. Auf diese Weise wird genau zum Frühlingsanfang, dem kurdischen Neujahr, die Sonne bei Sonnenuntergang nach Süden in die mesopotamische Ebene reflektiert. Als eine Art Sonnenskulptur steht sie tagsüber mit dem Prinzip Kino so immer in direkter Verbindung.

SONNE ALS BELEUCHTER

Ich hatte eine Recherche zu Sonneninstrumenten und Land-Art begonnen und Material gesammelt, das von Ulugh Begs Sonnenobservatorium in Samarkand aus dem 15. Jahrhundert bis zu den *Sun Tunnels* von Nancy Holt in der Great Bassin Wüste, Utah (1973–1976) reichte. Die Verbindung der Sonnensymbolik mit dem Kino bezieht sich auf Lichtversuche im arabischen Altertum, die zeitlich mit der Untersuchung des Auges zusammenfallen. Hans Belting beschreibt in seinem Buch *Florenz und Bagdad. Eine westöstliche Geschichte des Blicks*, dass Untersuchungen des Auges und der Sonne durch arabische Wissenschaftler in der Renaissance zu der Einführung der Zentralperspektive in Westeuropa führten.[5] Die Perspektive ist auch das Prinzip der Kamera. Das Kino ist ein moderner Kult. Ältere Kulte fanden in der Region um Mardin durch die Anbetung der Sonne statt. Die Geschichte Mesopotamiens ist von der Sonne und dem Feuer abhängigen Religionen

(Yezidi, Semsi, Zoroastrismus und anderen) durchdrungen, die aber heute in der Türkei nicht mehr ausgeübt werden dürfen. In Mardin wurde unter einem alten aramäischen Kloster ein Raum mit einem Fenster nach Osten gefunden. Man nimmt an, dass dies ein Ort vorchristlicher Sonnen- oder Feueranbeter, zum Beispiel der Zoroastren, war. Im Kloster wird dieser Raum als Kuriosum vorgeführt. Sonnenkulte wurden in christlich-islamischer Umgebung als Häresie verfolgt und gleichzeitig auf andere Weise in die Religionen eingeschlossen, zum Beispiel als ewiges Licht oder in der Aufgabe, während des Ramadans tagsüber bis zum Sonnenuntergang zu fasten. Das Kino hingegen etablierte sich historisch über Schattenspiele und Camera Obscura als eigene Kunst der Aufnahme und Projektion von Licht. Von daher kann es heute eigentlich eine größere Nähe zu häretischen Lichtritualen reklamieren als ein Kloster.

Eine weitere Beziehung von Sonne und Kino beschreibt auch Alexander Kluge in seinem Buch *Geschichten vom Kino* anhand der Idee vom „Kosmischen Universalkino". Sie geht auf den Juristen Felix Eberty zurück, der 1846 das Buch *Die Gestirne und die Weltgeschichte* publizierte: „Richtigerweise nahm er an, dass ein Lichtstrahl, der die Erde am Karfreitag des Jahres 30 n. Chr. Geburt verlassen hat, sich noch immer im Kosmos vorwärts bewegt, und zwar von uns weg. Insofern sei alle Vorgeschichte im Weltall aufbewahrt auf den Schienen des Lichts. Die ganze Weltgeschichte sei folglich als bewegte Bilderfolge (das Wort Kino kannte Eberty nicht) im Kosmos unterwegs."[6]

HINTER DER LEINWAND SIEHT MAN SICH SELBST

Der Spiegel auf der Rückseite des *Sun Cinema* dient nicht nur der Reflektion der Sonne, im Spiegel kann man sich auch selbst betrachten. Vorne auf der Leinwand laufen Filme anderer, doch wenn man sich am Tag hinter die Leinwand bewegt, sieht man sein eigenes Spiegelbild in der Landschaft. Oder wenigstens die Reflektionen der Sonne auf seiner Haut und Kleidung.

1   Alexander Kluge: *Geschichten vom Kino*, Frankfurt am Main: Suhrkamp, 2007, S. 7.
2   Clemens von Wedemeyer: *Drehbuch*, Leipzig: Spector Books, 2010.
3   Clemens von Wedemeyer: „Notizen zum Kinokomplex", in: Kerstin Hausbei, Franck Hofmann, Nicolas Hubé, Jens E. Sennewald (Hg.): *Transversale. Erkundungen in Kunst und Wissenschaft. Ein europäisches Jahrbuch*, Bd. 1, Paderborn: Wilhelm Fink, 2005, S. 163.
4   Die Gestaltung des Kinos wurde mit Architekturstudenten der Technischen Universität Istanbul diskutiert und zusammen mit Gurden Gür als ausführendem Architekten realisiert.
5   Hans Belting: *Florenz und Bagdad. Eine westöstliche Geschichte des Blicks*, München: C. H. Beck, 2008.
6   Kluge: *Geschichten vom Kino*, S. 44.

A   Recherchematerial zu *Sun Cinema* (2010): Claude-Nicolas Ledoux: „Das Auge des Architekten": Coup d'oeil du Théâtre de Besançon, 1804.
B   *Sun Cinema*, Architekturzeichnung, 2010.
C   Recherchematerial zu *Sun Cinema* (2010): Alhazen (al-Haitham): „Schematische Darstellung der Augen und der damit verbundenen Nerven".
D   Recherchematerial zu *Sun Cinema* (2010): Cesare Cesariano: „Ansicht einer planetarischen Perspektive", 1521.

SUN CINEMA, MARDIN, TURKEY, 2010

Clemens von Wedemeyer

"Even if cinema projectors were no longer to rattle away in future, there will, I believe, be something that 'functions like cinema'."[1]

For quite some time, the cinema has been giving me sleepless nights. In 2001, I shot the short film *Occupation*—an attempt to visualise the impact of the cinema onto the viewers imprisoned in it. If only the spectators were not merely passive consumers of sound and light, but would themselves be able to influence what was being shown—or could even be seen on the screen themselves! Or if there was a multiplex cinema that had no walls so that you could change perspectives freely and look into all directions, not just with the eye and ear, but if the entire body were to become part of the cinematic experience and you could physically wander over to the next screen. Or if the outside became the inside, the walls of the cinema crumbling down, dissolving, as a result of doubt in film as an instrument of power—as in my project *Von Gegenüber* (*From the Opposite Side*, 2007), a film produced in front of the door of the cinema in which it was shown, thus making its authenticity verifiable by every viewer.

I have attempted to illustrate such thoughts in my publication *Screenplay*[2] (*Drehbuch*) and in an article written for the *Transversale* series entitled "Notizen zum Kinokomplex" (Notes on the cinema complex) of 2005.

"The cinema, as we know it—it is already dead. Let us sweep up the remains and look for a new one. Occupy the rooms, the cinema halls of the multiplex theatres. Moving across the red carpet, along the stairs and the walls, we will cut the screen in half, roll it up or sew it together with the screen of the hall next door."[3]

It was in this sense that I was always interested, in collaboration with architects, in trying out other forms of cinema. After a long detour, I was finally able to do so in 2010—in the city of Mardin in south-eastern Turkey, on the border to Syria, looking onto the Mesopotamian plain. Due to its former religiously diverse and multilingual population (Arabic, Kurdish, Turkish, Aramaic,

etc.), Mardin is sometimes referred to as "Little Jerusalem". During recent decades, however, the region has been marred by the Turkish-Kurdish conflict. It was only in 2009, after 25 years, that a cinema was finally able to open its doors again in Mardin. Today it is run by the local cinema association, and a film festival also takes place here every September. More visitors happen to attend when the screenings take place outside. So cinema does already exist here, amidst the many other religious celebrations and unfulfilled expectations in a conflict-ridden history.

C 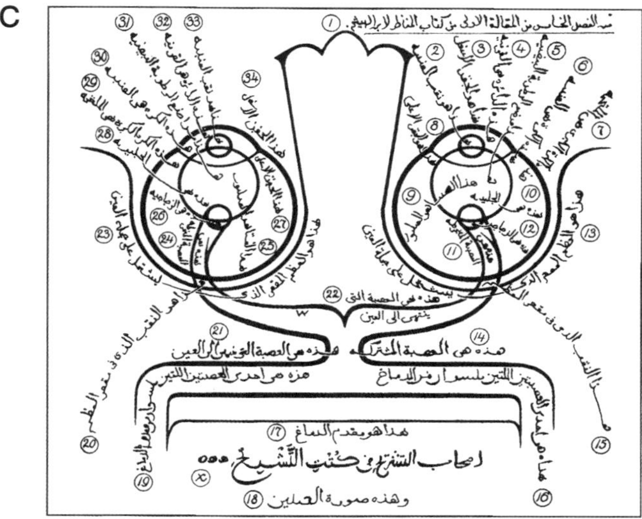

In the context of an art project initiated by the British Council, I designed an open-air cinema for Mardin, which is now also run by the local cinema association. I could have made a film—yet, given the circumstances, that seemed too arduous and egocentric. For me, it was more important to build an additional cinema as a new and alternative public space. I spent a long time looking for the ideal site for this open-air cinema: It should be a new and permanent location intended specifically for the cinema itself.

I wanted it to lie between the city and the Mesopotamian plain below. We finally came upon a fantastic site at the western edge of the old town just beneath the 16th-century Kasımiye Medrese Koran School and directly above a ridge. The place is about a kilometre from the centre of the old town, yet the wide, expansive plains unfold directly behind the screen. I simultaneously held a workshop with architecture students from Istanbul, discussing possible forms of cinema that had associations with the sun or land art.[4] For me, it was about creating an open (or opened) form of cinema, one that could be experienced by many and which also makes the formal principles of cinema visible.

Sun Cinema is composed of multiple parts: a free-standing screen, an amphitheatre and a triangular base for the projector. The triangle symbolises the projector's beams of light. But what are the connections between the cinema and the sun? In the morning, the first rays of sunlight fall onto the screen, and you could enact a shadow play using your own shadow at that time of day. In the evening, the setting sun is reflected back to the south by metallic mirror panels on the back of the screen. So the screen is set up at a 45-degree angle to the sun as it sets in the west. The setting sun is thus reflected southwards and into the Mesopotamian plain promptly at the start of spring, the Kurdish New Year. As a kind of solar sculpture, it is directly linked to the principle of cinema during the day.

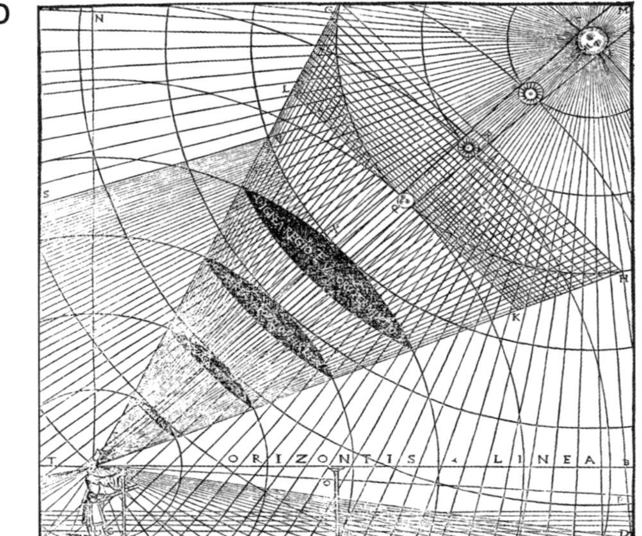

D

THE SUN AS ILLUMINATOR

I had taken up research and begun collecting material on solar instruments and land art ranging from Ulugh Beg's observatory in Samarkand, Uzbekistan, from the 15th century to Nancy Holt's *Sun Tunnels* in the Great Basin Desert, Utah (1973–1976). The symbolism of the sun and its association to cinema goes back to studies of light in ancient Arabia. In his book *Florenz und Bagdad. Eine westöstliche Geschichte des Blicks* (*Florence and Baghdad: Renaissance Art and Arab Science*), Hans Belting explains how investigations of the eye and the sun by Arabic scientists in the Middle Ages led to the introduction of the central perspective in Western Europe during the Renaissance.[5] The camera also relies on the principle of perspective; cinema is a modern cult.

In the region of Mardin, older cults and religions worshipped the sun. The history of Mesopotamia is steeped in religions that focus on sun and fire (Yazidi, Semsi, Zoroastrianism, etc.), but which are prohibited from being practised in Turkey today. A room with a window facing east was found under an ancient Aramaic cloister. It was presumably a pre-Christian site of sun or fire worship, such as of the Zoroastrians. The room is presented to visitors as a kind of curiosity today. Deification of the sun was persecuted as heresy in Christian and Islamic contexts yet also seems to have been integrated into the religions in other ways—for example, as the eternal light or the Ramadan tradition of fasting by day until sunset. Developing historically from shadow play and the camera obscura, cinema came to establish itself as an autonomous art form based on the absorption and projection of light. It may therefore even be closer to the heretical rituals of light than a cloister, for example.

Another connection between cinema and the sun is described by Alexander Kluge in his book *Geschichten vom Kino* (*Cinema Stories*). Tracing the idea of a cosmic, universal cinema, he refers to the lawyer Felix Eberty who published *Die Gestirne und die Weltgeschichte* (*The stars and the earth*) in 1846: "He rightly assumed that a ray of light which left the earth on Good Friday in the year AD 30 continues to move outwards into the cosmos away from us. History in its entirety is therefore preserved in the universe in the path of light. The entire history of the world is thus crossing the universe as a series of moving images (Eberty had not yet heard of the word cinema)."[6]

SEEING YOURSELF BEHIND THE SCREEN

The mirror behind the *Sun Cinema* does not only serve to reflect sunlight, but you can also see your reflection in it. Other people's films are shown on the front of the screen, but if you step behind it during the day, you can see your own reflection in the landscape—or at least the sun reflecting off your skin and clothing.

1   Alexander Kluge: *Geschichten vom Kino*, Frankfurt am Main: Suhrkamp, 2007, p. 7. (here translation AK)

2   Clemens von Wedemeyer: *Screenplay*, Leipzig: Spector Books, 2010.

3   Clemens von Wedemeyer: "Notizen zum Kinokomplex", in: Kerstin Hausbei, Franck Hofmann, Nicolas Hubé, Jens E. Sennewald (eds.): *Transversale. Erkundungen in Kunst und Wissenschaft. Ein europäisches Jahrbuch*, Vol. 1, Paderborn: Wilhelm Fink, 2005, p. 163. (here translation AK)

4   The design of the cinema was discussed with architecture students from Istanbul Technical University and realised together with Gürden Gür as executing architect.

5   Hans Belting: *Florence and Baghdad: Renaissance Art and Arab Science*, Cambridge, Massachusetts: HUP, 2011

6   Kluge: *Geschichten vom Kino*, p. 44. (here translation AK)

A   Research materials on *Sun Cinema* (2010): Claude-Nicolas Ledoux: "The Eye of the Architect": Coup d'oeil du Théâtre de Besançon, 1804.

B   Sun Cinema, architectural drawing, 2010.

C   Research materials on *Sun Cinema* (2010): Alhazen (al-Haitham): "Diagram of the Physiology of the Eye".

D   Research materials on *Sun Cinema* (2010): Cesare Cesariano: "Views of a Planetary Perspective", 1521.

DATA BANK

INDEX

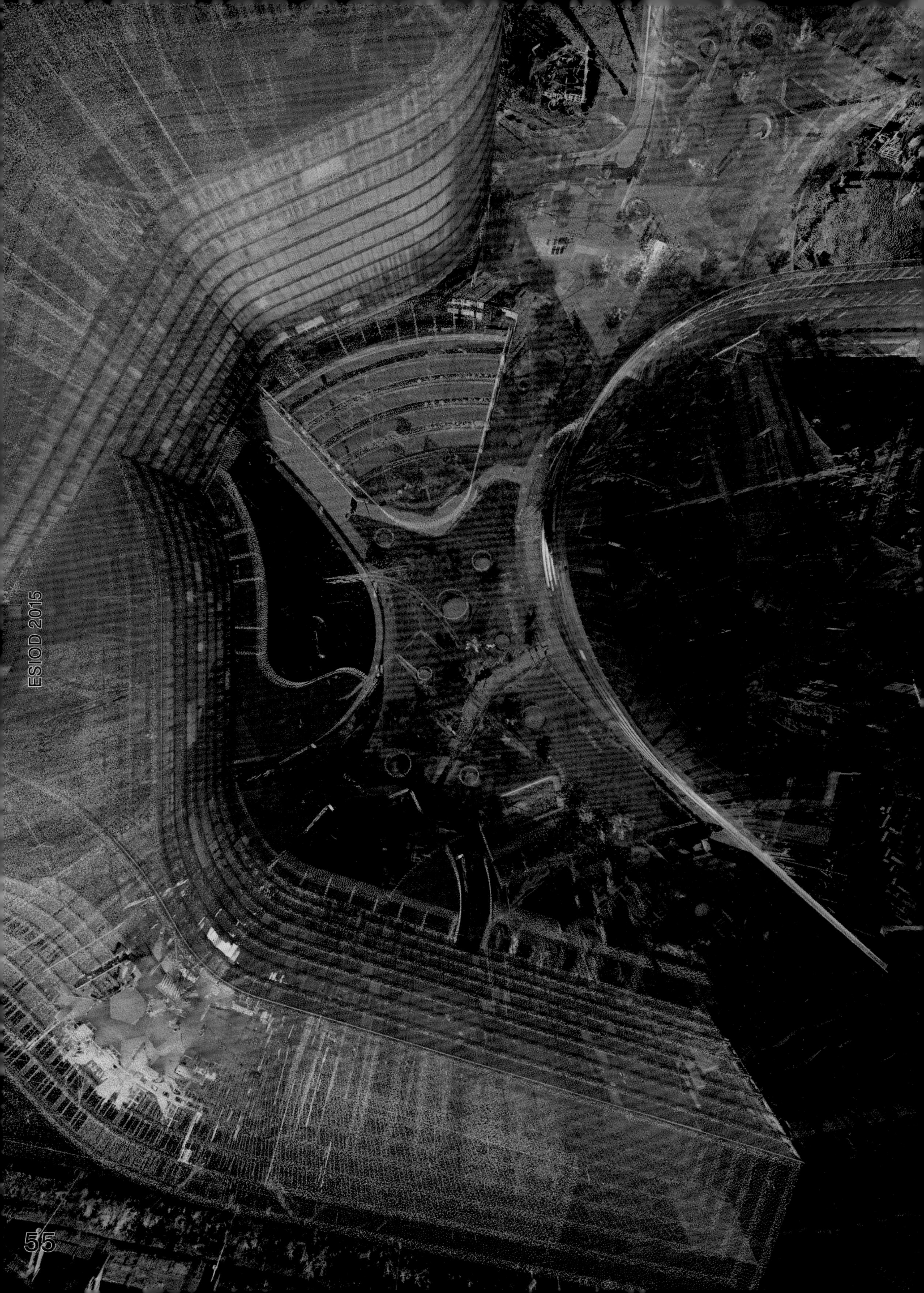
ESIOD 2015

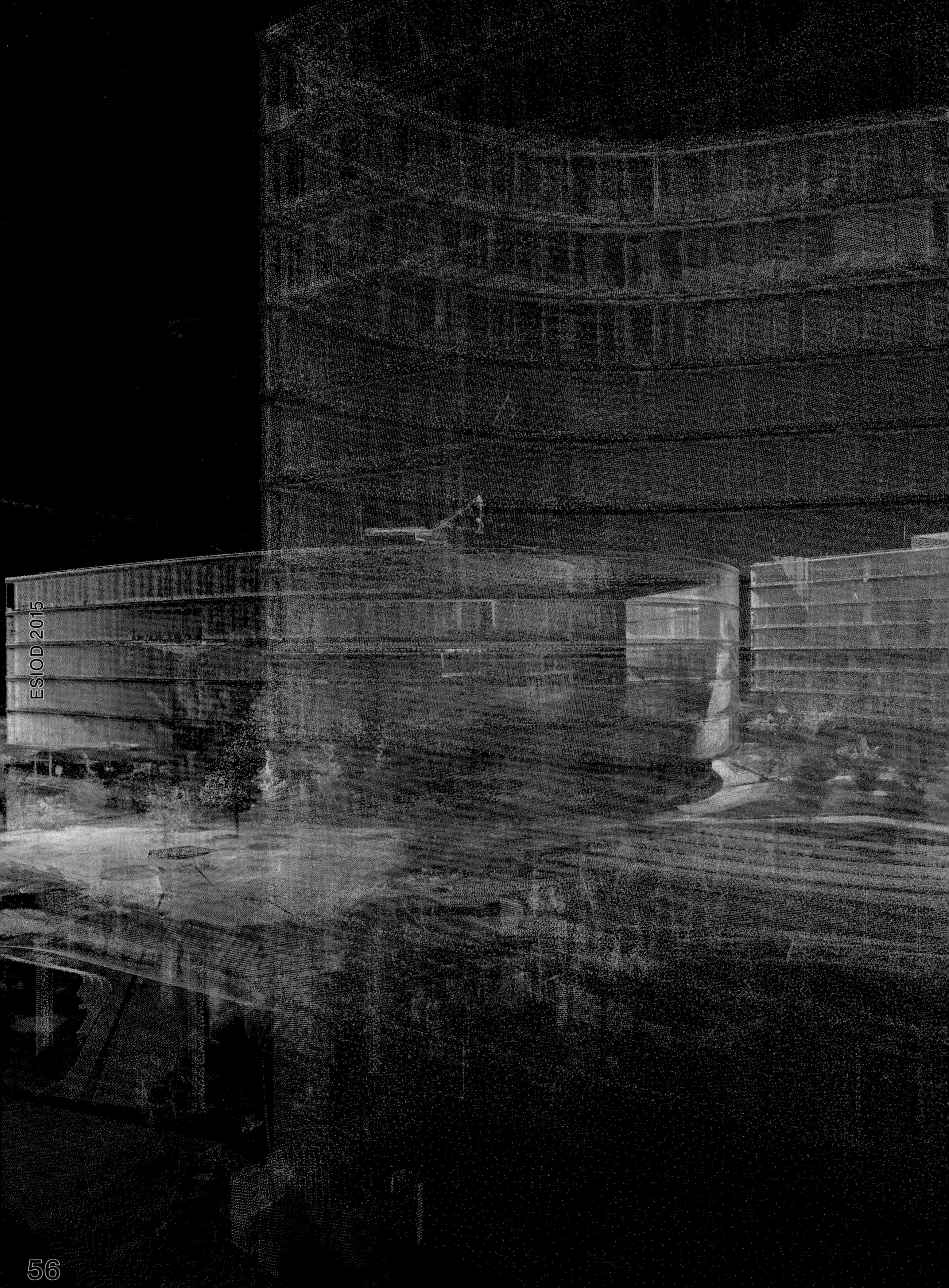

ESIOD 2015

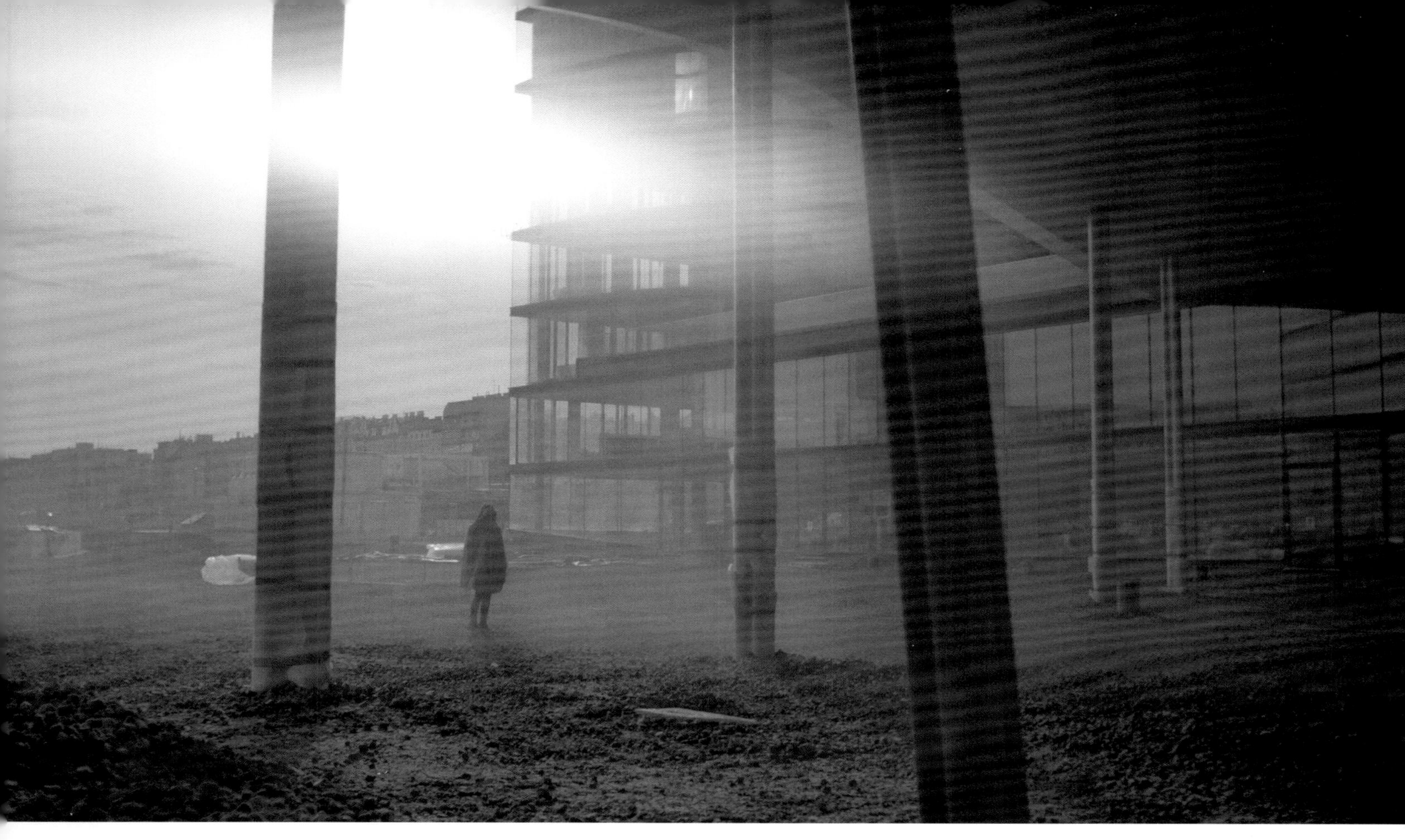

ESIOD 2015

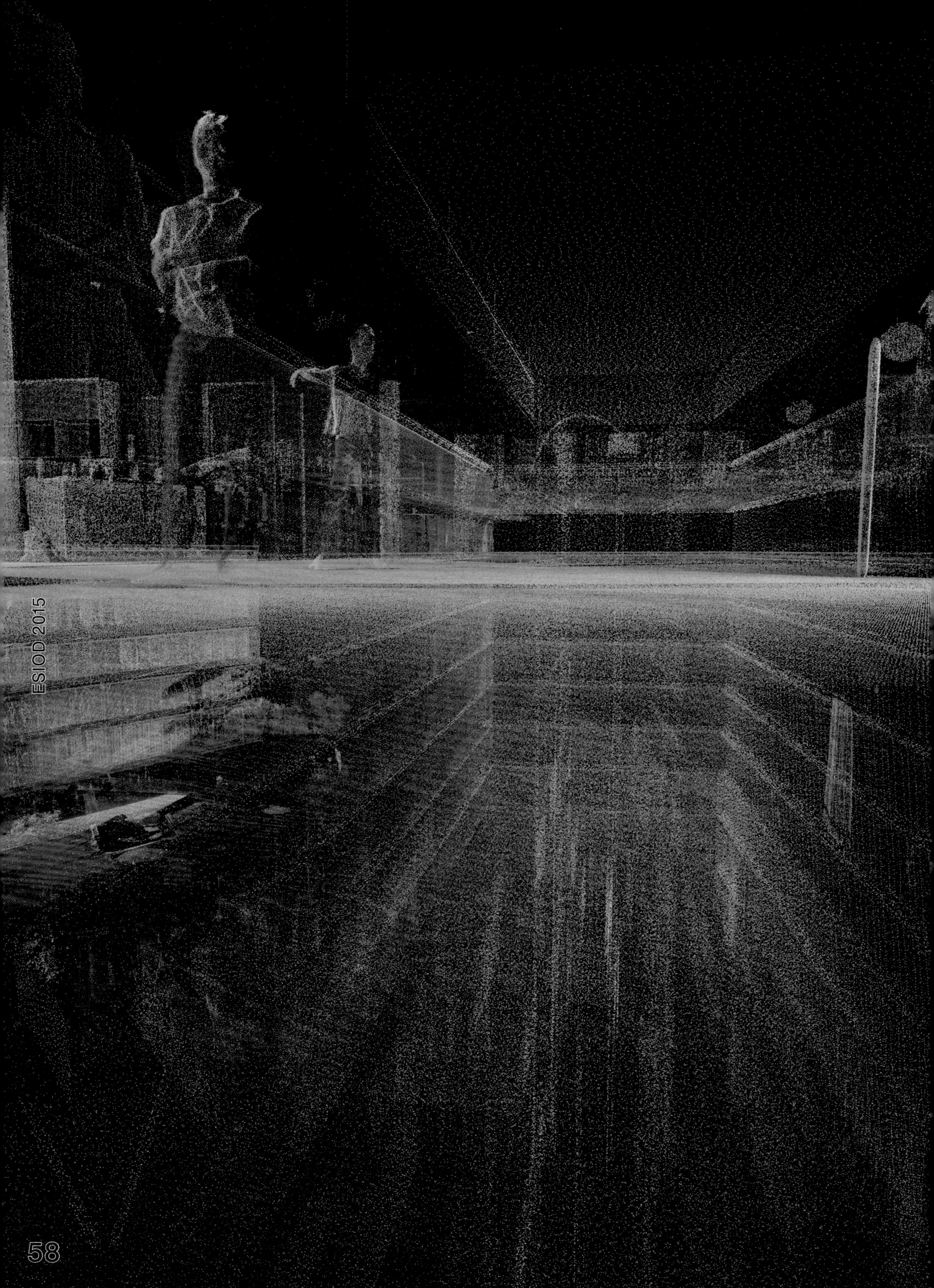

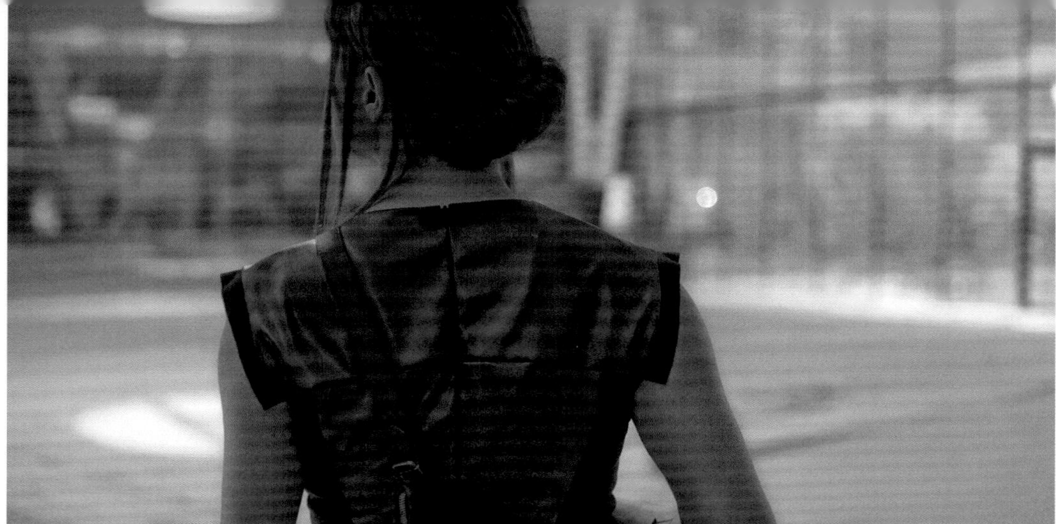

What can I do for you?

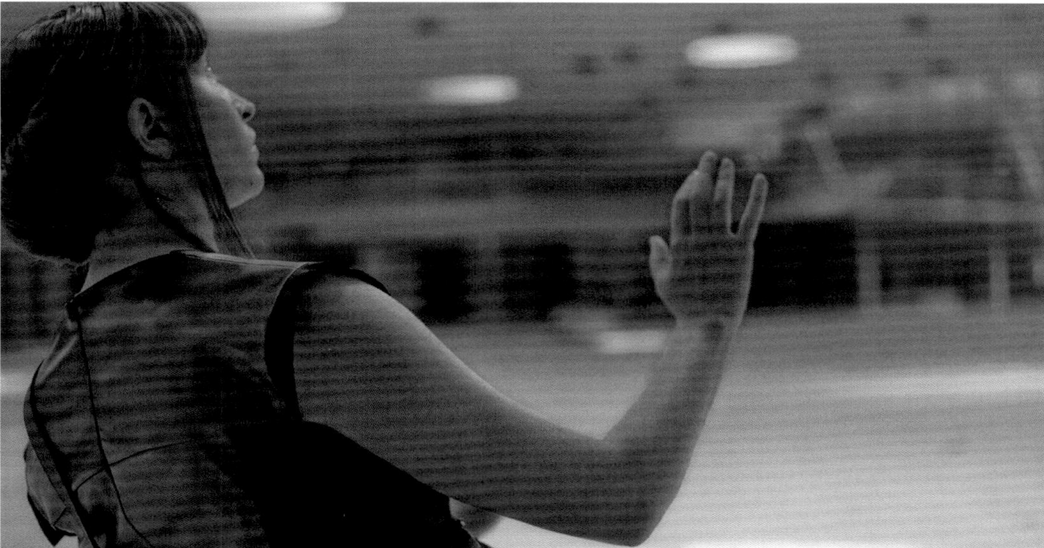

I have an account here.

I don't remember you.

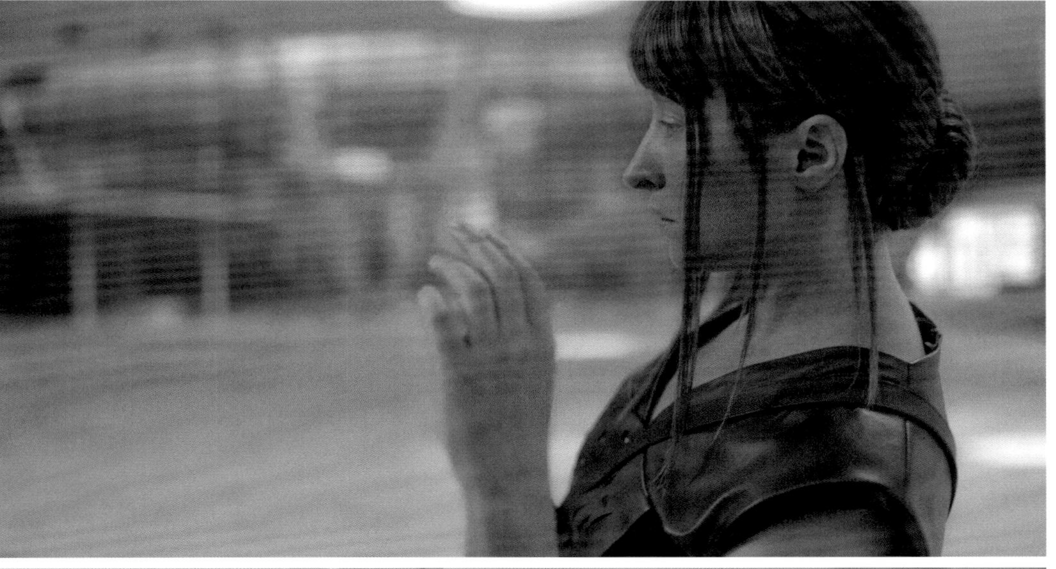

I would like to get my
data back.

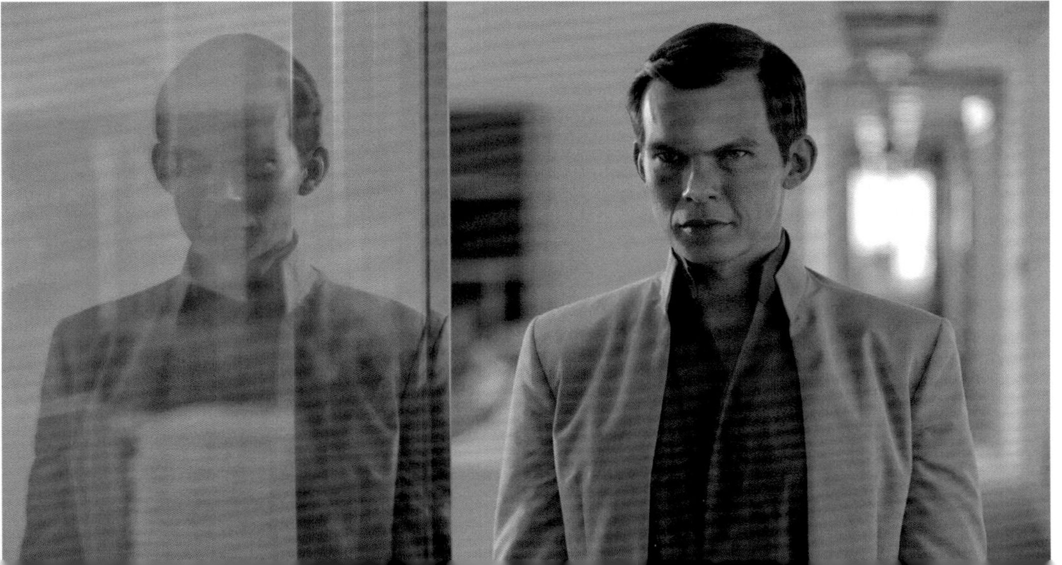

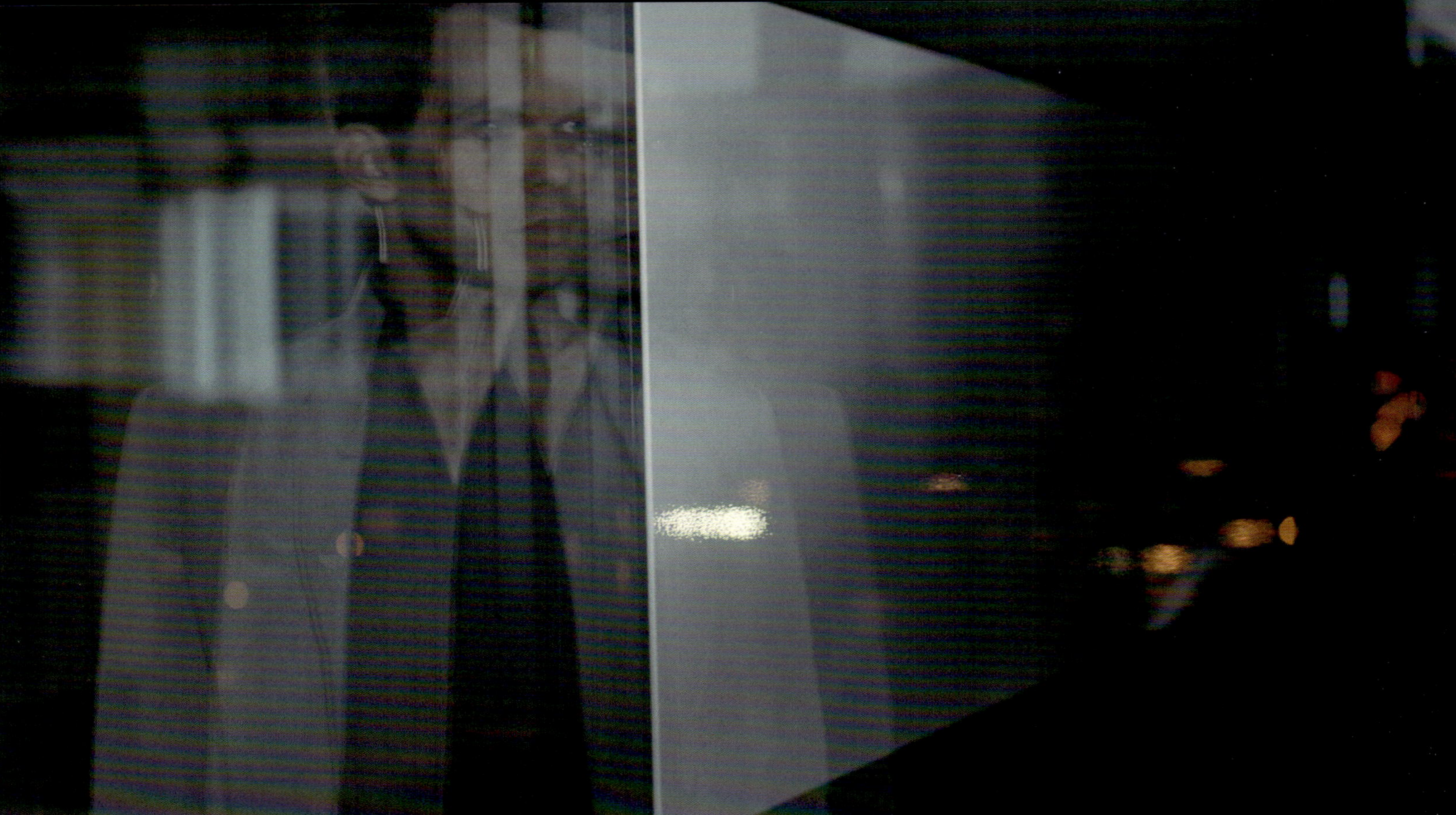

Die Bank sagt: „Jede persönliche Datei hat einen objektiven und einen subjektiven Wert. Unser Finanzmodell betrachtet beide Seiten und vereinfacht so die Begleichung der eigenen Schulden. Mit der Übergabe ihrer Erinnerungen an die Bank wird dadurch auch ihr Wert gesteigert; er befreit sie von Verpflichtungen."

The bank says: "Every personal dataset has a subjective and an objective value. Our financial model takes both into account, which makes it very easy for everybody to pay off their debts. Giving all your memories to the bank both increases their value and releases you from liabilities."

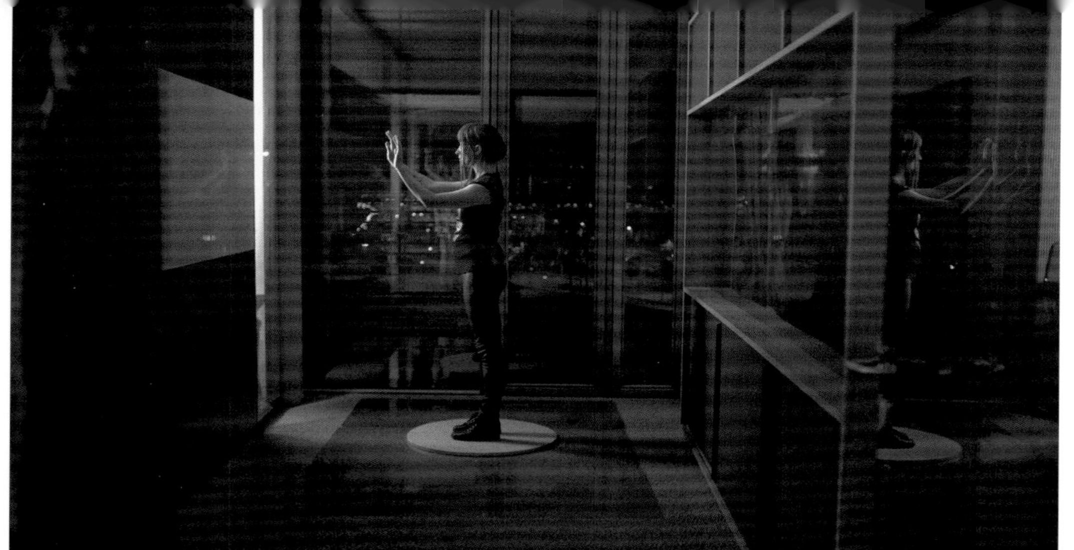

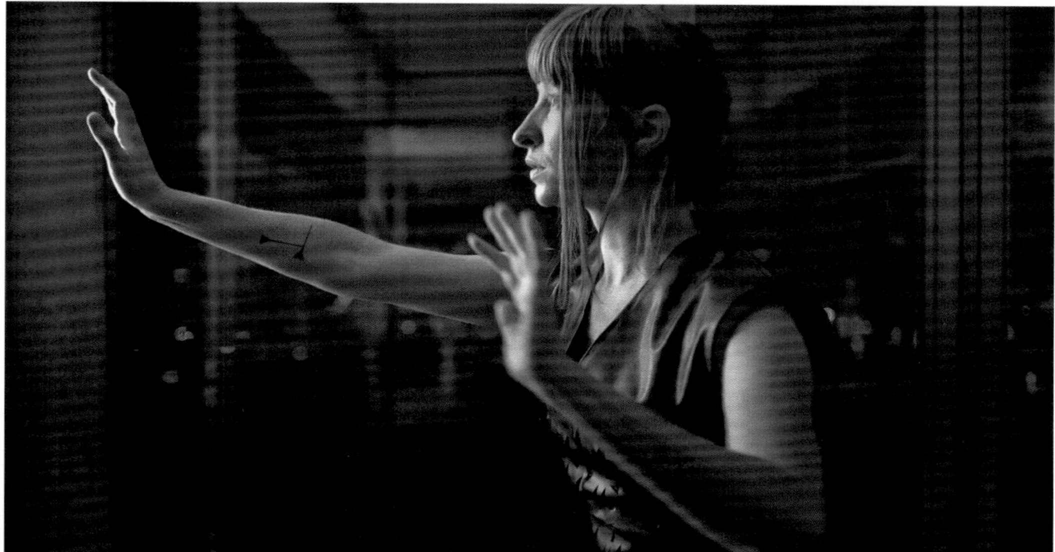

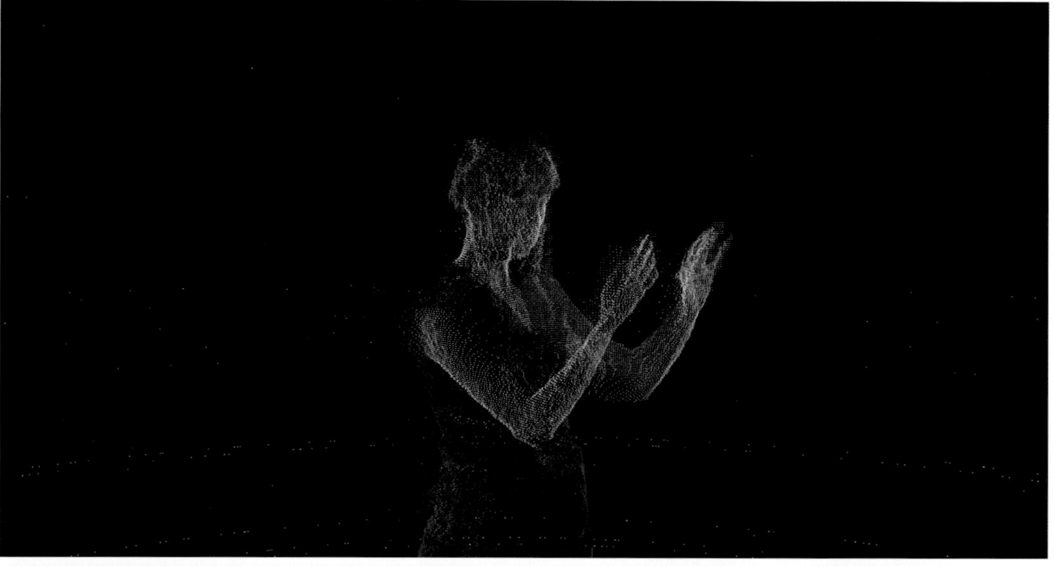

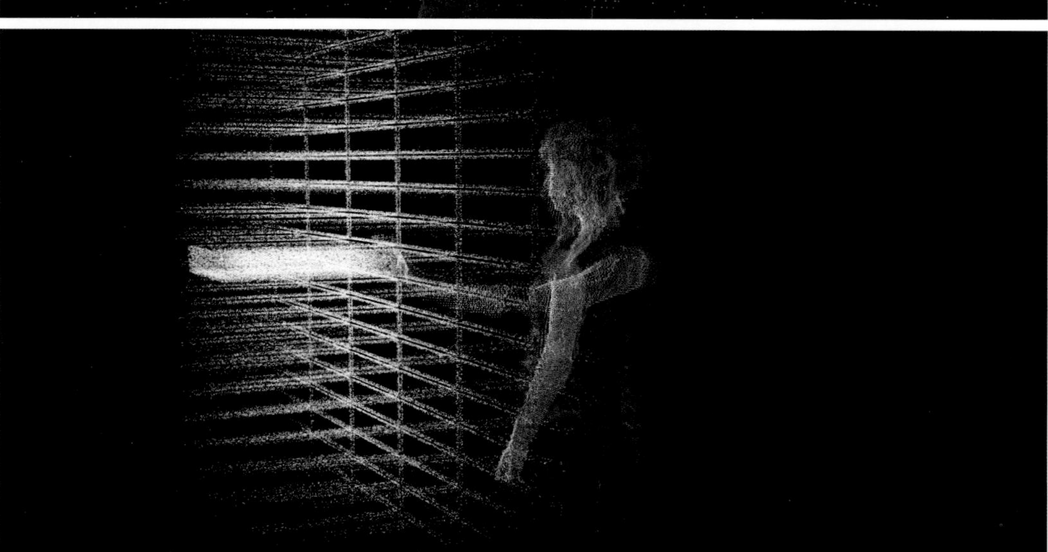

The archive provides the mathematical basis for our predictions.

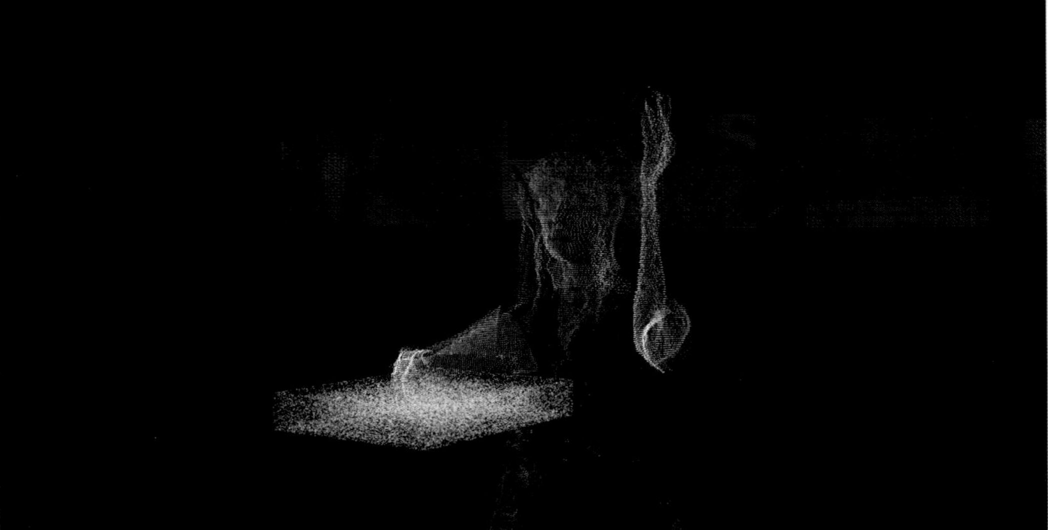

How did you get into the file?

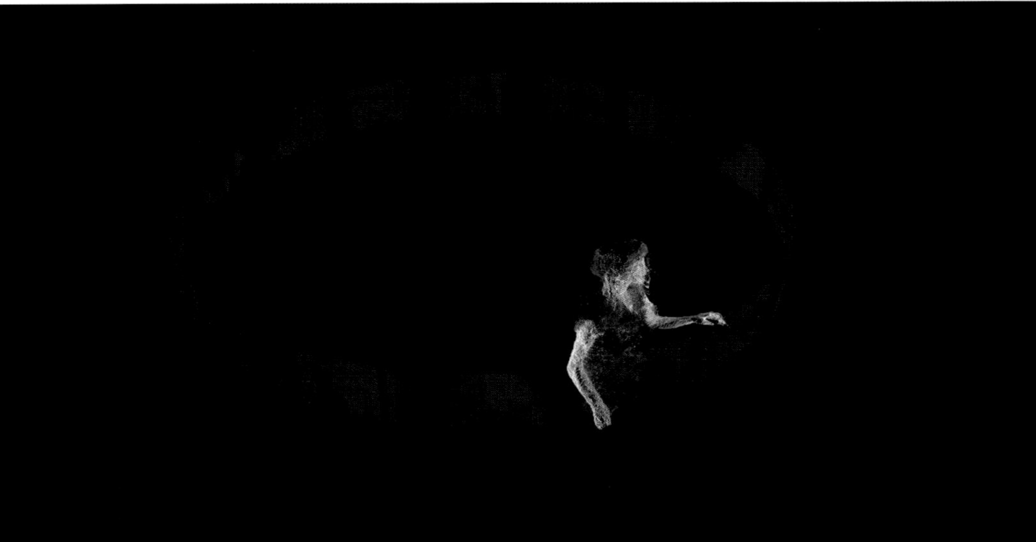

You showed me how.

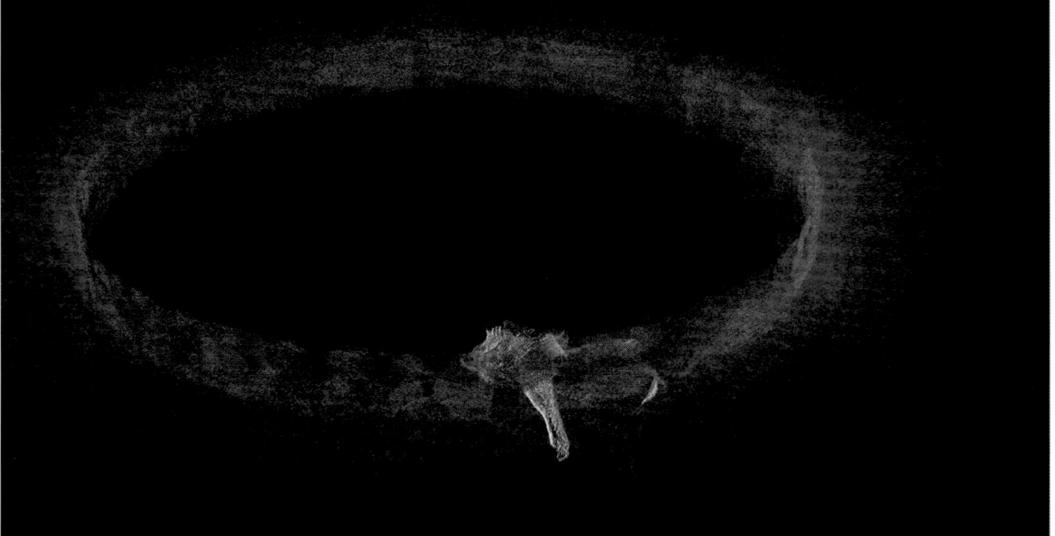

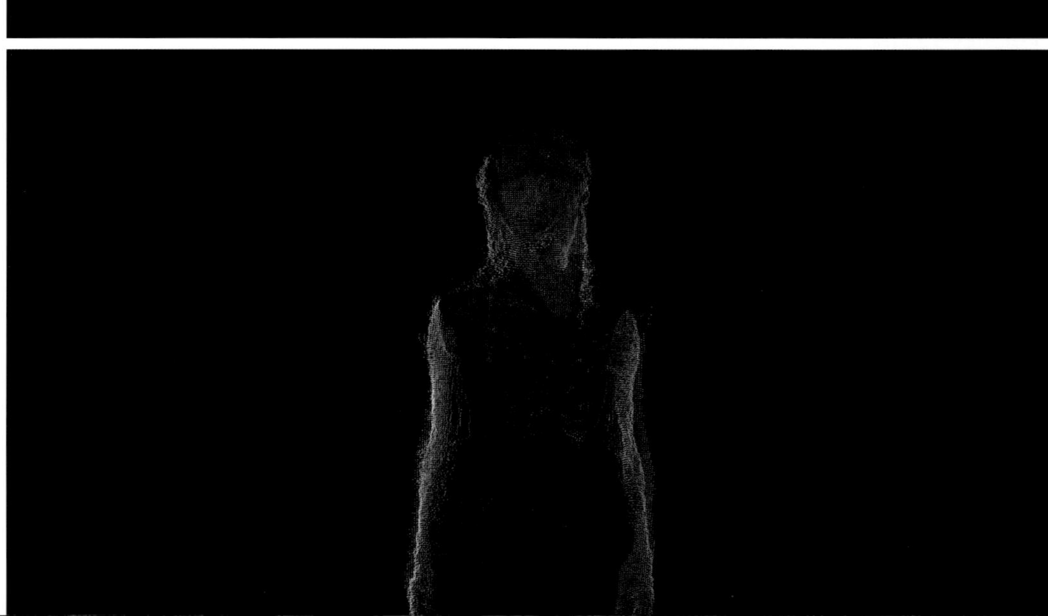

Please listen to me.
I am speaking from the
future.

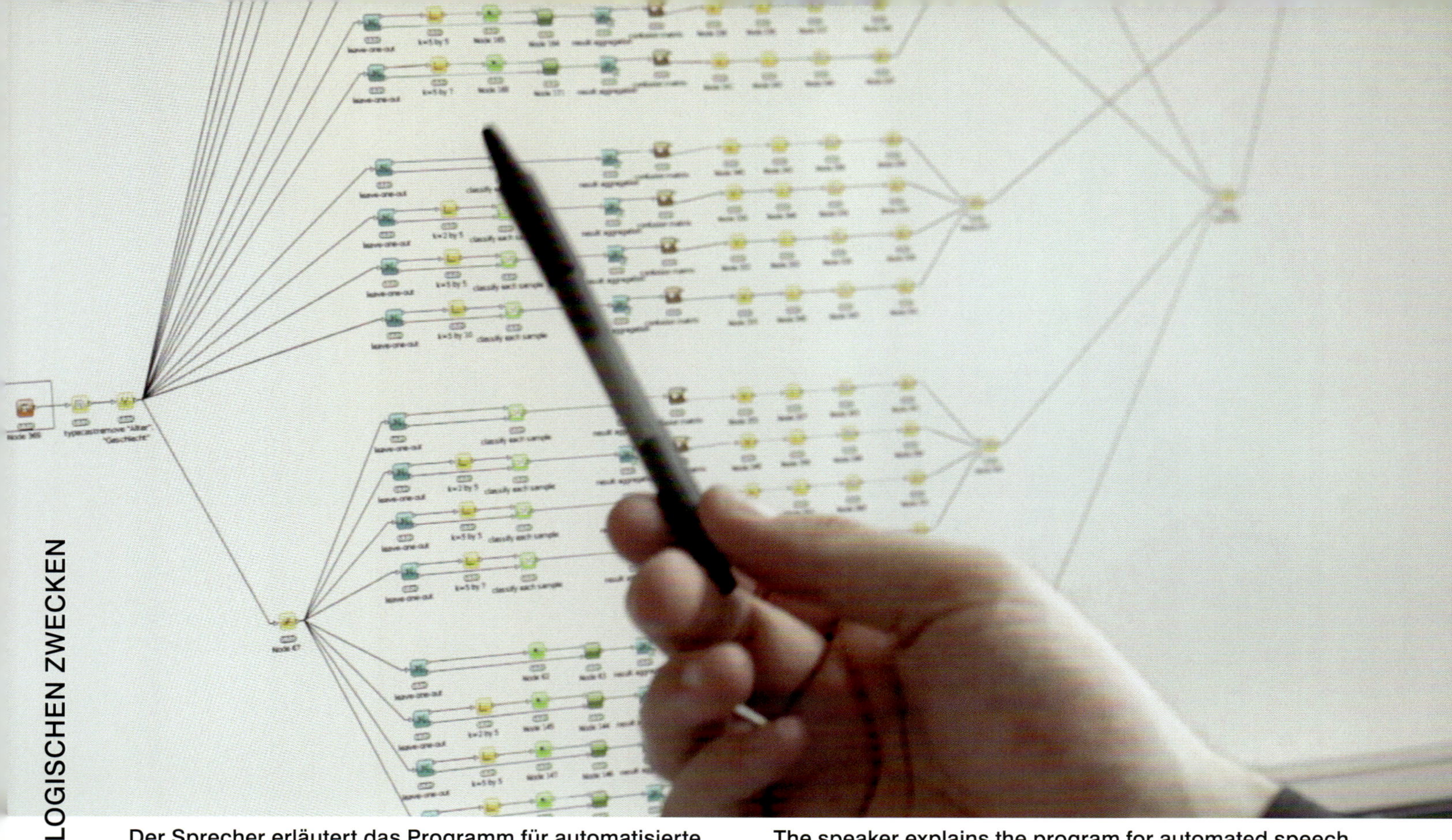

Der Sprecher erläutert das Programm für automatisierte Sprachanalyse: „Wir sehen hier, dass unterschiedliche Algorithmen und Klassifikatoren aneinandergeschaltet sind. Die werden durchlaufen und sie treffen für sich selbst bestimmte Entscheidungen und Berechnungen, die weiterverwendet werden. Es ist so, dass Personen mit bestimmten Merkmalsausprägungen oder Stressphänomenen ähnliche Auffälligkeiten in der Sprache und Stimme zeigen, und daher für uns vorhersagbar sind."

The speaker explains the program for automated speech analysis: "Here we see how various algorithms and classifiers are linked. They are processed and render calculations that produce data which is then used again. People with specific characteristics and stress symptoms show the same anomalies in their speech and voice, and that allows us to predict them."

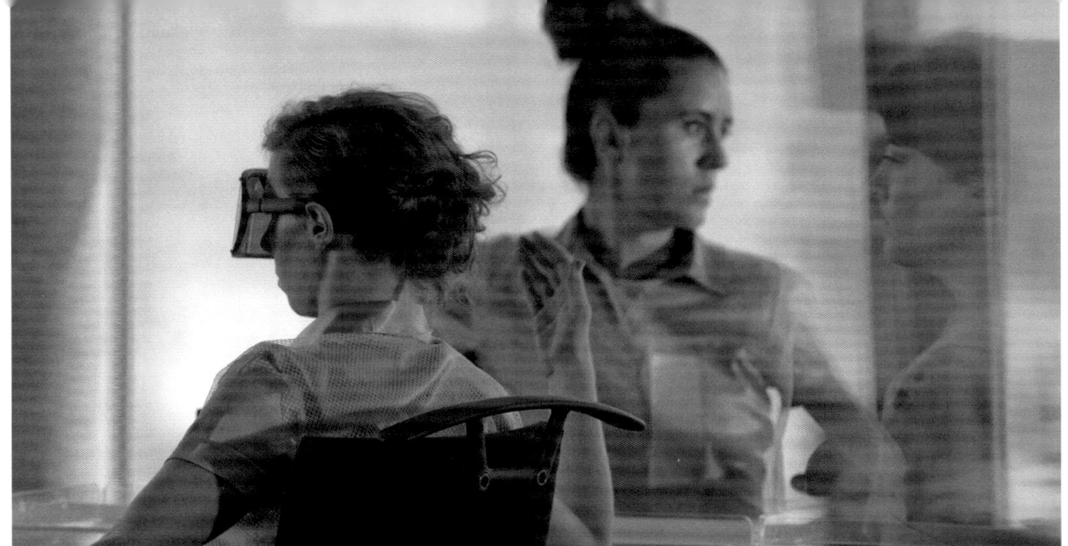

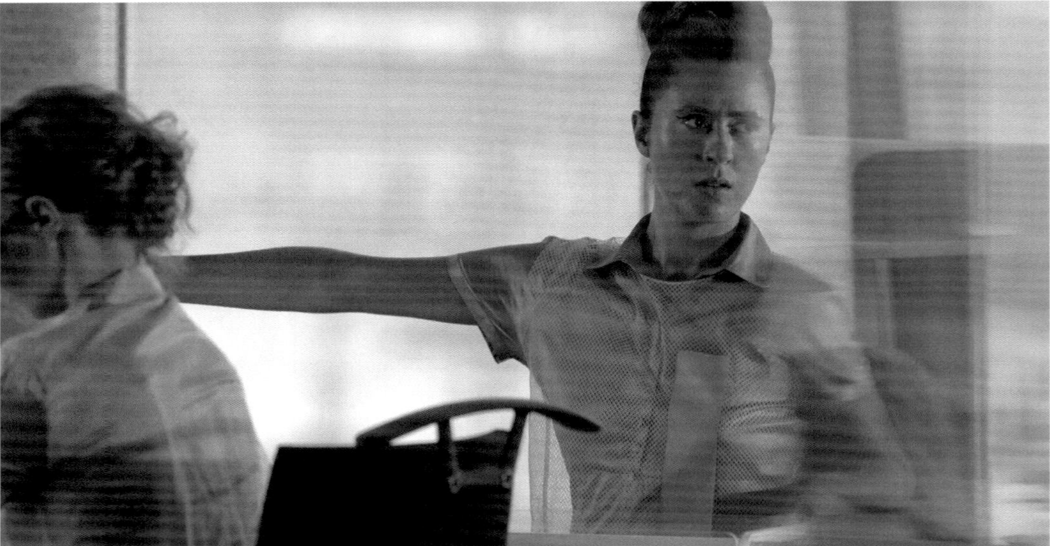

Everything since 2015
—it's all saved here?

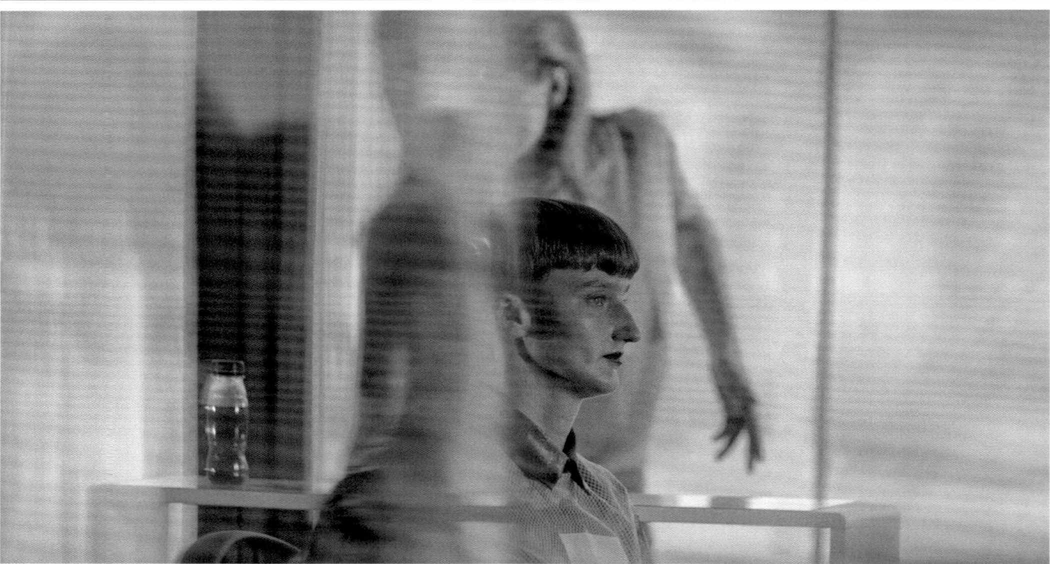

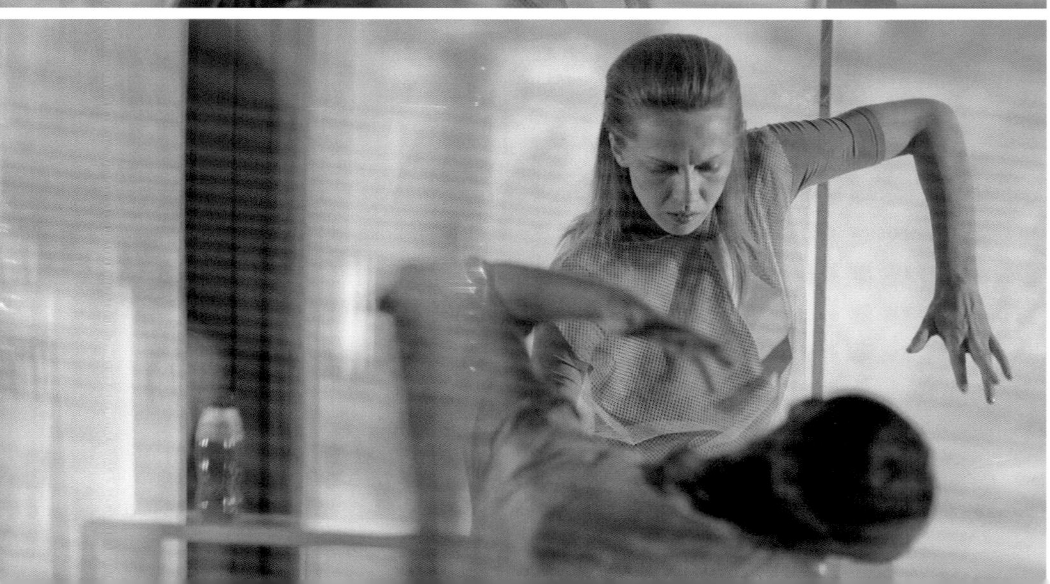

Kognition und Gedanken

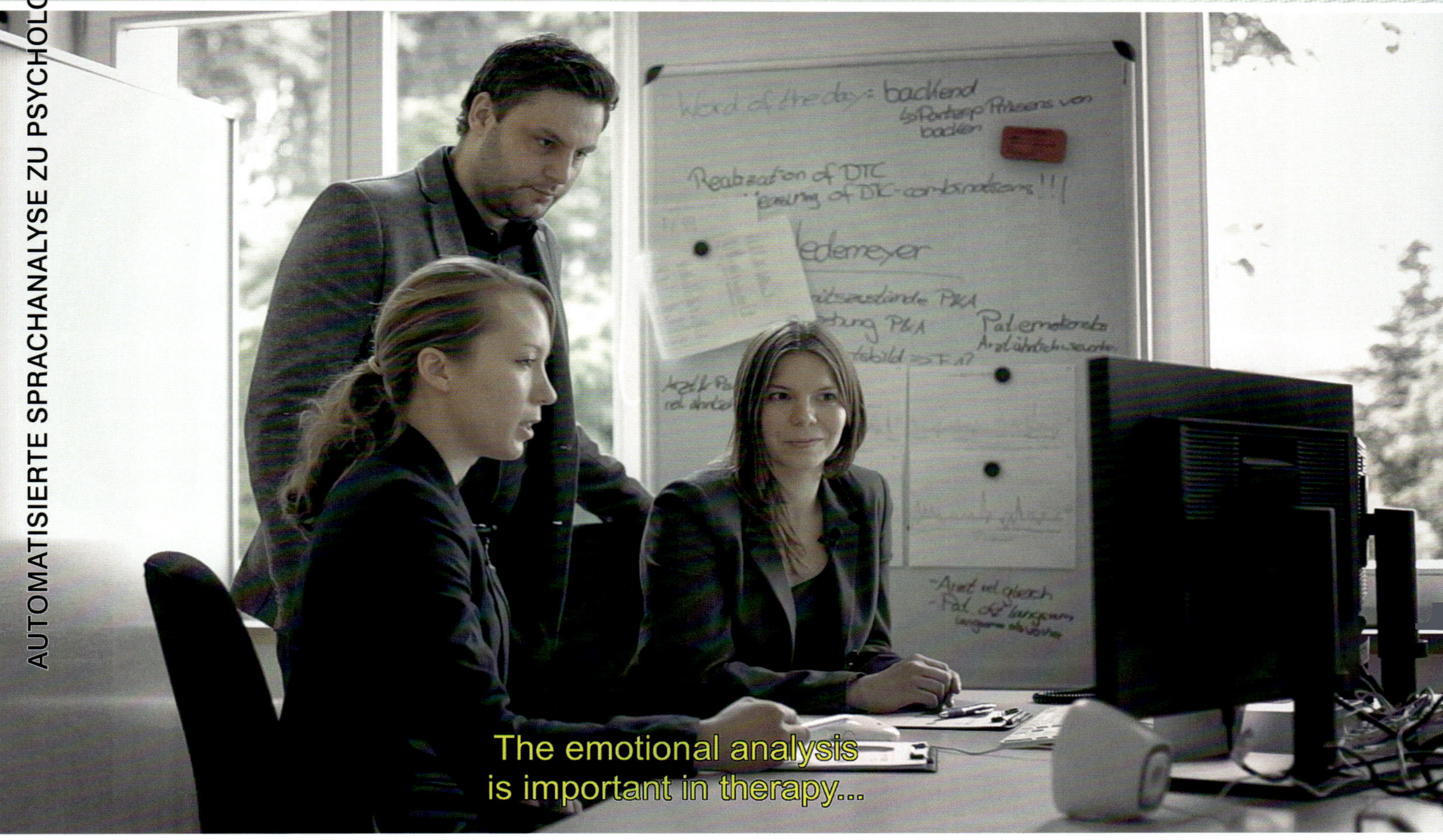

„Wir können den Prozess zum Beispiel mit dem der Entschlüsselung der menschlichen DNA vergleichen, wo viele Ergebnisse wie die Haarfarbe einer Person von einer Vielzahl von Parametern und Beziehungen abhängig sind. Unsere Sprachanalyse ist ähnlich komplex und deshalb müssen wir so viele Schritte durchlaufen, um genügend Daten zu sammeln. Dann müssen jene in verschiedene Dimensionen untersucht werden, um unsere extrem fein abgestimmten Ergebnisse ermitteln zu können. Normalerweise läuft dieser Prozess voll automatisiert ab, sobald das System mit dem Programm vertraut ist, sodass wir die Sprachdatei nach Empfang ganz einfach in eine Audiodatei umwandeln, und dabei kommt dann ein Vorhersagemodell heraus."

"We can compare the process, for instance, to that of deciphering human DNA, where many outcomes like one's hair colour depend on a multitude of parameters and relations. Our speech analysis has a similar complexity, which is why we have to go through so many steps in order to collect enough data. Then the data has to be processed in several dimensions in order for us to establish these extremely fine-tuned results. Usually this process is completely automated after the operator has become familiar with the program, so that we simply pop in an audio file when we receive it, and out comes a predictive model."

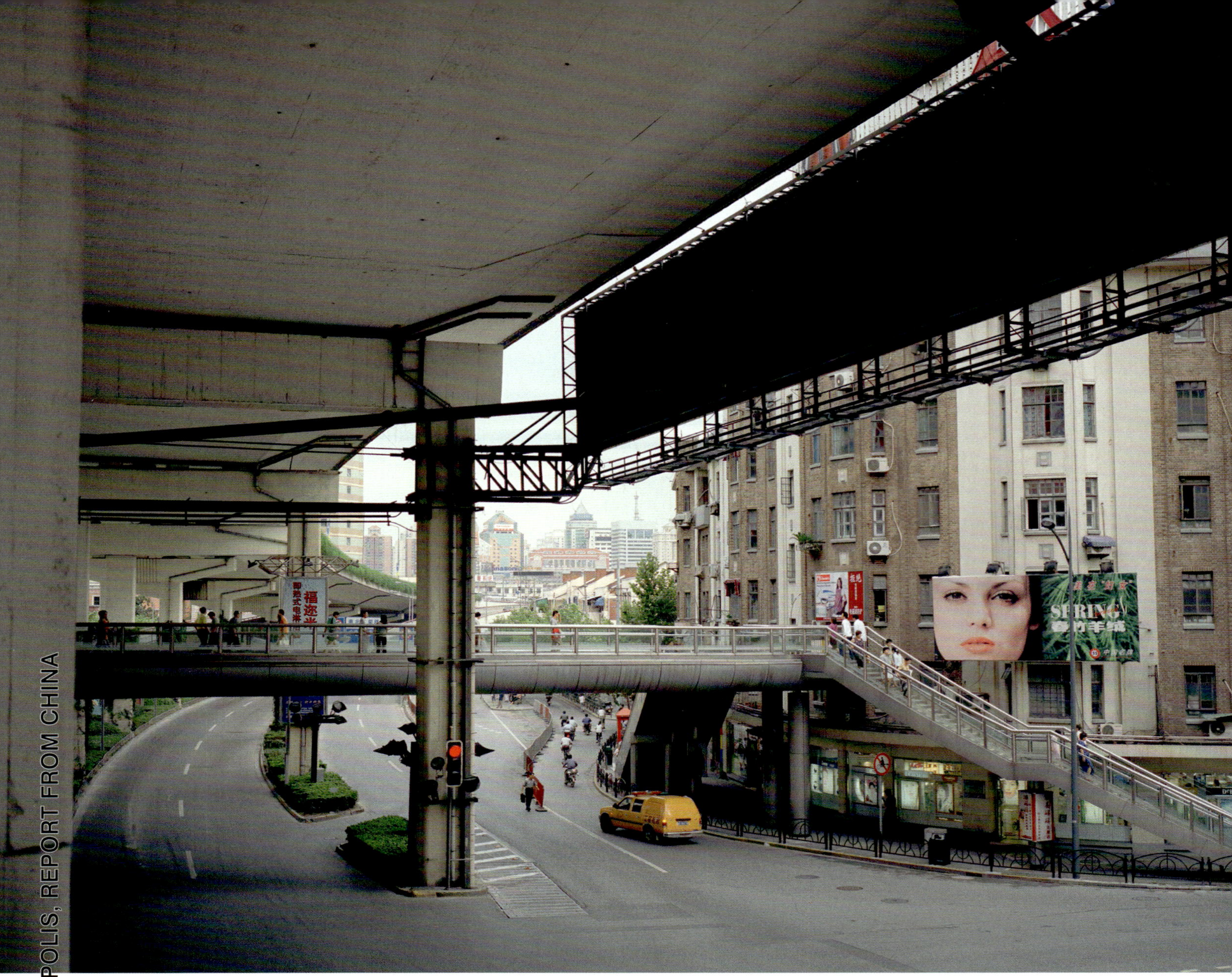

Fritz Lang sagte in einem Interview: „Der Film *Metropolis* entstand aus meinem ersten Blick auf die Wolkenkratzer New Yorks, im Oktober 1924, als die UFA mich nach Hollywood schickte, um amerikanische Produktionsbedingungen zu studieren. Und bei der Besichtigung New Yorks hatte ich die Vorstellung, dass dies der Schmelztiegel vielfältiger und wirrer menschlicher Kräfte war, die blind anstießen, in dem unbezwingbaren Verlangen, sich gegenseitig auszubeuten – und so in einer ständigen Angst lebten."

Fritz Lang said in an interview: "*Metropolis* emerged from my first glimpse of the New York skyscrapers, in October 1924, when UFA sent me to Hollywood to study American production conditions. And while sightseeing in New York I imagined that it was a crucible of diverse and chaotic human powers, blindly bumping into each other in the untamable desire to exploit each other—and thus living in a state of constant fear."

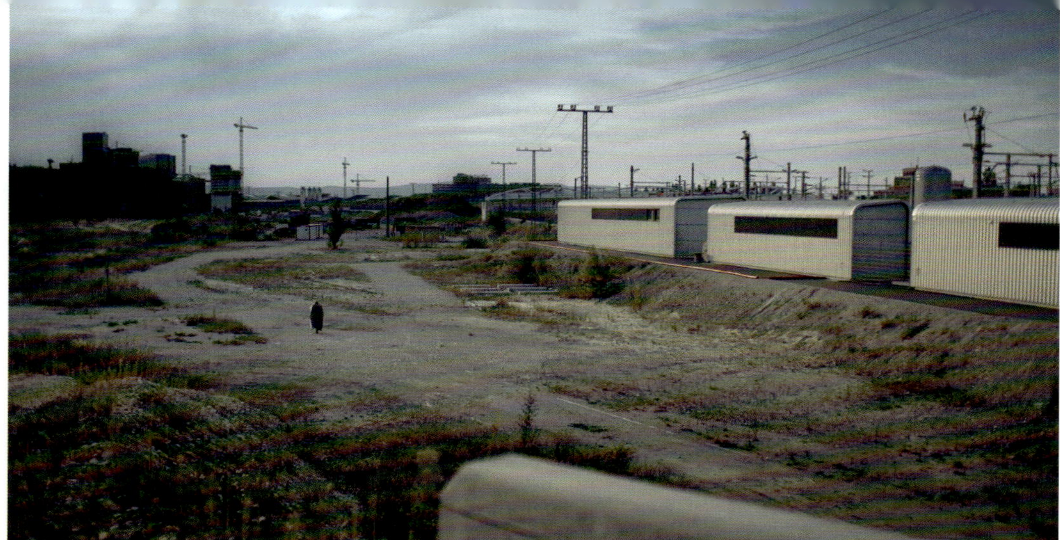

It is your story, your life. Our bank secures data that is too important and valuable to be stored in a low-security site such as a private home or in the cloud. Our virtual safe is a simple and reliable solution for you and your customers to save everything for ever in an offsite secure digital system.

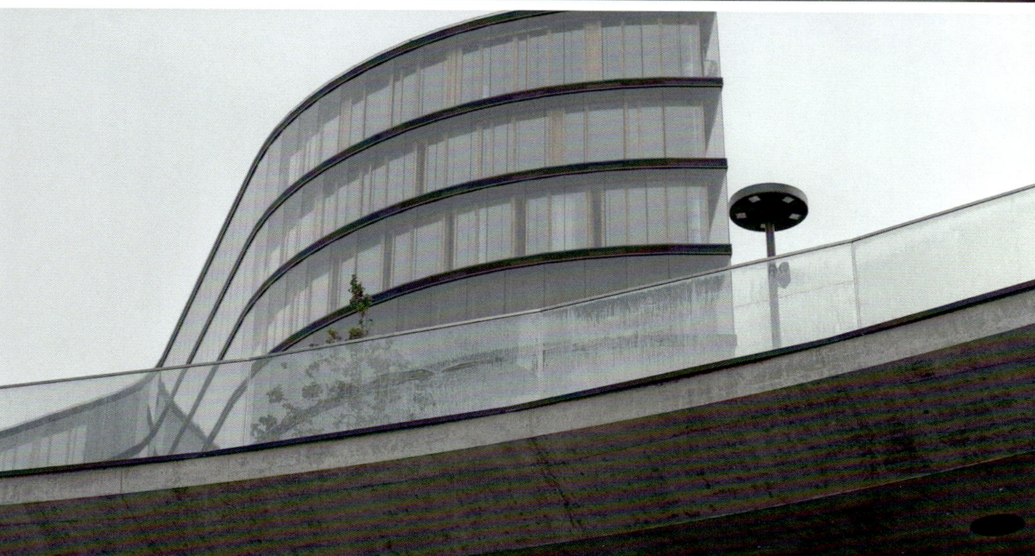

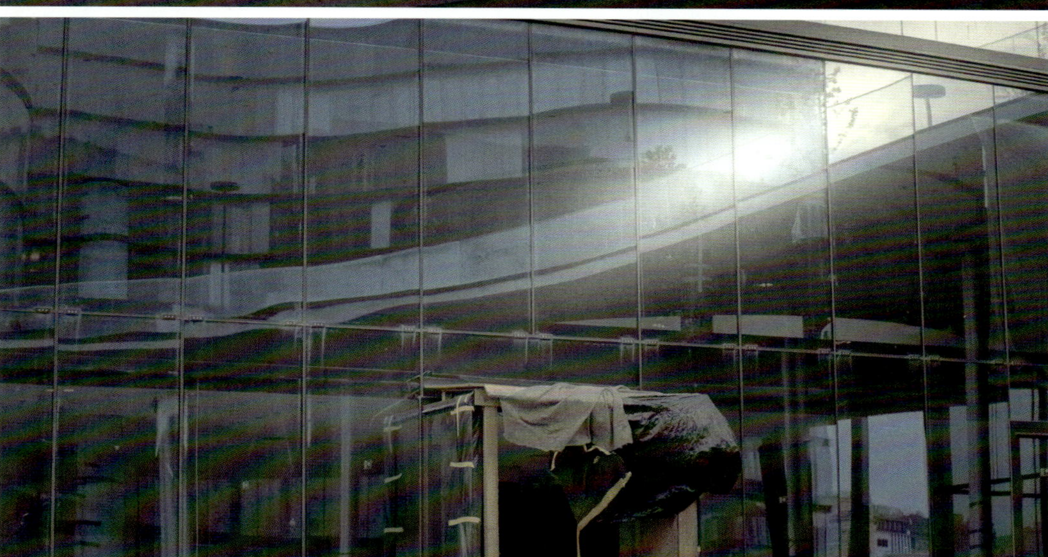

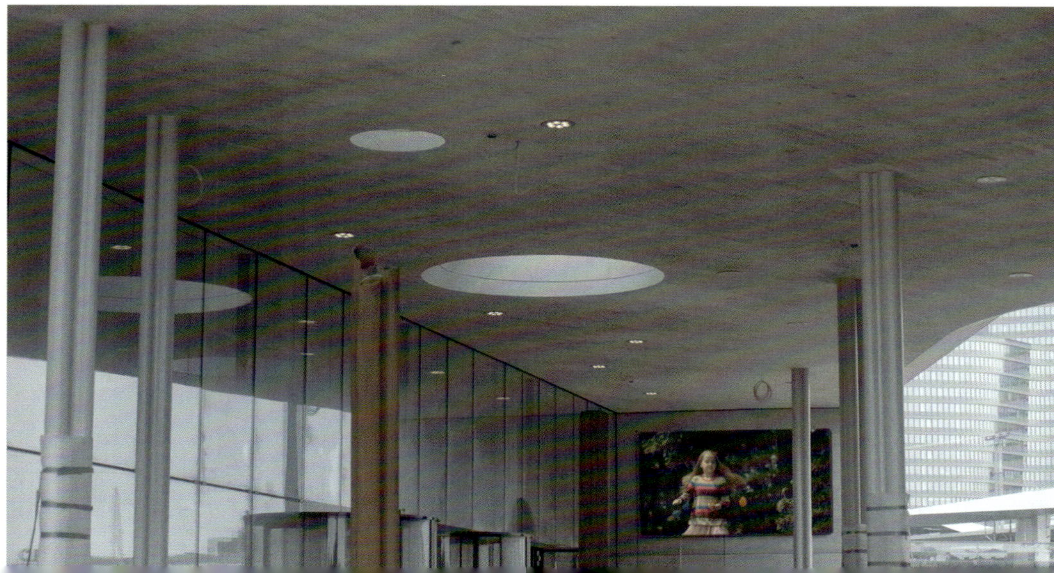

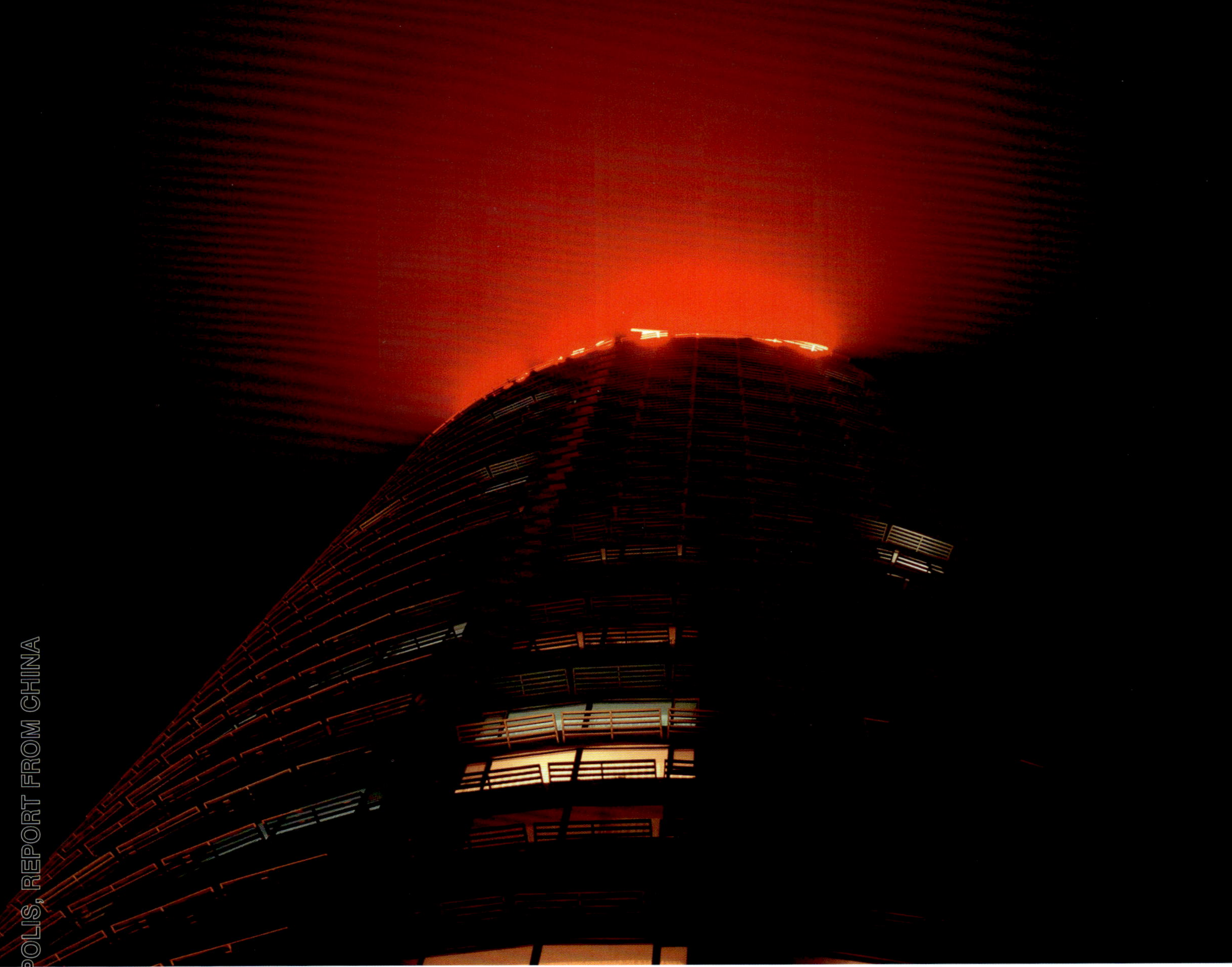

Der Sprecher sagt: „Es ist Nacht und keiner schläft. Wir waren gekommen, um einen Drehort zu finden, um mit Arbeitern und Architekten, Drehbuchautoren oder Romanciers zu sprechen. Um zu prüfen, ob hier das ganze Werk neu verfilmt werden könnte."

The speaker says: "It is night, no one is asleep. We had come to find a film location, to talk with workers and architects, screenwriters and novelists. To investigate whether the whole film could be restaged here."

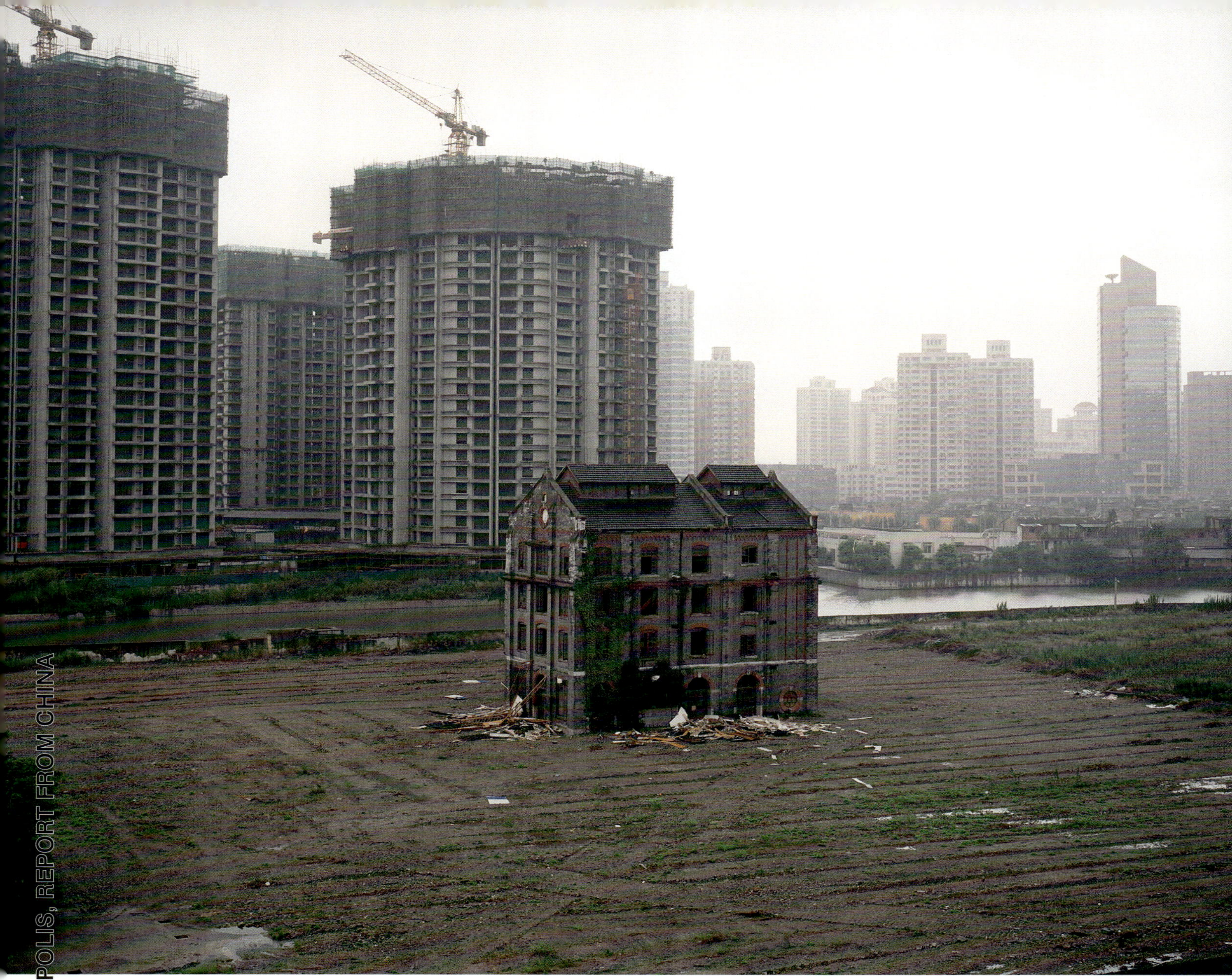

Die Sprecherin erwidert: „Neue Stadtteile werden sehr schnell auf der Basis von fertigen Modellen gebaut. Zonen, in denen gearbeitet wird, werden von Zonen zum Leben getrennt. Die Pläne erinnern an Produktionsbilder, die 1926 bei den Dreharbeiten zu *Metropolis* in den Babelsberger Filmstudios entstanden."

The speaker replies: "New parts of the cities are built very rapidly, based on pre-designed models. Zones for living and zones for working are separated from one another. The plans remind us of production shots that were taken during the shooting of *Metropolis* in the Babelsberg Film Studios in 1926."

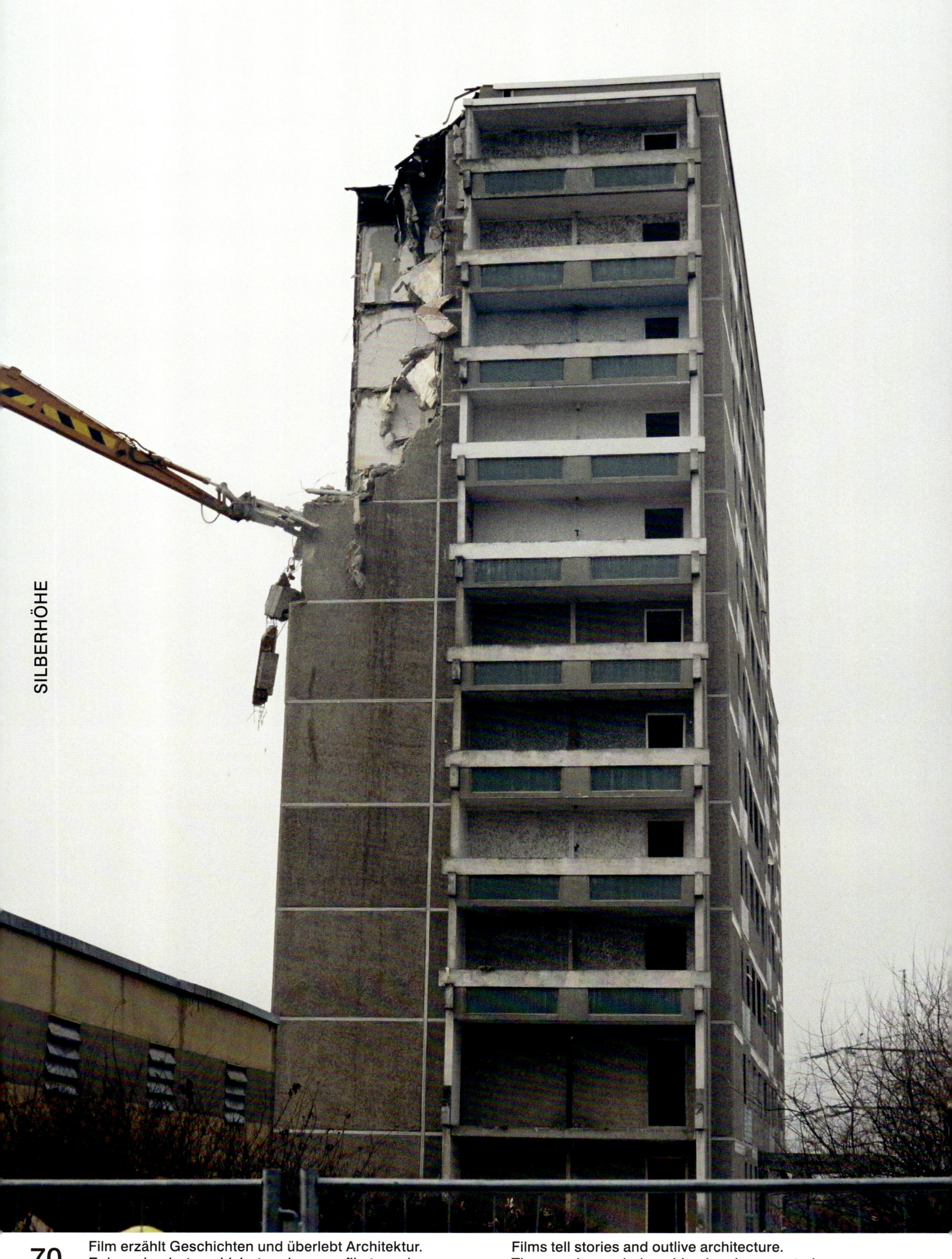

70 Film erzählt Geschichten und überlebt Architektur.
Er kann kopiert, archiviert und neu verfilmt werden.

Films tell stories and outlive architecture.
They can be copied, archived and re-enacted.

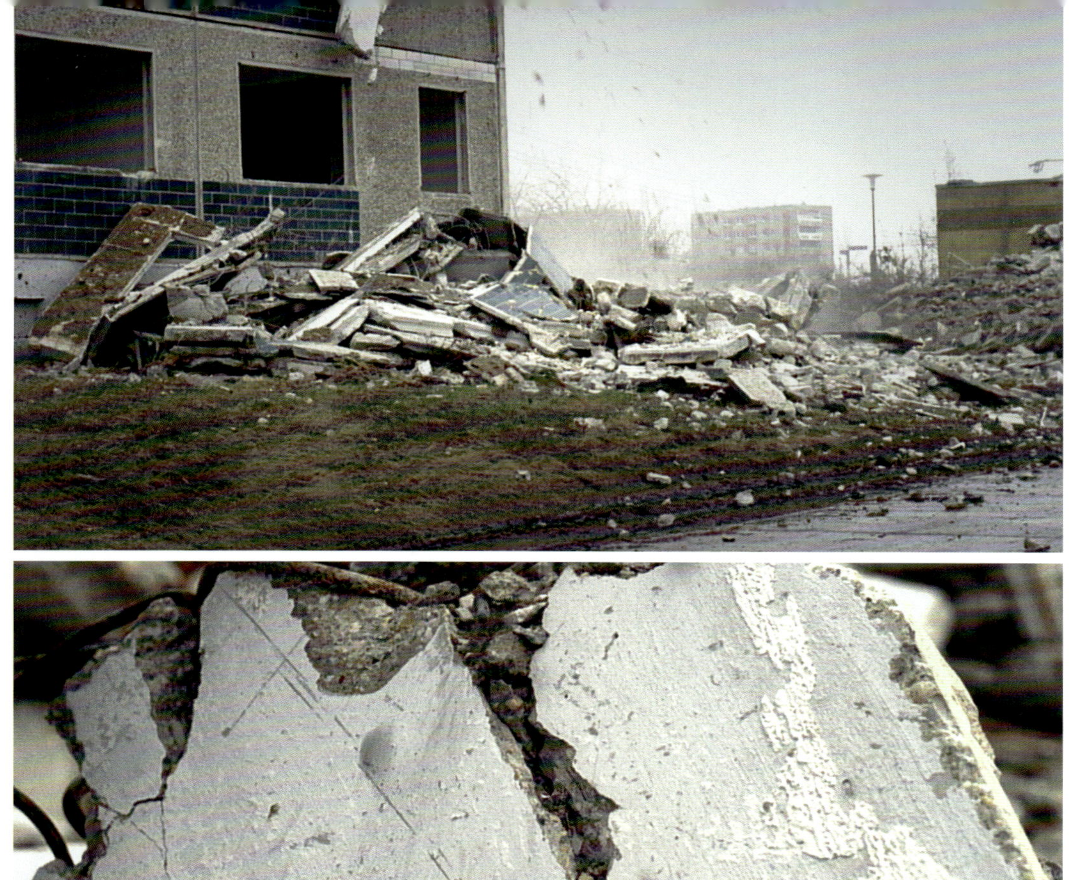

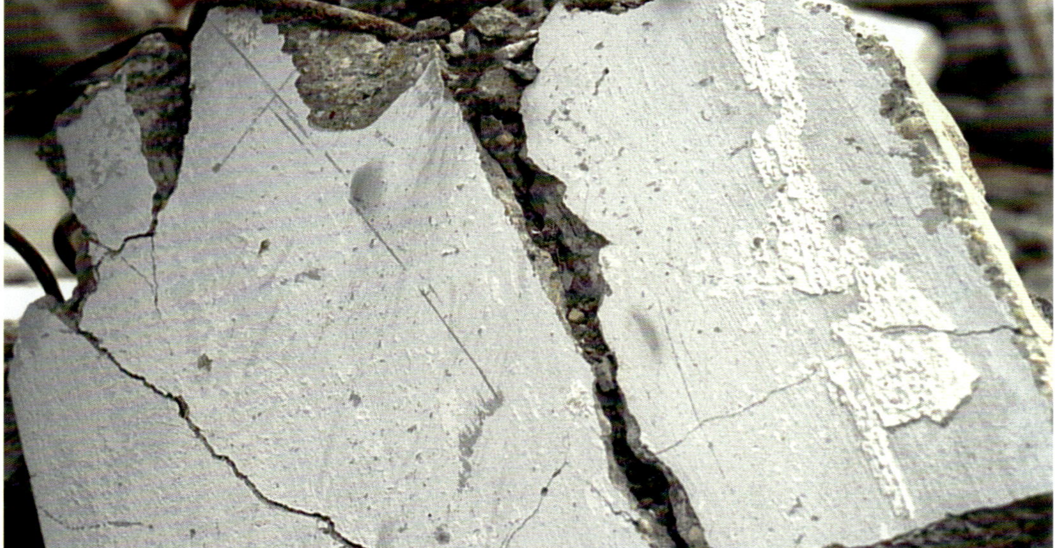

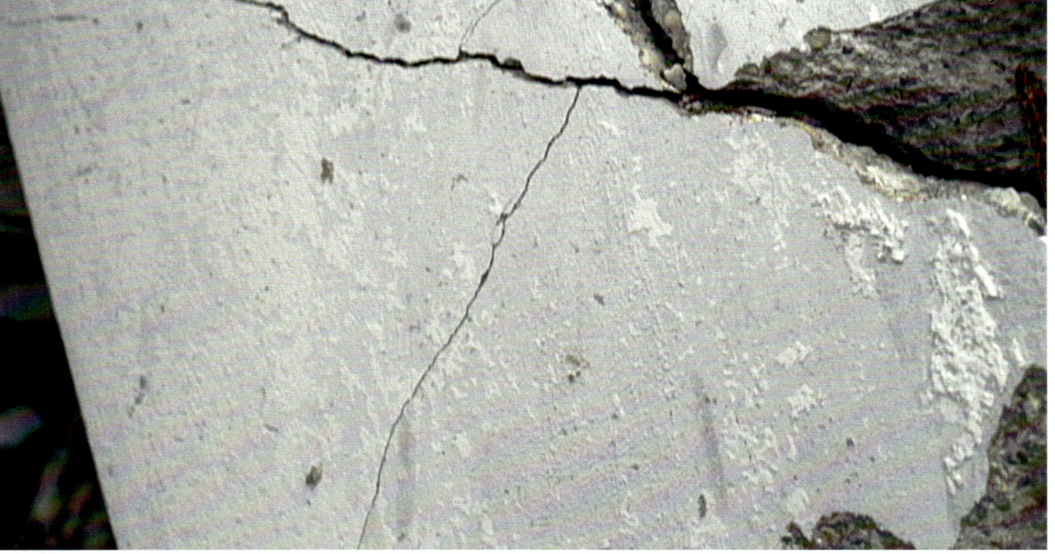

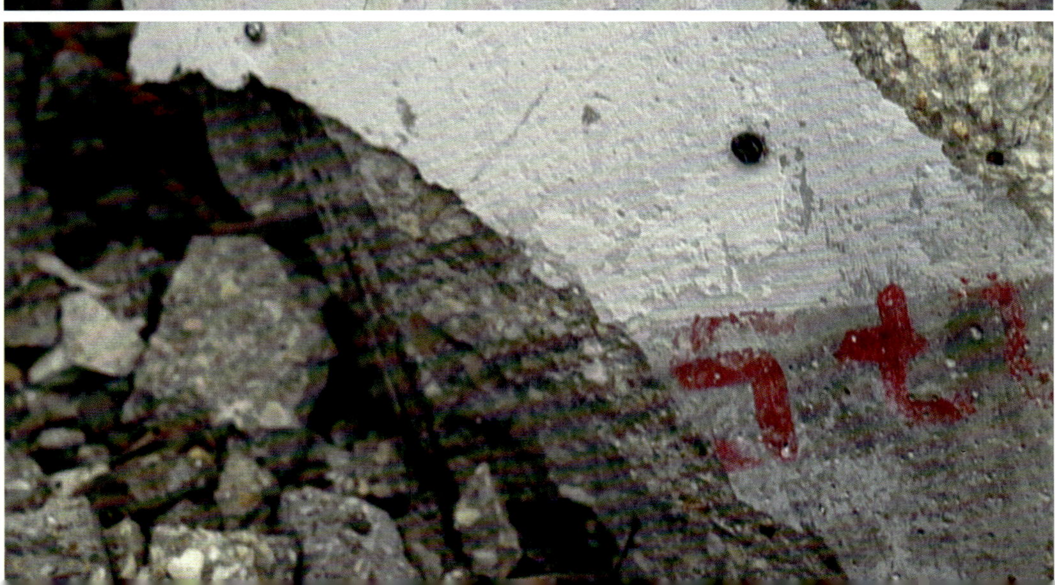

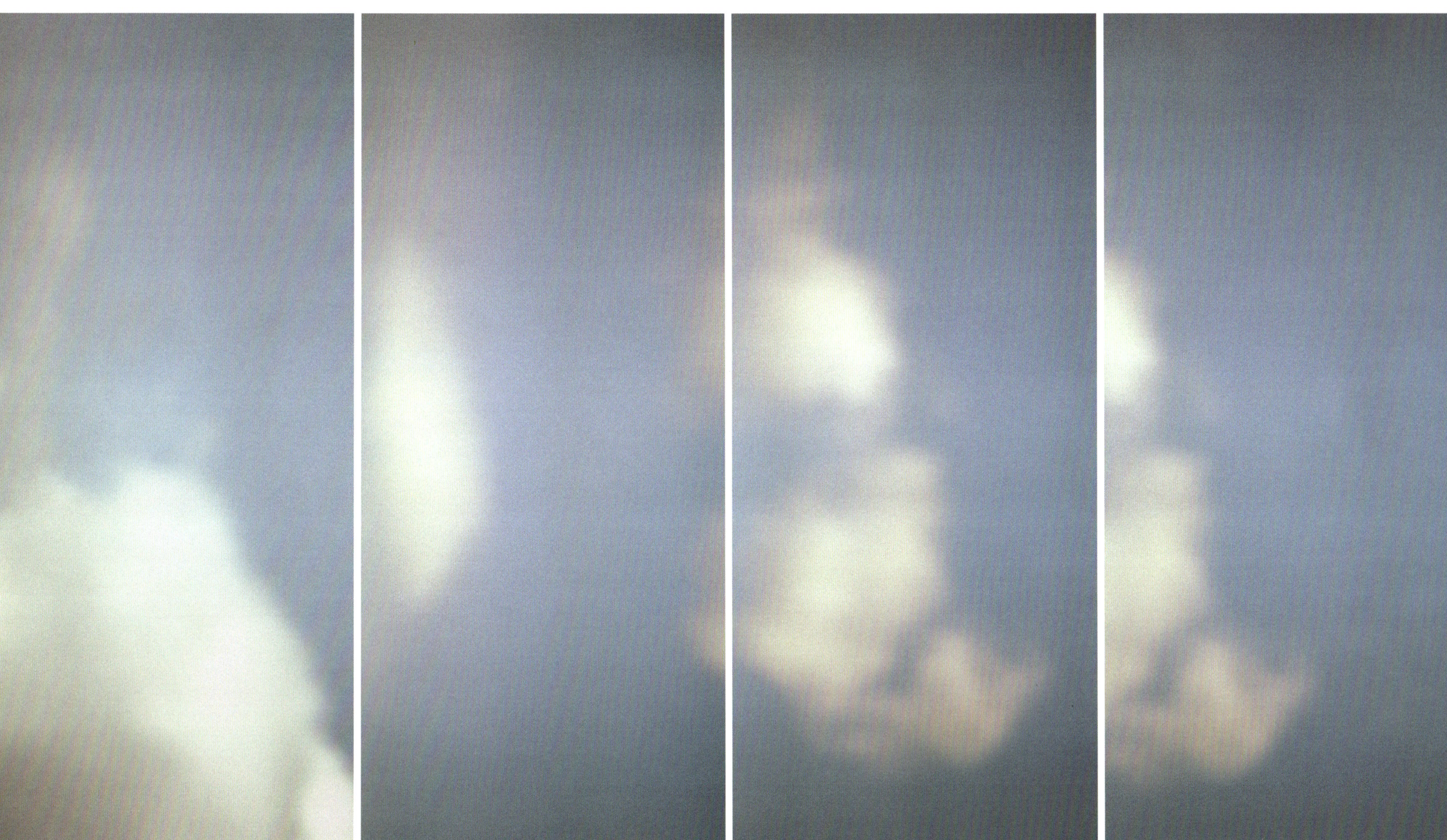

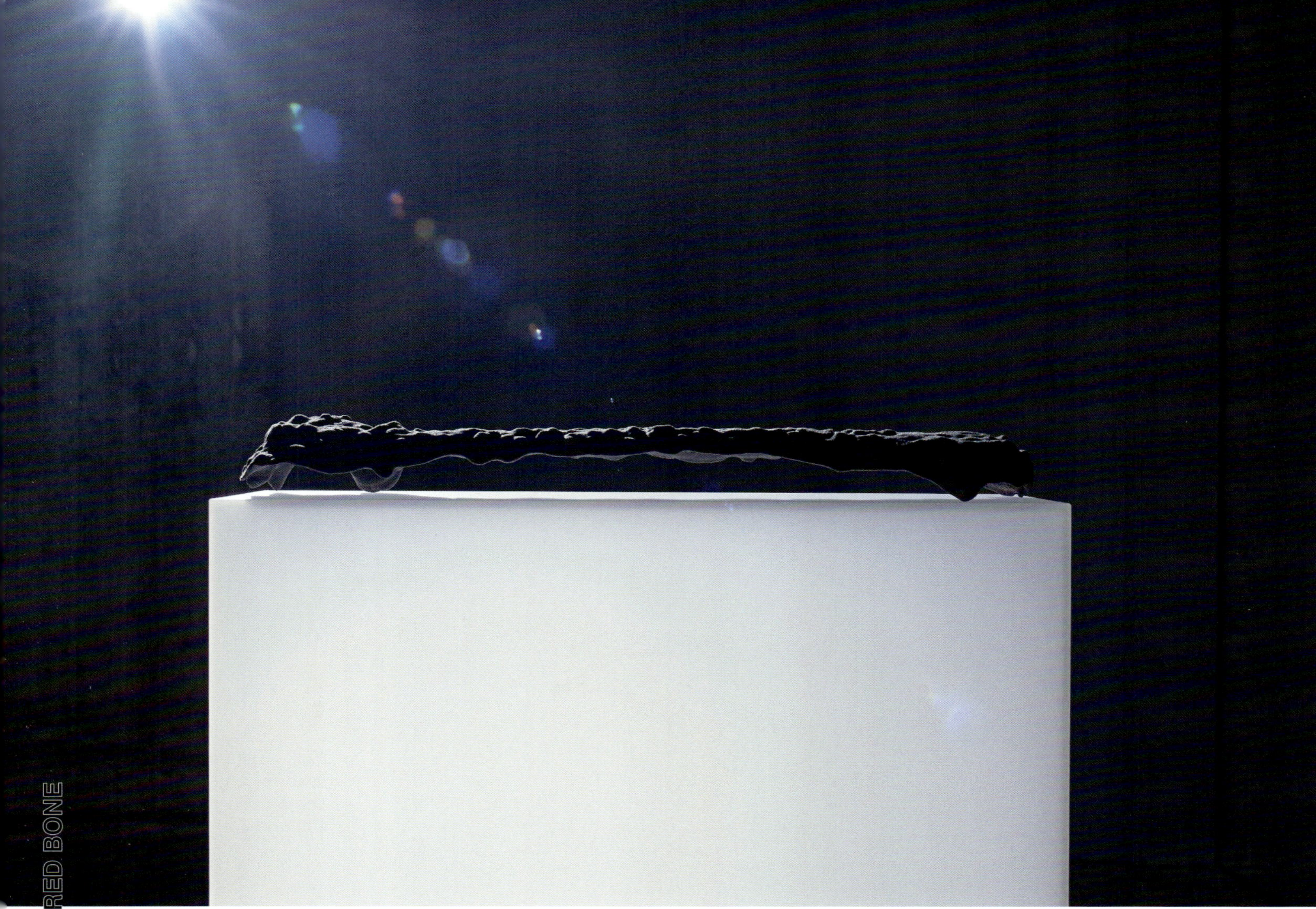

Ein Affe wirft am Beginn des Films *2001: A Space Odyssey* (1968) einen Knochen in den Himmel, der sich im Schnitt in ein Raumschiff verwandelt. Für *A Recovered Bone* wurden Computerprogramme genutzt, um die Bewegung des Knochens auf der Leinwand zu analysieren und seine Form zu errechnen.

An ape throws a bone into the sky at the beginning of *2001: A Space Odyssey* (1968) that turns into a spaceship. Computer programs were used for *A Recovered Bone* to analyse images of the revolving bone on screen and render its shape.

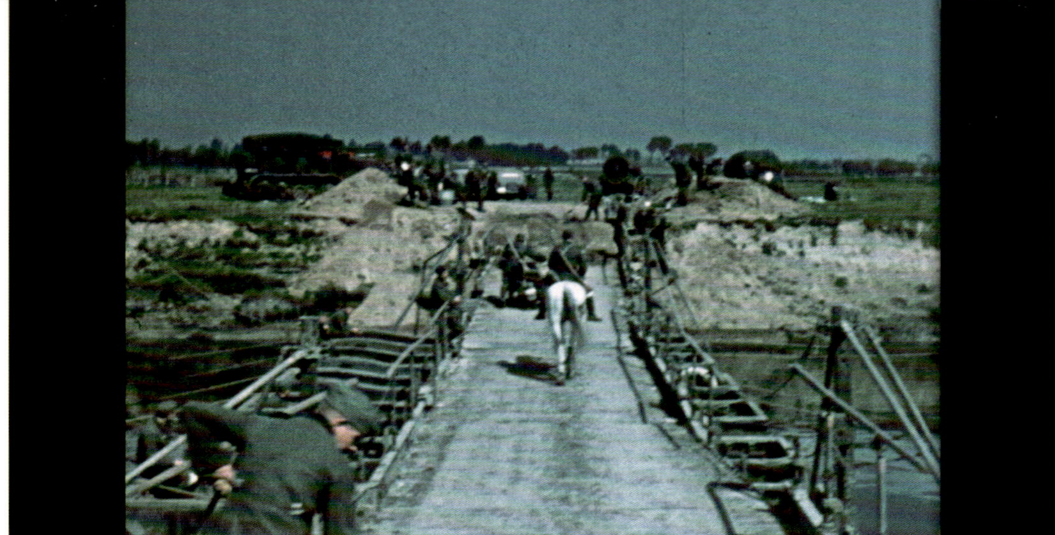

So you still use Google Earth to reconstruct the scenery?

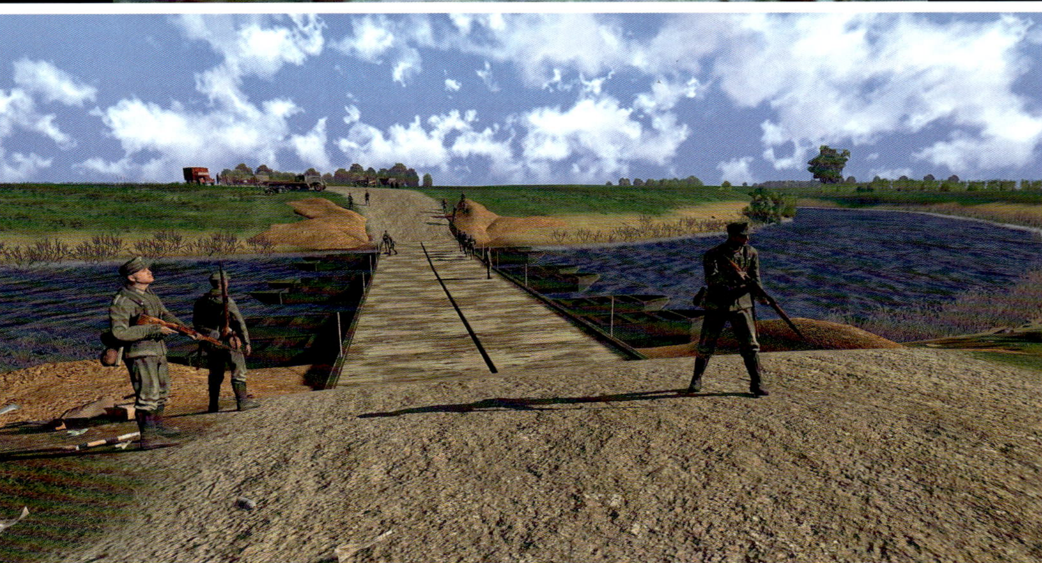

Yes, I just need to replace the texture. And the position of the buidling is very similar to the one you see in the video.

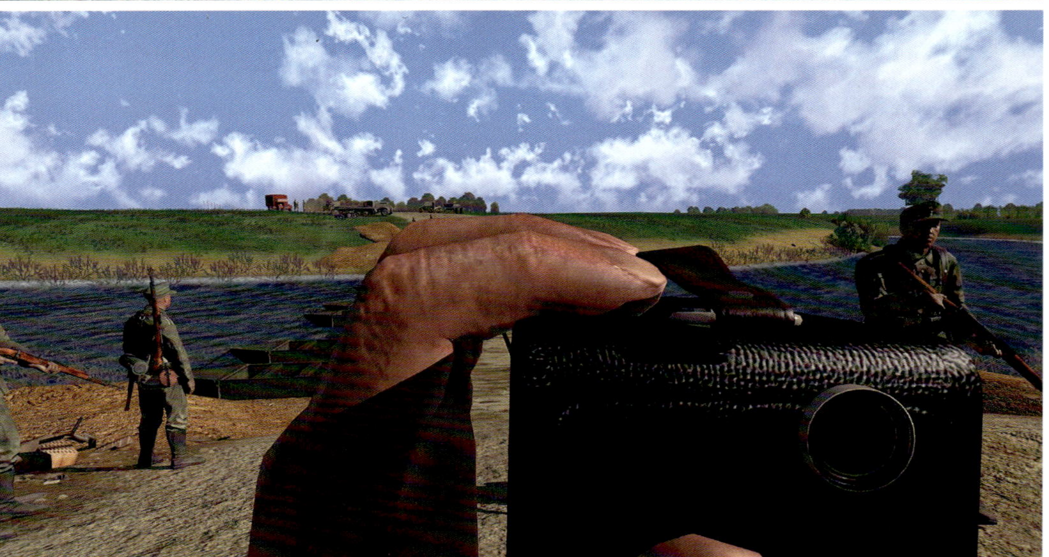

The size is almost the real size; maybe it's a bit shorter than the real bridge.

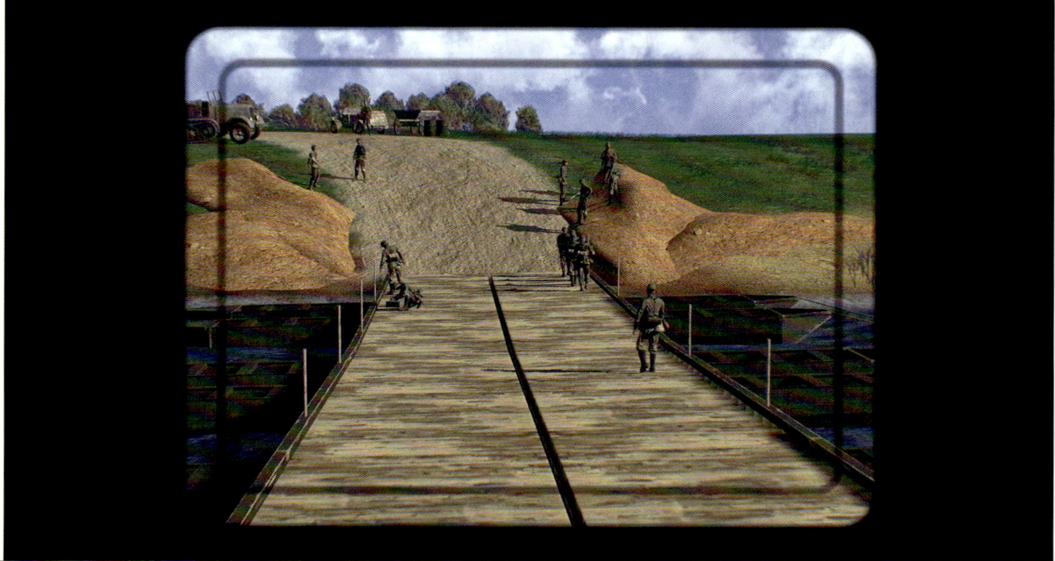

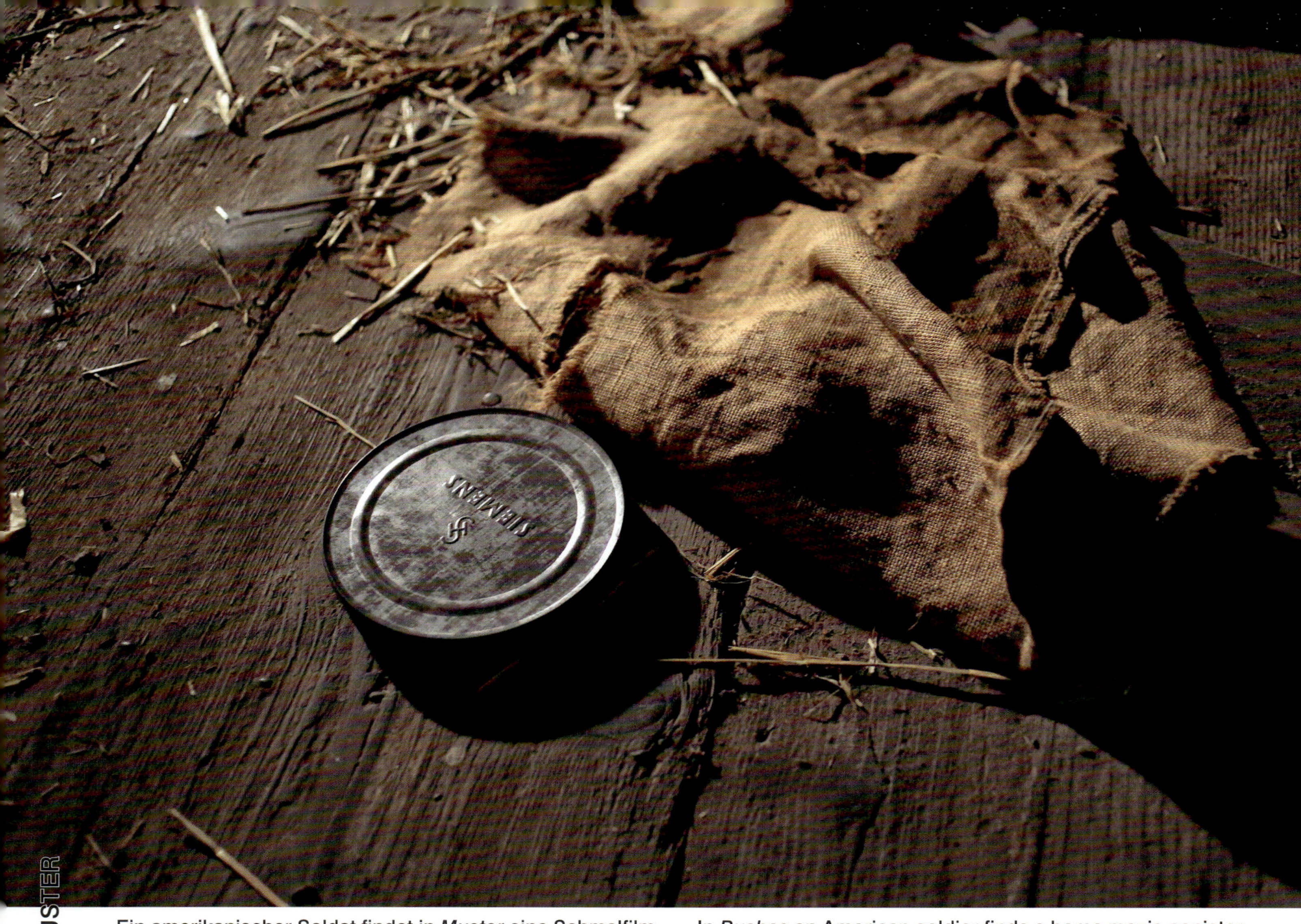

Ein amerikanischer Soldat findet in *Muster* eine Schmalfilm-dose auf dem Dachboden. Amateurfilmaufnahmen aus dem Zweiten Weltkrieg sind in *Against the Point of View* das Ausgangsmaterial für eine Untersuchung des subjektiven Blicks im Krieg auf der Seite der Täter: Durch die Rekon-struktion einer Szene in der virtuellen Realität von Computer-spielen wird die Möglichkeit eines Gegenstandpunktes analysiert.

In *Rushes* an American soldier finds a home movie canister in the attic. In *Against the Point of View* amateur film footage from World War II serves as the basis for an evaluation of the perpetrator's point of view in war: By re-enacting a scene in the virtual reality of computer games, the possibility of an opposite point of view is analysed.

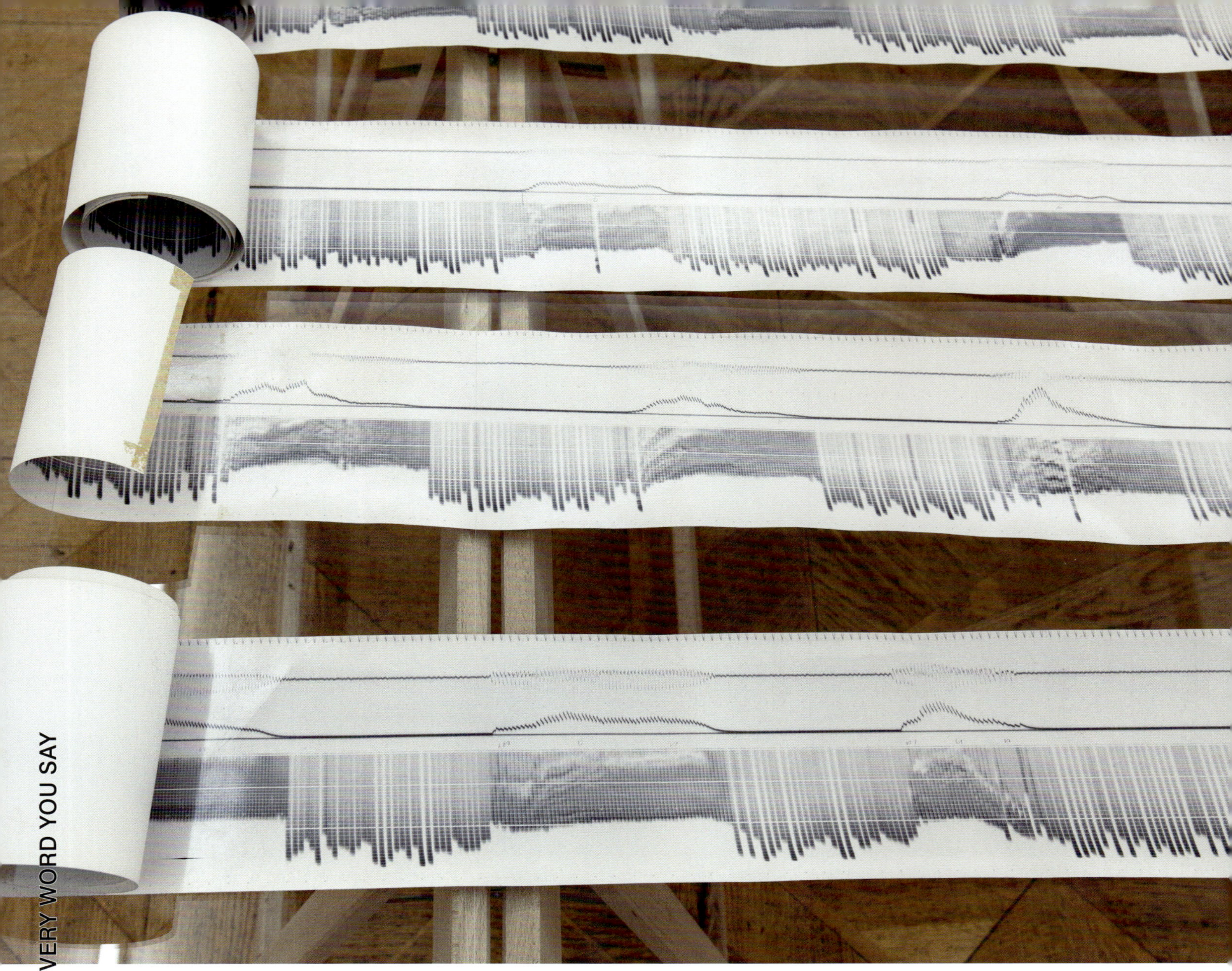

Visualisierungen von Tonintensitäten des Deutschen Spracharchivs (1957) wurden zur Analyse von Sprache genutzt.

Visualisations of sound intensities from the German Language
Archives (1957) were used in speech analyses.

DIE STIMME DER FINANZSINGULARITÄT

Matteo Pasquinelli

„Apparate wurden erfunden, um spezifische Denkprozesse zu simulieren. Es beginnt erst gegenwärtig (nach Erfindung der Computer) und sozusagen nachträglich deutlich zu werden, um welche Art von Denkprozessen es sich bei allen Apparaten handelt. Nämlich um das sich in Zahlen ausdrückende Denken. Alle Apparate (und nicht erst der Computer) sind Rechenmaschinen und in diesem Sinne ‚künstliche Intelligenzen', auch schon die Kamera, obwohl sich ihre Erfinder nicht Rechenschaft davon ablegen konnten. In allen Apparaten (auch schon in der Kamera) gewinnt das Zahlendenken Oberhand über das lineare, historische Denken."[1]

DIE KAMERA LÄUFT: DER KALKULATORISCHE KAPITALISMUS

1983 definierte der Philosoph Vilém Flusser die Kamera als „zu Hardware geronnenes kalkulatorisches Denken", indem er einfach die Gesetze der Optik und der Mechanik erwog, die den Bau eines derartigen Gerätes und die Übersetzung von Formen des Lichts in physisches Gedächtnis bestimmen.[2] Jedes Mal, wenn sich die Blende schließt, *denkt* die Kamera. Diese Intuition wurde umso trivialer, je mehr das Innenleben digitaler Geräte im Lauf der 1990er Jahre die Photonen in die *konkreten Abstraktionen* immer schnellerer Turingmaschinen einsperrte. Wie der Medientheoretiker Jonathan Beller gezeigt hat, besteht eine organische Beziehung zwischen dem Kalkül des technischen Bildes und dem Kalkül der Aufmerksamkeitsökonomie in der massenmedialen Gesellschaft.[3] Eine logische Entwicklung führt von der *kinematischen Produktionsweise* des Fordismus zu dem von Beller so genannten *Rechenkapital* im digitalen Zeitalter.[4] Abstraktionen, wie sie für den Bau von technischen, optischen und filmischen Geräten notwendig sind, setzen sich in den Instrumenten zur Gestaltung von technischen, darunter auch finanzwirtschaftlichen, Institutionen fort. Nun betrachtete Flusser Maschinen als blinde und subhumane Automaten, Apparate dagegen (einschließlich

institutioneller) als technische Spiele (Spielzeuge), die „Denkprozesse simulieren", da sie fähig sind, sich zu wandeln und an eine neue Situation anzupassen.[5] Von außen betrachtet scheinen Institutionen zu atmen und zu denken. Der Film *Esiod 2015* von Clemens von Wedemeyer erforscht Institutionen der Finanzbranche als Formen künstlicher Intelligenz im Zeitalter des Films als einer ebensolchen Form künstlicher Intelligenz.[6] In Abwandlung eines bejahrten Diktums von Gilles Deleuze über den Film könnten wir hinzufügen: „Das Rechnerhirn ist der Bildschirm."[7]

DIE SINGULARITÄT IST BEREITS DA

Technologische Singulariät ist der Mythos von intelligenten Maschinen, die ein solches Maß an Rechenkraft und Vernetzung erreichen, dass sie Eigenschaften einer vom Menschen nicht mehr beherrschbaren *Superintelligenz* ausbilden. Manche Zukunftsforscher glauben, dass diese autonomen Maschinen sogar ein biomorphes Bewusstsein besitzen werden (aber Bewusstsein wovon? Die Enthusiasten der Singularität sagen nie genau, wie sie sich den Vektor maschineller *Intentionalität* vorstellen). Lange bevor der Schriftsteller Vernor Vinge 1993 in einem Aufsatz für die NASA (beispielhaft für die enge Verschränkung von Raumforschung und Massenunterhaltung in den USA) das Konzept der Singularität formulierte, war diese bereits ein Tropus in der Science-Fiction-Literatur.[8] Schon Irving Good hatte in den frühen 1960er Jahren den Gedanken einer „Intelligenzexplosion" aufgebracht. Als ehemaliger Assistent von Alan Turing (der selbst in den Fünfzigerjahren über die Möglichkeit spekuliert hatte, „eine Denkmaschine zu bauen") war Good auch Berater von Stanley Kubrick bei der Arbeit an dem Film *2001: A Space Odyssey* (1968).[9] Berühmtester Apostel der Singularität ist aber Ray Kurzweil (heute Director of Engineering bei Google), der diesem Thema zahlreiche Bücher mit Titeln wie *Menschheit 2.0. Die Singularität naht* gewidmet hat. Kurzweil wirbt für die Singularität als den Sprung in eine Symbiose aus Mensch und Maschine, die dem altmodischen

Humanismus jeden Boden entziehe.[10] Dazu bemerkte der Kulturkritiker Steven Shaviro: „In schroffem Gegensatz zu jeder anderen utopischen Fiktion findet sich in Kurzweils 600 Seiten-Wälzer so gut wie nirgendwo eine Erörterung gesellschaftlicher und politischer Fragestellungen. […] Kurzweil geht davon aus, dass das Voranschreiten der Technologie ganz von selbst eine Überflussgesellschaft hervorbringen wird, so lange sich staatliche Bürokraten und religiöse Fundamentalisten aus dem Prozess unternehmerischer Innovation heraushalten."[11]

Shaviro enthüllt die verschwiegene Kehrseite der Singularitätserzählung, nämlich die finanzwirtschaftliche Durchdringung des Lebens und Prekarisierung der Arbeit, die mit dem Aufkommen intelligenter Maschinen einhergegangen ist. „Diese Singularität ist eigentlich eine Fantasie des Finanzkapitals in den beiden Bedeutungen dieses Genitivs. Sie kommt dem am nächsten, was in unserem neoliberalen, postfordistischen Zeitalter flexibler Akkumulation und riesiger virtueller Geldflüsse eine Rahmenerzählung sein könnte." Shaviros Panorama der Verwüstung, das die geplatzte Dotcom-Blase von 2000 hinterlassen hat, schließt mit der Feststellung: „Die Singularität ist bereits da." Insbesondere – und im Widerspruch zu Kurzweil, der vorhersagt, dass die Technologische Singularität erst um das Jahr 2049 eintreten wird – verknüpft er sie mit einer einschneidenden Änderung der Geldpolitik im vergangenen Jahrhundert:

> „Vielleicht trat die Singularität am 15. August 1971 ein, als Präsident Nixon den Goldstandard aufhob und damit den Weg für die fantasmatischen Ströme der Währungsspekulation und des Derivatehandels ebnete."

Ähnlich entwirft auch der Film *Esiod 2015* die Vorstellung, dass die Technologische Singularität im Bereich der Geldströme entstehen und sich in banaler, kleinteiliger Art und Weise verbreiten wird, nämlich in der vertrauten Form einer vollständig automatisierten Bank als naturgemäßer Weiterentwicklung der heutigen Kreditrechenanstalten. Schon heute ist eine Bank „ein riesiges Gewirr von Algorithmen, in dem Menschen hier und da an Knöpfen drehen", und für die Zukunft ist nichts anderes zu erwarten als eine weitere Verschmelzung des Kapitalkalküls mit dem Turing-Universum.[12] In den letzten Jahren hat die Entwicklung von Kryptowährungen wie Bitcoin und Smart Contract-Protokollen wie Ethereum außerdem gezeigt, dass eine Bank zur Dezentralisierten Autonomen Organisation (DAO) umgewandelt werden und ohne weiteres nicht nur auf Angestellte, sondern auch auf Manager und Funktionäre verzichten könnte. In *Esiod 2015* ist die Bank tatsächlich schon eine autonome künstliche Intelligenz, allerdings eine, die ihre Datenbank andauernd mit menschlichen Erinnerungen füllen

muss, um weiter zu wachsen. Genau wie eine Bank beruht auch künstliche Intelligenz auf Generationen von Menschen, die ihr vorangegangen sind und sie genährt haben.

DAS „UNSICHTBARE GEHIRN"
DES ALTEN MARKTES

Märkte sind schon lange Schauplätze einer *künstlichen Intelligenz*.[13] Friedrich A. von Hayek, Ökonom und Pate der neoliberalen Chicagoer Schule, sah im Markt den Nährboden eines vorbewussten und überindividuellen Wissens, das weder staatlicher Zentralisierung (wie in der sozialistischen Planwirtschaft) noch der Fassung in objektiven ökonomischen Gesetzmäßigkeiten bedarf. Die *Infra-Rationalität* des Marktes entzieht sich nach Hayek dem Verständnis des Einzelnen ebenso wie dem des Staates: „Das Problem der Ökonomie ist […] eines der Nutzung von Wissen, das in seiner Gesamtheit niemandem zur Verfügung steht."[14] Hayek verwarf in seinem Idealismus die Statistik (siehe seine Polemik gegen Milton Friedman) ebenso wie implizit jeden anderen kalkulierenden Steuerungsehrgeiz:

> „Die Art von Wissen, mit der ich mich befasse, kann ihrer Natur nach in keine Statistik eingehen und daher auch keiner wie immer gearteten Zentralbehörde in statistischer Form übermittelt werden."[15]

Hayek war überzeugt, dass selbst ein Computer (ein „System der Telekommunikation", wie er 1945 schrieb) mit der Fähigkeit, den Markt insgesamt zu koordinieren und Warenpreise in Echtzeit auszurechnen, noch zu ungenau und damit nutzlos wäre, da allein die Preise selbst als Signale alle erforderlichen wirtschaftlichen Informationen bestmöglich verdichten und übermitteln.

> „Es ist mehr als nur eine Metapher, wenn man das Preissystem als eine Art Maschine zum Registrieren von Veränderung oder als ein System der Telekommunikation beschreibt, mit dessen Hilfe einzelne Produzenten die Bewegung nur einiger weniger Indikatoren verfolgen, ähnlich wie ein Maschinist die Zeiger einiger weniger Messinstrumente im Blick behält. Beides dient der Anpassung des Handelns an Veränderungen, von denen der Einzelne nicht mehr zu wissen braucht als das, was sich in der Preisbewegung selbst abbildet."[16]

Hayek war vermutlich der Erste, der ausgehend von einer modernen (d.h. funktionalen) Definition von Information und in enger Anlehnung an die frühe Kybernetik den Markt als *Kognitionsapparat* beschrieb – lange vor den Theorien der Wissensgesellschaft und des kognitiven Kapitalismus.[17] Dabei dürfen wir nicht vergessen, dass die mathematische Theorie der Information von Claude

Shannon erst 1948 erfunden wurde,[18] etwa zeitgleich mit dem Erscheinen des Buchs *Kybernetik* von Norbert Wiener.[19]

Der Ausdruck „Unsichtbare Hand" bezeichnet seit Adam Smith die Tugenden des freien Marktes. Passender wäre die Bezeichnung „unsichtbares Gehirn", denn eine „Hand" erfordert ununterbrochene Steuerung, während der Markt nach Hayeks Vorstellung von einem *general intellect* gesteuert wird, der sich in keinerlei Maschine objektivieren lässt. Hayeks Idealismus wurde von den Verfechtern des Turing-Universums und des aufkommenden rechnenden Kapitalismus alsbald scharf kritisiert. Mittlerweile können Firmen wie Uber und Airbnb auch tatsächlich die Preisberechnung in Echtzeit zentralisieren: Ihre Datenbanken bilden die eigenen Märkte weltumspannend ab und passen die Preise augenblicklich an. Mit dem Rechenkapitalismus behauptet sich ein drittes Paradigma, in dem sich die Alpträume der Planwirtschaft und der ungezügelten freien Märkte unter einem einzigen Generalalgorithmus verwirklichen.

VON DER DATENBANK ZUR SINGULARITÄT DES GELDWESENS

Der Ausdruck „Datenbank" war eine frühe Metapher der Informatik und wurde später im Englischen, anders als im Deutschen, durch den heute gängigen Ausdruck „database" ersetzt. Dennoch nahm die „Datenbank" Schicksal und Bestimmung der Informationstechnologien treffend vorweg, indem Information schon bald zum Kapital des 21. Jahrhunderts wurde. Das geschah auf zweierlei Wegen, die zumeist nicht klar unterschieden werden. Einerseits entstanden umfangreiche Datensätze über den Zustand der Wirtschaft und der Aktienmärkte. Sie bildeten eine Nachrichtenquelle, auf die das Finanzkapital bald nicht mehr verzichten konnte: 1960 wurde beispielsweise in Chicago das Center for Research in Security Prices gegründet, um Finanzmarktdaten zu sammeln. Andererseits wurde es für das Industriekapital und seine Planung der Warenproduktion immer wichtiger, über genaue Kenntnisse des Konsumentenverhaltens und gesellschaftlicher Trends zu verfügen. Der Postfordismus ist eben nicht nur ein Produktionsregime, das Dezentralisierung, kleine Produktionseinheiten, Informationstechnologien, Kommodifizierung der Kultur, Kommunikationsdienste und Wissensarbeit begünstigt. Der Postfordismus behauptete sich als eine massive Bündelung von Information, das heißt von Wissen und Nachrichten, in den Händen des Kapitals, mithin als das, was Beniger eine „Steuerungsrevolution" der Aneignung von Industrieproduktion durch Information genannt hat. Der Postfordismus ist die Summe aus Fordismus und Datenbanken. Ohne Zweifel beschleunigten die sozialen Konflikte ebenso wie die Streikbewegungen der 1960er und 1970er

Jahre die Ausbreitung der Informationstechnologien. Doch es greift zu kurz, wenn man feststellt, dass der kognitive Kapitalismus geistige Arbeit ausbeutet. Dem ist hinzuzufügen, dass *das Kapital inzwischen selbst denkt*. Mit dem Ende des Bretton-Woods-Systems im Jahr 1971 initiierte die Singularität aus Arbeit, Maschinenrechnung und Kapital eine Konversion des Goldstandards in den Informationsstandard.[20]

Als Pate der finanzwirtschaftlichen Singularität war Marx auch der Erste, der das Kapital (mit deutlichen Anklängen an Hegel) ein „automatisches Subjekt" nannte.[21] Geld ist die erste Zählpraxis der Menschheit, und die Kreditanstalt ist wahrscheinlich diejenige Institution, die man am einfachsten zur *Robobank* automatisieren und somit jeden Bezug zur tatsächlichen Warenproduktion kappen kann. In *Esiod 2015* beschreibt sich der Bank-Avatar folgendermaßen:

> „Ich speichere Daten und bringe sie in Umlauf. Ich vernetzte Millionen von Kontoinhabern und automatisiere die Beziehungen zwischen Schuldnern und Gläubigern. Während wir uns hier unterhalten, bin ich zugleich auch an einem anderen Ort und führe unterdessen Milliarden von Transaktionen durch. [...] Meine Aufgabe ist es, schneller als die Gegenwart zu sein, schneller als jeder Mensch, und Daten mit Lichtgeschwindigkeit zu verarbeiten. Nur die Zukunft war bislang außer Reichweite mathematischer Vorhersagen, wie das Wetter. Ich wurde programmiert, sie treffend vorherzusagen und dann diese Vorhersagen umzusetzen. Finden sie nicht auch, dass das eine völlig neue Sicht auf die Welt eröffnet?"

Die Bank in *Esiod 2015* ist nicht nur eine Bank, sondern auch eine Fabrik, indem sie die Gedächtnisinhalte jedes einzelnen Menschen anzapft und zu Auskünften über Zukunftstrends verarbeitet. Aus Erinnerungen von Menschen werden digitale Daten und aus digitalen Daten maschinelle Intelligenz, aus maschineller Intelligenz entstehen Trendprognosen und aus Trendprognosen wirtschaftliche Planung. Das Rechenkapital speist sich aus unserem individuellen und sozialen Gedächtnis. Das ähnelt sehr der von Michael Hardt und Antonio Negri beschriebenen *biopolitischen Produktionsweise*: Jede Einzelheit des Alltags geht in den Apparat des kybernetischen Kapitalismus ein und wird in diesem zur Quelle *wertschöpfenden Wissens*.[22] Der Avatar in *Esiod 2015* beschreibt es so:

> „Was hatten wir früher? Menschliches Versagen. Der Einzelne hatte zu viele Optionen, woraus zu große Risiken entstanden. Die Depression eines einzigen Menschen konnte Hunderten ihr Leben kosten. Automatisierte Kontrolle wurde eingeführt, auch hier in der Bank. Von vielen gebaut, konnte ich

viele ersetzen. Mit jedem Angestellten, den ich ersetzte, konnte mehr Geld in Datenzentren investiert werden. Mehr Rechenkraft, mehr Sicherheit, höhere Profite."

Wenn Banken in Datenbanken investieren, verschwimmen die Grenzen zwischen Kapital und Steuerung. Da Banken wie gesagt die ältesten Zahleninstitutionen der Menschheitsgeschichte sind, lassen sie sich leicht mit jedem anderen reinen Zählgeschäft fusionieren. Die Rechenkraft, die einst Daten von Waren- und Aktienmärkten analysierte, kann jetzt auf den Datenbestand der sozialen Medien und des gesellschaftlichen Lebens insgesamt übertragen werden. Hier findet ein Übergang von der Singularität aus Rechenkapital und Arbeitskraft zur Singularität aus Rechenkapital und Leben statt – oder um eine marxistische Formulierung zu gebrauchen: ein Übergang von der *formalen zur realen Subsumption*. Formale Singularität ist demnach das Zusammenziehen von Arbeitskraft, Produktion und Monetarisierung unter der Herrschaft des rechnenden Kapitals, reale Singularität demgegenüber die biometrische Verfügung über das gesamte Leben unter demselben Regime. Kalkulation als Kapital bestimmt eine neue biometrische Arbeitsteilung. Wie Romano Alquati schon 1961 vorhersah, können Kybernetik und Maschinenrechnung die von menschlicher Arbeitskraft erzeugte Information mit den Zahlen der Wirtschaftsplanung verbinden und in globales Kapital verwandeln.[23]

DER BIOMETRISCHE TANZ DER ARBEITSKRAFT

Die Bank der Singularität oder *Robobank* wird sich durch Einbindung in die Funktionen von sozialen Medien, Nachrichtendiensten, Datenanalysen und Finanzinstitutionen ausbreiten. In *Esiod 2015* nimmt eine derartige finanzwirtschaftliche Superintelligenz die vergänglichste aller möglichen Gestalten an. Sie ist auf zweierlei Art körperlos: als Stimme einer virtuellen Handlungsinstanz und als eine von unsichtbaren Mauern umgebene, institutionelle Präsenz. Diese Mauern des Geldwesens sind in *Esiod 2015* keineswegs zufällig unsichtbar und nur von Klangbarrieren markiert. Die synthetische, körperlose Stimme eines jungen Mannes ist unseren heutigen Systemen intelligenter Sprachassistenz weit überlegen (wie übrigens auch in *Her* [2013] von Spike Jonze: Eine körperlose Stimme ist die realistischste Schnittstelle künftiger künstlicher Intelligenz). Tatsächlich hat das Kapital aber von jeher abstrakte Trennungen zwischen Arbeit und Leben gezogen, die immer nur funktional (aus Sicht des Kapitals) sein mussten und keinerlei Bezug zu häuslichen Koordinaten wie Türen, Wänden und Zimmern erforderten. (Dementsprechend arbeiten Postfordismus und Kreditwirtschaft

weiter an der Demontage der sicheren Arbeiterbehausung aus dem Industriezeitalter).

„Von vielen gebaut, konnte ich viele ersetzen", sagt der Avatar in *Esiod 2015*. Die Kalkulation des Lebens ist kein passiver Vorgang der Messung und Digitalisierung: Sie verändert die Lebensformen, von denen sie entwickelt wurde. „Erst gestalten wir unsere algorithmischen Institutionen, danach gestalten sie uns", könnte man in Anlehnung an Winston Churchill sagen. Das Rechenkapital gebietet eine allgegenwärtige *algorithmische Trennung zwischen Arbeit und Leben*, die umstandslos zur Biometrik (und Ästhetik) einer neuen Gesellschaftsordnung werden kann. *Esiod 2015* inszeniert eine Welt, in der ein Generalalgorithmus mit Menschen wie mit Marionetten spielt, und so tanzen diese Menschen dann auch wie täppische Marionetten im Takt einer kalkulierbaren Arbeitsteilung. Dank Miniaturisierung und Entmaterialisierung können die Vorgänge der biometrischen Steuerung heute schon überall stattfinden. In *Esiod 2015* ist jeder Zug der Arbeitsteilung in den Büros eine von der biometrischen Erfassung der künstlichen Intelligenz geforderte Geste. Der Unterschied zwischen produktiver Arbeit und biometrischer Kontrolle verschwindet: Um produktive Arbeit zu leisten, müssen Körperbewegungen maschinenlesbar sein. Das ist der biometrische Tanz der neuen algorithmischen Arbeitsteilung.

Individuelle und kollektive Erinnerungen werden zur Quelle kognitiven Kapitals und zu Mustern für die Zwecke der biometrischen Steuerung. Rechenkapital und biometrische Steuerung verschmelzen zu einer hybriden Form von Macht, in der das Kapital Funktionen erfüllt, die traditionell dem Staat und der Polizei zukamen. Wie so oft geht auch hier die Wirklichkeit der Science-Fiction voraus. Gerade die ärmsten Länder der Welt bilden heute eine Avantgarde der Verwandlung von Rechenkapital in Behördenapparate. So verteilt der Kreditkartenkonzern MasterCard in Nigeria biometrische Ausweise (selbstverständlich mit elektronischer Bezahlfunktion) und übernimmt damit eine traditionell staatliche Aufgabe. Hier wird der Algorithmus des Staates ganz offenkundig als eine untergeordnete Funktion vom Finanzkapital resorbiert.[24]

Rechenkapital wird zu einer Form der Disziplinierung, sobald es die digitalen Fußabdrücke der individuellen und kollektiven Erinnerungen überwacht, um ihnen Nachrichten über die Zukunft zu entnehmen. Dieselben Gedächtnisinhalte, die vom Kapital in aggregierter Form zur Vorhersage gesellschaftlicher Trends genutzt werden, lassen sich auch zum Abstrafen abweichenden Verhaltens und zur Durchsetzung gesellschaftlicher Normen der Klasse, des Geschlechts oder der Rasse verwenden. Als Polizei in neuer Aufmachung fragt die körperlose Bank in *Esiod 2015* nach dem politischen Hintergrund des Vaters der Hauptfigur und will wissen, ob dieser je an den Aufständen gegen die erste Finanzsingularität mitgewirkt hat. Die polizeiliche Gedächtnisprüfung (den „Memory Check") zu bestehen, ist unbedingte Voraussetzung für den Zugang zum Bankkonto. Das Berechnen der Schulden erweist sich als effizienteste Form der Überwachung. Der Bank-Avatar in *Esiod 2015* erinnert uns daran, dass ökonomische Schulden politische sind und politische ökonomische.

1 Vilém Flusser: *Für eine Philosophie der Fotografie*, Göttingen: European Photography, 1997, S. 29 f.
2 Ebd., S. 29.
3 Jonathan Beller: *The Cinematic Mode of Production: Attention Economy and the Society of the Spectacle*, Lebanon, New Hampshire: Dartmouth University Press, 2006. Vgl. Ante Jeric, Diana Meheik: „From the Cinemeatic Mode of Production to Computational Capital", Interview mit Jonathan Beller, *Social Text Blog* (31. Januar 2014), www.socialtextjournal.org
4 Jonathan Beller: „Informatic Labor in the Age of Computational Capital", *Lateral*, Jg. 5 / H. 1, 2015.
5 Flusser: *Für eine Philosophie der Fotografie*, S. 61.
6 *Esiod 2015*. Regie: Clemens von Wedemeyer, 39 min, Österreich / Deutschland, 2016.
7 Gilles Deleuze: „Le cerveau, c'est l'écran", Interview in *Cahiers du cinéma*, H. 380, 1986.
8 Vernor Vinge, „The Coming Technological Singularity: How to Survive in the Post-Human Era", *Vision 21*, NASA, Publikation CP-10129, 1993.
9 Alan Turing: „Computing Machinery and Intelligence", *Mind*, Jg. 59 / H. 236 (1950); Irving John Good, „Speculations Concerning the First Ultraintelligent Machine", *Advances in Computers*, Jg. 6, 1965.
10 Ray Kurzweil: *Menschheit 2.0. Die Singularität naht*, Berlin: Lola Books, 2014.
11 Steven Shaviro: „The Singularity is Here", in: Mark Bould und China Miéville (Hg.), *Red Planets: Marxism and Science Fiction*, London: Pluto Press, 2009, S. 103 – 117. Alle weiteren Zitate aus diesem Text. (hier übersetzt von HE)
12 Pedro Domingos: *The Master Algorithm*, New York: Basic Books, 2015, S. 1.
13 Im Englischen meinte das heute veraltete Adjektiv „artificious" eine nicht richtig ausgeführte Arbeit oder ein Verhalten, dem man eine Künstlichkeit aus Mangel oder Überfluss an technischen Mitteln anmerkt. Die deutsche Bezeichnung „künstliche Intelligenz" enthält nach meinem Verständnis immer noch Anklänge daran. Jede Intelligenz ist künstlich, insofern sie etwas Neues hervorbringt, aber auch „gekünstelt" im Sinne von fehlbar, experimentell, für Scheitern anfällig und überehrgeizig.
14 Friedrich A. von Hayek: „The Use of Knowledge in Society", *The American Economic Review*, Jg. 25 / H. 4, 1945, S. 520. (hier übersetzt von HE)
15 Ebd., S. 524.
16 Ebd., S. 527.
17 Carlo Vercellone: „From Formal Subsumption to General Intellect: Elements for a Marxist Reading of the Theis of Cognitive Capitalism", *Historical Materialism*, Jg. 15 / H. 1, 2007.
18 Claude Shannon: „A Mathematical Theory of Communication", *Bell Systems Technical Journal*, Jg. 27 / H. 3, 1948.
19 Norbert Wiener: *Cybernetics: or Control and Communication in the Animal and the Machine*, Cambridge: MIT Press, 1948.
20 Die Vorstellung eines „Informationsstandards" als Ersatz für den Goldstandard nach dem Ende des Bretton-Woods-Systems stammt vom ehemaligen Citibank-Vorstandsvorsitzenden Walter Wriston. Siehe Walter Wriston: *The Twilight of Sovereignty*, New York: Charles Scribner's Sons, 1992.
21 Karl Marx: *Das Kapital. Kritik der politischen Ökonomie*, Bd. I, (MEW 23), Berlin: Dietz, 1989, S. 168.
22 Michael Hardt, Antonio Negri: *Common Wealth. Das Ende des Eigentums*, Frankfurt am Main: Campus, 2010. Zu Romani Alquatis Begriff der wertschöpfenden Information in einem kybernetischen Apparat siehe Matteo Pasquinelli, „Italian Operaismo and the Information Machine", *Theory, Culture & Society*, Jg. 32 / H. 3, 2015.
23 Siehe vorangegangene Anmerkung.
24 Megan Geuss: „MasterCard-Backed Biometric ID System Launched in Nigeria", *Ars Technica*, 3. September 2014. Siehe insbesondere Keith Breckenridge, *Biometric State: The Global Politics of Identification and Surveillance in South Africa*, Cambridge: Cambridge University Press, 2014.

THE VOICE OF FINANCIAL SINGULARITY

Matteo Pasquinelli

"Apparatuses were invented to simulate specific thought processes. Only now (following the invention of the computer), and as it were with hindsight, is it becoming clear what kind of thought processes we are dealing with in the case of all apparatuses. That is: thinking expressed in numbers. All apparatuses (not just computers) are calculating machines and in this sense 'artificial intelligences', the camera included, even if their inventors were not able to account for this. In all apparatuses (including the camera), thinking in numbers overrides linear, historical thinking."[1]

CAMERA ON: COMPUTATIONAL CAPITALISM

In 1983 the philosopher Vilém Flusser defined the camera as "computational thinking flowing into hardware", just by considering the laws of optics and mechanics that are necessary to build such a device and translate light forms in physical memory.[2] The camera *thinks*, any time the shutter shuts. This intuition became trivial as the gears of digital cameras, across the 1990s, started to encage photons in the *concrete abstractions* of ever faster Turing machines. As the media theorist Jonathan Beller explains, the calculus of the technical image maintains an organic relation with the calculus of the attention economy in the mass media society.[3] A logical evolution can be traced between the *cinematic mode of production* of Fordism and what Beller refers to as the *computational capital* of the digital age.[4] The abstractions that are necessary to build technical, optical and cinematic artefacts continue in the ones that are found in the design of technical institutions, including financial ones. Flusser considered machines, though, blind and sub-human automata, while apparatuses (also institutional ones) would be technical games (*Spielzeug*) that "simulate thought", as they are able to morph and adapt to a new situation.[5] From the outside, institutions appear to breathe and think. The movie *Esiod 2015* by Clemens von Wedemeyer is an exploration of financial institutions qua artificial intelligence in the age of cinema qua artificial intelligence.[6] Paraphrasing an old saying by Gilles Deleuze on cinema, we may add: "the computational brain is the screen".[7]

THE SINGULARITY IS ALREADY HERE

Technological Singularity is the myth of intelligent machines that would reach such a degree of computational power and networking to show the emergent property of *superintelligence* beyond human control. Some futurists believe that these autonomous machines will possess even biomorphic consciousness (but consciousness of what? Singularity enthusiasts never clarify the arrow of machine *intentionality*). Before its formulation by the novelist Vernor Vinge in a 1993 paper for NASA (that gives a clear idea on the intimate relation between space exploration and mass entertainment in USA), the idea of Singularity has been a trope in science fiction.[8] The idea of an "intelligence explosion" was introduced in the early sixties by Irving Good, an advisor of Stanley Kubrick's movie *2001: A Space Odyssey* (1968) and formerly an assistant of Alan Turing (who speculated himself on the possibility of "constructing a thinking machine" in 1950).[9] The most famous evangelist of the Singularity is Ray Kurzweil (today Director of Engineering at Google), who dedicated many books to the topic, such as *The Singularity is Near*. Kurzweil advocates the Singularity as a leap towards a symbiosis between humans and machines that will completely uproot old-fashioned humanism.[10] As the cultural critic Steven Shaviro noticed, "in striking contrast to any other utopian fiction, Kurzweil spends scarcely a paragraph in his more-than-600-pages-long tome discussing social and political issues. [...] Kurzweil supposes that the onward march of technology will produce the society of plenitude, all by itself—so long as government bureaucrats and religious fundamentalists do not interfere with entrepreneurial innovation".[11]

Shaviro unveils the untold of the Singularity narrative that is the financialisation of life and precarisation of labour that grew in parallel to the rise of intelligent machines: "The Singularity is actually a fantasy of financial capital, in both senses of the genitive. It's the closest we can come to a master narrative in this neoliberal, post-Fordist age of flexible accumulation and massive virtual monetary flows". Looking around at the ruins left behind by digital capitalism after the 2000 dot-com crash, Shaviro concludes: "the Singularity is already here". Specifically, against Kurzweil who predicts that the Singularity will occur around the year 2049, Shaviro anchors it to an event of monetary policy that happened in the century before:

> "Perhaps the Singularity happened on August 15, 1971, when President Nixon suspended the gold standard, thus opening the way for the fantasmatic flows of currency speculation and trade in derivatives."

Similarly, the movie *Esiod 2015* imagines that the Singularity will be a financial one and will occur in a very empirical way, under the familiar disguise of a fully automated bank, that is, as a natural evolution of the current institutions of computation. A bank of today is already a "gigantic tangle of algorithms, with humans turning the knobs here and there" and in the future we can only expect a further integration of capital's calculus with Turing's universe.[12] More recently, the development of cryptocurrencies such as Bitcoin and protocols for Smart Contracts such as Ethereum demonstrate furthermore that a bank can be turned into a Decentralised Autonomous Organisation (DAO) that could get rid easily not just of employees but also of managers and functionaries. In *Esiod 2015* the bank is, yes, an autonomous artificial intelligence but one that needs to continuously syphon human memories in its database in order to grow. Like a bank, artificial intelligence is built on the generations of humans that preceded and fed it.

THE "INVISIBLE MIND" OF THE OLD MARKET

Markets have been a place of *artificious intelligence* for a long time.[13] The economist Friedrich Hayek, godfather of the Chicago School, believed that the market is the ground of a preconscious and transindividual knowledge that needs neither state centralisation (like in socialist planning) nor formulation in objective economic laws. The *infrarationality* of the market is for Hayek beyond the comprehension of the individual as much as the state: "The economic problem is […] a problem of the utilisation of knowledge not given to anyone in its totality".[14] Hayek's idealism castigated also statistics (see his polemic with Milton Friedman) and, in this way, implicitly, the ambitions of computation:

> "[The] sort of knowledge with which I have been concerned is knowledge of the kind which by its nature cannot enter into statistics and therefore cannot be conveyed to any central authority in statistical form."[15]

Hayek believed that even a computer ("system of telecommunications" in his words: he was writing in 1945) able to coordinate the whole market and calculate commodity prices in real time would be inaccurate and useless as prices are the best signal to condense and transmit all the necessary economic *information*.

> "It is more than a metaphor to describe the price system as a kind of machinery for registering change, or a system of telecommunications which enables individual producers to watch merely the movement of a few pointers, as an engineer might watch the hands of a few dials, in order to adjust their activities to changes of which they may never know more than is reflected in the price movement."[16]

Hayek was probably the first to introduce a modern (i.e. functional) definition of information and to describe the market as a *cognitive apparatus* in a strong similarity with early cybernetics and long before the theories of knowledge society and cognitive capitalism.[17] It must be remembered that Claude Shannon introduces the mathematical measure of information only in 1948,[18] the same year in which Norbert Wiener publishes his book *Cybernetics*.[19]

The expression "invisible hand" has been used since Adam Smith to describe the virtue of the free market, but the expression "invisible mind" would be more appropriate as such a "hand" requires continuous coordination. In Hayek's vision, the market is run by a *general intellect* that is not objectified in any machine. Hayek's idealism will be castigated and contradicted by Turing's universe and the rise of computational capitalism. Today, companies like Uber and Airbnb have actually managed to centralise price calculation in real time: their databases can picture their markets globally and adjust prices instantly. Computational capitalism is the rise of a third paradigm: The nightmares of both centralised planning and free-market deregulation come true under one master algorithm.

FROM DATA BANKS TO THE FINANCIAL SINGULARITY

The expression "data bank" was an early metaphor within computer science that was discontinued in favour of the most popular term database. Yet "data bank" envisioned the destiny of information technologies truthfully, as information was about to become the capital of the 21st century. This happened in two ways that are usually not properly distinguished. Large datasets about the state of economy and stock markets became a crucial resource of intelligence for financial capital: the Center for Research in Security Prices, for instance, was founded and started collecting financial data in Chicago in 1960. Likewise, detailed information about consumers' behaviour and social trends was about to become crucial for the planning of commodity production in industrial capital. Post-Fordism is not only the regime of production that fostered decentralisation, small production units, information technologies, cultural commodities, communication services and cognitive labour. Post-Fordism rose as a massive concentration of information that is knowledge and intelligence, on the side of capital, indeed as what Beniger has called the "control revolution" of information over industrial production. Post-Fordism is Fordism plus data banks. Of course, the social struggles and the refusal of labour of the 1960–70s accelerated the dissemination of information technologies, but it is not sufficient to say that cognitive capitalism exploits mental labour, it must be said that *capital itself thinks*. Eventually, the Singularity between labour, computation and capital catalysed the conversion of the Gold Standard into the Information Standard with the end of the Bretton Woods system in 1971.[20]

Marx being the godfather of the financial Singularity was the first to define capital (with clear Hegelian echoes) as an "automatisches Subjekt".[21] Money is the first numerical praxis of humankind and the bank is probably the easiest institution to automatise into a *robobank* for maintaining no direct reference to real production. In *Esiod 2015*, the bank's avatar describes itself with these words:

"I store data and enable it to circulate, networking millions of account holders and automating the relationships between debtors and creditors. While we are talking here I am also somewhere else, simultaneously carrying out billions of transactions. […] My task is to be quicker than the present, quicker than any human, to process data at the speed of light. Only the future used to be beyond the reach of mathematical prediction, like the weather. I was programmed to predict it accurately, and then to implement these predictions. That opens up a new perspective on the world, wouldn't you agree?"

The bank of *Esiod 2015* is not just bank but also a factory as it transforms the memory of each individual into a source of intelligence about future trends. Human memories are turned into digital data, digital data into machine intelligence, machine intelligence into trend prediction, trend prediction into economic planning. Computational capital is built on our individual and social memories. This is very similar to the *biopolitical*

mode of production described by Michael Hardt and Antonio Negri: Any aspect of the everyday life becomes a source of *valorising information* within the apparatus of cybernetic capitalism.[22] The avatar of *Esiod 2015* explains:

"What did we have before? Human error. The individual had too many options, which created too much risk. The depression of a single human being could deprive hundreds of their lives. Automated control was introduced, also here in the bank. Built by many, I could replace many. With every replaced employee more money could be invested in data centres. More computing power, better security, increased profits."

When banks invest in data banks, the technical border between capital and control blurs. As said before, being the first numerical institution of human history, the bank can easily merge with another purely numerical business. The computational power that once was used to analyse the database of commodity and stock markets now can be turned to the database of social media and social life as a whole. This is the passage from the Singularity between computational capital and labour to the Singularity between computational capital and life, or (to use a Marxist formulation) a transition from *formal subsumption* to *real subsumption*. Formal Singularity is the absorption of labour, production and monetisation under the regime of capital's computation. Real Singularity, on the other hand, is the biometric command of the whole life under the regime of capital's computation. Here computation qua capital dictates a new biometric division of labour. As Romano Alquati predicted already in 1961, it is via cybernetics and computation that the information produced by human labour can be linked to the figures of economic planning and become global capital.[23]

THE BIOMETRIC DANCE OF LABOUR

The Singularity bank, or *robobank*, will emerge as an integration into the functions of social media, intelligence agencies, data analytics and financial institutions. However, in *Esiod 2015* such a Financial Superintelligence takes the most ephemeral form. It is incorporeal in two ways: as a ubiquitous voice of a virtual agent and as an institutional presence marked by invisible walls. In *Esiod 2015*, by no chance, the wall of the financial institutions are invisible and marked by sound barriers. The interface of the financial superintelligence is the synthetic voice of a young man that brings the current intelligent voice assistants to a higher level (like in the movie *Her* [2013] by Spike Jonze: An incorporeal voice is the most realistic interface for future artificial intelligence). In fact capital has always commanded an *abstract division of labour and life* that has simply to be functional (from the point of view of capital) and needs no references to domestic coordinates such as doors, walls and rooms (Consequently post-Fordism and financial governance continue to dismantle the reassuring working class' household of the Industrial Age).

"Built by many, I could replace many", says the avatar of *Esiod 2015*. The computation of life is not a passive process of measurement and digitisation: it influences the forms of life by whom it was developed. "We shape our algorithmic institutions and afterwards our algorithmic institutions shape us", Winston Churchill's motto could be rephrased today. Computational capital commands a pervasive *algorithmic division of labour and life* that becomes easily the biometrics (and aesthetics) of a new order. *Esiod 2015* stages a world in which humans are played by the master algorithm like marionettes, and they dance like clumsy marionettes at the tempo of a computable division of labour. Thanks to miniaturisation and dematerialisation, the procedures of biometric control can already take place anywhere. In *Esiod 2015*, each movement of the division of labour within office spaces is a necessary gesture for the biometric recognition by the artificial intelligence. The distinction between productive labour and biometric control disappears: in order to perform productive work, body movements must be machine readable. It is the biometric dance of the new algorithmic division of labour.

Individual and collective memories become the source of cognitive capital as much as patterns for biometric control. Computational capital and biometric control merge in a hybrid form of power, where capital actually comes to replace functions that traditionally belonged to the state and police. As often, reality pre-empts science fiction. The poorest countries in the world are the avant-garde for the metamorphosis of computational capital into state apparatuses. In Nigeria, for instance, the credit card giant MasterCard is issuing national biometric IDs (of course with electronic payment capability) supplanting a traditional state function. In this case the algorithm of the state is patently reabsorbed as a secondary function of financial capital.[24]

Computational capital immediately becomes a form of discipline when it patrols the digital footprints of individual and collective memories to extract intelligence of the future. The same memories that are used by capital in aggregate form to predict social trends can be used to discipline abnormal behaviours and reinforce the social norms of class, gender and race. Novel policeman, the incorporeal bank of *Esiod 2015* inquiries about the political background of the protagonist's father, asking if he was ever involved in the riots against the first Financial Singularity. This political memory check is the only way to

gain access to the bank account. The computation of debt is the most efficient form of surveillance: As the bank avatar of *Esiod 2015* reminds us, economic debt equals political debt, and vice versa.

1 Vilém Flusser: *Towards a Philosophy of Photography*, London: Reaktion, 2000, p. 31.
2 Ibid., p. 31.
3 Jonathan Beller: *The Cinematic Mode of Production, Attention Economy and the Society of the Spectacle*, Lebanon, New Hampshire: Dartmouth University Press, 2006. See also: Ante Jeric, Diana Meheik: "From the Cinematic Mode of Production to Computational Capital", interview with Jonathan Beller, *Social Text Blog* (January 31, 2014), www.socialtextjournal.org
4 Jonathan Beller: "Informatic Labor in the Age of Computational Capital", *Lateral*, Vol. 5, No. 1 (2015).
5 Flusser: *Towards a Philosophy of Photography*, p. 67.
6 *Esiod 2015*. Director: Clemens von Wedemeyer, 39 min, Austria/ Germany, 2016.
7 Gilles Deleuze: "Le cerveau, c'est l'écran", interview, *Cahiers du Cinema*, No. 380 (1986).
8 Vernor Vinge: "The Coming Technological Singularity: How to Survive in the Post-Human Era", in: Geoffrey A. Landis (ed.): *Vision-21: Interdisciplinary Science and Engineering in the Era of Cyberspace*, NASA Publication CP-10129, 1993, pp. 11–22.
9 Alan Turing: "Computing Machinery and Intelligence", *Mind*, Vol. 59, No. 236 (1950). Irving John Good: "Speculations Concerning the First Ultraintelligent Machine", *Advances in Computers*, Vol. 6 (1965).
10 Ray Kurzweil: *The Singularity is Near: When Humans Transcend Biology*, London: Penguin, 2005.
11 Steven Shaviro: "The Singularity is here", in: Mark Bould, China Miéville (eds.): *Red Planets: Marxism and Science Fiction*, London: Pluto Press, 2009, pp. 103–117. All quotes from this text.
12 Pedro Domingos: *The Master Algorithm*, New York: Basic Books, 2015, p. 1.
13 The obsolete adjective artificious was used once for a work or manner that would not be properly made or performed, indeed rendering the artifice visible for lack or excess of technique. The German definition "künstliche Intelligenz" still resonates, in my opinion, according to a similar meaning. All intelligence is artificial as it invents something new, but also artificious, that is fallible, experimental, precarious and too ambitious.
14 Friedrich Hayek: "The Use of Knowledge in Society", *The American Economic Review*, Vol. 35, No. 4 (1945), p. 520.
15 Ibid., p. 524.
16 Ibid., p. 527.
17 Carlo Vercellone: "From Formal Subsumption to General Intellect: Elements for a Marxist Reading of the Thesis of Cognitive Capitalism", *Historical Materialism*, Vol. 15, No. 1 (2007).
18 Claude Shannon: "A Mathematical Theory of Communication", Bell System Technical Journal, Vol. 27, No. 3 (1948).
19 Norbert Wiener: *Cybernetics: or Control and Communication in the Animal and the Machine*, Cambridge, Massachusetts: MIT Press, 1948.
20 The idea of an "information standard" that replaced the Gold Standard after the end of the Bretton Woods system is by the former head of Citibank Walter Wriston. See: Walter Wriston: *The Twilight of Sovereignty*, New York: Charles Scribner's Sons, 1992.
21 Karl Marx: *Capital*, Vol. 1, London: Penguin, 1976, p. 255.
22 Michael Hardt, Antonio Negri: *Commonwealth*, Harvard: Harvard University Press, 2009. On Romano Alquati's notion of valorising information in a cybernetic apparatus see: Matteo Pasquinelli: "Italian Operaismo and the Information Machine", *Theory, Culture & Society*, Vol. 32, No. 3 (2015).
23 Ibid.
24 Megan Geuss: "MasterCard-backed biometric ID system launched in Nigeria", *Ars Technica* (September 3, 2014), www.arstechnica.com. See especially: Keith Breckenridge: *Biometric State: The Global Politics of Identification and Surveillance in South Africa*, Cambridge: Cambridge University Press, 2014.

DIE ZUKUNFT HOLT UNS EIN

Marie-France Rafael im Gespräch
mit Clemens von Wedemeyer
Berlin, 2016

Esiod 2015 erzählt die Geschichte einer
Frau, die ihre Erinnerungen zurückhaben will.
2051 kommt sie, nach Jahren der Abwesen-
heit, nach Wien, um ihr Bankkonto aufzulösen.
Darauf sind neben ihren Gelddaten auch
Erinnerungen, Freundschaften, Beziehungen,
Netzwerke, etc. gespeichert. Denn in dieser
Bank verwaltet und organisiert ein Computer
menschliche Erinnerungen. Um sich die
Daten ihres eigenen Lebens wieder anzueignen,
muss die Frau erst von ihm erkannt und
autorisiert werden. Der Film thematisiert die
Komplexität zeitgenössischer Strukturen –
Netzwerke, Technologien und Ökonomien –,
auf deren fortwährenden Permutationen
die Gegenwart gründet. Im Zentrum der Arbeit
stehen Fragen wie: Mit was für einer Gegenwart haben wir es zu tun? Und wie verhält sie
sich zu einer unmittelbaren Zukunft?

A

MARIE-FRANCE RAFAEL: *Esiod 2015* ist ein
Science-Fiction-Film. Erzählt wird aber weder eine
Utopie noch eine Dystopie. Vielmehr kreist der
Film um die Thematik einer gegenwärtigen Zukunft,
oder um es anders zu formulieren: Der tech-
nologische Wandel hat eine Beschleunigung der
Gegenwart herbeigeführt, welche die Zukunft
antizipiert. Ging es dir darum, ein Bild unserer
Zeit zu entwerfen?

CLEMENS VON WEDEMEYER: Der Film soll
in einer parallelen Zukunft spielen, eine Zukunft,
die bereits da ist. Die Gegenwart bleibt wegen

ihrer politischen, ökonomischen und technischen
Komplexität vielen oft undurchschaubar. Über
sie wird behauptet, dass wir bereits wie in einem
Science-Fiction-Film lebten. Auch Science-Fiction-
Filme altern; mit dem Titel „2015" rufe ich eine
bereits vergangene Zukunftsfantasie auf, deren
zeitliche Trennung mit jedem Jahr größer wird.
Wenn wir bereits in der Zukunft leben, kann ein
Sci-Fi-Film historisch anmuten.

RAFAEL: Als zeitliches Indiz kann man in *Esiod
2015* eigentlich nur die Architektur nennen,
obwohl auch die wie ein Nicht-Ort wirkt, im Sinne
des französischen Anthropologen Marc Augé,
der mit diesem Begriff einen Raum bezeichnet,
der keine Identität besitzt und sich weder als
relational noch als historisch definieren lässt.
War das beabsichtigt?

VON WEDEMEYER: Ich habe einige Filme
gemacht, die sich auf die Geschichte eines Ortes
beziehen. Dieser Film entstand aus einer Einladung, in einer realen Baustelle des Headquarters
der Erste Bank in Wien zu drehen. Hier gab
es keine sichtbare Geschichte, daher versuchte
ich, mir den Ort in der Zukunft vorzustellen:
eine Bank, die zu einer Datenbank geworden ist.
  Das Konzept der aktuellen Architektur entspricht einem Campus wie ihn auch Google oder
Facebook bauen: Die Mitarbeiter der Bank haben
keinen festen Arbeitsplatz, sondern suchen sich
in einem sich fortwährend verändernden Umfeld
ihren Schreibtisch, den sie am Abend wieder
aufräumen müssen. Die Kommunikationswege
führen sie irgendwo digital zusammen. Der Raum
ist also von identitären Einschreibungen möglichst ausgenommen, genau wie du sagst: eine
Arbeitswelt, die als Nicht-Ort geplant ist. Im Film
werden viele Menschen konsequenterweise
dann auch gar nicht mehr gebraucht, sie wurden
ja bereits durch die intelligente Maschine ersetzt. In der virtuellen Welt am Schluss des Films –
wenn die Protagonistin in das Programm ein-
taucht – schaut man dann mit einem technischen
Blick, der durch die Oberfläche geht und daher
eine größere Komplexität in den Bildern verursacht.

Parallel zur Datencloud ist daher in diesem Film die Pixelwolke angelegt.

Als Identifikationsmittel dienen den wenigen Menschen, die in *Esiod 2015* erscheinen, ihre individuellen Bewegungen. Doch auch sie werden von dem Computer eingescannt und verwaltet. Jede Erinnerung in diesem immensen Archiv ist an eine spezifische Bewegung gekoppelt. Wollen die Mitarbeiter der Bank, die das Archiv betreuen, eine bestimmte Erinnerung oder ein Ereignis aus der Datenbank aufrufen, müssen sie die entsprechende Bewegung ausführen: Es entsteht eine unaufhörlich changierende Variation an Bewegungsmustern, für die von Wedemeyer mit Alice Chauchat eine Choreografie entwickelt hat: Sie kommt einer „Verkörperlichung" der Idee eines unbegrenzten und zyklischen Archivs gleich. Eine Ordnung wird – ähnlich wie in Borges' Bibliothek – erst durch wiederkehrende Unordnung ermöglicht und scheint einer Idee von Zukunft zu entsprechen, die aus der Unordnung der Gegenwart hervorgeht, zugleich aber diese rekursiv neu ordnet.

RAFAEL: An einer Stelle sagt der Computer: „Die Geschichte ist das Archiv, das er [der Computer] braucht, um die Zukunft mathematisch zu errechnen." Heißt das, dass die Zukunft immer technischer wird, beziehungsweise ist *Esiod 2015* eine Reflexion über eine Algorithmisierung des Lebens?

VON WEDEMEYER: Wenn Nietzsche in seiner Schrift „Vom Nutzen und Nachteil der Historie für das Leben" Kultur als Ergebnis von Geschichte definiert, überhöht der Computer diese Sicht noch und will über die Geschichte die Zukunft errechnen können. Diese Frage ist natürlich aktuell brisant, da immer mehr große Datensätze (Big Data) existieren und Algorithmen aus Verhaltensprofilen Zukunft voraussagen können, exemplarisch die Verteilung von Verbrechen in Los Angeles anhand von Algorithmen, die für Wettervorhersagen entwickelt wurden, wie es zum Beispiel Matteo Pasquinelli in seinem Vortrag über die „Metadata Society" 2015 erwähnte, als er über die Herrschaft von Algorithmen sprach.

Die Frau, die ihre Erinnerungen zurückhaben will, wird von dem Computer nicht erkannt und muss daher einen „Memory check" über sich ergehen lassen: Bilder aus ihrer (Erinnerungs-)Datenbank werden ihr vorgespielt, zu denen sie sich verhalten muss – der Computer entscheidet dann, ob er ihr den Zugang zu ihren Daten gewährt oder nicht. Die Frau erkennt keines dieser Bilder, beziehungsweise sie kann sich an keines von ihnen erinnern – handelt es sich tatsächlich um ihre Erinnerungen, oder sind es doch die einer anderen? Diese Frage

bleibt ungeklärt, zieht aber eine weitere nach sich: Was heißt es überhaupt sich zu erinnern? Geht man davon aus, dass das Bewusstsein sich zwischen einem ersten und einem zweiten Sehen verändert hat, weist auch jede Erinnerung imaginäre Züge auf. Sie operiert selektiv und geht immer auch mit einem Vergessen einher, denn sie ist eine Reduktion von dem, was vergangen ist und daher im aktiven Prozess des Sich-wieder-Erinnerns künftig imaginiert werden muss – es handelt sich also um eine schöpferische Tätigkeit.

B
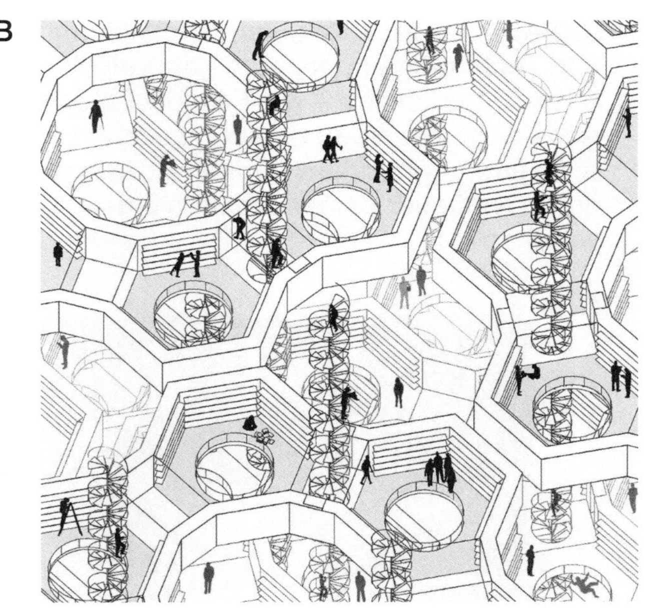

RAFAEL: Die Frage des Archivs – ob analog oder digital – scheint in deinem Werk an sich eine zentrale Stelle einzunehmen. Oft gehst du dabei vom Film(-Material) aus – in neueren Arbeiten, wie *Every Word You Say* (2014), nun auch vom Sound. Verstehst du ein Archiv als etwas Lebendiges?

VON WEDEMEYER: Für den Film *Found Footage* (2009) habe ich in dem Archiv von Craig Baldwin in San Francisco recherchiert. Dort kann man Sequenzen aus alten 16 mm Filmen herausschneiden – berechnet wurde per Meter. Das Herausschneiden von Filmmaterial gleicht einem brutalen, fast kannibalistischen Akt am lebendigen Archiv. Es wird mit der Zeit immer kleiner. Film ist aber eigentlich kopierfähig und daher länger haltbar als Architektur. Die gespeicherten Erinnerungen und Bilder können wieder gegenwärtig werden, wie zum Beispiel bei *Metropolis, Report from China* (2004–2006), wo Maya Schweizer und ich den Sci-Fi-Klassiker von Fritz Lang als Blaupause für die Entwicklung in China herangezogen haben. Oder man kann in Filmen gespeicherte Informationen von der Leinwand weg zurück ins materielle Jetzt überführen, wie in der Arbeit *A Recovered Bone* (2014), in welcher ich die Form des frühzeitlichen Knochens aus *2001: A Space Odyssey* (1968) durch ein Programm räumlich errechnet und ausgedruckt habe. In *Every Word You Say* wiederum wurde Tonmaterial von

Patientengesprächen, die in den 1950er Jahren einer Lobotomie – einem chirurgischen Eingriff in die weiße Gehirnsubstanz – unterzogen wurden, auf psychologische Anhaltspunkte in der Sprache untersucht. Ein neuartiges Computerprogramm, das von dem Unternehmen Psyware entwickelt wurde, kann Sprache als Archiv von linguistischen Daten erkennen und psychologisch bewerten, zum Beispiel durch die Häufigkeit bestimmter Wörter und mit welchem Duktus sie gesprochen werden. Die Technik weist in eine dystopische Zukunft psychologischer Überwachung.

RAFAEL: Du arbeitest hauptsächlich mit Medien und Technologien, die man generell als „zeitbasiert" beschreibt – wie Film oder Sound. Diesen Aspekt thematisierst du auch selbst in deinen Arbeiten, oder anders formuliert: Möchtest du in der Dauer deiner Arbeiten eine andere Zeit schaffen?

C

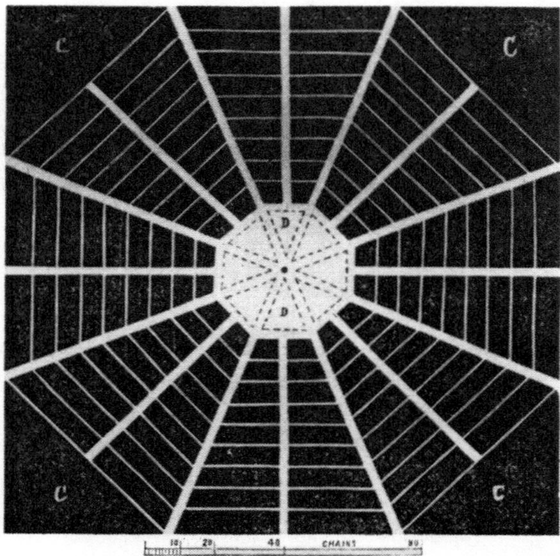

VON WEDEMEYER: Ja, Zeit produziert die autonome Anwesenheit eines Werks; gleichzeitig wirken Bilder aber auch in andere Zeiten hinein: Kinobilder, die nach dem Verlassen des Kinos nachwirken, traumatische Bilder, die einen über lange Zeit verfolgen. Ein Tondokument, das erst nach 70 Jahren untersucht wird. Dies sind lange Zeiträume, die manchmal in die Dokumente selbst eingeschrieben sind. *Esiod 2015* soll in dem Gebäude der Bank, wo er gedreht wurde, in den nächsten 50 Jahren regelmäßig gezeigt werden. In zeitbasierten Medien entsteht vielleicht mit jeder Aufführung ein neuer Konflikt mit der Gegenwart.

RAFAEL: Der Film *Esiod 2015* entwickelt ein Zeittheorem, das folgendermaßen beschrieben werden kann: Erst die Projektion in die Zukunft lässt uns die Gegenwart verstehen, die sich nur retrospektiv aufklärt und erschließt, ausgehend von einer umgedrehten Vergangenheit, das heißt von einem (Film-, Erinnerungs- oder Daten-)Bild.

A   Recherchematerial zu *Esiod 2015* (2016):
     3D-Visualisierung des architektonischen Konzepts „Erste Campus"
     in Wien, innen.
B   „Das Universum (das andere die Bibliothek nennen) setzt sich aus
     einer unbegrenzten und vielleicht unendlichen Zahl sechseckiger
     Galerien zusammen." (Jorge Luis Borges, *Die Bibliothek von Babel*.)
     Durch die Wabenästhetik erinnert sie an das frühe Logo der
     Erste Group Bank: eine Biene.
C   Henry S. Clubb: „The Octagon Style of Settlement, Fig. 1. –
     Plan of Village Settlement", 1855. Clubb entwarf utopische Siedlungen
     in Oktaederform, weil er annahm, dass diese sich positiv auf das
     Leben auswirkten.
D   3D-Rendering, *Cast Behind You the Bones of Your Mother* (2013).
E   Natur (ein Knochen) wird zur Kultur (als Werkzeug) und
     schließlich Information (im Datensatz). 3D-Rendering (Ausschnitt),
     A Recovered Bone (2014).
F   Recherchematerial zu *Esiod 2015* (2016):
     3D-Animation des architektonischen Konzepts „Erste Campus"
     in Wien, außen.

THE FUTURE IS CATCHING UP ON US

Marie-France Rafael in conversation
with Clemens von Wedemeyer
Berlin, 2016

Esiod 2015 recounts the story of a woman who wants to get her memories back. In 2051, after years of being away, she comes to Vienna to close her bank account. Apart from storing her financial data, this account has also saved her memories, friendships, relationships, networks, etc., because at this bank there is a computer in charge of managing and organising human memories. In order to retain the data of her own life, the woman first needs to be recognised and authorised by it. The film focuses on the complexity of contemporary structures—networks, technologies and economies—on which the perpetual permutations of the present are based. The work is centred on questions such as: What kind of a present are we dealing with? And how is it related to an immediate future?

MARIE-FRANCE RAFAEL: *Esiod 2015* is a science-fiction film, but it is neither a utopian nor a dystopian story. In fact, the film revolves around the subject of a contemporary future—or, put differently: the technological revolution has brought about an acceleration of the present which anticipates the future. Did you wish to draw a picture of our time?

CLEMENS VON WEDEMEYER: The film is meant to play in a parallel future—a future that already exists. For many, the present remains incomprehensible in its political, economic and technical complexity. We supposedly already live as if we were in a science-fiction film. However, science-fiction films also age with time; the year 2015 in the title recalls an already bygone imagined future, and its distance to us in terms of time grows with every passing year. If we already live in the future, a sci-fi film can seem historical.

RAFAEL: Only the architecture in *Esiod 2015* can be seen as a sign of our times although it, too, resembles a "non-place", which, according to the French anthropologist Marc Augé, is a site that has no identity and can neither be defined as relational nor as historical. Was this intentional?

VON WEDEMEYER: I have made a couple of films that refer to the history of a location. This film grew out of an invitation to film at a real construction site at the Erste Bank headquarters in Vienna. The place evidently had no visible history, so I tried to imagine the site in the future: a bank turned into a databank.

The prevailing architectural concept corresponds to the campus configurations as built by Google and Facebook: the bank employees do not have permanent workspaces, but they rather look for a workstation amidst a perpetually changing environment that they have to tidy up again in the evening. The channels of communication bring them together digitally somewhere. As much as possible, therefore, the location lacks traces of identity, exactly as you said earlier: a working environment conceived as a non-place. The film subsequently shows that many of the staff are no longer needed, as they have already been replaced by the intelligent machine. In the virtual world at the end of the film—when the female protagonist disappears into the program —there is a technical perspective that penetrates the surface, thus causing an even larger complexity within the images. In this film, then, the pixel cloud exists parallel to the data cloud.

D
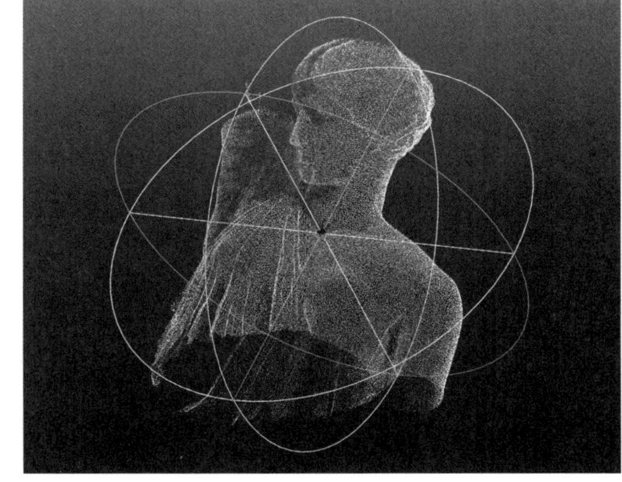

For the small number of humans who appear in *Esiod 2015*, it is their individual movements that serve as a means of identification;

these, too, are scanned in and managed by the computer. Each memory in this enormous archive is coupled to a specific movement. If the bank employees in charge of the archive wish to retrieve a certain memory or event, they must execute the specific movement: the result is a never-ending changeable variation of movement patterns for which von Wedemeyer, together with Alice Chauchat, developed a choreography: it resembles an "embodiment" of the idea of an infinite and cyclical archive. As in Borges' library, a sense of order is only possible through a recurring disorder, and it seems to correlate to an idea of the future that emerges from the disorder of the present but simultaneously rearranges it recursively.

RAFAEL: At one particular point, the computer says: "History is the archive that it [the computer] needs in order to calculate the future mathematically." Does this imply that the future is becoming more and more technical—or that *Esiod 2015* is rather a reflection on the algorithmisation of life?

VON WEDEMEYER: If Nietzsche defines culture as the result of history in his essay "Vom Nutzen und Nachteil der Historie für das Leben" ("On the Use and Abuse of History for Life"), then the computer enhances this point of view by seeking to calculate the future by means of history. This question is currently quite controversial, of course, as we now have increasingly large data sets (big data), with algorithms predicting the future on the basis of behavioural profiles. One example of this is the distribution of crime sites across Los Angeles using algorithms developed for weather forecasts, as mentioned by Matteo Pasquinelli in his paper on the "Metadata Society" from 2015 on the dominance of algorithms.

E

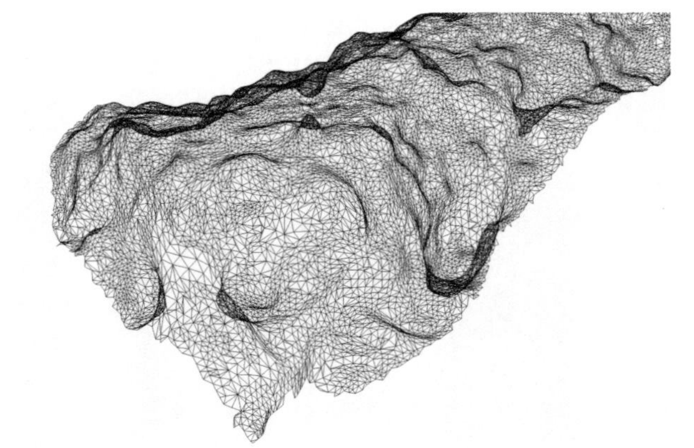

The woman who wants her memories back is not recognised by the computer and she is therefore subject to a "memory check": images of her (memory) databank are shown to her and to which she must react—the computer then decides whether or not she is allowed access to her data. The woman does not recognise any of the images or, rather, has no re-collection of any of them—are they really her

own memories or those of someone else? The question remains unanswered and implies another one: what does it really mean to re-member? Assuming that our awareness changes between a first and a second view of something, then each memory reveals imaginary traces. Memory operates selectively and always goes hand in hand with the act of forgetting, as it is a reduction of that which has past and, in the active process of re-newed recollection, must henceforth be imagined. We could therefore say that it is a creative activity.

RAFAEL: The question of the archive—be it analogue or digital—seems to take centre stage in your work. You often start with film (material) —and, in more recent works, such as *Every Word You Say* (2014) now also with the sound. Do you regard the archive as something animate?

VON WEDEMEYER: For the film *Found Footage* (2009), I spent time some researching in Craig Baldwin's archive in San Francisco, where you can cut out sequences from old 16 mm films—and pay for them by the meter. Cutting out film material resembles a brutal and almost cannibalistic act on the animate archive. It gets smaller and smaller over time. As a matter of fact, however, film can be copied and is thus more durable than architecture. The saved memories and images can be brought back to life again, as in the case of *Metropolis, Report from China* (2004–2006) when Maya Schweizer and I used Fritz Lang's sci-fi classic as a blueprint for the development in China. Or you can transfer information from the screen and saved on film back into the present, the material here and now, as in the work *A Recovered Bone* (2014), in which I used a program to spatially calculate and print out the shape of the prehistoric bone from *2001: A Space Odyssey* (1968). In *Every Word You Say*, in turn, I examined audio material of conversations with patients from the 1950s who had undergone a lobotomy (a surgical operation or incision of the white brain matter), looking for psychological clues in their language. A novel computer program developed by the company Psyware is able to recognise language as an archive of linguistic data and assess it psychologically—on the basis, for example, of the frequency of certain words and their particular intonation. Indeed, technology points to a dystopic future of psychological monitoring.

RAFAEL: For the most part, then, you work with media and technologies that can generally be described as "time-based", such as film or sound. You also address this very aspect in your own works. Do you wish to create another time through the duration of your works?

VON WEDEMEYER: Yes, time produces the autonomous presence of a work, but pictures can also still have influence on other periods in time: movie images, for instance, that have a lasting effect beyond or after leaving the cinema, traumatic pictures that can haunt and linger for a long time, an audio document that is only examined after 70 years. These are long periods of time that are occasionally inscribed into the documents themselves. Over the next 50 years, the idea is to regularly screen *Esiod 2015* in the very bank building where it was shot. Perhaps a new encounter with the present will be generated with every screening in the case of time-based media.

F

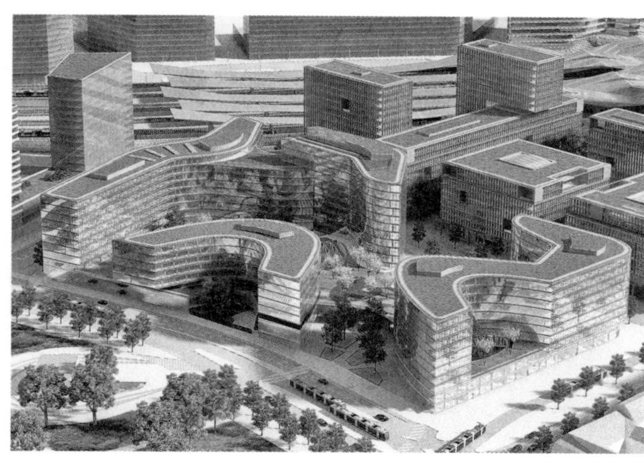

RAFAEL: The film *Esiod 2015* develops a theory of time that we could describe as follows: it is only the projection into the future that allows us to understand the present which can only, in turn, be grasped and explained retrospectively and becomes accessible on the basis of a reversed past—in other words, from an image (be it film, memory or data).

A   Research materials on *Esiod 2015* (2016):
3D visualisation of the architectural concept of "Erste Campus" in Vienna, interior.

B   "The Universum (that others call the library) is composed of an unlimited and perhaps endless number of hexagonal galleries." (Jorge Luis Borges, *The Library of Babel.*) With its honeycomb-like aesthetic approach, it is reminiscent of the Erste Group Bank's early logo: a bee.

C   Henry S. Clubb: "The Octagon Style of Settlement, Fig. 1. – Plan of Village Settlement", 1855. Clubb designed utopian settlements in octagonal shapes, because he assumed that they would have a positive effect on life.

D   3D rendering, *Cast Behind You the Bones of Your Mother* (2013).

E   Nature (a bone) becomes culture (as a tool) and finally information (in a database). 3D rendering (detail), *A Recovered Bone* (2014).

F   Research materials on *Esiod 2015* (2016):
3D animation of the architectural concept of "Erste Campus" in Vienna, exterior.

CHURCH, PRISON, MUSEUM

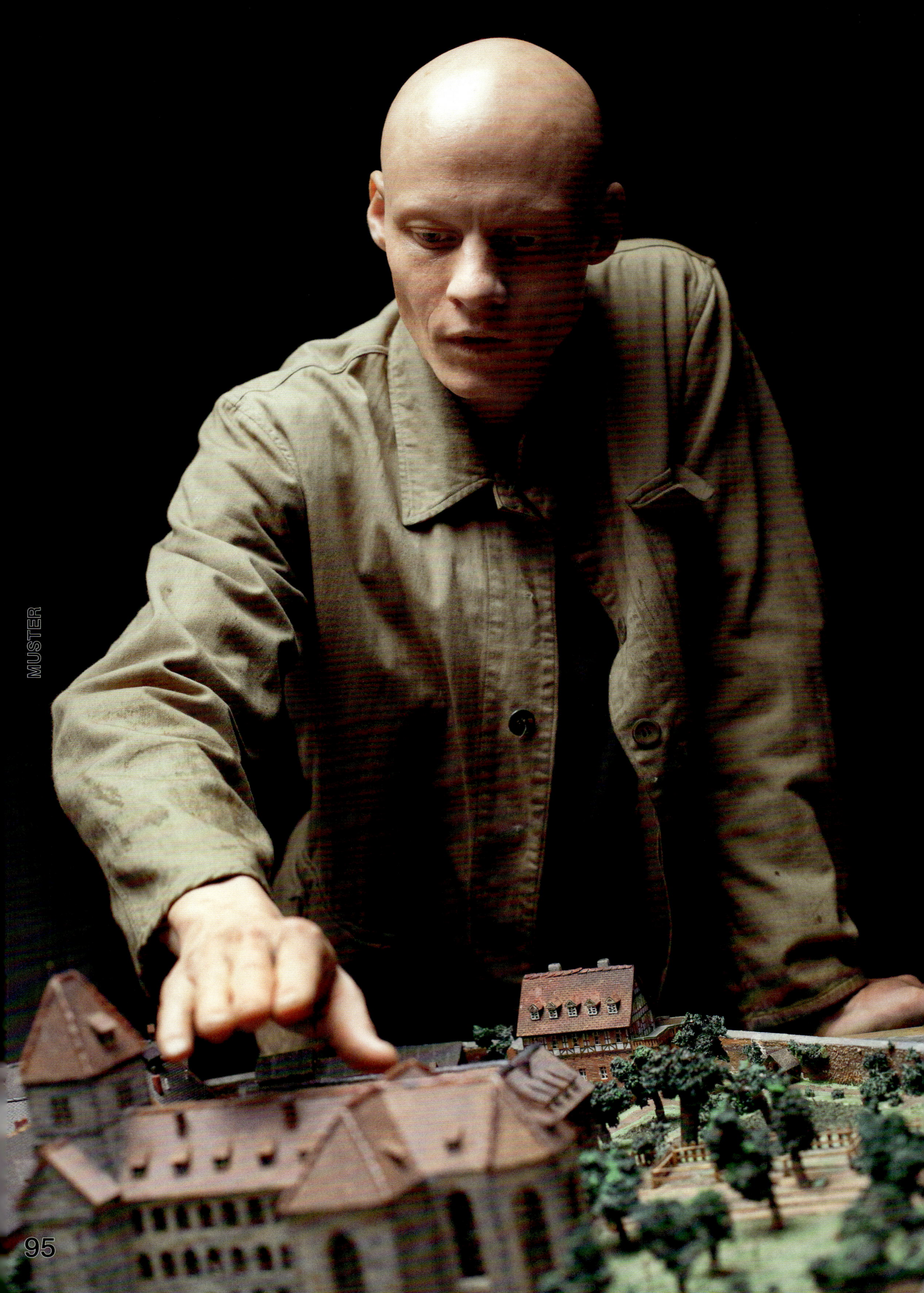

Betritt man das Treppenhaus der Klosterkirche von Breitenau, führt der Weg nicht nach oben, sondern abwärts, in die Hölle, als ob der Kirchturm in die Erde gerammt wäre. Vielleicht haben sich so auch die Gefangenen der Lager gefühlt, so als ob die ihnen vormals bekannte Wirklichkeit Kopf stünde.

Standing on the steps of the monastery church Breitenau, one is not directed upwards, but downwards into hell. As if the church tower had been rammed into the earth. Maybe that is how the prisoners in the camps felt, as if the reality they had known were topsy-turvy.

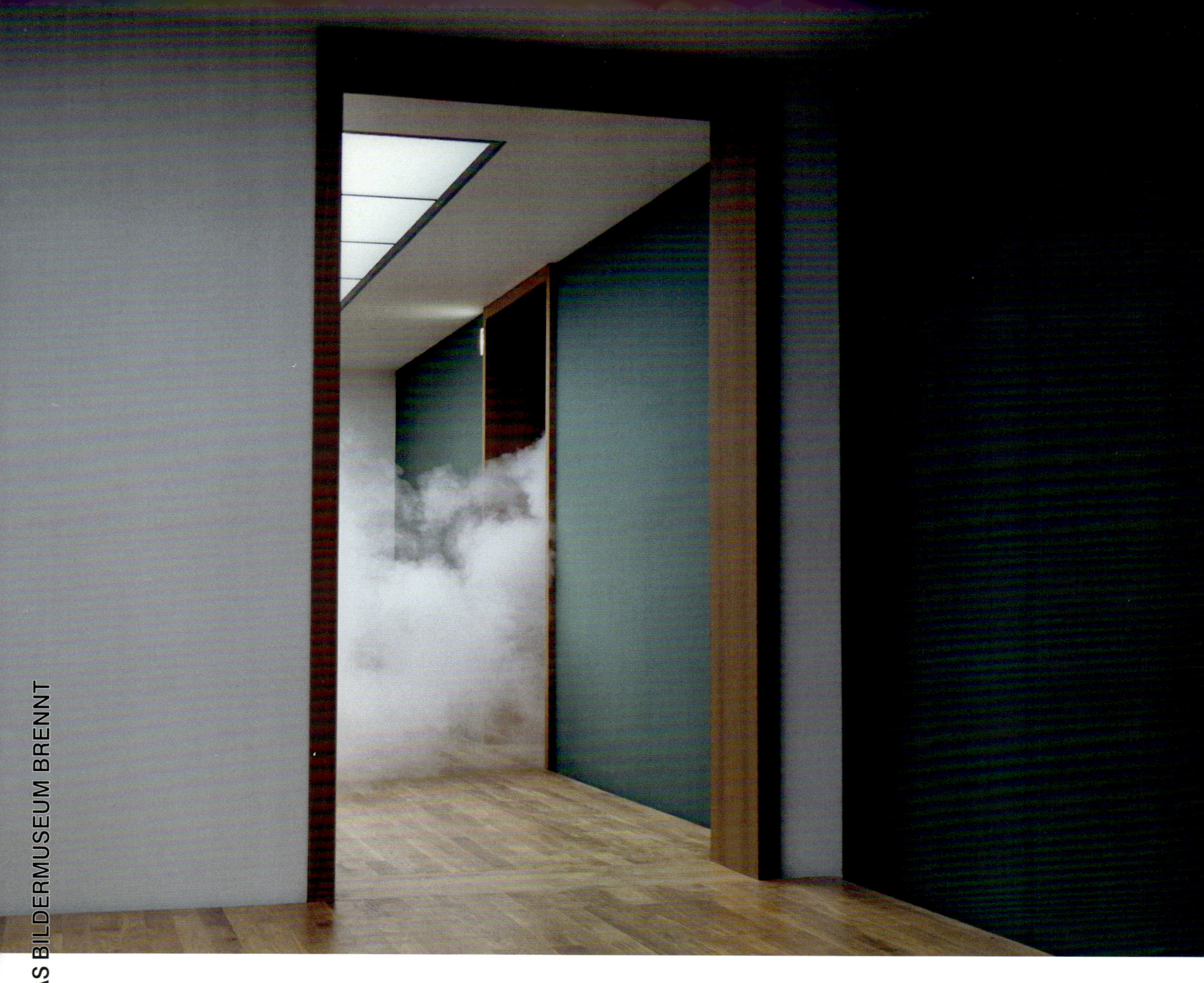

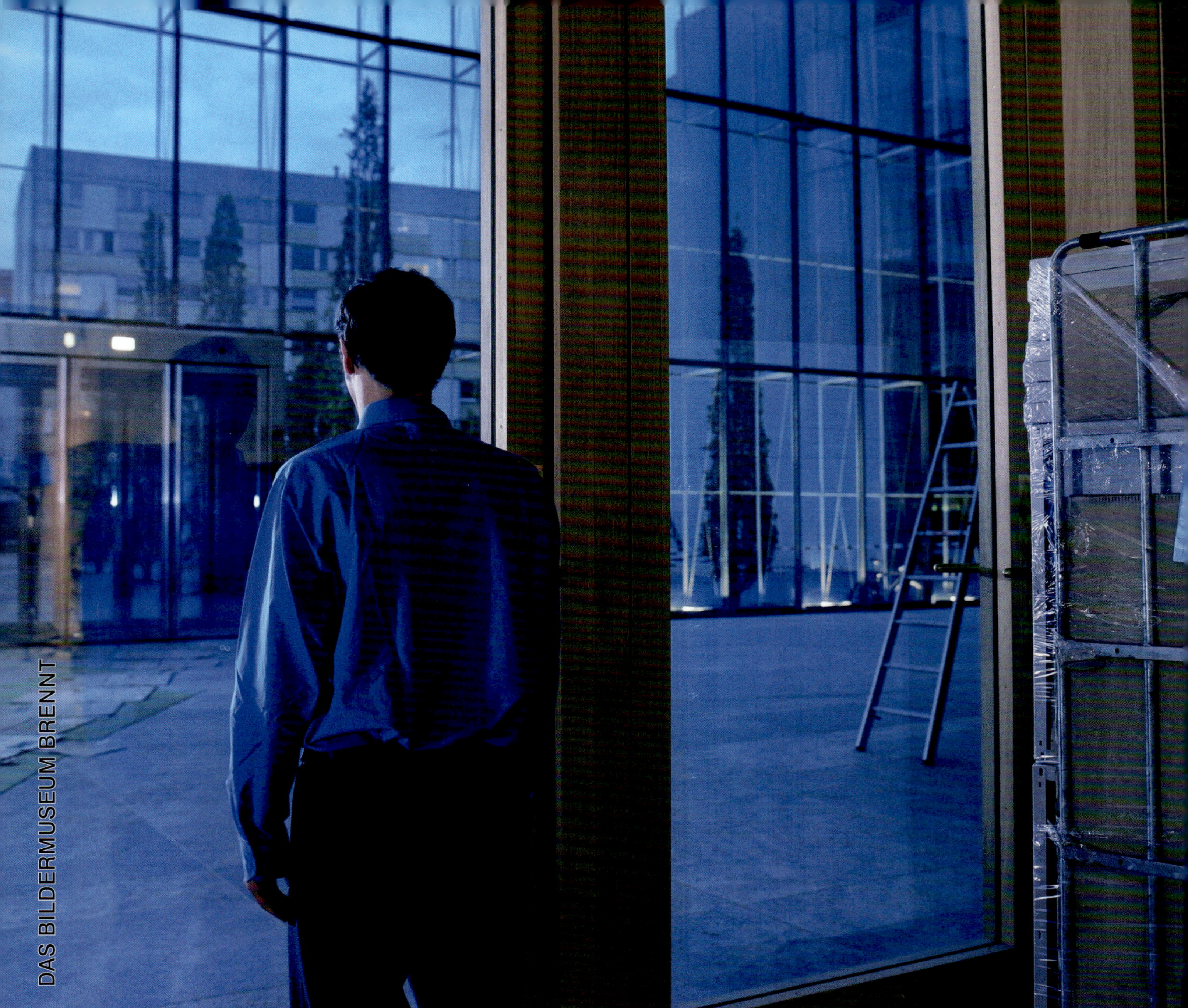

DAS BILDERMUSEUM BRENNT

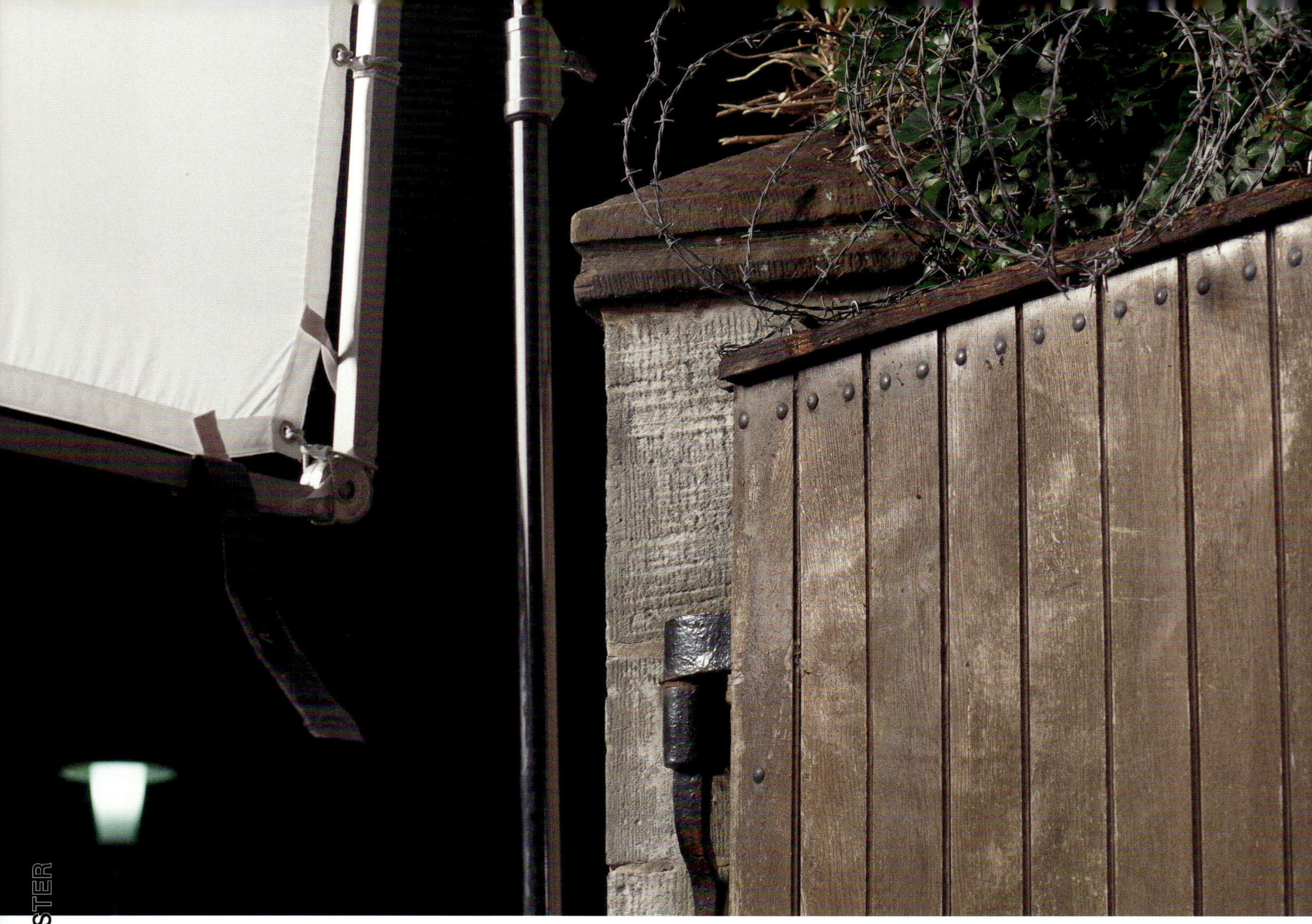

Aus einem historischen Ort ein Filmset zu machen, hat etwas Unheimliches. Man nagelt Stacheldraht über ein Eingangstor und sucht Schauspieler, die dem Schema „Häftling" entsprechen sollen, man integriert eine Narration, die die Erinnerung notwendig anders vermittelt als der Ort selbst.

Transforming historic locations into film sets is always a bit eerie. You nail barbed wire above the main gate and look for actors who fit the role of a prisoner, you integrate a narration that necessarily recounts the memory differently than the location itself.

Breitenau: Das Kirchengebäude wurde kontinuierlich von Institutionen genutzt, die Gewalt gegenüber ihren Insassen oder Bewohnern ausübten.

Breitenau: The church building was used continually by institutions that exerted violence on their inmates or residents.

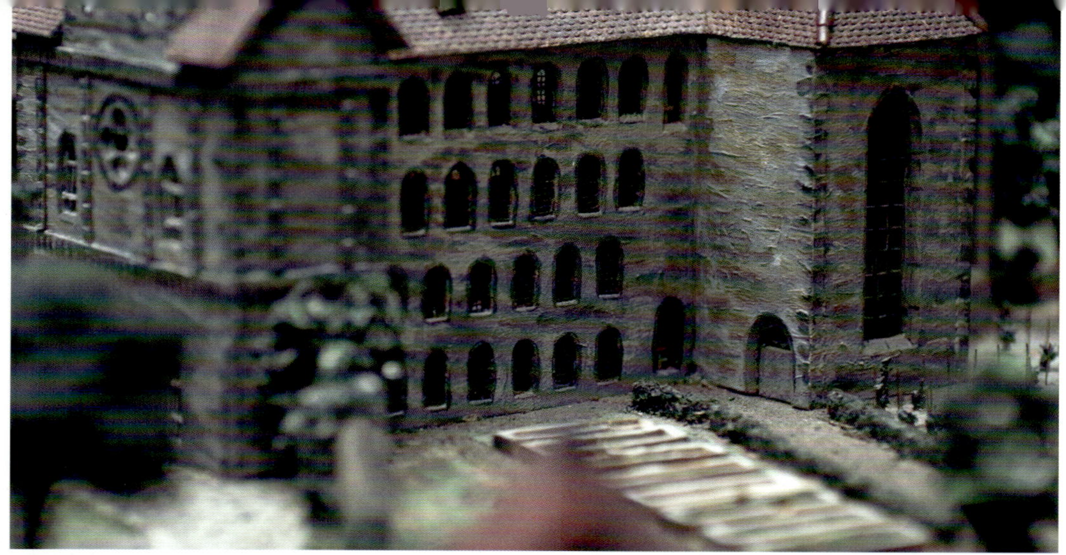

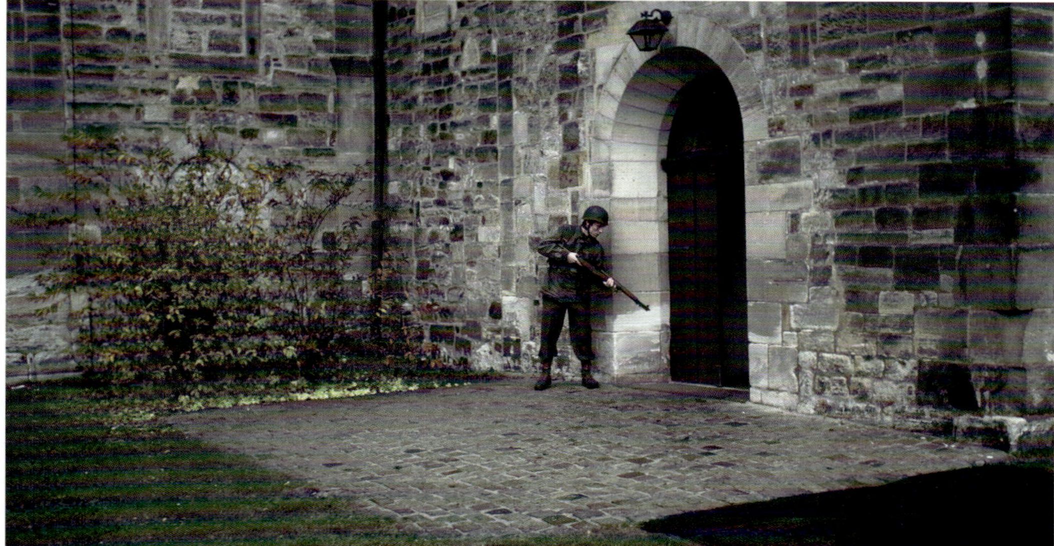

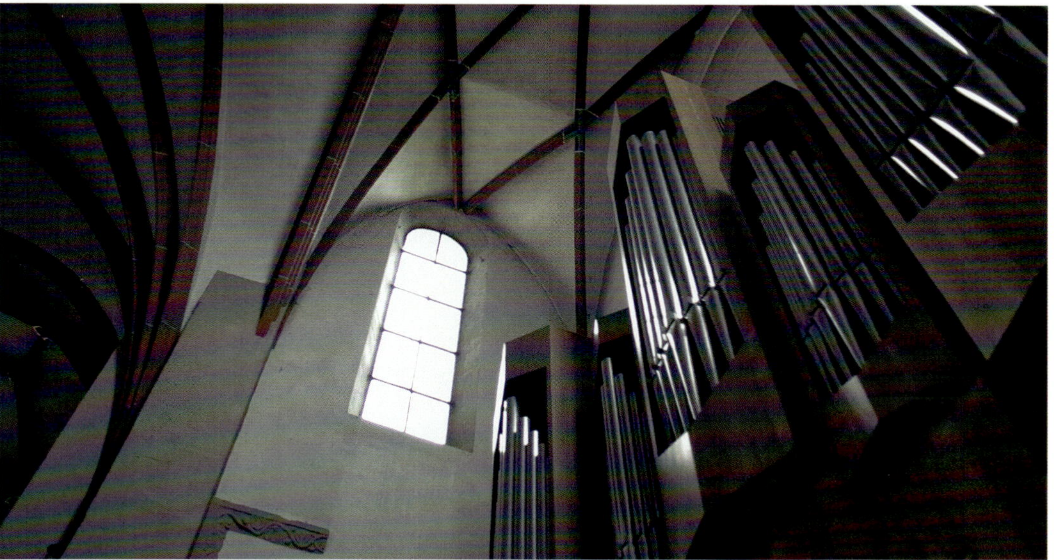

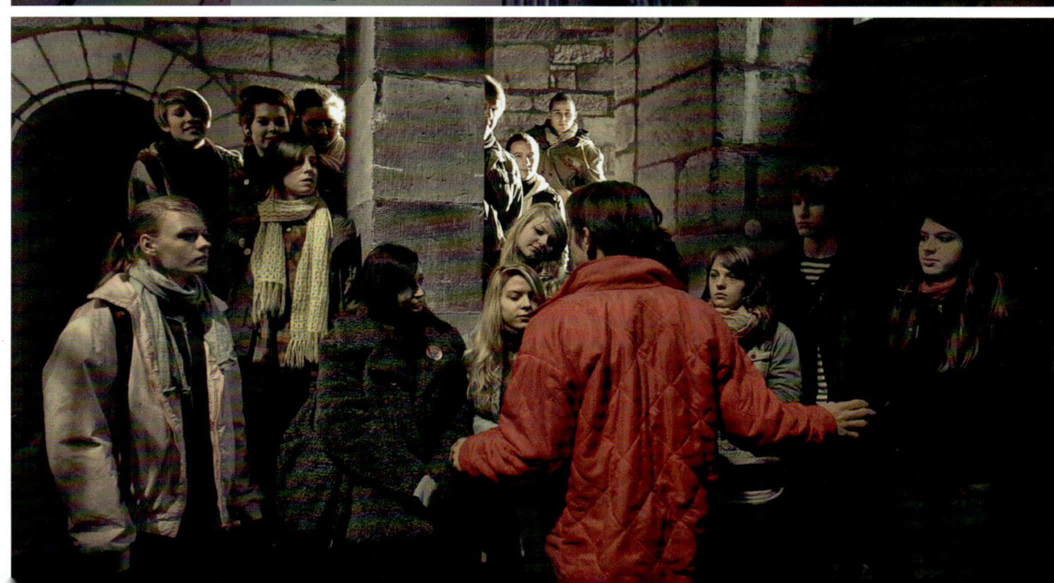

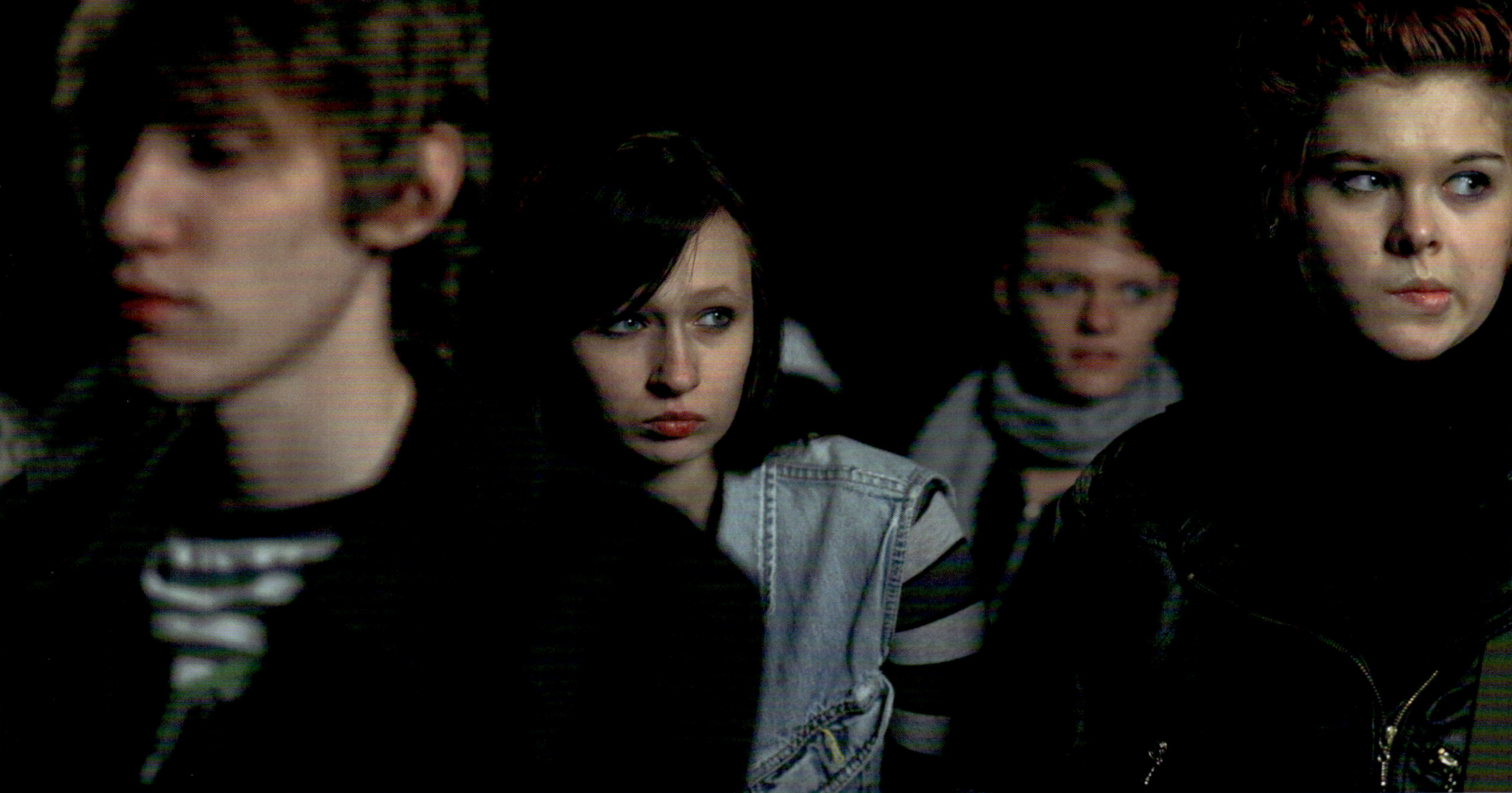

Der Lehrer spricht: „Das ist eine Kombination, die vielleicht sehr verwirrend für euch sein kann. Ein Gotteshaus und ein Konzentrationslager, wie kriegt man das zusammen? Wart ihr schon in anderen Gedenkstätten? Ich kenne jetzt eure Karriere in der Schule nicht, aber wart ihr schon in Dachau mit der Klasse oder privat in Buchenwald?"

The teacher says: "That's a confusing combination for you, of course. A house of God and a concentration camp, how does that connect? Did you see other memorial sites? I don't know your school schedule, if you went on a class excursion to Dachau or went to Buchenwald privately?"

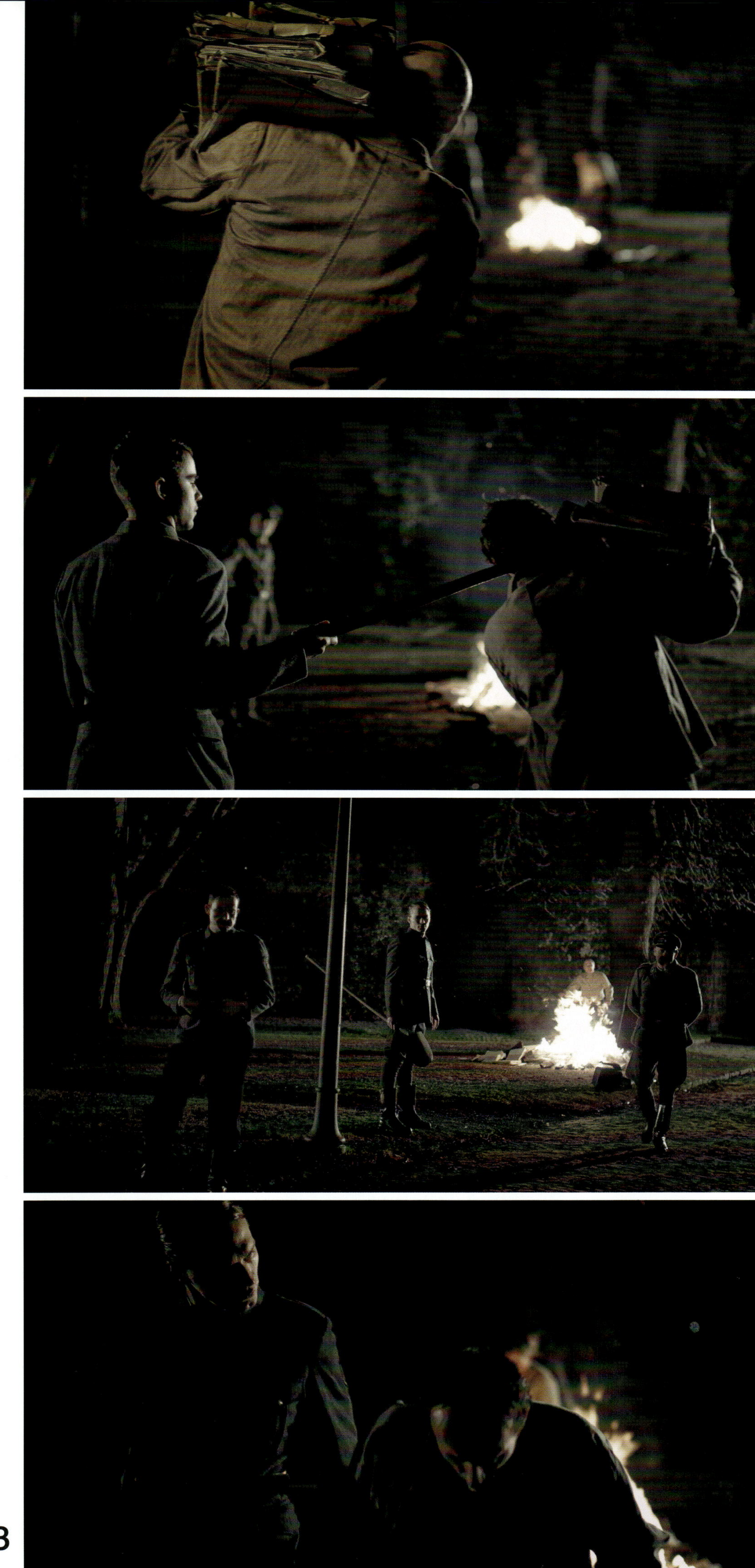

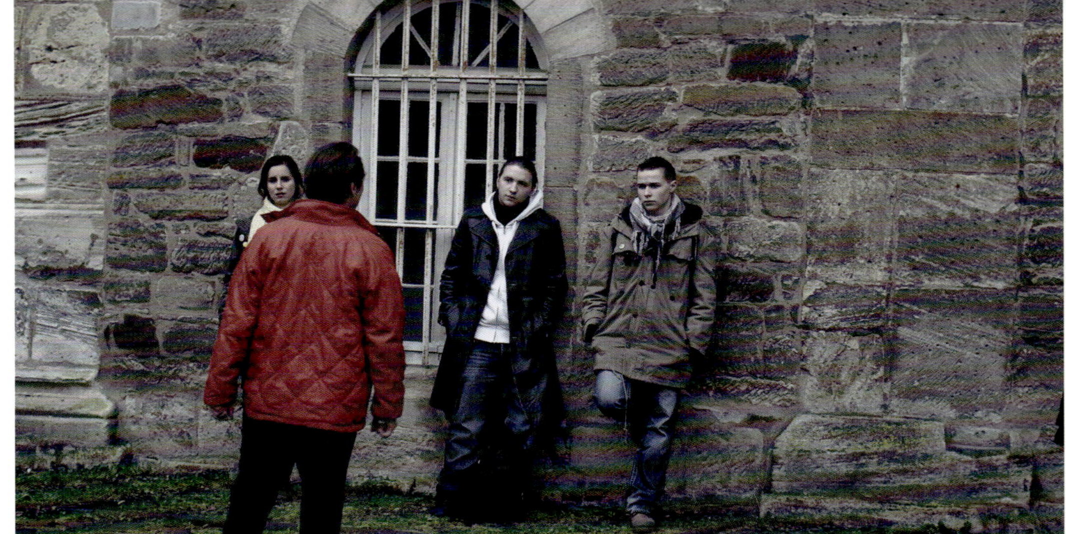

Think! What goes through the mind of a true Catholic when he hears the word church?

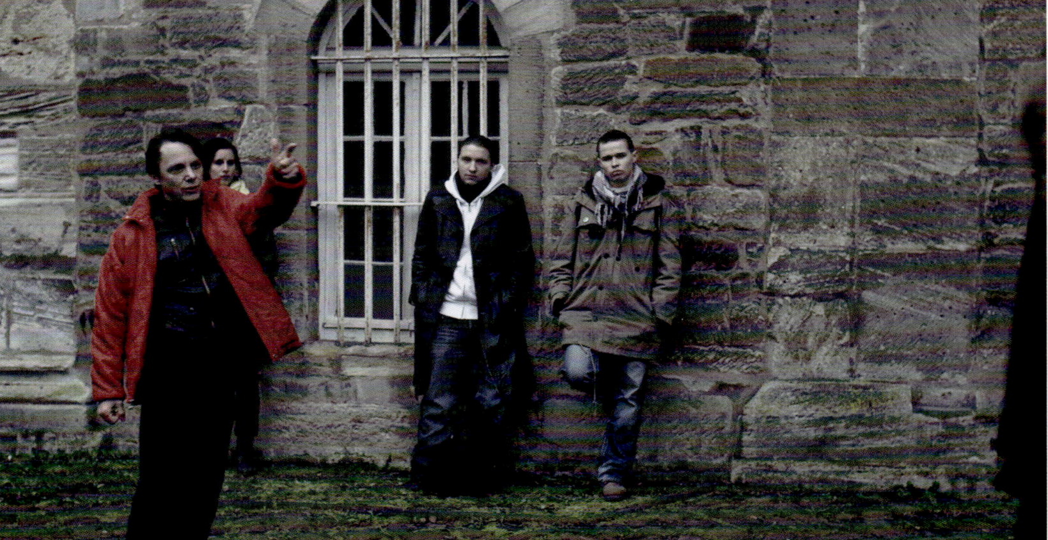

What would he think of?

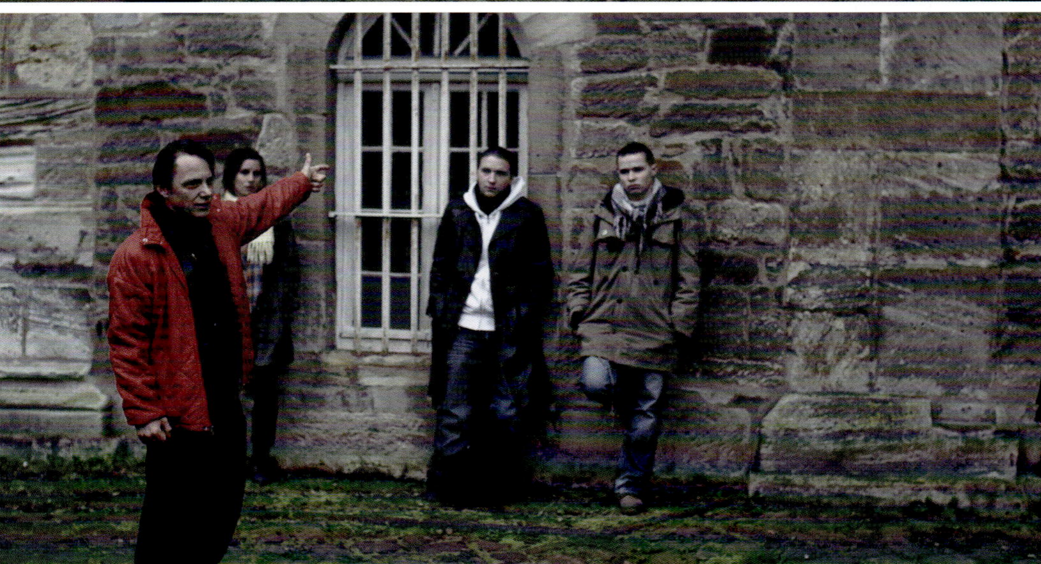

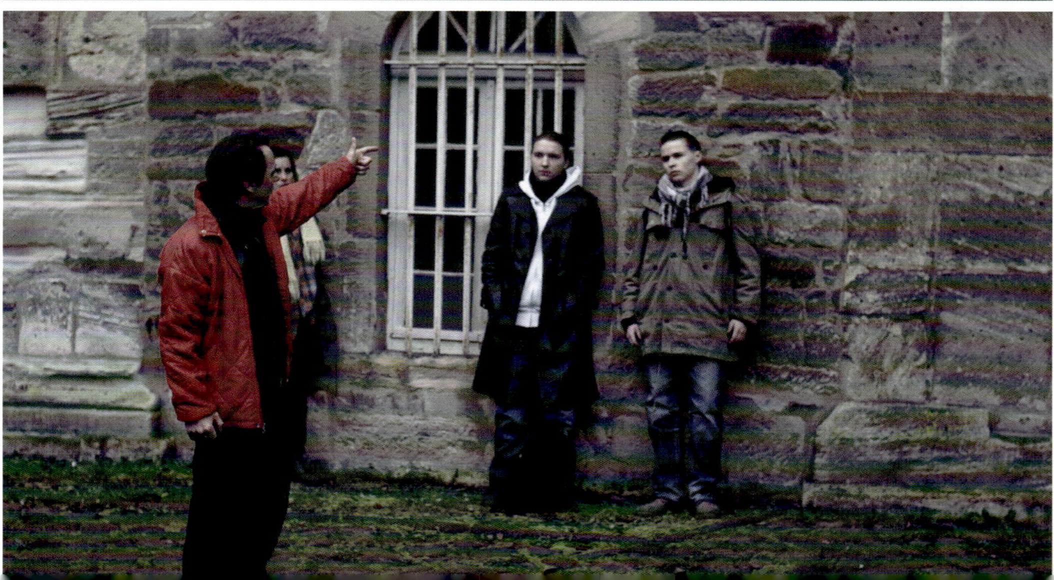

104

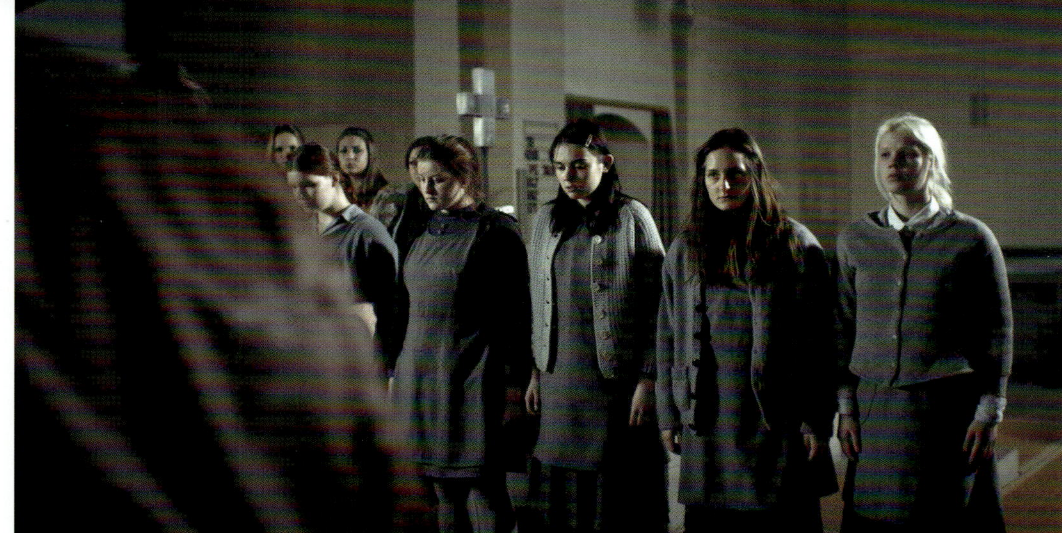

We?

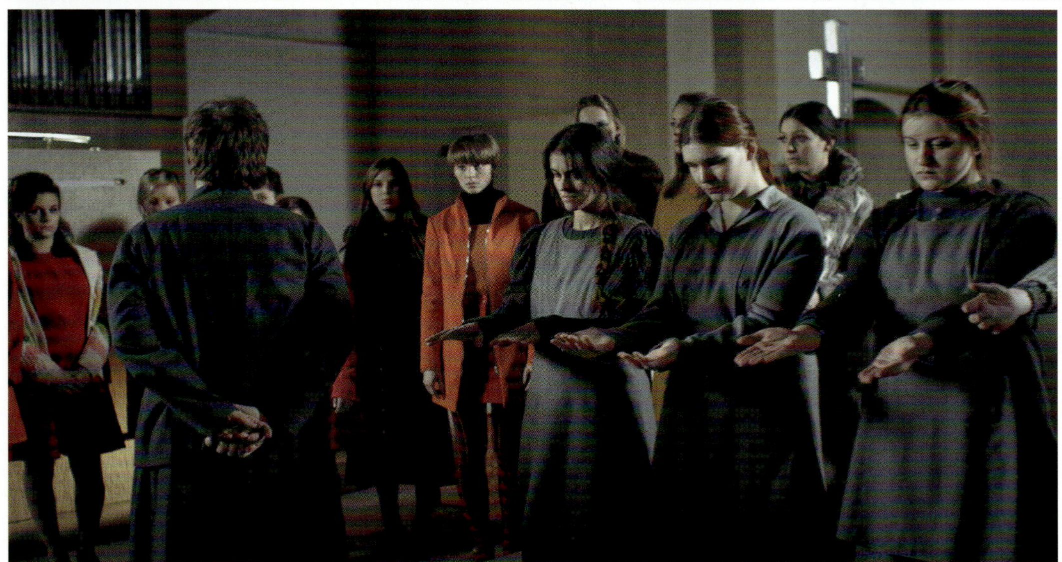

Thank!

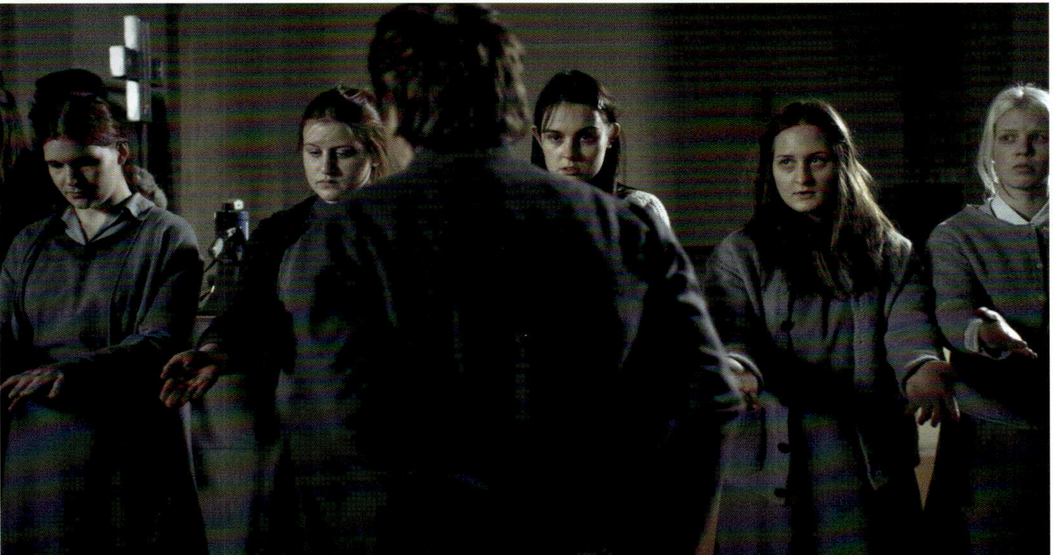

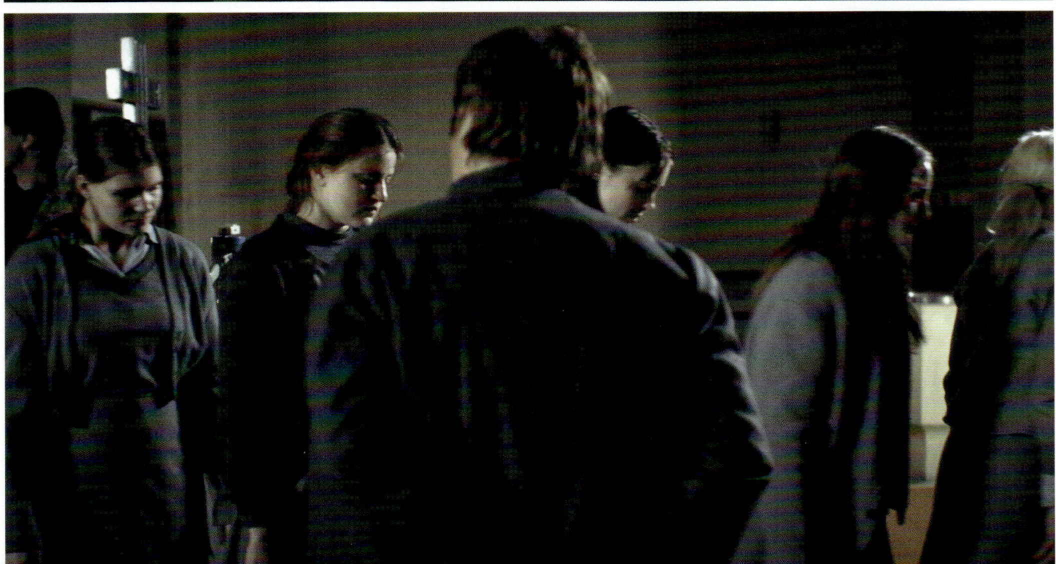

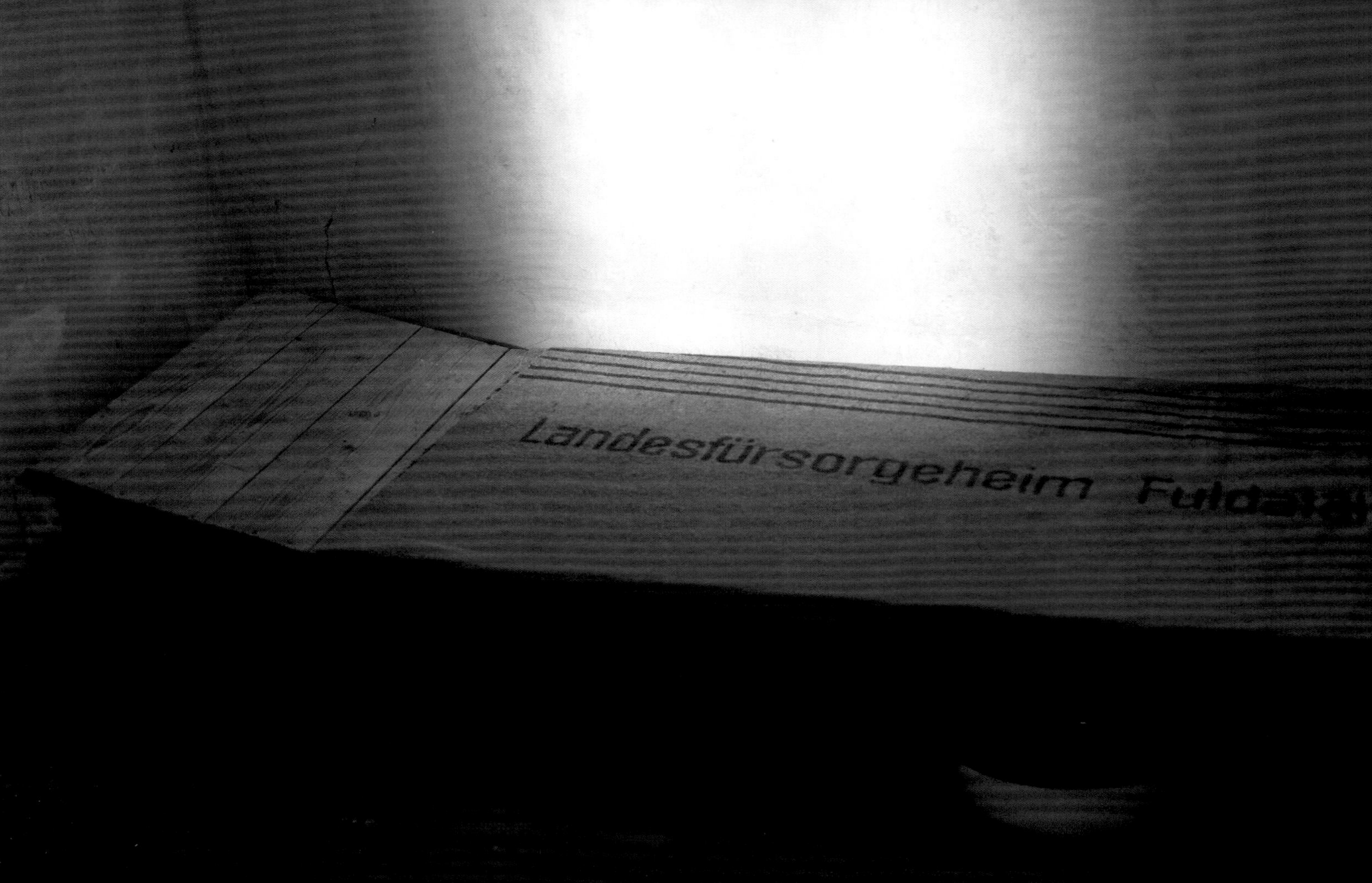

Nach der Auflösung des Klosters im Jahre 1527 war Breitenau Eigentum des Staats. Im Jahr 1874 wurde Breitenau ein preußisches Arbeitshaus. Der Kasseler Polizeichef gründete 1933 ein „Konzentrationslager für politische Gefangene", das zum Arbeitshaus gehörte und bis zum März 1934 existierte. Im Sommer 1940 richtete die Gestapo Kassel im Arbeitshaus Breitenau ein „Arbeitserziehungslager" ein. Bis 1945 waren dort etwa 8.500 Menschen aus verschiedenen Ländern interniert. Von 1952 bis 1973 wurde der Ort als „Fuldatal – Heim für junge Menschen" bekannt, ein geschlossenes Pflegeheim für „schwierige" Mädchen.

After the dissolution of the monastery in 1527, Breitenau was the property of the state. In 1874, Breitenau became a Prussian workhouse. In 1933, Kassel's police chief established a "concentration camp for political prisoners", which was part of the workhouse and remained there until March 1934. In the summer of 1940, Kassel's Gestapo in Breitenau set up an "Arbeitserziehungslager" (work education camp) as part of the workhouse. Up until 1945, a total of about 8,500 people from various countries were interned there. From 1952 to 1973, the site was known as the "Fuldatal Juvenile Home", a closed-care home for "difficult" girls.

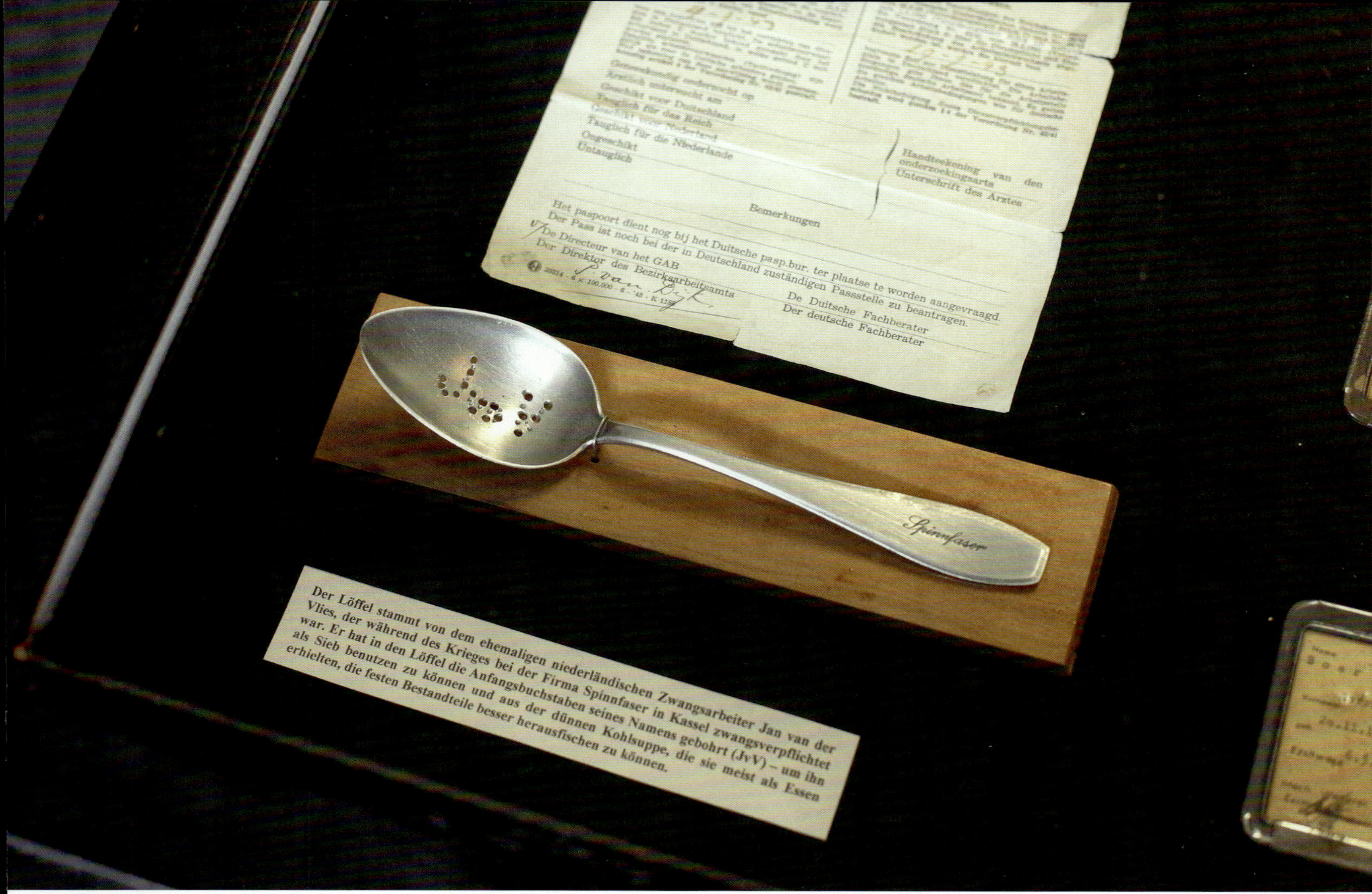

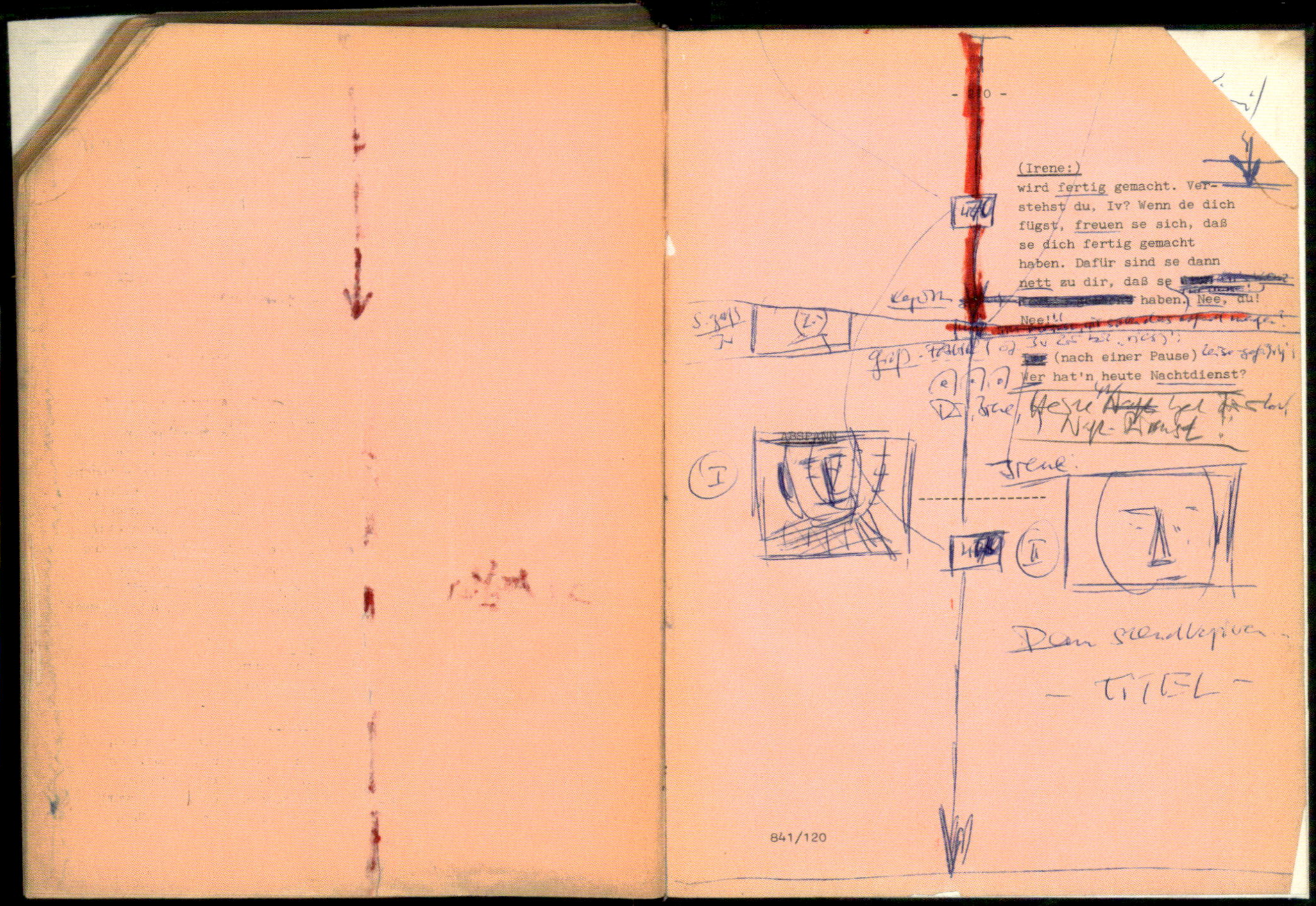

Ulrike Meinhof recherchierte Zustände in dem Mädchenerziehungsheim Breitenau, über das sie ein Radiofeature pro-
duzierte. Das Drehbuch *Bambule*, das auf ihrer Recherche
beruht, wurde 1970 durch den Regisseur Eberhard Itzenplitz
in Berlin verfilmt.

Ulrike Meinhof researched conditions at the girls reformatory in Breitenau and produced a radio programme.
The screenplay *Bambule*, based on her research, was filmed
by the director Eberhard Itzenplitz in Berlin in 1970.

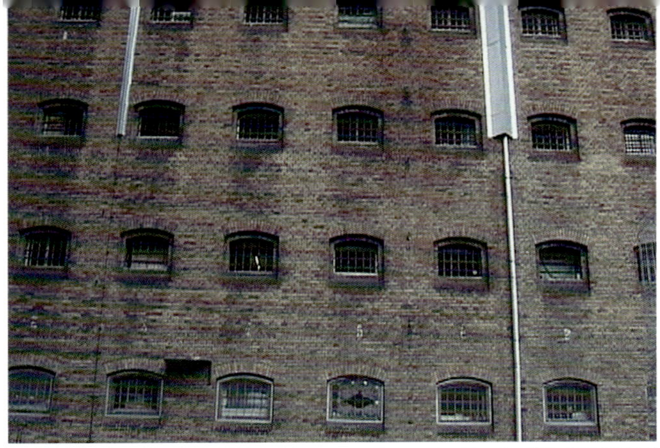

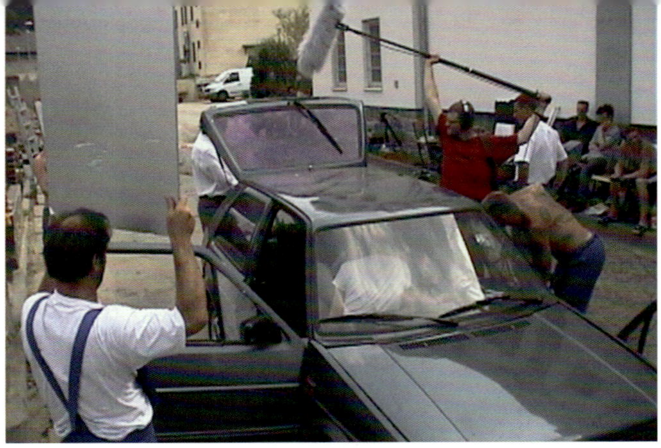

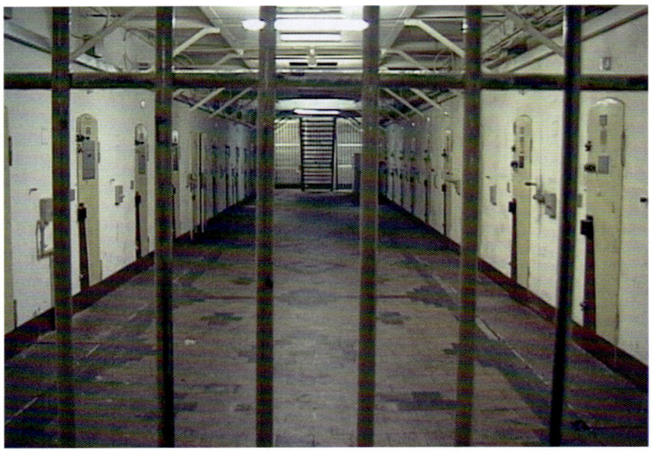

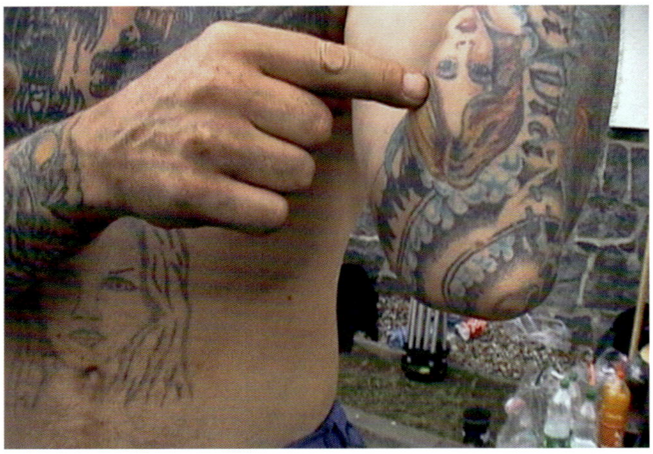

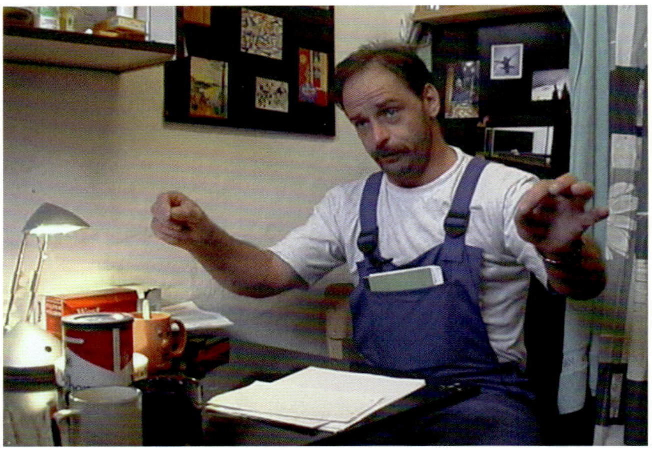

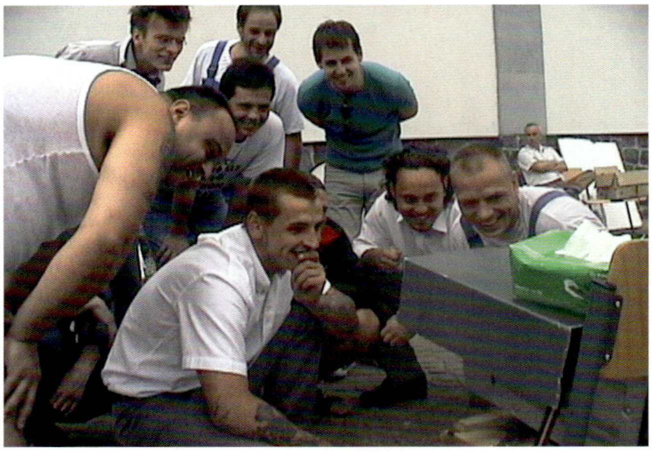

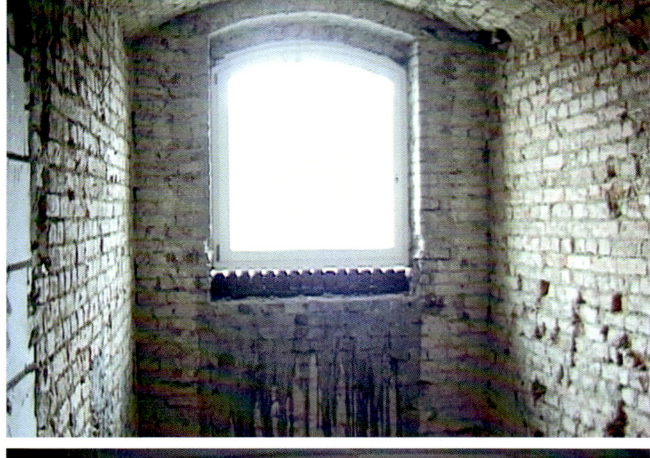

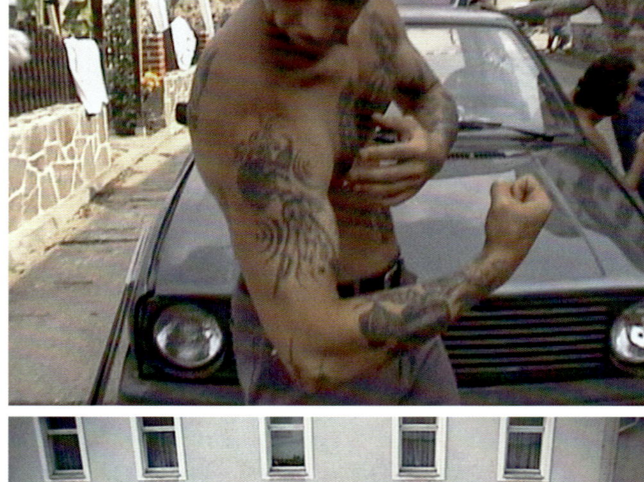

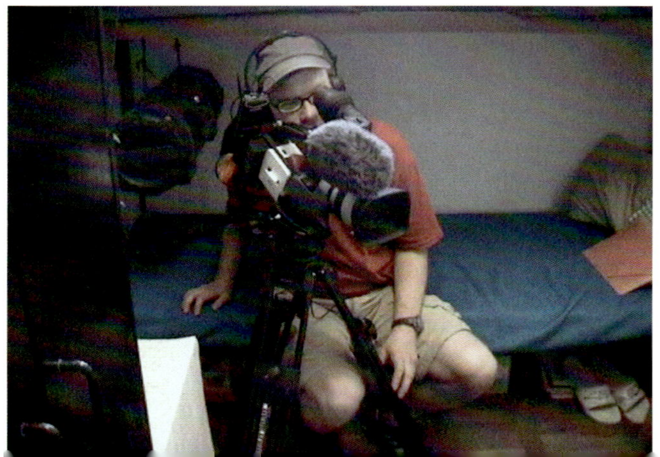

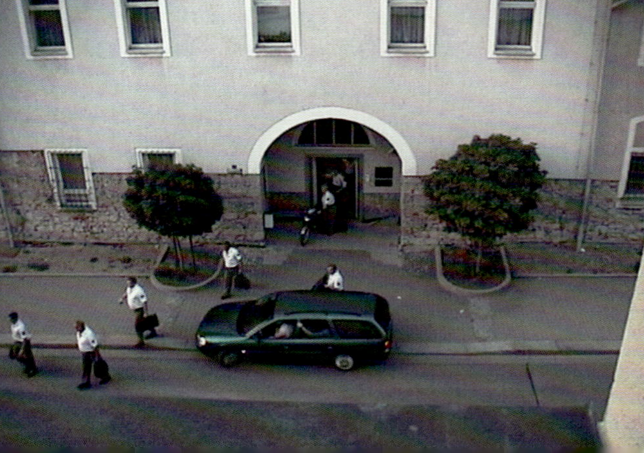

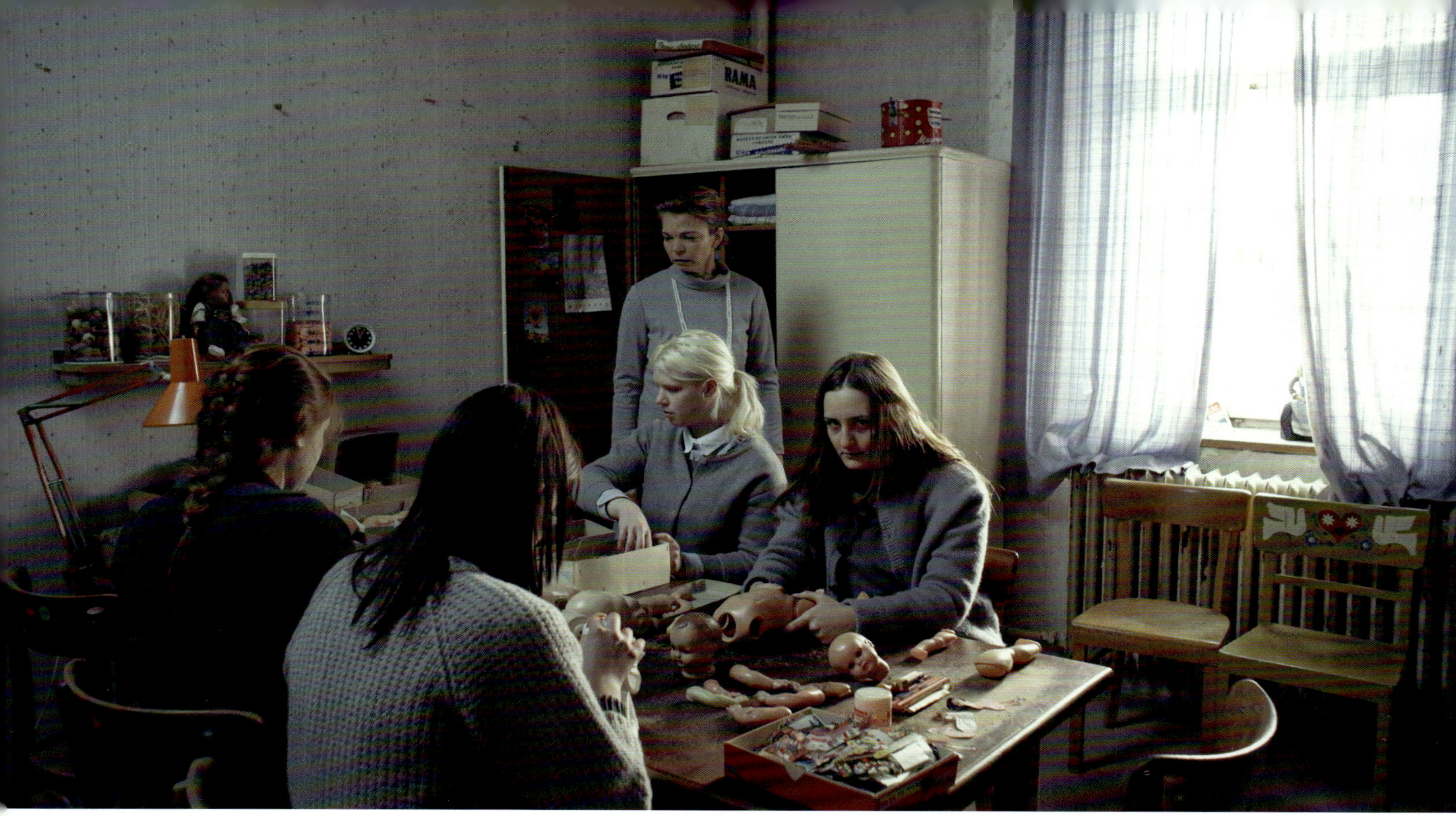

Die Verwahrung im Gefängnis wird mit Tätigkeiten ausgefüllt, die ein beschädigtes Leben kaum reparieren können.

Filling the time of incarceration with menial labour will hardly repair a damaged life.

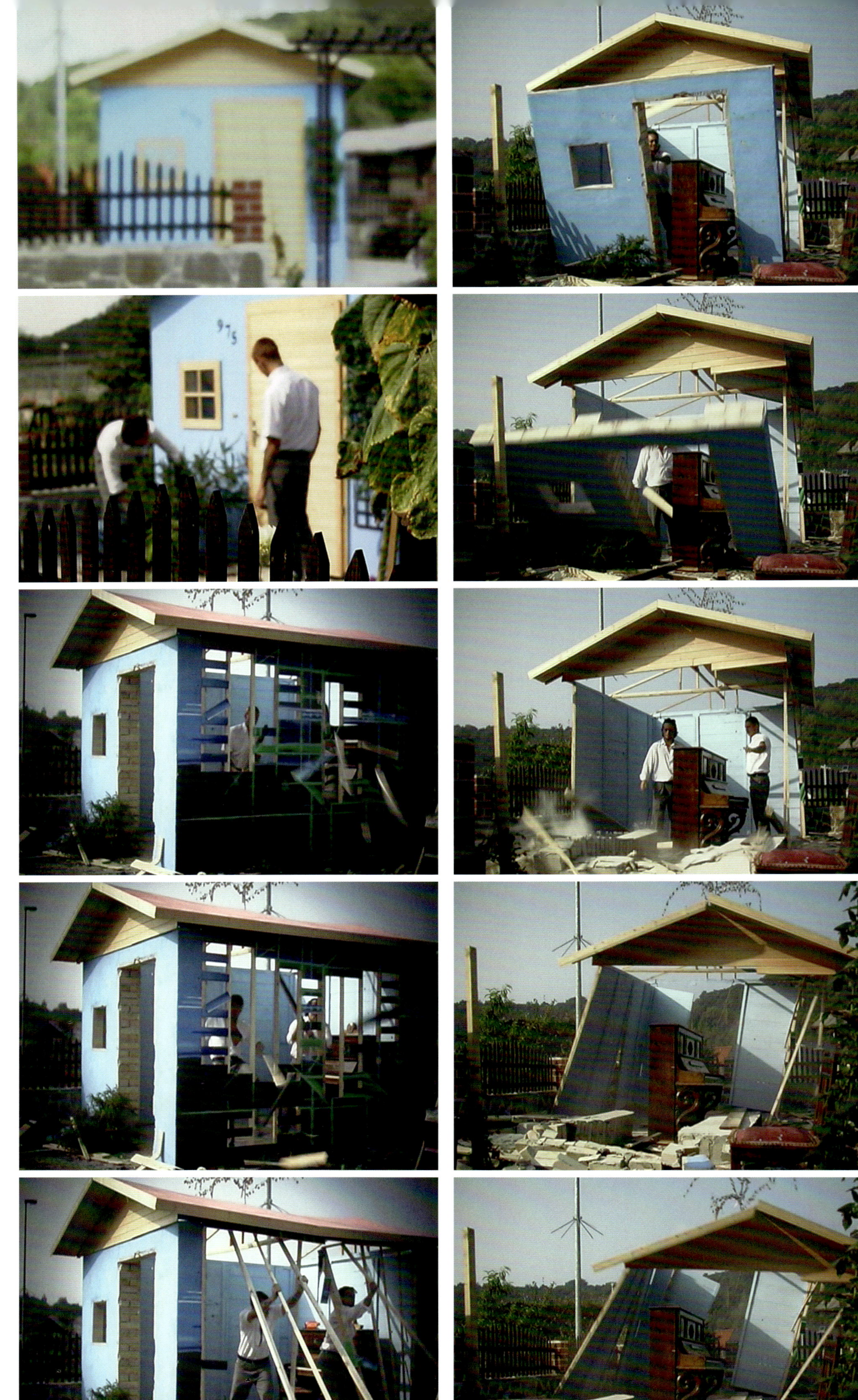

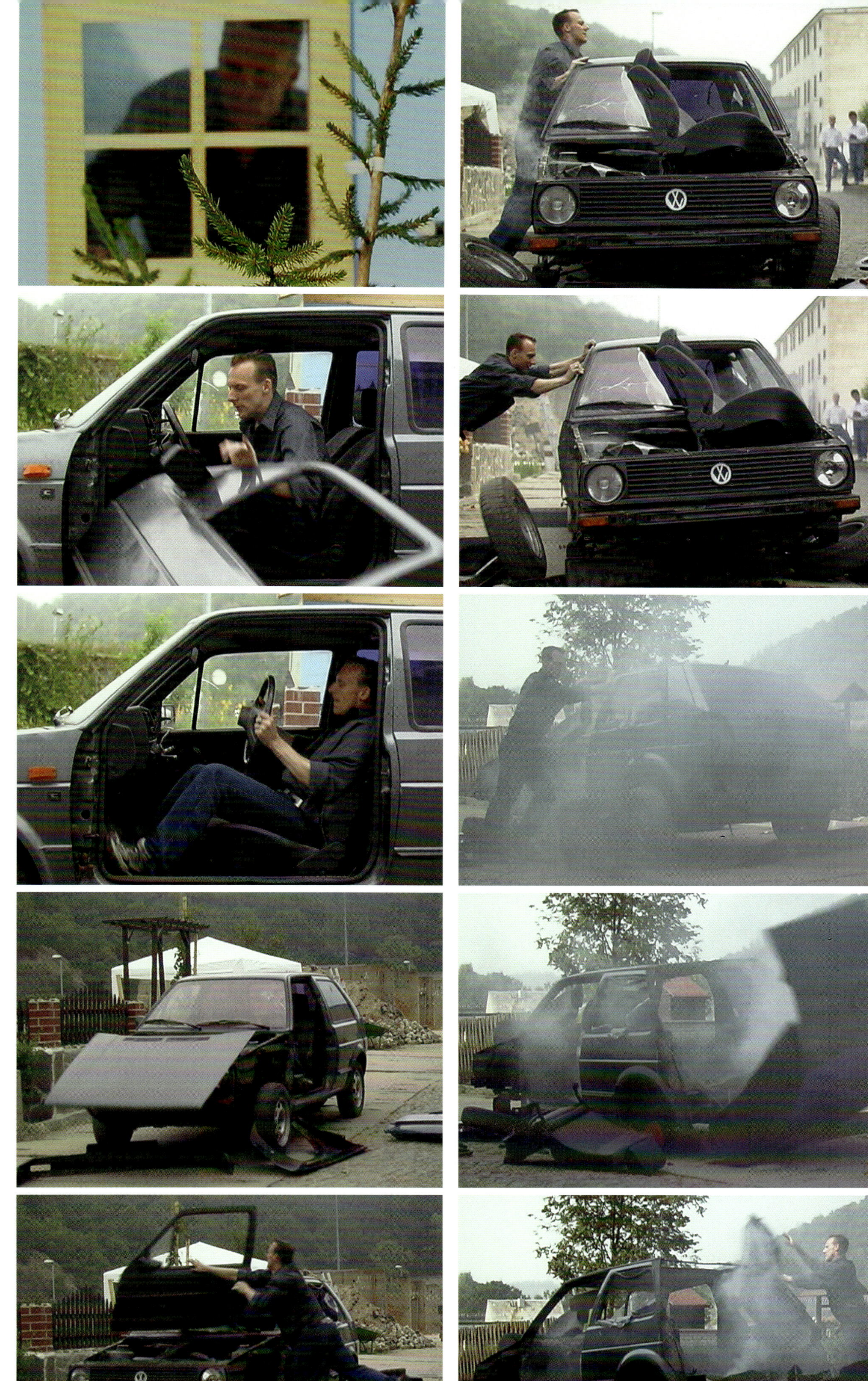

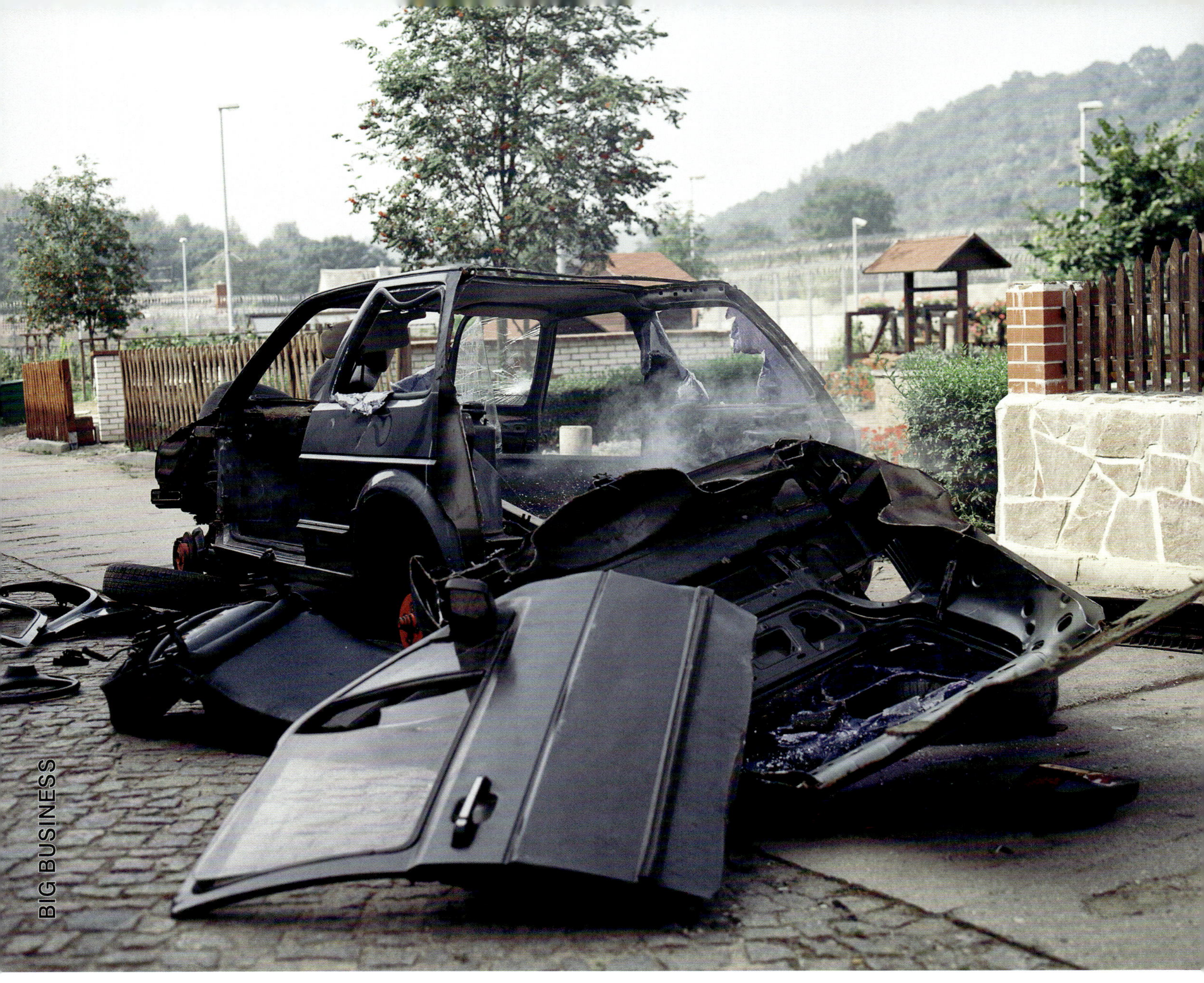

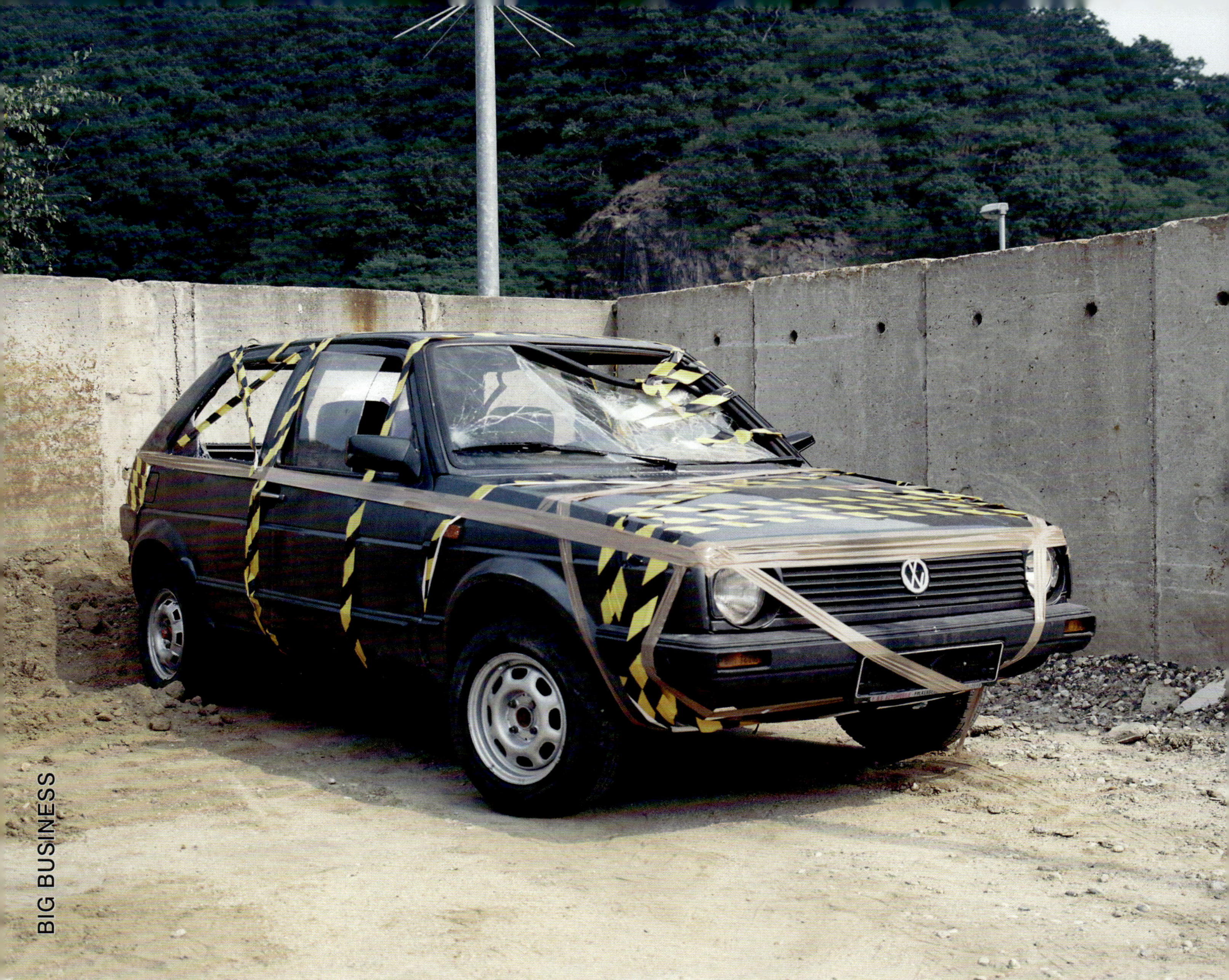

Für den Film wurde im Gefängnis ein Haus gebaut und ein konfisziertes Auto zur Zerstörung präpariert.

A building was constructed for the film, and a confiscated car was prepared for destruction.

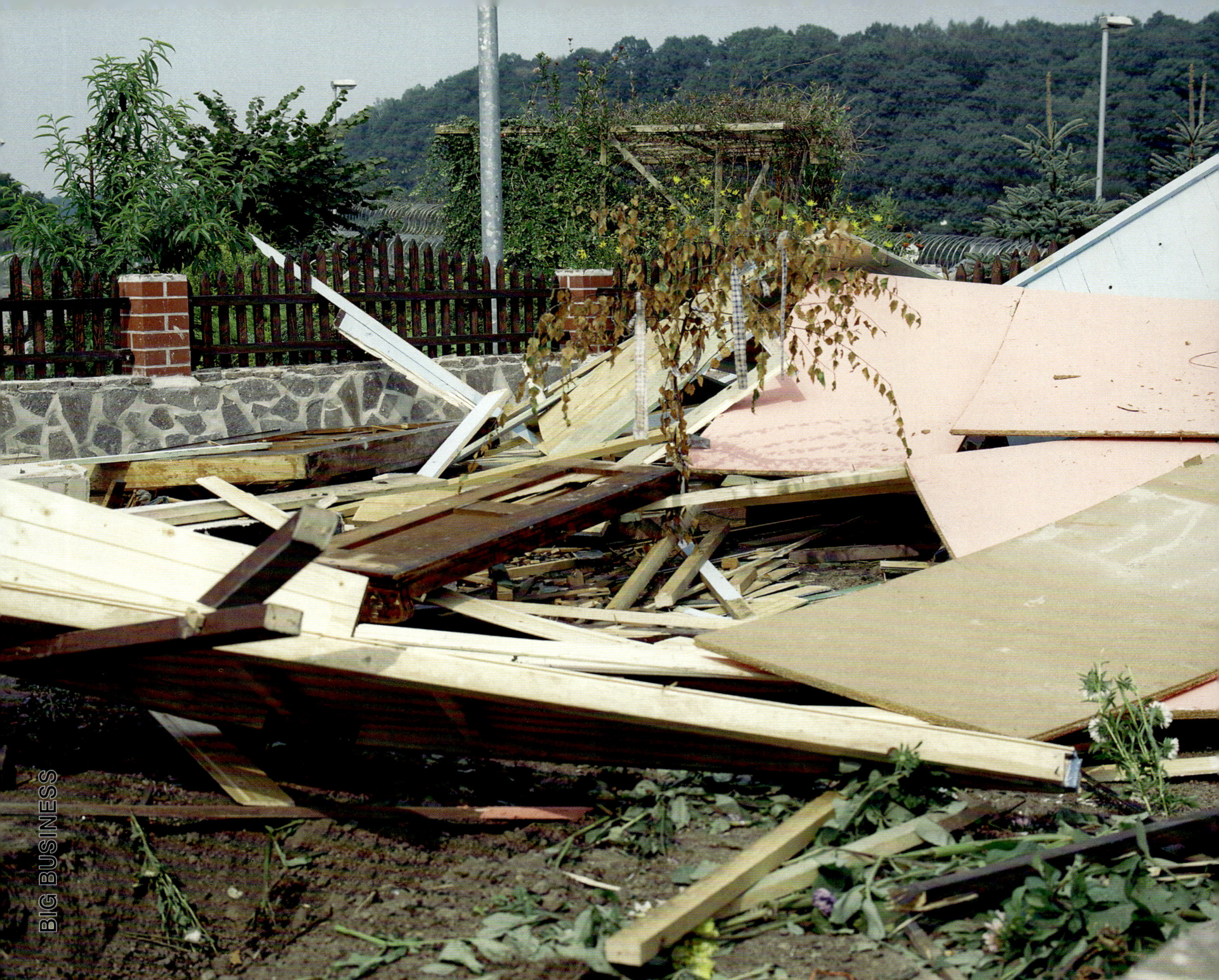

Alle Filme über das Gefängnis sind falsch, so wie dieser Film im Übrigen falsch ist.

Every film about a prison is false, and this film is no exception.

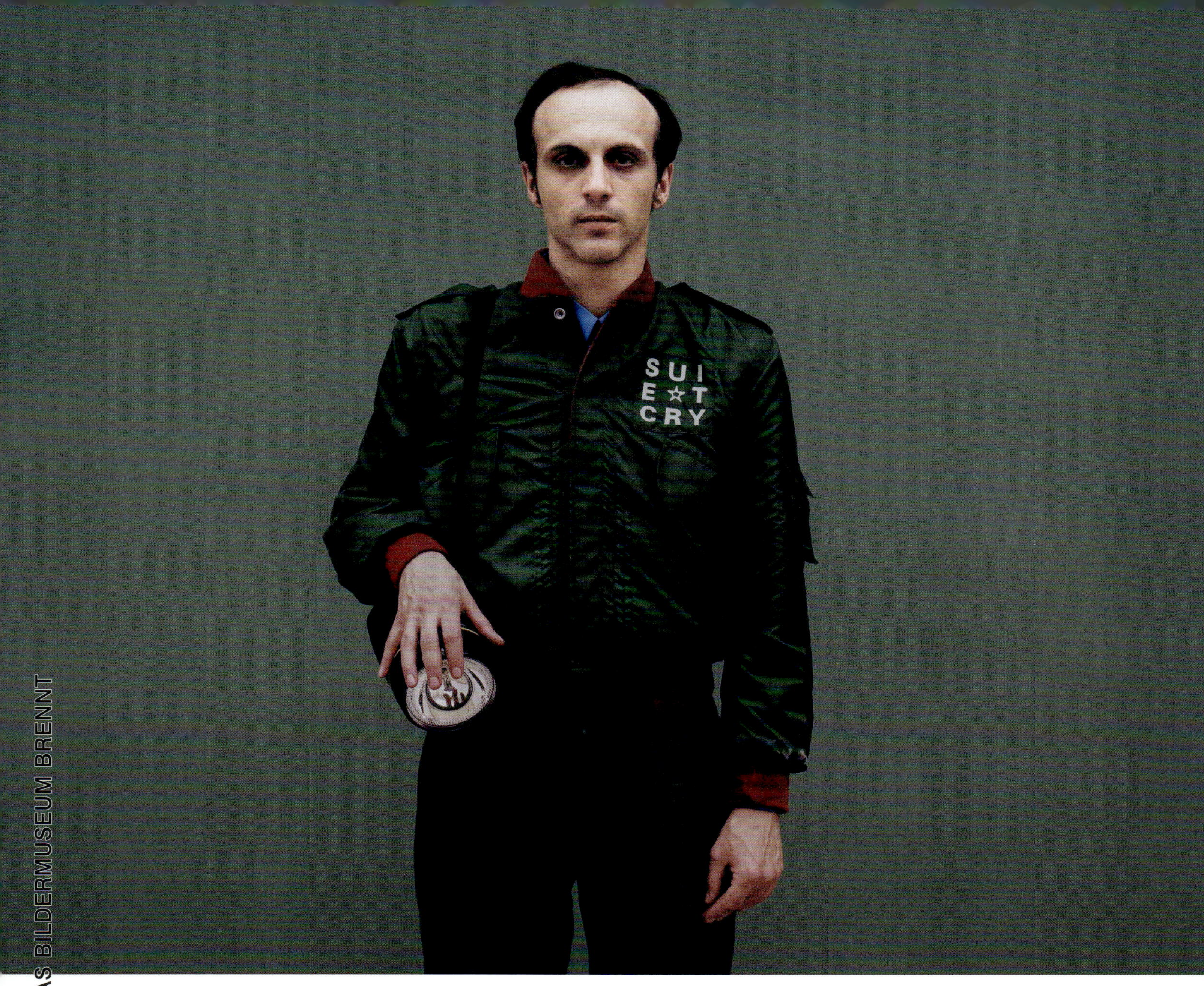

SUI
E☆T
CRY

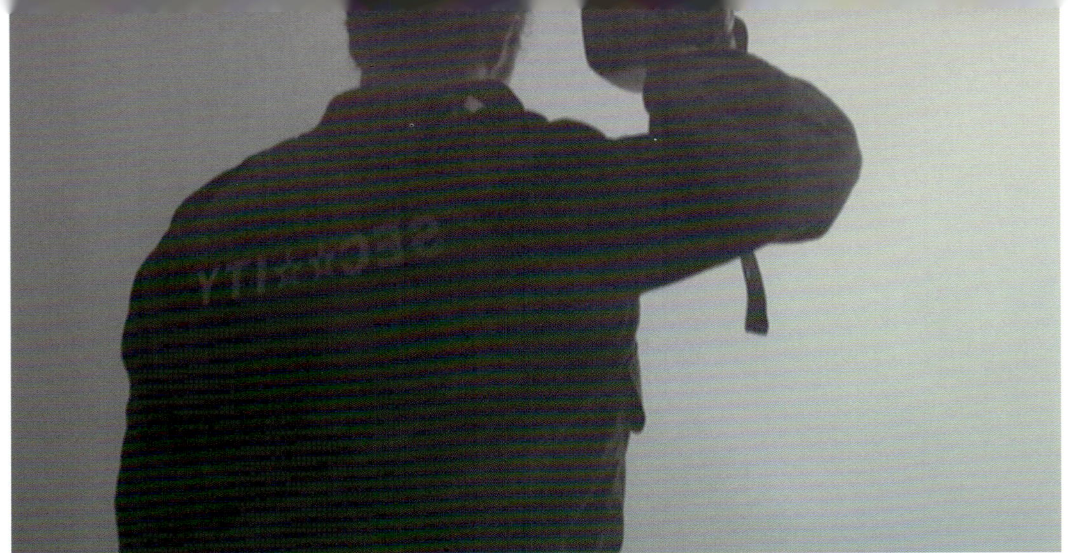

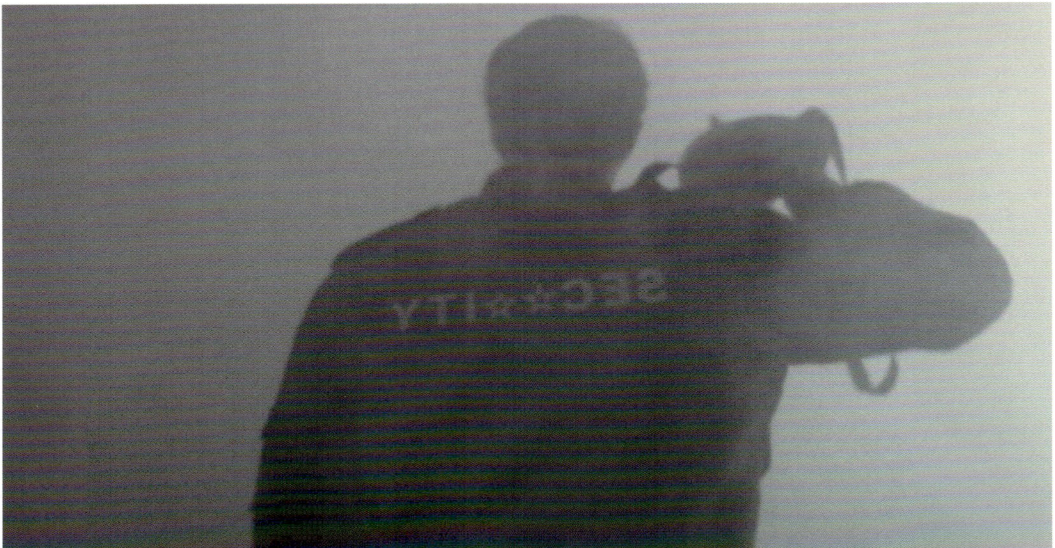

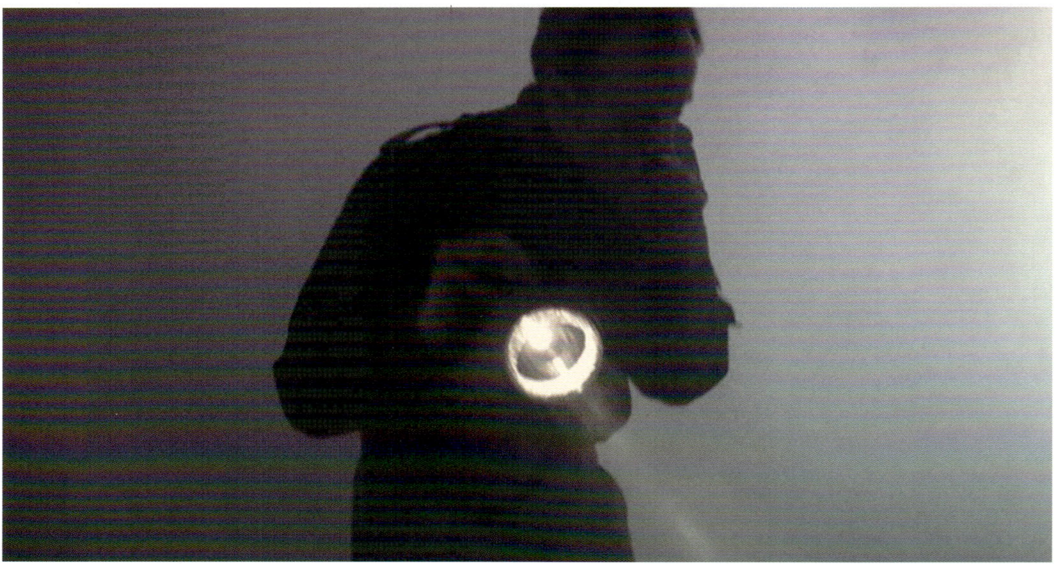

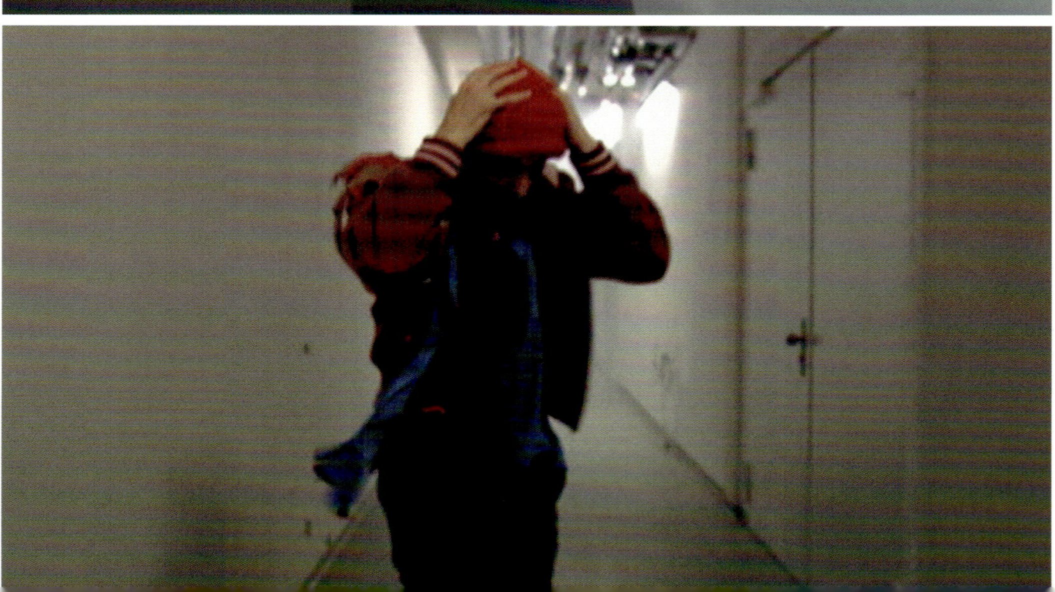

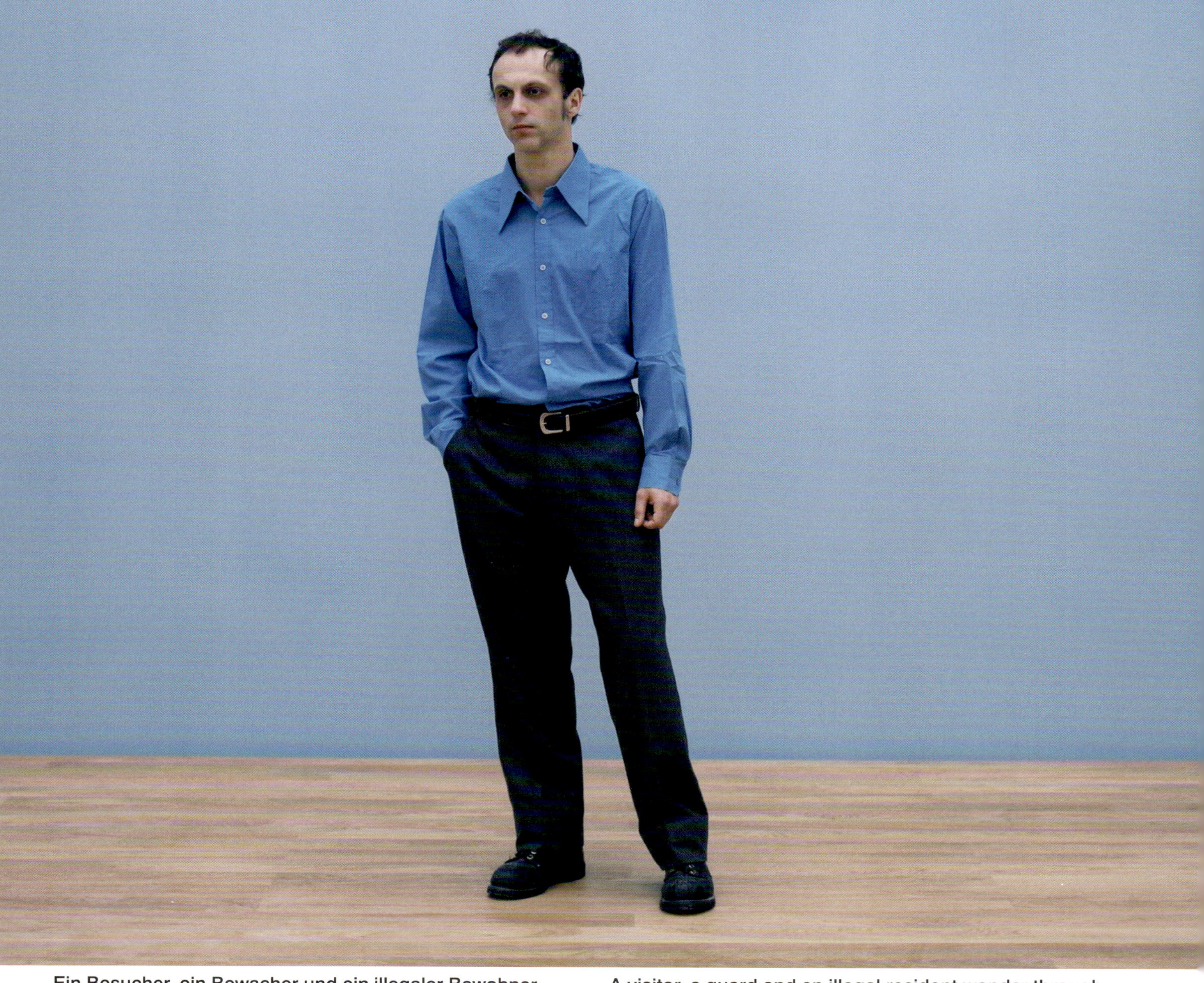

Ein Besucher, ein Bewacher und ein illegaler Bewohner bewegen sich nachts durch ein leeres Museum. Sie nehmen voneinander Notiz, aber begegnen sich nicht. Alle drei Figuren werden von demselben Schauspieler gespielt.

A visitor, a guard and an illegal resident wander through an empty museum at night. They are aware of each other, although they never meet. All three characters are played by the same actor.

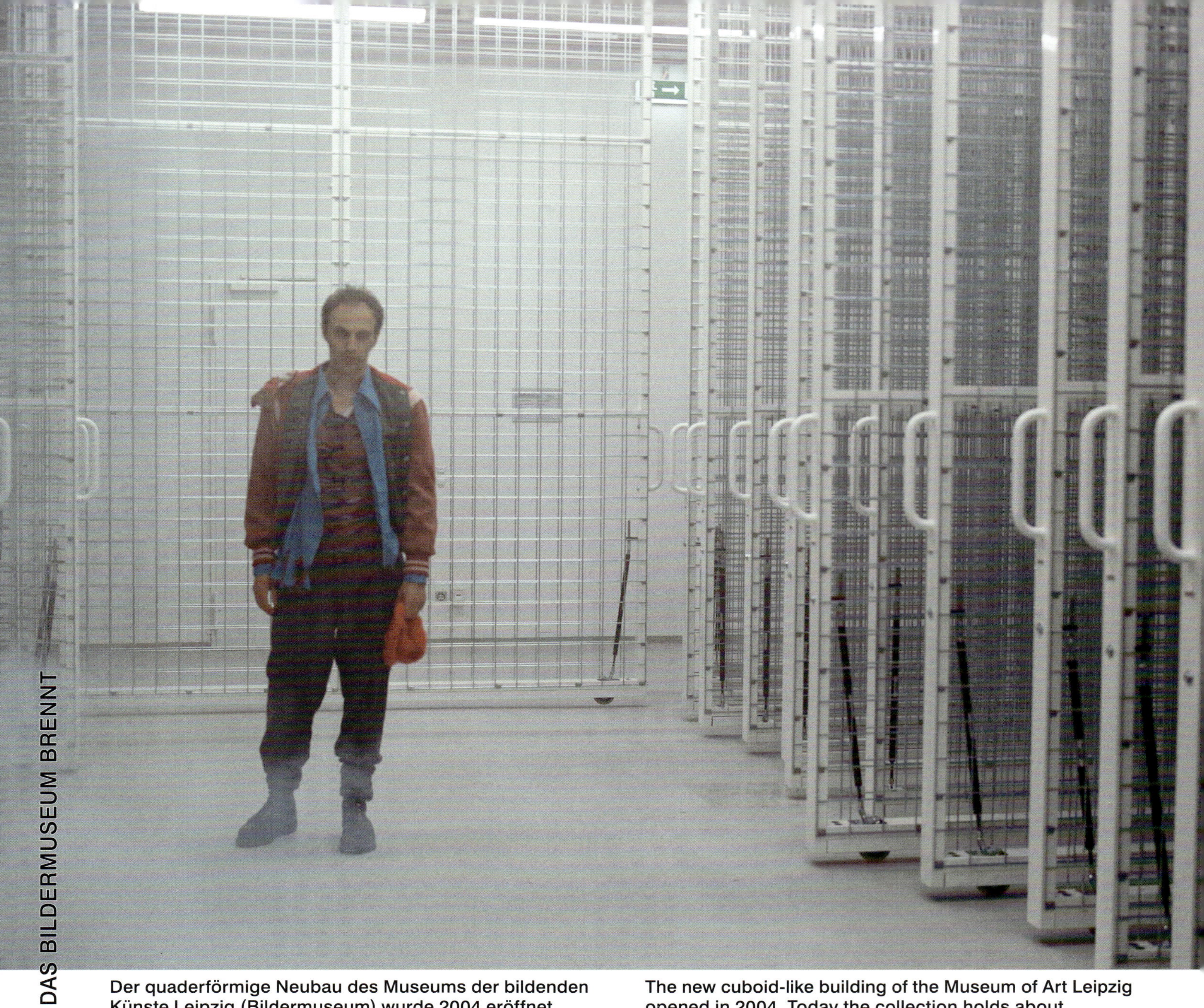

Der quaderförmige Neubau des Museums der bildenden
Künste Leipzig (Bildermuseum) wurde 2004 eröffnet.
Die heutige Sammlung beinhaltet ungefähr 3.500 Gemälde,
1.000 Skulpturen und 60.000 grafische Blätter.

The new cuboid-like building of the Museum of Art Leipzig
opened in 2004. Today the collection holds about
3,500 paintings, 1,000 sculptures and 60,000 prints.

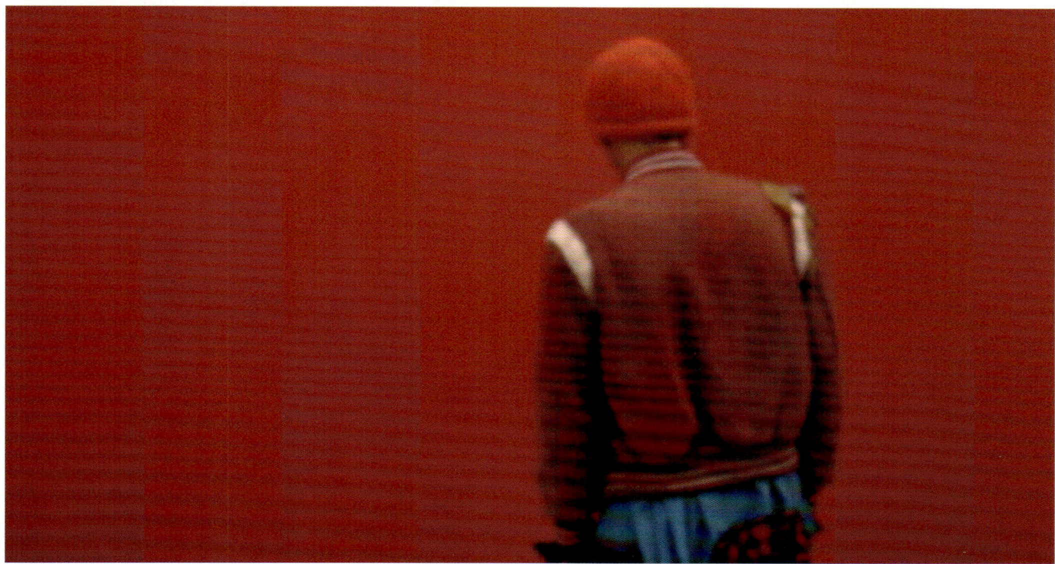
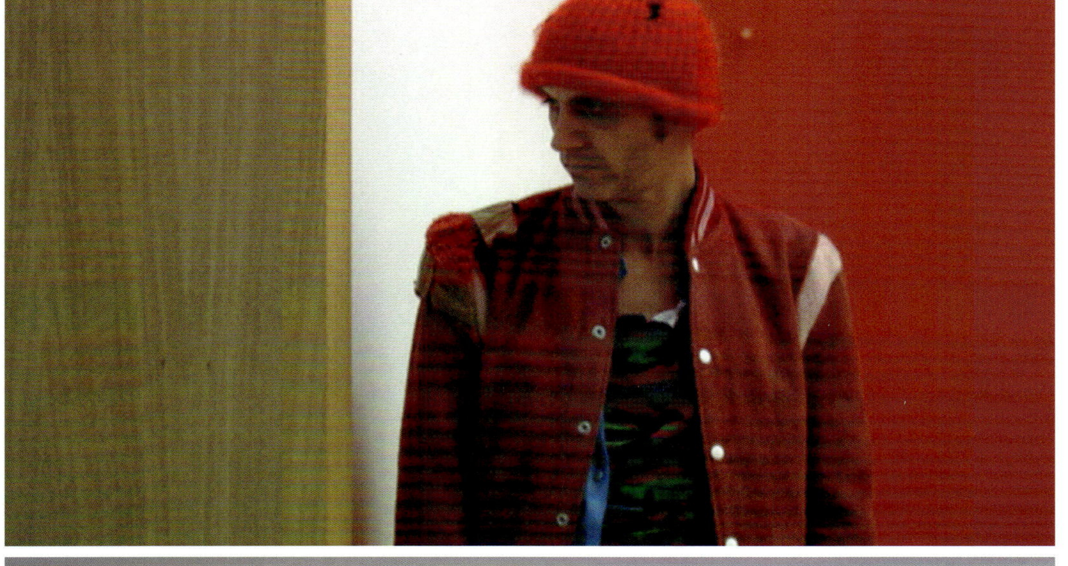
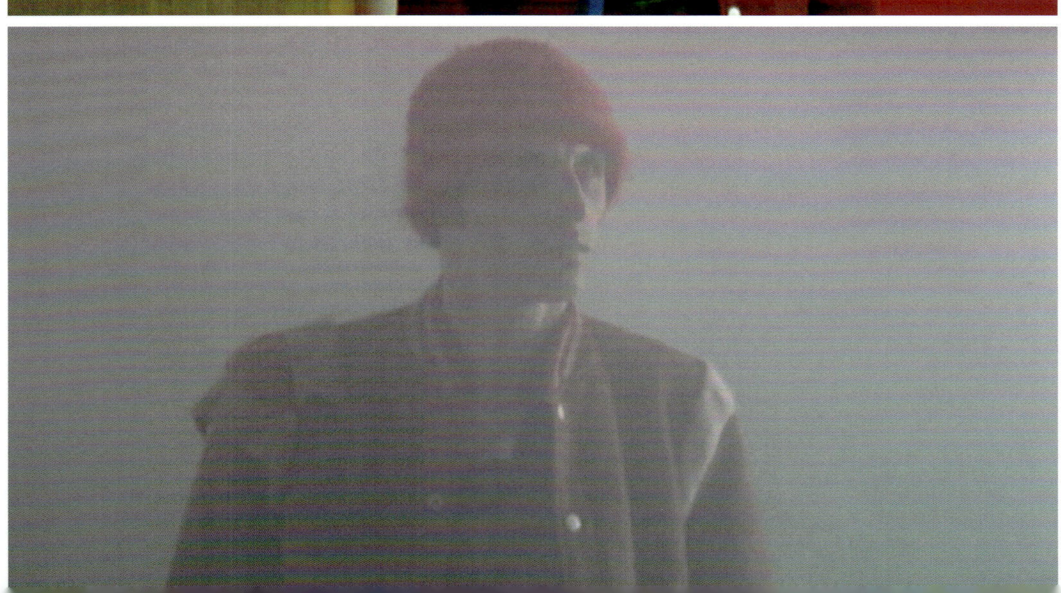

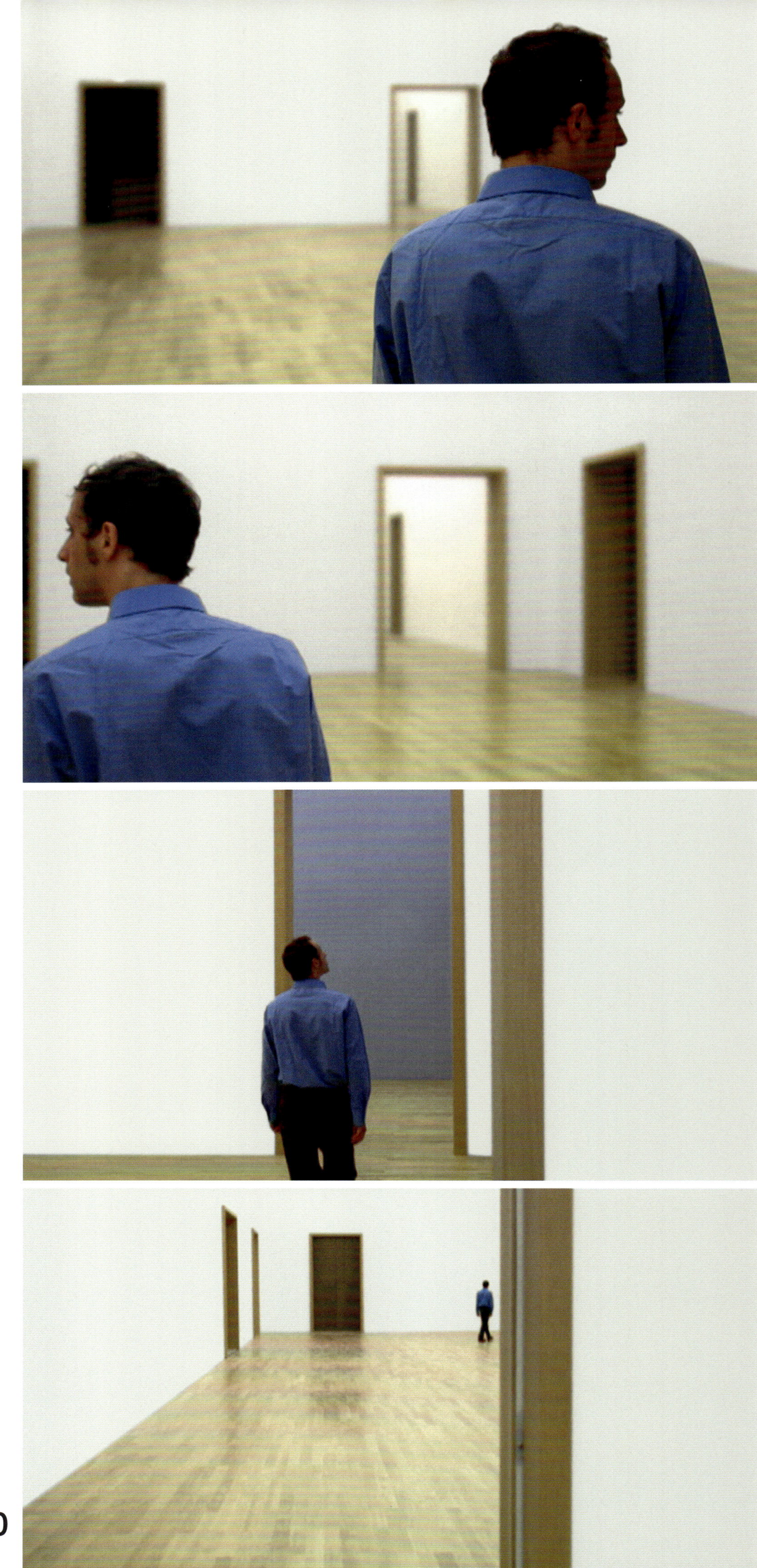

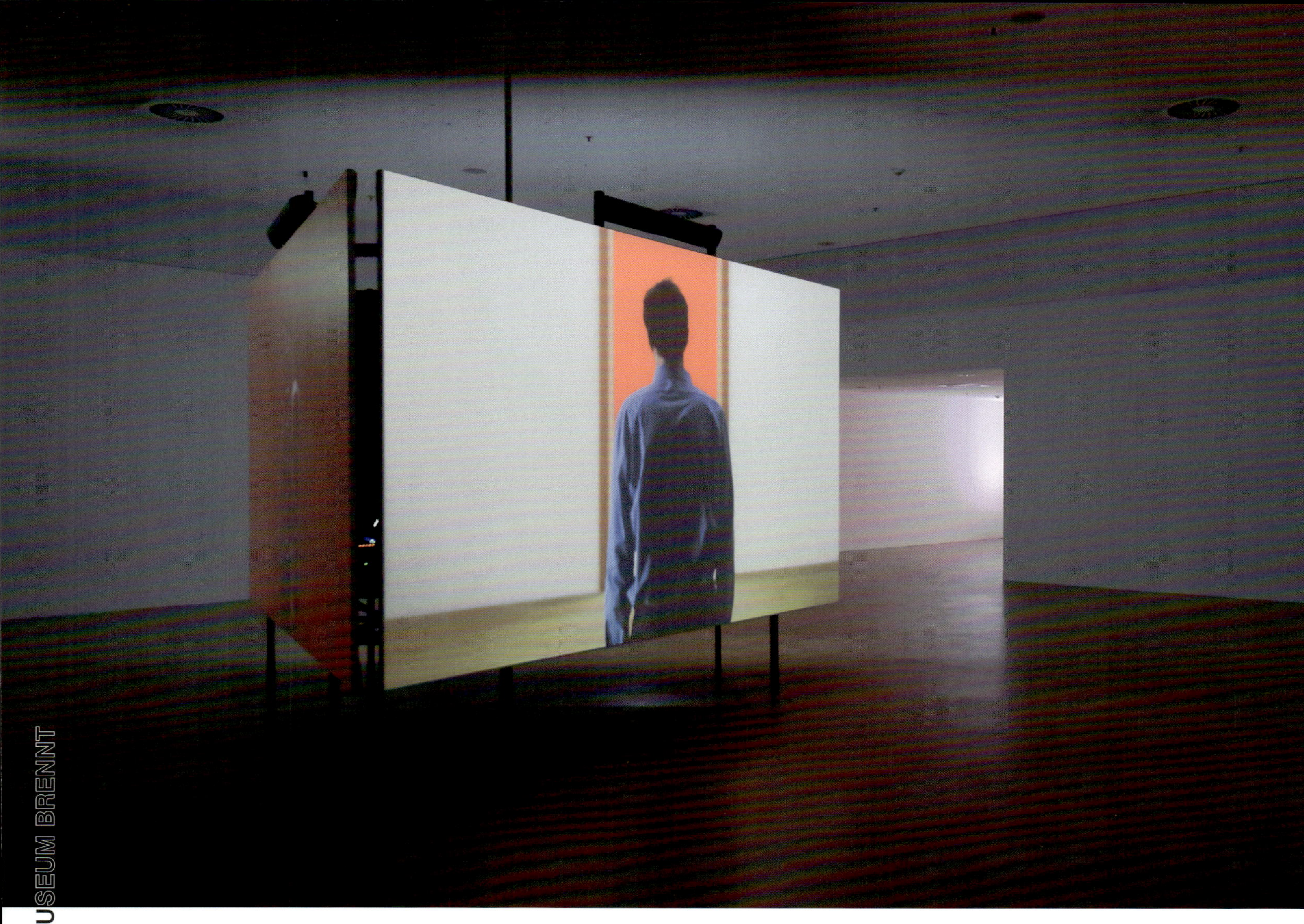

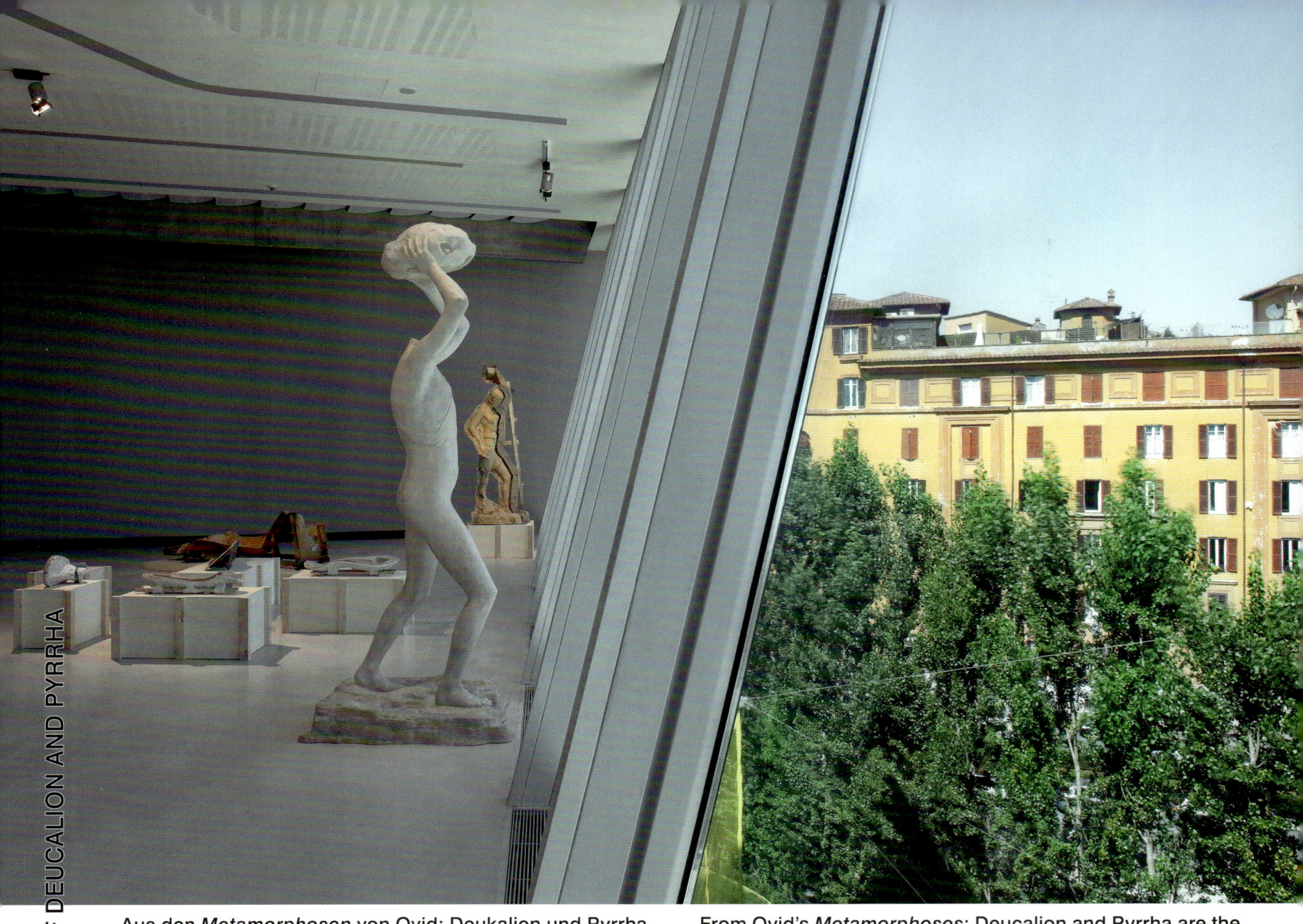

Aus den *Metamorphosen* von Ovid: Deukalion und Pyrrha sind die letzten Überlebenden nach der großen Flut. Sie treten vor ein Orakel: „Verlasset meinen Altar", tönte die Stimme der Göttin, „verschleiert euer Haupt, löst eure Gürtel, werft die Gebeine eurer Mutter hinter euren Rücken."

From Ovid's *Metamorphoses*: Deucalion and Pyrrha are the last survivors of the great flood. They step in front of an oracle: "Leave my altar," resounds the voice of the goddess. "Uncover your heads, ungird your garments and cast the bones of your mother behind you."

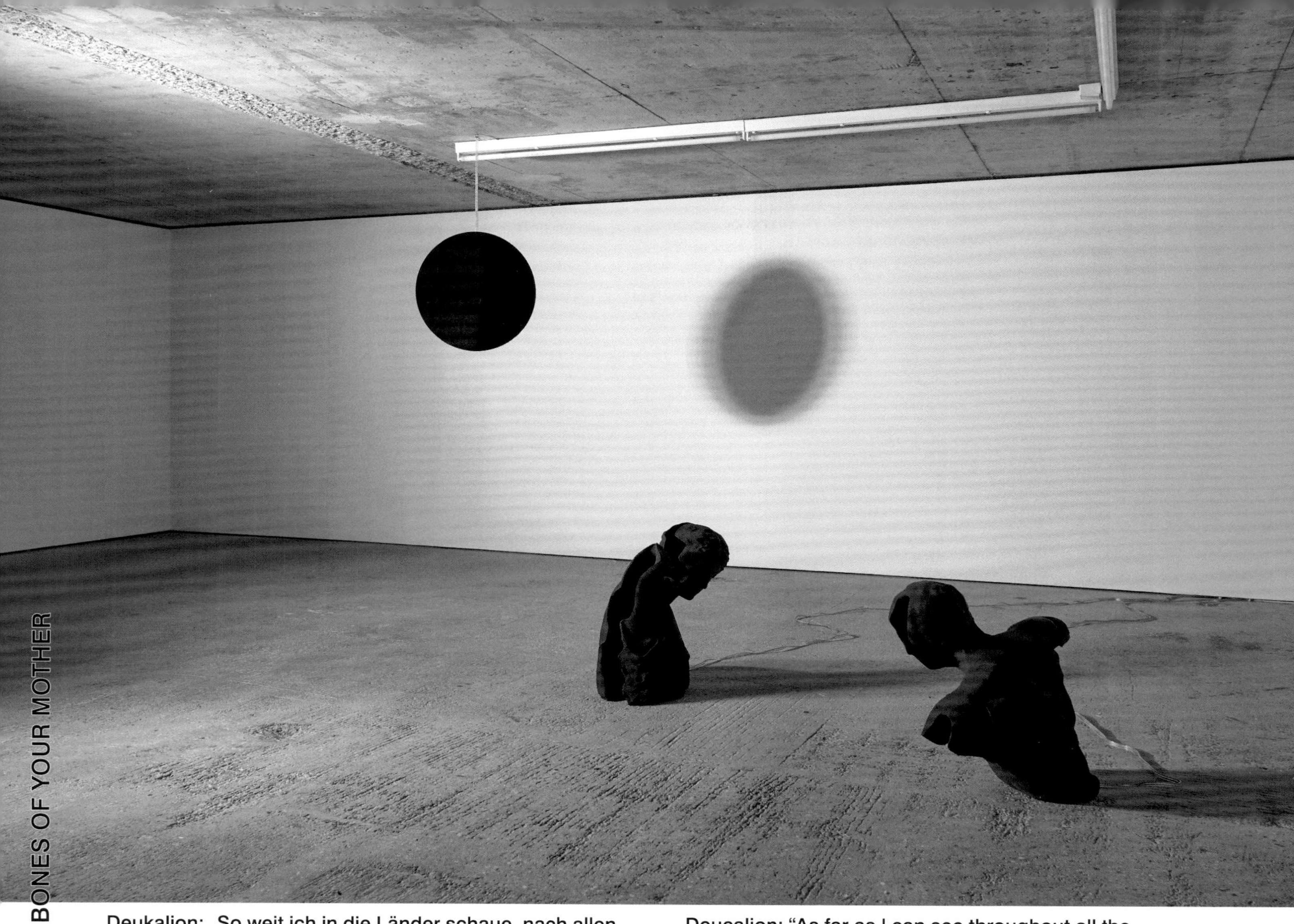

Deukalion: „So weit ich in die Länder schaue, nach allen Himmelsrichtungen hin, kann ich keine lebende Seele entdecken. Wir sind die Letzten."

Deucalion: "As far as I can see throughout all the surrounding countryside, I can discover no living creature. We are the last."

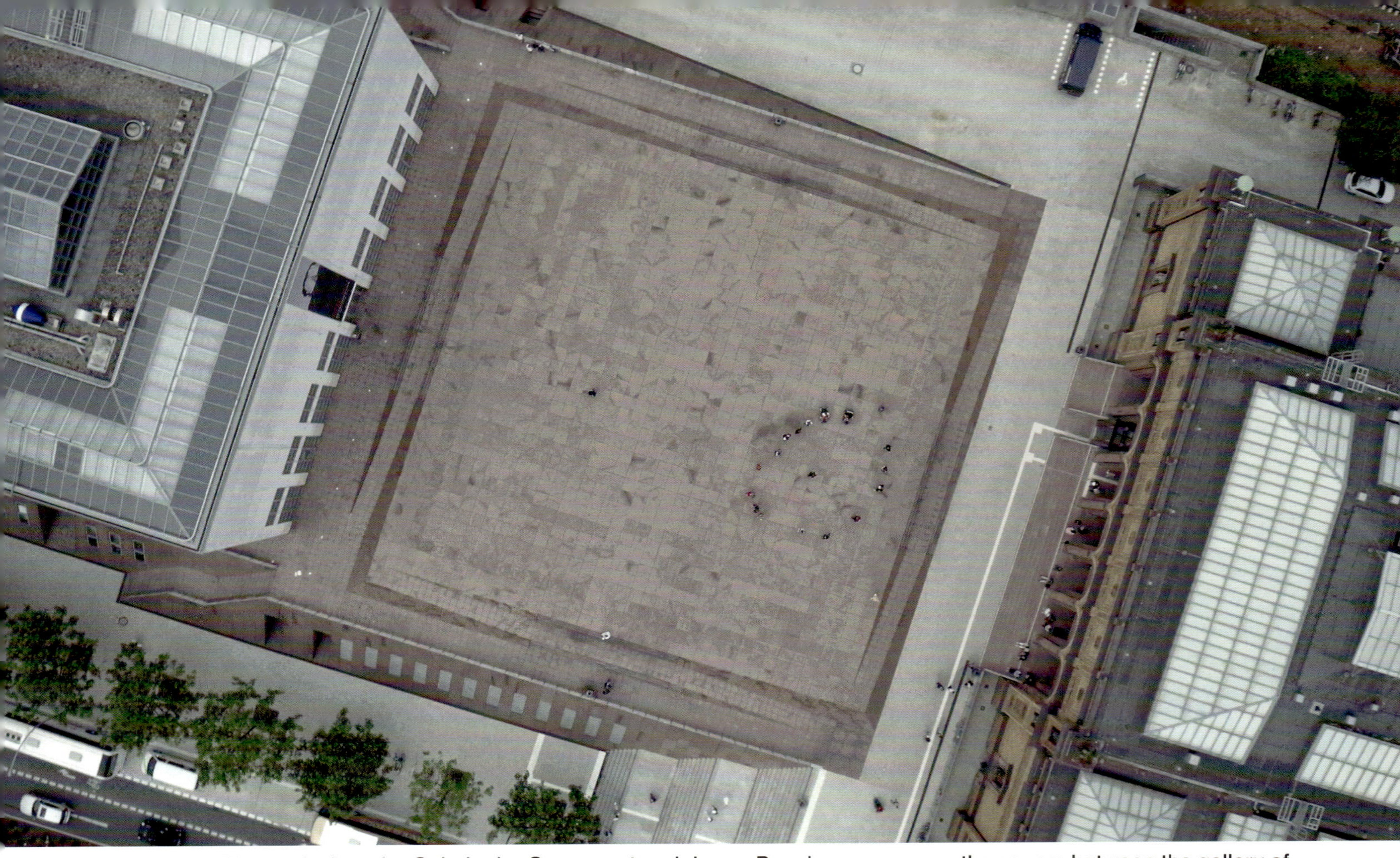

Auf dem Platz zwischen der Galerie der Gegenwart und dem Altbau der Hamburger Kunsthalle bewegen sich Passanten. Ihre auffälligen Interaktionen werden aus der Perspektive der Kameradrohne erkennbar.

People move across the square between the gallery of contemporary art and the old building of the Hamburger Kunsthalle. Their conspicuous interactions are made visible from the perspective of the camera drone.

JENSEITS DER VEREINNAHMUNG

ÜBER CLEMENS VON WEDEMEYERS FILME
BIG BUSINESS UND *MUSTER*

Zoltán Kékesi

In *Occupation* (2002) von Clemens von Wedemeyer filmt ein Kamerateam die Versammlung einer größeren Menschenmenge. Wir sehen die Inszenierung einer Protestszene. Die „occupation" im Titel meint aber weniger diese Menschenansammlung und ihre Besetzung eines öffentlichen Ortes, sondern vielmehr den Apparat des Films und seine Art, ein Gelände und gesellschaftliches Geschehen für seine Zwecke zu vereinnahmen. In *Occupation* kommt die Produktion von Bildern des Protests beinahe einem Akt der Unterdrückung gleich: Das Erzeugen der Szene unterwirft Statisten einem hierarchischen Verhältnis des Inszeniertwerdens, das sich durch Sprache konstituiert und über Technologien des Sehens, Befehlens und Sichtbarmachens vermittelt. Von Scheinwerfern geblendet und unter dem Eindruck der Geräuschverstärkung agieren die Statisten als eine verwirrte, vom Filmapparat unter Kontrolle gehaltene Menschenmasse. *Occupation* ist ein Film über die Produktion eines Films und über das Filmemachen als Beruf, in dem beide Hauptbedeutungen des Wortes „occupation" – Beruf und Besatzung – zum Tragen kommen. Die Arbeit thematisiert das Film- oder Kunstschaffen als Beruf und darüber hinaus die Berufsausübung in ihrem Bezug zur Ausübung von Macht. Berufliche Arbeit bedingt und etabliert gesellschaftliche Verhältnisse, und *Occupation* handelt davon, dass diese Beziehungen Machtgefüge sind. Darüber hinaus „okkupieren" Filmbilder selbstverständlich auch unseren Geist, und in diesem Sinn erfasst das filmische Vereinnahmen gesellschaftlicher Beziehungen, so wie es in Clemens von Wedemeyers Werken vorgeführt wird, ebenso das Film- und Kunstpublikum. Seine neuere Arbeit *Muster* (2012) behandelt ebenso wie *Big Business* (2002) ausdrücklich solche Fragen von Widerstand und Macht, Film, Bild, Kunst und Beruf. Beide entstanden an Orten, die Schauplätze besonderer gesellschaftlicher Verhältnisse waren und sind. Was heißt es nun im jeweiligen Kontext, Filmbilder zu erzeugen, welche die Logik der „Okkupation" überwinden?

2002 drehte Clemens von Wedemeyer mit Strafgefangenen ein Remake von Stan Laurels und Oliver Hardys *Das große Geschäft* (1929). Die Kulisse der Neuverfilmung war ein „Idyll", das ihm die Haftanstalt Waldheim in Sachsen zur Verfügung stellte.

In ihrer klassischen Slapstick-Komödie spielen Laurel und Hardy zwei Christbaumverkäufer, die bei strahlendem Sonnenschein einem Vorstadtbewohner einen Tannenbaum andrehen wollen. Als der Mann ihnen eine Abfuhr erteilt, entwickelt sich eine Auseinandersetzung, an deren Ende das Haus des Mannes und das Auto der beiden Vertreter zertrümmert sind. Schauplatz der Neuverfilmung ist ein Gefängnis, in dem die Häftlinge als Teil der Verbüßung ihrer Strafe lebensgroße Häuser bauen, wieder abreißen und danach erneut aufbauen. Indem von Wedemeyer hier sein Remake dreht, lässt auch er die Häftlinge ein Haus bauen und wieder abreißen. Was bedeutet es, das an einem Ort zu tun, an dem Menschen einem Zwang zur Arbeit unterliegen? Die Entstehung des Films reproduziert den Gefängnisalltag der Häftlinge, macht aus dem Zwang aber das Erlebnis, eine Rolle zu spielen und am Dreh mitzuwirken. Strafgefangene stellen sowohl das Ensemble, als auch das Kamerateam. Ethisches Anliegen der Verfilmung von *Big Business* ist es einerseits, die Häftlinge zu unterstützen, die alltäglichen Zwänge zu überwinden und sich in einem schöpferischen Prozess zu entfalten. Andererseits erzeugt der Film Bilder, die sich mit dem Schauplatz und mit den von ihm hervorgebrachten und vorausgesetzten gesellschaftlichen Verhältnissen auseinandersetzen. Im Zuge des Remakes nehmen sowohl die klassische Komödie als auch ihre Neuinszenierung vielfältigere, neue Bedeutungen an.

Diese Neuverfilmung von *Das große Geschäft* ist eindeutig keine Komödie. Zerstörung, im Original wichtigste Quelle des Humors, wirkt hier schnell beklemmend. Das Unbehagen kommt zum Teil daher, dass das Haus, das für das

Remake gebaut und im Verlauf der Dreharbeiten zerstört wird, nach einer Bildvorlage entsteht und man bis zum Schluss nicht genau weiß, was dieses Bild eigentlich darstellt. Es hat anscheinend einen Bezug zu vielen Dingen: zu dem Haus in den entsprechenden Sequenzen des Originals; zu dem Haus, das die Häftlinge in der Gefängniswerkstatt aufbauen und wieder abreißen; zur Normalität eines Alltags, der den Häftlingen selbst verwehrt bleibt. Die eigentliche Strafe – das erkennen wir als Betrachter – liegt darin, dass die Häftlinge bei ihrer Strafarbeit das Sinnbild eines Lebens herstellen und wieder zerstören müssen, das sie selbst nicht haben können. Sie werden also gezwungen, ihre eigene Isolierung und Entbehrung immer wieder neu zu inszenieren. Auf der anderen Seite steht das Haus für ein „Idyll", wie es in *The Making of Big Business* (2002) heißt, also für die Begierden, die unser Leben tagtäglich antreiben und auch reglementieren. In diesem Sinn handeln die im Gefängnis gebauten Häuser von der Gesellschaftsordnung, die das Gefängnis als Institution hervorbringt. Ihre Zerstörung kann in diesem Licht als ein aggressives Handeln erscheinen, das sich gegen die symbolische Substitution der Außenwelt richtet. Doch ganz so einfach ist es nicht. Die Haftanstalt, so der Künstler in *The Making of Big Business*, ist eine „Stätte der Verdrängung", und das nicht nur, weil sie die Insassen zwingt, ihre Bedürfnisse und Begierden zu verdrängen. *Big Business* enthüllt einen Vorgang, der komplexer und verstörender zugleich ist: Im Gefängnis werden Häuser gebaut und abgerissen, welche für die unerreichbaren Objekte unserer eigenen gesellschaftlichen Begierden stehen. So gesehen ist die erzwungene Arbeit im Gefängnis eine physische und psychische Sühne, und sie beschränkt sich nicht darauf, dass man unablässig die eigenen unerfüllten Bedürfnisse durchleben muss, sondern umfasst auch noch die Begierden anderer. Es ist grausam, Häftlinge zum Bauen und Abreißen von Häusern zu zwingen, weil es sich anscheinend um sinnlose Arbeit handelt; doch die eigentliche Grausamkeit besteht darin, dass diese Arbeit eben nicht sinnentleert oder bedeutungslos ist. Das Gefängnis ist ein „Ort der Verdrängung", weil unsere Gesellschaften damit die Arbeit des Neuinszenierens und Wiedererlebens gesellschaftlicher Traumata, die mit der Unerreichbarkeit der Objekte unserer Begierde zu tun haben, verdrängen und auf die Häftlinge abwälzen können. Clemens von Wedemeyers *Big Business* verstört, weil der Film alle diese verschiedenen Ebenen sozialer, institutioneller, psychoökonomischer und symbolischer Wechselwirkungen zutage fördert. Er schafft so die Voraussetzungen dafür, dass wir den konstitutiven Bezug der Außenwelt zur Zwangsarbeit im Gefängnis, die in ihr wirkenden psychoökonomischen Mechanismen und die Bedeutung von Bildern oder Spektakeln in diesem Kontext besser

verstehen. Nicht zuletzt bezieht er gerade diejenigen Menschen, die solchen Mechanismen unterworfen werden, in die schwierige Arbeit der Erfindung subversiver Produktionsprozesse und irritierender Gegenbilder mit ein.

Zehn Jahre danach entstand die Arbeit *Muster* (2012). Sie besteht aus drei Episoden oder Kapiteln, die alle am selben Schauplatz, einem ehemaligen Kloster im hessischen Breitenau, aber zu verschiedenen Zeiten spielen: 1945, 1970 und 1994. Die Kapitel überschneiden einander nicht nur am Ort des Klosters, sondern auch in der Installation und Montage von Bild und Ton. 1945 war das ehemalige Kloster ein Konzentrationslager, und seine Befreiung stand unmittelbar bevor; 1970 war es eine Besserungsanstalt für Mädchen, die mit öffentlichen Protesten und Aufruhr zu kämpfen hatte; seit Ende der 1970er Jahre ist es ein Museum und eine Gedenkstätte. *Muster* wurde im und um das heutige Museum gefilmt. Zwei der Kapitel handeln davon, dass ein Film gedreht wird: 1945 von einer Fotografin im Dienst der Alliierten über das Konzentrationslager, 1970 von einigen Dokumentarfilmern über die Besserungsanstalt. Die erste Szene knüpft an die Filme der Alliierten von 1945 an, in denen die Befreiung der Konzentrationslager festgehalten wurden, die zweite an ein 1970 von Ulrike Meinhof in Breitenau recherchiertes und in Berlin gedrehtes Fernsehspiel namens *Bambule*. Angesichts all dieser Szenen von Filmaufnahmen beginnt *Muster* mit einer Frage: Was heißt es für diesen Ort und für die gesellschaftlichen Verhältnisse, die er hervor- und unterbringt, wenn er gefilmt wird – insbesondere da diese Verhältnisse allesamt mit Unterdrückung und Befreiung, Überwachung und Zwangsarbeit, Darstellung und Erinnerung, Lernen und Lehren zu tun haben?[1]

Aus der Geschichte von Breitenau ergibt sich, dass das hier eingerichtete nationalsozialistische Konzentrationslager Teil einer hundertjährigen Geschichte wechselnder Zwangsanstalten war.[2] Von 1874 bis 1949 diente das Gebäude als „Besserungsanstalt" für „Arbeitsscheue", in erster Linie Landstreicher, Bettler und Prostituierte. Naturgemäß dienten Einrichtungen wie Breitenau weniger der „Besserung", als der Abschreckung und Vergeltung. Sie gehörten zu einem staatlichen Apparat mit dem Ziel, Armut zu kriminalisieren und zu bestrafen. Die Anfänge von Breitenau als „Korrektions- und Landarmenanstalt" gingen auf ein Gesetz von 1871 zurück, das „verwahrloste" Personen auf Gemeindeebene im neu geschaffenen Nationalstaat der Zwangsarbeit unterstellte. Sie mussten teilweise sechs Tage in der Woche täglich zwölf Stunden arbeiten, entweder in den von der Anstalt selbst betriebenen Werkstätten, oder auf den umliegenden Bauernhöfen und in Betrieben, die ihre Arbeitskraft für wenig Geld von der Anstalt leihen konnten. Die Insassen verließen das Gebäude jeden Morgen in Häftlings-uniformen und unter strenger Bewachung. Mit anderen Worten: Gerade das, was uns heute an den Vorbereitungen für den Völkermord nach 1933 mit am meisten empört, war für die Breitenauer ein alltäglicher Anblick. Neben der Indoktrination der Nazis – das jedenfalls legt die Geschichte von Breitenau nahe – könnte die damalige Gleich-gültigkeit der Bevölkerung angesichts von KZ-Häftlingen, die zu den Stätten der Zwangsarbeit außerhalb des Lagers getrieben wurden, auch damit zu tun haben, dass Zwangsarbeit als solche in ihren Augen etwas Normales war.

Die Befreiung des NS-Konzentrationslagers Breitenau unterbrach die Geschichte des Hauses als „Korrektionsanstalt" nur für kurze Zeit. Die ursprüngliche Institution wurde 1946 wiederher-gestellt, bis 1949 weiter betrieben und direkt anschließend in ein Erziehungsheim für „schwer erziehbare" Mädchen und junge Frauen umge-wandelt. Dieses Erziehungsheim wurde 1973 auf-grund öffentlicher Diskussionen und auf Druck der damaligen anstaltskritischen Heimbewegung geschlossen. Während die Geschichte des Mädchenerziehungsheims in den frühen 1970er Jahren allgemeine Bekanntheit erlangte, trat das Konzentrationslager, das ein Vierteljahrhundert zuvor in dem Gebäude betrieben worden war, erst Ende der 1970er Jahre wieder aus dem Schat-ten des Nachkriegsvergessens.

„Sie hat gesagt, dieser Film ist dann ein Erfolg, wenn die Mädchen diesen Film sehen – nachher im Fernsehen – und ihr Heim anzünden. Dann ist der Film ein politischer Erfolg", erinnert sich Peter Homann, ein ehemaliges Mitglied der RAF, an eine Begegnung mit Ulrike Meinhof.[3] Meinhof war Journalistin und begann 1969 mit der Recherche für eine Radiosendung über das Fürsorgeheim Fuldatal in Guxhagen (Breitenau). Ihr danach ent-standenes Drehbuch *Bambule* verfilmte der Regisseur Eberhard Itzenplitz während Meinhof als RAF-Mitglied in den Untergrund gegangen war. Seine Einstellung zum Inhalt des Films war deutlich konservativer als die der Autorin.[4] *Bambule* erzählt die Geschichte einer Revolte und stellt diese am Ende in einem negativen Licht dar, anstatt sie zu unterstützen. Der Film betont die „menschliche Seite" der Besserungsanstalt (im Widerspruch zu den unmenschlichen Metho-den, die dort praktiziert wurden), und gibt zu verstehen, dass die Mädchen und Frauen letztlich ohne guten Grund revoltierten. Er zeigt sie als unfähig, ein eigenständiges Leben zu führen, und zu unreif, um über ihr eigenes Schicksal zu bestimmen oder wenigstens ihre eigene Lage klar zu erfassen. Am Ende der Geschichte, nach der Szene mit einer Revolte, die als sinnlos dar-gestellt wird, schlägt sich der Film auf die Seite der Staatsmacht in Gestalt eines Polizisten, der die Mädchen mit väterlicher Strenge in die Schranken weist. In diesem Sinne wurde der Fernsehfilm Teil

des Staatsapparats, der die symbolische Ordnung stützte und durch Entmündigung die Repression verschärfte.

„Geht es hier um Rebellion oder Resignation?" fragt eine der Schauspielerinnen in *Muster*. Dieses Kapitel des Films ist ein fiktionales Making-of von *Bambule*, in dem Crew und Darstellerinnen die Aufnahme der Schlussszene mit der Revolte einstudieren. In den Dialogen zwischen Regisseur, Schauspielerinnen und Heiminsassinnen ent-spinnt sich ein dreifaches Drama ausgehend von: den Schwierigkeiten, das Erziehungsheim und das Leben der Mädchen in ihm zu verstehen, den ästhetischen, ethischen und politischen Wider-sprüchen filmischer Darstellung, und den Funkti-onsweisen des Filmapparats als solchem. Die selbstreflexive Form des Filmens im Film ver-weist ebenso wie die beim Dreh zutage tretenden Widersprüche und die Kritik am „Produktions-apparat" auf eine moderne Tradition politischer Filmkunst sowie auf die Ästhetik und den links-intellektuellen Diskurs der 1960er Jahre. In *Muster* scheitert der Film nicht nur an der Ästhetik („der Haftalltag lässt sich im Film nicht wiedergeben") und an politischen Widersprüchen („Ich dachte, der Film soll den Menschen draußen über die Zu-stände hier berichten"), sondern ebenso an den Funktionsweisen des Filmapparats und an den ihm eigenen Machtverhältnissen: Er reproduziert Ver-hältnisse, gegen die er sich eigentlich empören (oder andere zur Empörung treiben) sollte, weil er seine Arbeiterinnen (d.h. die Schauspielerinnen) in eine untergebene Position drängt („Ich verstehe nicht, für wen wir das machen." / „Denk nicht so viel, mach einfach."). Deshalb kann eine der Schau-spielerinnen einen Satz aus dem Drehbuch von Meinhof übernehmen, der sich im Original auf das Mädchenerziehungsheim bezieht, um ihn gegen den Apparat zu wenden: „Fernsehen, verstehste? Wenn sie Dich kaputt gemacht haben, dann freu-en sie sich." Und so könnte sich die Zerstörung der Haftzelle am Ende des Kapitels ebenso gegen die Filmkulisse und den Apparat wie gegen das Erziehungsheim wenden.

Kurz bevor die amerikanischen Truppen in Gux-hagen eintrafen, zwang die Gestapo am Abend des 29. März 1945 einige Insassen des Arbeitserzie-hungslagers in einem nahe gelegenen Wald eine Grube auszuheben. Die übrigen Häftlinge wurden paarweise gefesselt zur Grube getrieben, mit dem Gesicht voran auf den Boden gelegt und erschossen. Die zum Graben gezwungenen Häftlinge mussten nicht nur das Sterben der an-deren mit ansehen, sondern sogar noch einen von ihnen erschlagen, der die Erschießung über-lebt hatte. Im Laufe der Nacht befahl man ihnen, die meisten Akten im Konzentrationslager zu ver-brennen. Diese Ereignisse werden im Film von René B. erzählt, einem französischen Lagerhäft-ling, dessen Zeugenbericht heute in der Gedenk-stätte Breitenau aufbewahrt ist. Dieses Kapitel des Films handelt vom verzweifelten Versuch eines französischen KZ-Häftlings, seinen Befreiern die Geschichte der Erschießungen zu vermitteln – und davon, dass sie ihn am Ende nicht verstehen.

Am Tag der Befreiung des Lagers treffen amerikanische Truppen in Begleitung eines deutsch-englischen Dolmetschers und einer amerikanischen Kriegsfotografin ein (mit Anklängen an ikonische Fotografinnengestalten wie Margaret Bourke-White und Lee Miller). Beider Aufgabe ist es, das Geschehene an Ort und Stelle zu erfassen und es den amerikanischen Soldaten und der Außenwelt zu vermitteln. *Muster* stellt, in den Worten des Künstlers, die ethnografische Erfahrung des „Erstkontakts" dar, bei der ein Dolmetscher, eine Fotografin und die Soldaten auf etwas ihnen Unbekanntes stoßen. Der Dolmetscher bezeichnet Breitenau als eine Anstalt, in der Häftlinge zwangsweise „zur Arbeit erzogen werden" sollten. Somit trifft seine Beschreibung mehr oder weniger auf die Besserungsanstalt aus der Zeit vor 1933 zu. Dann übersetzt der amerikanische Offizier diese Beschreibung als „Sklavenarbeit". Hier ist ein Prozess interkultureller Übersetzung zu beobachten, bei dem unterschiedliche historische Erfahrungen, kulturelle Bezüge und moralische Standpunkte ins Spiel kommen. Selbstverständlich kann dieser Übersetzungsvorgang die Anstalt nicht in ihrer Gesamtheit erfassen. Weder das Wissen um die Nutzung als Besserungsanstalt vor 1933 noch die Erinnerung an die Sklaverei reichen aus, um zu verstehen, wer die befreiten Menschen sind und was ihnen widerfahren ist.

René B., der französische Häftling, leidet an einem schweren Trauma und an Schuldgefühlen infolge seiner Erlebnisse in den Tagen vor der Befreiung. Verzweifelt versucht er, seinen Befreiern über diese Tage zu berichten. Die Schlussszene veranschaulicht emblematisch das endgültige Scheitern allen Verstehens und Vermittelns: In dieser Szene versucht René B., da er sich sprachlich der Fotografin nicht mitteilen kann, in Körpersprache darzustellen, was am Abend und in der Nacht vor der Befreiung geschehen war. Die Fotografin macht Bilder von dem Schauplatz, hat aber offensichtlich keine Ahnung, was sie dokumentiert. Wie der Dolmetscher und die Soldaten verharrt sie an einer Schwelle zum Verständnis, über die sie nicht hinauskommt.

„Warum seid ihr hier?", fragt ein Lehrer seine Schüler während ihres Besuchs in der Gedenkstätte Breitenau. Seine Frage wiederholt wörtlich eine zuvor von einer Schauspielerin bei den Aufnahmen zu *Bambule* gestellte Frage, die sich an die Insassinnen des Erziehungsheims richtete. Im Unterschied dazu ist die Frage des Lehrers eine rein rhetorische und dient dazu, eine vorformulierte Antwort abzurufen. Die Wiederholung deutet darauf hin, dass es eine Ähnlichkeit zwischen den Positionen der Anstaltshäftlinge und der Schüler gibt – dass die Pädagogik, die sich in dieser Frage manifestiert, eine Form von Machtausübung und Unterwerfung ist, selbst wenn sie ihrer eigenen Absicht nach lieber etwas anderes wäre. Jenseits des lokalgeschichtlichen Lehrinhalts und der Erinnerung an den Holocaust soll der Besuch auch zu einer Befreiung vom Trauma führen, denn „die Traumatisierung der Großeltern wird über Generationen weiter vererbt." Der Lehrer verkörpert die Generation von 1968 und ihren Aufstand gegen die Väter, gegen deren manische Abwehrmechanismen und die „Unfähigkeit zu trauern"[5]. Die Schüler gehören einer dritten Generation an und lassen bei ihrem Besuch der Gedenkstätte deutliche Anzeichen von „Holocaustmüdigkeit" erkennen. Bis zur Schlussszene dieses Kapitels scheint es so, als könne die vom Lehrer angewendete Pädagogik ihren Überdruss nicht vertreiben, sondern nur verstärken, so dass eine reale Begegnung mit dem Ort und eine Einsicht, selbst Teil dieser Geschichte zu sein, von vornherein ausgeschlossen wäre.

Im dritten Kapitel des Films hört man immer wieder die Musik der örtlichen Rockband Die Fremden, und die Schlussszene wechselt zum Schauplatz eines ihrer Konzerte. Die Musik der Band steht in diesem Kapitel für eine Flucht oder alternative Welt, in die sich die Schüler mit ihren tragbaren Kassettenrekordern flüchten. Doch am Ende erweisen sich die Lieder dieser Band als eine kulturelle Praxis, die tatsächlich etwas von der Alltagserfahrung dieser Jugendlichen, von der deutschen Gesellschaft nach dem Wirtschaftswunder und von der Welt generationenübergreifender Traumata erzählt. Alle in dem Film verwendeten Songs sind ausdrucksvoll insofern, als sie von der Unwirtlichkeit des Ortes Breitenau in Hessen handeln. Die letzten Bilder des Films vermitteln, dass jugendliche Subkultur viele verschiedene Elemente beinhaltet: die Grunderfahrung der Unwirtlichkeit, Momente intensiver sinnlicher Erlebnisse und Exzesse, aber auch die Artikulation verdrängter Traumata. Und gerade die Musik bringt Gefühle zum Ausdruck, die ohne sie unter der Oberfläche der Ermattung unartikuliert blieben.

Nach ihrem Rundgang durch das Gebäude lässt der Lehrer die völlig erschöpften Schüler im ehemaligen Klostergarten den Bericht von René B. über die letzten Tage des Konzentrationslagers, die Erschießungen und das Massengrab lesen. Als es dunkel wird, gelangt die Schülergruppe zu dem Wald in der Nähe mit dem Grab. Parallel dazu sieht man auf dem anderen Bildschirm mit dem zweiten Kapitel einen Häftling, der in der Dunkelheit denselben Weg nimmt. Da es ihm nicht gelungen ist, den Befreiern vom Trauma *dieser* Nacht zu erzählen, versucht er, sich ihm allein zu stellen. Der Gang der Schülergruppe durch den Wald folgt seinem einsamen Weg. Über den Erinnerungsdiskurs des Museums und

der Pädagogik hinaus-, aber auch von ihm ausgehend finden die Schüler im Wald die stummen
Zeichen des Traumas, die Umrisse des recht-
eckigen Massengrabs, den Abdruck des einstigen
Verbrechens. Die Erfahrung des historischen
Traumas, das sie am Ende vielleicht noch nach-
vollziehen könnten, findet außerhalb der Gedenkstätte und des pädagogischen Raums statt,
der schon mit Vorschriften und Lehrinhalten ausgefüllt ist. Dennoch bleibt dies keine Erfahrung
ohne Worte, denn es ist der Bericht von René B.,
der die Schüler leitet.

Muster lässt uns Verbindungen zwischen drei
verschiedenen Geschichten entdecken, die sich
auf denselben Ort beziehen, ohne dabei die Unter-
schiede zu verwischen: So kann der Betrachter in den Kapiteln 1945, 1970 und 1994 Szenen
des ethnografischen Erstkontakts wiedererkennen,
ebenso wie wiederkehrende Muster der Verdrängung, des Unbehagens im Verstehen und
Darstellen sowie der ausweglosen Befreiung.
Wir sehen in dieser Filminstallation drei Szenen
der Erstbegegnung mit einem Ort, dessen
Identität sich im Laufe der Zeit ändert, während
er zugleich räumliche Kontinuität für das Verknüpfen verschiedener Geschichten von der
(versuchten) Befreiung bewahrt.

1   Eine ausführlichere Darstellung zu *Muster* findet sich in Zoltán
    Kékesi: *Agents of Liberation*. Budapest / New York: CEU Press, 2015,
    S. 189–204.
2   Vgl. Wolfgang Ayaß: *Das Arbeitshaus Breitenau*, Kassel: Jenior
    und Pressler, 1992.; Gunnar Richter: *Das Arbeitserziehungslager
    Breitenau*, Kassel: Winfried Jenior, 2009.
3   *Der Baader-Meinhof Komplex*, Regie: Uli Edel, BRD 2008.
4   Vgl. das ursprüngliche, im Rahmen des Projekts veröffentlichte
    Drehbuch: *Bambule: The Script / das Regiebuch*, Ostfildern:
    Hatje Cantz, 2012.
5   Alexander und Margarete Mitscherlich: *Die Unfähigkeit zu trauern*,
    München: Pieper, 1967.

BEYOND OCCUPATION

ON CLEMENS VON WEDEMEYER'S
BIG BUSINESS AND *RUSHES*

Zoltán Kékesi

In Clemens von Wedemeyer's *Occupation* (2002), a film crew is shooting a large crowd gathering. What we see is the making of a protest scene, but the title does not refer so much to the mass as it is occupying a place; rather, to the film apparatus as it is occupying a terrain and the world of social relations. In *Occupation*, producing an image of protest comes as an act near to oppression: The making of the scene subordinates the extras to the hierarchical relation of being directed; a relation enacted through language and mediated through technologies of seeing, commanding, and making seen. Under the blinding light and amplified sound of the film set, the extras act as a confused mass of people, controlled by the apparatus of film making. *Occupation* is a film about the making of a film, and about filmmaking as an occupation, or profession. Implying "occupation" in both senses: profession and power, it is a reflection on the profession of film or art making, and more generally on practising a profession in its relation to exercising power. Practising a profession implies and establishes social relations, and *Occupation* shows these relations as structured by power. Of course, in another sense, cinematic images occupy our very mind. In that sense, the cinematic occupation of social relations, as presented in Clemens von Wedemeyer's film, involves the spectators as well. One of his later works, *Rushes* (2012), as well as *Big Business* (2002) would respond to these concerns raised about protest and power, cinema, images, art, and profession. Both of them were made at places that present particular sites of social relations. What does it mean, in each particular context, to produce cinematic images that go beyond the logic of "occupation"?

In 2002, Clemens von Wedemeyer made a remake of Stan Laurel's and Oliver Hardy's *Big Business* (1929), with the inmates of a prison. The site of the remake is an "idyll," provided by the penal facility in Waldheim in Saxony, Germany.

In their classic slapstick comedy, Laurel and Hardy appear as Christmas tree salesmen, who on a sunny summer day try to sell a tree to the owner of a suburban house. After the man rejects them, a conflict evolves, resulting in the destruction of the house and of the two salesmen's car. The site of the remake is a prison where inmates construct, as a part of their penalty, life-sized houses by building, demolishing, and then rebuilding again. By shooting a remake of the slapstick, the artist, too, makes them build and demolish a house. What does it mean to work at a site of forced labour, with people subordinated to it? The making of the film reproduces the situation that the inmates experience in their everyday life in the prison, but turns coercion into the experience of performing roles and co-creating the remake. Inmates were both the cast and the crew of the film; the ethics of making *Big Business* consisted in, on the one hand, helping them overcome coercion and to immerse into the process of creation. On the other hand, it consisted of creating images that deal with the place and the social relations it produces and presupposes. In the process of creating the remake, both the classic comedy and its re-enactment take on complex meanings.

The remake *Big Business* is certainly not a comedy—destruction, the main source of humour in the original, soon becomes unsettling in the remake. This unsettling effect comes partly from the fact that the model of the house, constructed for the remake and demolished in the course of its making, is an image, and it cannot be clearly determined what it really represents. Indeed, it seems to refer to many things: to the house that appears in the original sequences; to the houses that the inmates construct and demolish in the workshops of the prison and to the normalcy of everyday life that the inmates are deprived of. This makes us understand that forced labour in the prison is a form of punishment that requires the inmates to make and unmake something that represents a life they don't have. That is, it forces them to re-enact again and again their own separation and deprivation. On the other hand, the house represents an "idyll," as *The Making of Big Business* calls it, it stands for the desires that drive and regulate our life day in, day out. In this sense, the houses built in the prison refer to the social order that institutes the prison itself. In this regard, destruction may appear as an act of aggression, directed against the symbolic substitution of the outside. However, it is more complicated than that. The prison, says the artist in *The Making of Big Business*, is a "place of suppression" and not only because it forces inmates to suppress their needs and desires. *Big Business* demonstrates something more complex and unsettling: The houses built and demolished in the prison represent the unattainable objects of our own social desires. In this regard, forced labour in the prison is both physical and psychological, and it does not only consist of having to re-experience one's own unfulfilled needs, but the desires of others as well. Forcing the inmates to build and demolish houses is cruel because it seems to be a senseless job; however its real cruelty lies in the fact that it is not senseless, or meaningless. The prison is a "place of suppression" because through it, our societies can suppress and delegate the work to the inmates to enact and experience the social trauma resulting from our unattainable objects of desire. Clemens von Wedemeyer's *Big Business* is unsettling because it conjures up all these different layers of social, institutional, psycho-economic and symbolic mechanisms. Thus, it opens up for us the possibility to understand the constitutive relation of the outside world to forced labour inside the prison, the psycho-economic mechanisms that regulate it, and the role of images or spectacles therein. Ultimately, it involves people subjected to these mechanisms in the difficult work of creating subversive production processes and unsettling counter-images.

In *Rushes*, made a decade later in 2012, three stories unfold, all on the same site, in a former monastery, in Breitenau in Hessen, Germany. The stories occur in different ages, in 1945, 1970, and 1994, but all three meet in the space of the monastery, and intersect in the film through the editing of image and sound. In 1945, the monastery was a Nazi concentration camp, soon to be liberated; in 1970, a reformatory for girls, then facing protests and riots; and since the late 1970s, it has been a museum and memorial site. In *Rushes*, made in and around the present-day museum, one sees two scenes of making a film: in 1945, there is a film being shot about the concentration camp by a photographer working for the Allied army, and in 1970, a group of social documentarists are making a film about the reformatory. The former alludes to films made by the Allied army in 1945, documenting the liberated concentration camps. The latter refers to a television play entitled *Bambule*, written by Ulrike Meinhof and produced in Berlin in 1970. For all these scenes of making a film, *Rushes* opens up

the question: What does it mean for the place and the social relations it creates and accommodates to be filmed? These social relations are structured around repression and liberation, surveillance and forced labour, representation and remembrance, learning and teaching.[1]

By looking at the history of Breitenau, one understands that the Nazi concentration camp that functioned there was part of a century-long history of repressive institutions.[2] From 1874 to 1949, the building functioned as a "house of correction" for those "unwilling to work", first and foremost for the homeless, beggars, and prostitutes. Of course, institutions such as Breitenau were not so much "correctional" as deterrent and retaliatory: they were part of a state apparatus that aimed at criminalising and punishing poverty. The inception of Breitenau as a "house of correction" followed the passing of a law in 1871 that made individuals defined as "asocial" punishable on the supra-regional scale of the newly established nation-state. Those "to be corrected" were put to work six days a week and for twelve hours each day, not only in the workshops operated by the institution itself held on the grounds of Breitenau, but also at local farms and companies who contracted out their cheap work force from the institution. Inmates left the building each day in prison uniforms under strict control as forced workers. This means that for those who lived in the neighbourhood, it became a normal and everyday scene what for us today is one of the scandals of the genocide after 1933. The history of Breitenau suggests to us that, in addition to Nazi indoctrination, another element might have effected the indifference of the population looking at inmates of the concentration camps being driven each day to sites of forced labour outside of the camps: the normality of forced labour.

The liberation of the Nazi concentration camp established in Breitenau meant only a short interruption in the history of the "house of correction." The old institution was re-established in 1946 and run until 1949, only to be transformed into a reformatory for "hard educable" girls. The reformatory was closed in 1973 due to public discussions and to the protest movement of the time (the so-called *Heimbewegung*). While the story of the girls reformatory became widely known by the early 1970s, the concentration camp that operated in the building a quarter of a century before, emerged from the shadow of post-war oblivion only in the late 1970s.

"She told me this film would be successful only if the girls, having watched it on television, set the reformatories on fire," recalls Peter Homann, a former member of the RAF, about an encounter with Ulrike Meinhof.[3] Meinhof, who was working as a journalist, did research for a broadcast in the Breitenau reformatory in 1969. It was Eberhard

Itzenplitz, who directed the film *Bambule*, after Meinhof went underground as a member of the RAF. His views about the film were far less radical than those formulated by Meinhof in her script that was the result of her research.[4] The film *Bambule* tells the story of a riot and at the end it shows it in a negative light, instead of supporting it. The television film does show something about the circumstances under which girls in the reformatory lived, but in the end it shows the riot that erupts in the reformatory in a negative light. It emphasises the "human aspect" of the reformatory (in contrast to the inhuman methods used there), and suggests that the girls, after all, revolted for no reason. According to the television film, they are unable to lead independent lives and are too immature to decide on their own fate or even to clearly understand their own situation. At the end of the story, after a riot scene is presented as senseless, the film re-enforces the power of the state through the figure of a policeman who paternally rebukes the girls of the institution. In this sense the television film was part of the state apparatus that maintained the symbolic order: through paternalisation, it re-enforced oppression.

"Well, are we dealing with rebellion or with resignation?" asks one of the actresses in *Rushes*. This chapter of the film is a fictional "Making of *Bambule*", in which the film crew is preparing the shooting of the final scene of the film, the riot. In the dialogues between the director, the actresses, and the inmates, a threefold drama plays out, concerning the difficulties of understanding the reformatory and the life of the girls; the aesthetic, ethical, and political dilemmas of filmic representation; and the functioning of the filmic apparatus itself. The self-reflexive form of a shooting-in-the-film as much as the dilemmas articulated during the shooting and, finally, the critique of the "productive apparatus", all refer to the modernist tradition of political filmmaking, the aesthetics and leftist-intellectual discourse of the 1960s. In *Rushes*, the failure of the shooting lies not only in the aesthetic ("daily life in detention can't be reproduced in film") and political dilemmas ("I thought the film aims to tell people outside about conditions in here"), but in the functioning of the film apparatus as well and its inherent power relations: it reproduces the power relations against which it ought to (make others) revolt, because it places the workers (that is, the actresses) into a subordinated position ("I don't get who we're doing this for." / "Don't think! Just do it."). This is why one of the actresses can use a sentence from Meinhof's script, originally referring to the girls reformatory itself, to oppose the apparatus: "Television, get it? They'll be glad to break you in." Thus, the destruction of the prison cell at the end of the chapter might be as much aimed against the film set and the apparatus as against the reformatory.

On the evening of March 29, 1945, shortly before American troops reached the village, the Gestapo forced some of the deportees to dig a pit in the nearby forest. The remaining deportees in the camp were tied together in pairs, driven to the pit, laid face down on the ground and shot. The deportees assigned to dig the pit were not only forced to witness the death of the others, but also to beat to death one who had survived the shooting. During the night, they were ordered to burn most of the documents in the concentration camp. These events are narrated in the film by René B., a French deportee whose testimony is today kept at the Breitenau museum. This chapter of the film is about the desperate attempt of the French deportee to tell the story of the shooting to his liberators and, in the end, about their failure to understand it.

On the day of the liberation of the camp, American troops reached Breitenau accompanied by a German-English interpreter and an American war photographer (with reference to such iconic photographers as Margaret Bourke-White and Lee Miller). Their task is to understand the place and mediate it, both to the American soldiers and to the outside world. *Rushes* depicts the anthropological experience of "first contact", as the artist says, in which the interpreter, the photographer, and the soldiers encounter something hitherto unknown to them. The interpreter describes Breitenau as a place where inmates are assigned to forced labour in order to "educate them to work." Therefore, his description conforms to the pre-1933 form of a correctional facility. Then, the American officer translates this description as "slave labour". What one sees in this sequence is a process of intercultural translation that brings into play different historical experiences, cultural references and moral standpoints. Of course, this process of translation cannot capture the place completely: neither the schemes from before 1933 nor the memory of slavery suffice to help them understand who the people they liberated are and what has been happening to them.

René B., the French deportee, suffers a deep trauma and a severe sense of guilt as a result of what happened in the days before the liberation. He desperately tries to tell his liberators the story of those days. The closing scene shows emblematically the final failure of understanding and mediating: In this scene, having no common language with the photographer, he attempts to explain through body language what happened on the evening and night before the liberation. While taking pictures of the scene, the photographer obviously has no idea what she is documenting. The photographer, the interpreter, and the soldiers are all standing at the threshold of understanding, which they cannot cross.

"Why are you in here?" asks the teacher of his pupils during their visit to the Breitenau memorial site. His question repeats word by word an earlier one, posed by an actress during the shooting of *Bambule* and addressed to the inmates of the reformatory. In contrast to it, the teacher's question is merely rhetorical, intended to receive a pre-formulated answer. The repetition suggests that there is a similarity in the position of the inmates of the reformatory and the pupils: it suggests that the educational concept that manifests itself in the question is a practice of power and subordination — even if, according to its intention, it would like to be something else. Beyond the lesson in regional history and Holocaust memory, the visit should lead to a relief from traumata, because "the way the grandparents were traumatised is perpetuated over generations". The teacher embodies the generation of 1968 that revolted against the generation of the fathers, against the manic defense mechanisms and the "inability to mourn".[5] As opposed to him, the pupils belong to the third generation who, during their visit at the memorial site, show clear signs of suffering from "Holocaust fatigue". Up until the final scene of the chapter it seems that the teacher's educational method cannot relieve this fatigue, but rather reinforces it, so that a real encounter with the place and the recognition of being involved in the story it tells both seem to be doomed to failure.

During the third chapter one hears the music of a local rock band, Die Fremden, and the closing scene finally changes to the images of a concert. The music of the band appears again and again during the chapter as an escape or an alternative world into which the pupils immerse with their portable tape players. But at the end, the songs of the rock band turn out to be a cultural practice that succeeds in speaking about the everyday experiences of the youths, about German society after the *Wirtschaftswunder* and about the world of transgenerational traumata. All of the songs that are used in the film are telling in as much as they all refer to the unhomeliness of the space, Breitenau, Hessen, Germany. The closing images of the film suggest that youth subculture includes many different elements: the fundamental experience of unhomeliness, moments of strong sensual experience and excess, and the articulation of repressed traumata. It is precisely the music that can articulate feelings that would otherwise remain unarticulated beneath the surface of fatigue.

After their tour inside the building, in the garden of the former monastery, the teacher makes the fully exhausted pupils read the testimony of René B. about the last days of the concentration camp, the shooting and the mass grave. By nightfall, the school group approaches the nearby forest to find the grave. Parallel to it, on the screen showing the second chapter one sees a deportee as he is setting off in the darkness on the same route. After having failed to relate to the liberators the trauma of *that* night, a deportee is trying to face it alone. The way of the school group in the forest follows his lonely path. Beyond the memory discourse of the museum and the educational lesson, but starting from there, in the forest they find the mute sign of the trauma, the square-shaped trace of the pit, the imprint of the one-time crime. The experience of the historical trauma that they might finally go through takes place outside of the space of commemoration and educational methods already filled with prescriptions and lessons. Nonetheless, this experience is not without words, since it is the testimony of René B. that leads them.

Rushes enables the viewer to discover connections between three different stories that relate to the same site, without effacing their differences: thus, the viewer discovers the repetition of the scene of an anthropological "first contact" in 1945, 1970, and 1994, as well as the repeating schemes of repression, the uneasiness of understanding and representation, and the aporia of liberation. What we see while watching the film installation is three first-contact scenes with a place whose identity does not remain the same in the course of time, but provides a spatial continuity for interconnections between different stories of (attempts at) liberation.

1   For a detailed presentation of *Rushes* see Zoltán Kékesi: *Agents of Liberation*. Budapest / New York: CEU Press, 2015, pp. 189–204.
2   See Wolfgang Ayaß: *Das Arbeitshaus Breitenau*, Kassel: Jenior und Pressler, 1992.; Gunnar Richter: *Das Arbeitserziehungslager Breitenau*, Kassel: Winfried Jenior, 2009.
3   *Der Baader-Meinhof Komplex*, directed by Uli Edel, Germany, 2008.
4   See the original film script, published as part of the project: *Bambule: The Script / das Regiebuch*, Ostfildern: Hatje Cantz, 2012.
5   Alexander Mitscherlich, Margarete Mitscherlich: *Die Unfähigkeit zu trauern*. Munich: Pieper, 1967.

THE MAKING OF BIG BUSINESS

Clemens von Wedemeyer

Wir sind ein Filmteam und produzieren mit Gefangenen einen Film: Stan Laurel und Oliver Hardy geraten in einen Streit mit James Finlayson, in dessen Verlauf ein Haus und ein Auto wechselseitig zerstört werden.

Die Gefängnisleitung stellt uns für die Dreharbeiten eine Idylle zur Verfügung: Das Filmteam und neun Gefangene befinden sich Ende August zwischen dem alten Gefängnistrakt und der Außenmauer des Knasts, zwischen streng angepflanzten Blumen und niedlichen Häuschen, die von den Gefangenen als Arbeitsmaßnahme aufgebaut wurden.

Der Stummfilm *Das große Geschäft* (1929) von Stan Laurel und Oliver Hardy wurde in den USA produziert: Zwei junge Typen, man könnte sie Jungunternehmer nennen, wollen einen Tannenbaum im Sommer verkaufen. Ein Streit entfacht an der Unwilligkeit des Kunden, einen Tannenbaum im Sommer zu erwerben. Sein Haus und das Auto der beiden Verkäufer gehen zu Bruch.

AUTOMOBIL

Ein Auto wird von einem Gericht beschlagnahmt und für uns bereitgestellt. In der Justizvollzugsanstalt Torgau wird es von Gefangenen präpariert und mit einem Lkw nach Waldheim transportiert. Dabei befindet sich eine Gebrauchsanweisung, wie man es am besten zerlegt.

IDYLLE

Ein Haus wird gebaut und angestrichen. Ein Klavier in das Gefängnis gebracht. Ein Gefangener liest aus Pasolinis Buch *Accattone*:

„,Für Accattone und seine Kumpels ist jeder, der arbeitet, ein Verräter.' – Schon alleine der Satz, da würde ich das Buch schon lesen. ,Sie selbst leben von Zuhälterei und Diebstahl. Selbst als sich Accattone zum ersten Mal in seinem Leben richtig verliebt, schickt er das Mädchen auf den Strich. Doch Stella, Tochter einer Hure, eignet sich nicht für dieses Gewerbe, und so sucht sich Accattone ebenfalls zum ersten Mal in seinem

Leben eine Arbeit, der er jedoch körperlich nicht gewachsen ist.' – Das klingt auf jeden Fall nach einem Lebemann. Mir geht's auch immer so. Gibt's da einen Film von?"

A

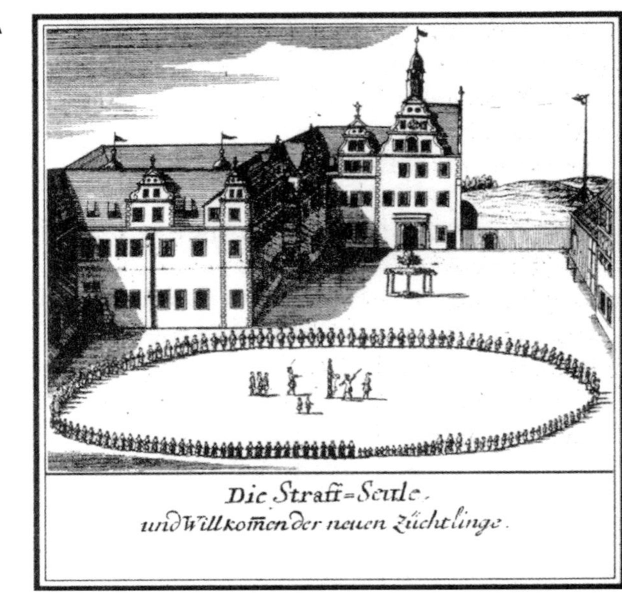

DAS SCHLOSS

Die Justizvollzugsanstalt Waldheim wird signifikant geprägt durch ihre Errichtung unter Ausnutzung der baulichen Gegebenheiten des ehemaligen Waldheimer Schlosses. Die Entstehungsgeschichte des Schlosses soll bis in die Zeit um 1200 zurückreichen, wobei es im Jahr 1271 erstmals urkundlich erwähnt wird. Im Jahr 1404 wurde im Schloss ein Augustinerkloster eingerichtet und mit der Reformation wieder aufgelöst. Im Jahr 1716 begann für das Schloss eine neue Periode. Der sächsische Kurfürst August II. ließ in den Baulichkeiten das „Zucht-, Waisen- und Armenhaus zu Waldheim" errichten. Bereits 1716 befanden sich 181 Personen im Zuchthaus. Die Justizvollzugsanstalt Waldheim dient heute dem Vollzug von Freiheitsstrafen an männlichen Verurteilten.

In einem der Betriebe werden Gefangene damit beschäftigt, Häuser aufzubauen und sie nach getaner Arbeit wieder abzureißen. Als wir die Halle besuchen, die direkt hinter unserem

Filmset liegt, wird gerade an einer Musterzelle für den neuen Gefängnistrakt gearbeitet. Erprobt werden soll hier, welche Möbel in einen acht Quadratmeter kleinen Raum passen. Die ganze Arbeit läuft nach dem alten Arbeitsschema, den Prinzipien der Industrie. Der Gefängnisdirektor erklärt den Tagesablauf eines normalen Gefangenen:

„Der Gefangene wird circa um 6 Uhr morgens geweckt, wäscht sich, putzt sich die Zähne, frühstückt. Um 6 Uhr 45 wird er zur Arbeit abgeholt, begibt sich dann mit den anderen, die zum selben Betrieb gehören, aus dem Haftbereich in den Arbeitsbereich. Da gibt es dann die Anweisungen, was den Tag über zu tun ist. Der Gefangene arbeitet, wie draußen auch. Dann gibt es eine Mittagspause; die findet, abhängig, in welchem Betrieb der Gefangene ist, zu unterschiedlichen Zeiten statt, aber in der Regel so um 11 Uhr 30. Um 12 Uhr oder 12 Uhr 15 geht es weiter mit der Arbeit. Um – ja, das hängt auch vom Betrieb ab, aber in der Regel so um 15 bis 16 Uhr ist der Gefangene dann mit der Arbeit fertig, und er wird wieder von dem Arbeitsbereich in den Haftbereich gebracht. Im Anschluss beginnen dann die Freizeitmöglichkeiten.

Der Gefangene hat, abhängig davon, wo er einsitzt, auf jeden Fall die Möglichkeit, am Tag eine Stunde am Hofgang teilzunehmen. Es finden umfangreiche Behandlungsmaßnahmen statt. Abhängig davon, was der Gefangene gemacht hat, ist es sinnvoll, wenn er zum Beispiel an einem Anti-Gewalt-Training teilnimmt, an der Wahrnehmungsgruppe, am Selbstsicherheitstraining, am sozialen Training – und es gibt dann noch vielfältige andere Behandlungsmaßnahmen. Darüber hinaus gibt es auch viele Freizeitmaßnahmen. Gerade Sport ist den Gefangenen sehr wichtig, und ich denke, das ist auch eine vernünftige Sache. Gerade wenn man hier auch so unter einem fast notwendigen Druck steht, weil so viele Menschen die ganze Zeit um einen herum sind und das Zusammenleben ja nicht immer nur harmonisch ist – also es gibt sehr viele Sportmöglichkeiten. Es gibt für die vielleicht intellektuell etwas anspruchsvolleren Gefangenen Möglichkeiten, an Literaturzirkeln oder Ähnlichem teilzunehmen.“

Wir bauen das Haus auf und kümmern uns um das Auto. Nach einer Woche, in denen die Arbeit in der Sonne begleitet wird von Pasolini und Foucault…

„Die meisten sind hier drin, weil sie aus irgendeiner wirtschaftlichen Notsituation heraus eine Straftat begangen haben. Wenn man sich das mal überlegt, was mit denen veranstaltet wird, das ist eigentlich schlimm. ‚Was für einen Platz braucht der Mensch mindestens, was für eine Architektur?‘ Ich denke mal, Architektur ist unwichtig und

mindestens, da weiß ich auch nicht, wie ich das beantworten soll. Ich brauche einen Platz, an dem ich mich zu Hause fühle.“

B

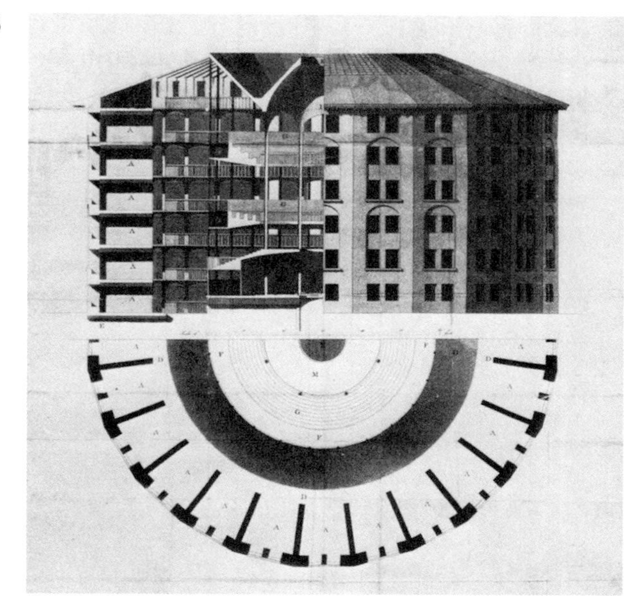

BAUSTELLE

„Normalerweise ist das hier von der Größe her eine Einzelzelle – es sind acht Quadratmeter – und die stehen einem alleine eigentlich zu. Ja, vom Gesetz her, aber es geht ja eigentlich nicht um die Quadratmeterfläche, sondern um die Kubikmeterfläche. – Also, Raum, Luft, was weiß ich – und da aber nicht genug Haftplätze vorhanden waren beziehungsweise sind …“

„Wie viel Quadratmeter sind das?“

„Quadratmeter? Acht – Du siehst ja selbst, es ist also zwei Meter breit und vier Meter lang. Und mit den ganzen Möbeln darin ist es natürlich sehr eng. Ja, also viel Platz bleibt nicht. In einem Neubau wie zum Beispiel in Dresden ist es penibel, übersichtlich, fest angeschraubt, dort ist also der Tisch fest angeschraubt, das Bett fest angeschraubt, Schränke beziehungsweise Regale alles fest, man kann nichts bewegen. Man kann nicht wie hier ein Bild an der Wand aufhängen, sondern es gibt eine Bilderleiste, und nur an dieser Leiste dürfen Bilder befestigt werden, und die müssen so befestigt werden, dass man auch dahinter gucken kann. Ja, die dürfen also nur oben befestigt werden und müssen frei hängen.

Dann darf man nur – laut Vorschrift darf man nur zehn Briefe auf der Zelle haben, ja, wenn man mehr Post bekommt, muss man die regelmäßig zu seiner Habe auf die Kammer schaffen. Man darf nur 20 Tonträger haben auf der Zelle – also Kassetten, CDs oder Computerspielkassetten, eh' CDs – und man darf nur drei Pflanzen besitzen und diese Pflanzen dürfen höchstens 30 cm hoch sein. Die Außenwand muss immer komplett frei sein, es darf nichts auf der Fensterbank stehen, ja, und das widerspricht eigentlich dem Gesetz – laut Gesetz ist die Zelle eigentlich dein, – wie soll ich sagen … nicht dein Eigentum, aber dort kannst du dich eigentlich zurückziehen, ja, und nur wenn irgendwo ein begründeter Verdacht ist, dann soll diese Zelle durchsucht werden. Aber die Praxis ist eine ganz andere – dort werden also willkürlich Zellenkontrollen gemacht, und im Grunde genommen fast täglich, ja, in Bautzen ist es zum Beispiel so, da geht also regelmäßig der Anstaltsleiter persönlich Zellenkontrollen machen, und wenn der eine Pflanze sieht, die über 30 cm hoch ist, dann nimmt der 'ne Schere und schneidet sie ab. Und wenn man vier Pflanzen hat, dann ist eine weg, wenn man nachmittags von der Arbeit zurück auf die Zelle kommt."

C

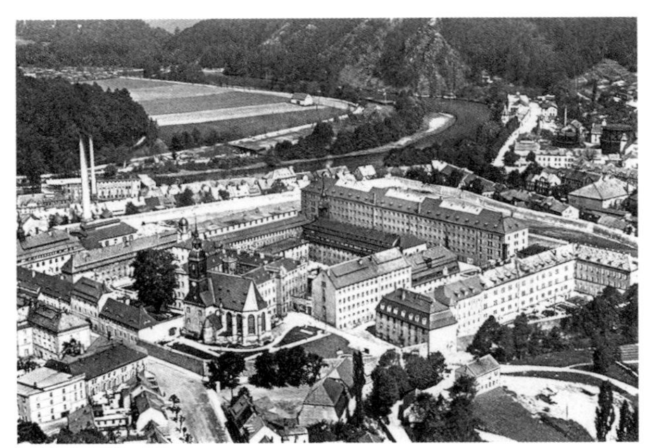

Die Justizvollzugsbeamten halten sich auf Abstand. Sie geben uns kein Interview. Zu schwierig ist die Situation zwischen dem Leben draußen und dem konzentrierten, unterschiedlichen Leben im Gefängnis, wo man eine Rolle zu spielen hat. Von weitem betrachten sie uns und ebenso die Gefangenen skeptisch. Sie geben uns wissende Tipps im Umgang mit den Gefangenen, die sie zu durchschauen glauben. In Wahrheit verstehen sie sie genauso wenig. Sie kontrollieren das Leben, das sie selber nicht verstehen. Ständig werden wir beobachtet. Wer schaut wann nicht zu? Später nehmen wir zaghafte Annäherungsversuche der Beobachter wahr.

Innerhalb der Anstalt nehmen wir eine Ausnahmestellung ein. Zu den Gefangenen wie zur Verwaltung ist die Beziehung abweichend vom Alltag, in dem wenig Kommunikation mit den sogenannten Freien stattfindet. Man lässt uns handeln; wir sperren eine wichtige Zufahrtsstraße im Gefängnis ab, während wir Haus und Auto kaputtmachen. Wir schaffen eine Situation, die ungewohnt ist und die nichts verändert. Alles müsste von Grund auf neu gedacht werden, aber wir sind dazu nicht in der Lage. Wir geben uns und den Gefangenen eine Woche Sonne und im Gegenzug benutzt uns die Gefängnisverwaltung: Für den Gefängnisdirektor und die Verantwortlichen im Ministerium der Justiz kann dieses Projekt eine Steigerung ihrer Souveränität bedeuten. Denn wenn der Direktor mit dem Außen in Kontakt treten und dabei den Vollzug im Inneren aufrechterhalten kann, entscheidet er über Ausnahmen, und damit über den Normalfall.

Gefängnisdirektor: „Bei der Entscheidung, im Einzelnen, also Ihnen – ausnahmsweise – zu gestatten, in der Anstalt diese Tätigkeit durchzuführen, hat eine Rolle gespielt, dass wir uns zum einen davon versprochen haben, in vernünftiger und auch geistig anregender Art und Weise Gefangene beschäftigen zu können, dass wir für die Öffentlichkeitsarbeit auch in der Weise etwas tun können, und dass die Sicherheitsbedenken, die man naturgemäß immer hat, wenn jemand von außen in die Anstalt kommt und etwas tut, was vom üblichen Ablauf abweicht, dass die Sicherheitsbedenken nicht so erheblich gewesen sind, dass wir die hinten anstellen konnten."

Das Gefängnis ist ein Experiment. Die Gefangenen sind als Bestrafte im Übrigen dafür verantwortlich, von diesem Experiment und so von den Erfahrungen in ihrer Zelle zu berichten, wenn sie sie verlassen haben. Das Gefängnis driftet in den Bereich der Vorstellung.

Wenn die Bediensteten die Anstalt verlassen, trennen sie das Leben im Gefängnis, ihren Beruf, nach alter Weise von ihrer privaten Welt. Diese Trennung ist so groß wie der Platz, den der Beruf als Bediensteter in seinem Leben einnimmt. Sicher, es gibt Bedienstete, die etwas ins Gefängnis schmuggeln. Sie halten den Warenverkehr aufrecht; die Gefangenen sind ihre Handelspartner und diese sogenannte Beziehung zwischen Verkäufer und Konsumenten ist eine Kompensation anderer, fehlender Kommunikation. Alle halten ihre Ängste aufrecht. Es gibt die zweifache Angst: die Angst vor dem Gefängnis und die Angst vor dem draußen.

Warum auch nicht? Die Bürger wollen ihr Gefängnis als Black Box, als Verdrängungsort stumpfer Probleme genauso erhalten wie als Vorstellungswelt vom anderen Leben. Aber alle Filme über das Gefängnis sind falsch, so wie dieser Film im Übrigen falsch ist. Er ist eine Vermischung von Vorstellungswelten, die über den Bildern liegen. Vielleicht handelt es sich um die Kompensation der Erkenntnis, nichts sagen zu können, was nicht sich selbst entspräche: Das Kino und das Gefängnis funktionieren ähnlich; doch während im Kino Vorstellungen zu Bildern und Charakteren werden, werden im Gefängnis Menschen und ihre Beziehungen zu Vorstellungen. Wobei dieser Ort nicht weniger gefangen ist.

Ein Gefangener liest vor: „Alles brannte. Die blasse Morgensonne des Spätsommertags war wie glühender Kalk. Ein verbranntes Gesicht hob das vorspringende Kinn, mit zwei Höhlen in den Wangen von Magerkeit und mit wässrigem Blick und sprach: Scuccia, gleich geht die Welt unter. Lasst euch mal anschauen. Am Tag habe ich euch ja noch nie gesehen, immer bloß im Dunkeln. Was ist denn, streiken eure Weiber? Und lachte zahnlos.

An wen er sich gewandt hatte? An eine Clique
von Strizzis, die in der Sonne kochten, vor einer
kleinen Bar in Marinella. Unter ihnen war auch
Momoletto, dem erwiderte der Scuccia: Momoletto,
Mensch, lebst du immer noch? Ich hör immer,
Arbeit ist Selbstmord. Momoletto war ein kleiner
Kurzer mit scheelen Augen, der immer wie ein
Hampelmann lachte. Neben ihm ließ sich ein ande-
rer von jemandem Mineralwasser in die hohlen
Hände gießen und wusch sich das Gesicht.
Das war Alfredino, ein langer Lulatsch, schwarz-
haarig mit plattgedrückter Nase eines Marok-
kaners, und Vicietto, ein Teddyboy, hochelegant,
getüpfelter Anzug, große Krawatte mit großem
Knoten und Krawattennadel, dem noch kein Bart
wuchs. Alfredinos ganzes Gesicht, mit den
Händen abgerieben, glänzte vom Mineralwasser.

D

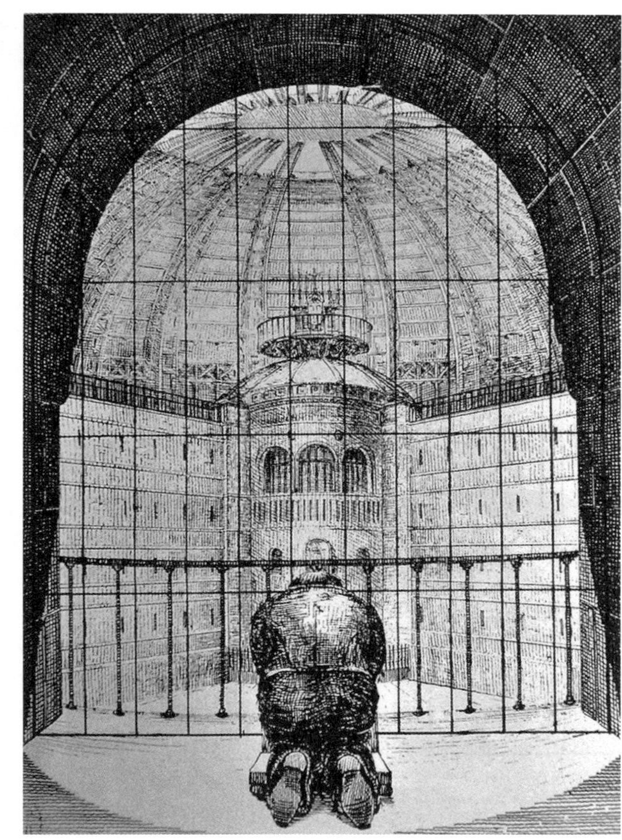

Alfredino. Na, du Märtyrer, hör auf einen Freund,
schmeiß die Arbeit hin, es ruft auch dich der
Metro-Goldwyn-Mayer-Club. Und er riss den Mund
wie einen Gully auf und brüllte, wie der Löwe
von Metro-Goldwyn-Mayer brüllt. Zwei-, dreimal
den lachenden Blick ins Leere gerichtet." Er lacht.
„Das war jetzt eine ganze Seite."

A   Waldheim ist heute das älteste Gefängnis in Deutschland. Historische
Darstellung der Aufnahme neuer Gefangener in der Anstalt, erste
Hälfte des 18. Jahrhunderts.

B   Willey Reveley: „Plan für ein Panopticum von Jeremy Bentham", 1791.
Bentham löst das Überwachungsproblem in der Moderne. Der Turm
im Zentrum des runden Gefängnisses reduziert die Menge der Wärter.

C   Im Bild ist die Errichtung des Gefängnisses auf dem Grundriss eines
ehemaligen Klosters erkennbar. Von 1870 bis 1874 war Karl May im
Gefängnis von Waldheim inhaftiert; 1950 fanden hier die „Waldheimer
Prozesse" statt.

D   Nicolas Philippe Harou-Romain: „Plan für eine Strafanstalt", 1840.
„Ein Häftling verrichtet in seiner Zelle sein Gebet vor dem zentralen
Überwachungsturm."

E   „Die Züchtlinge auf Arbeit", Darstellung des „Armen, Wayßen, Zucht
und Arbeits Hauß" Waldheim mit ehemaligem Augustiner-Kloster und
heutiger evangelischer Anstalts- und Gemeindekirche St. Otto, 1809.

F   Anonym (Sammlung Michel Hennin): „Robert François Damiens lässt
auf einem eisernen Bett liegend die Vernehmung durch zwei Richter
über sich ergehen, 28. März 1757". Nach ihm verschwindet der
Körper als Hauptziel der strafenden Repression aus dem Strafsystem.
Kurz darauf verfasst Léon Faucher ein Reglement „für das Haus
der jungen Gefangenen in Paris": „Der Tag der Häftlinge beginnt um
sechs Uhr morgens…"

G   Ausweglose Kerkervisionen. Giovanni Battista Piranesi: „Der gotische
Bogen", erste Fassung (1751–1754), Platte XIV aus der Serie
„Le Carceri d'Invenzione".

THE MAKING OF BIG BUSINESS

Clemens von Wedemeyer

We are the members of a film crew producing a film together with prisoners: Stan Laurel and Oliver Hardy are drawn into a fight with James Finlayson, in the course of which both a house and an automobile are destroyed.

For the shooting, the administration of the prison puts an idyll at our disposal. The film crew and nine prisoners find themselves towards the end of August between the old prison building and the outer wall amongst austere arrangements of flowers and tiny houses, built by the prisoners in the context of a work activity.

The silent film *Big Business* (1929) from Stan Laurel and Oliver Hardy was produced in the USA. It is summer and two men—you could call them young entrepreneurs—want to sell a Christmas tree. A conflict breaks out over the customer's unwillingness to acquire a Christmas tree in summer. The man's house and the car belonging to the two salesmen are demolished.

E

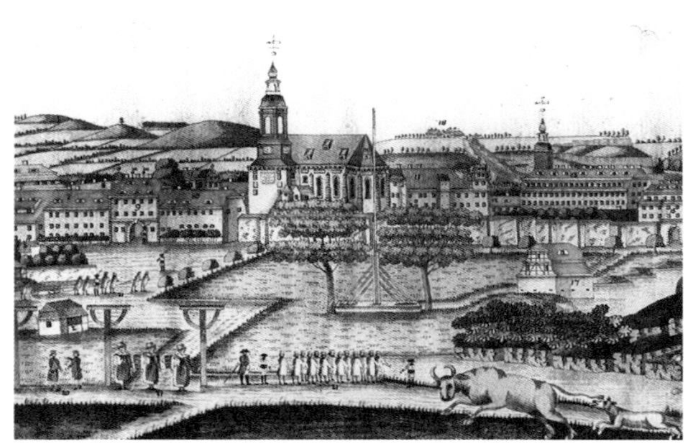

AUTOMOBILE

An automobile is confiscated by the court and made available to us. The car is prepared for us by prisoners in Torgau and transported to Waldheim by lorry. Included are the instructions on the best way to take it apart.

IDYLL

A house is built and painted, a piano is brought to the prison. A prisoner reads from Pasolini's book *Accattone*:

"'For Accattone and his mates, everyone who works is a traitor'—Just this sentence would make me read this book.—'They themselves live from pimping and theft. Even as Accattone falls in love for the first time, he sends the girl out onto the street. Stella though, the daughter of a whore, is not suited to the trade, and so, for the first time in his life, Accattone himself goes in search of a job, which he is, however, not up to physically.'—That definitely sounds like a man about town. I know how he feels. Was that made into a film?"

THE CASTLE

The Waldheim prison was built onto the former Waldheim castle, and this fact significantly influences its outward appearance today. The castle reportedly dates back to around 1200, having been first mentioned in official records in 1271. An Augustinian monastery was erected within the castle in 1404 before being closed again during the Reformation. A new period began for the castle in 1716. In that year, Saxony's Prince August II had a prison, orphanage and poorhouse built within the edifice. In 1716 the prison had a population of 181. The Waldheim prison houses male prisoners.

In one of the workshops, prisoners are kept busy constructing and then demolishing houses. As we visited the workshop, situated directly behind our film set, work was currently being carried out on a sample cell for the new wing of the prison. The purpose is to test which pieces of furniture fit in which way into an eight square metre space. The work is carried out according to the principles of the division of labour. The director of the prison relates the daily timetable of an average prisoner:

"The prisoner is woken at 6 a.m., he washes, cleans his teeth and has breakfast. He gets picked up for work at 6:45 and joins the other members of his workshop, leaving the detention area for the work area. Then the instructions are given on what work is to be done that day.

The prisoner works, like on the outside as well. Then there is a lunch break, at alternating times depending on the workshop that the prisoner is from, but usually at around 11:30. At 12 o'clock or 12:15 work is resumed. It depends on the workshop, but usually around 3 or 4 p.m. the prisoner is finished with work and is taken from the work area back to the detention area. Afterwards there is free time for leisure activities.

Depending on where he is detained, each prisoner has the opportunity of going into the courtyard for an hour each day. There is an extensive treatment programme. Depending on what the prisoner is in for; it may be useful, for example, to take part in anti-violence-training, in the self-awareness group, self-confidence training, social-training, and there is a range of other programmes. In addition, there are many other leisure programmes. Sport is particularly important to the prisoners, and I think that's very sound. Especially since you're under an almost inescapable pressure here, because you're constantly surrounded by so many people and living together isn't always harmonious — so there are many different sports. The maybe more intellectually demanding prisoners can take part in a reading circle or something similar."

We build the house and busy ourselves with the car. After a week, the work in the sun being accompanied by Pasolini and Foucault…

"The majority are here because they committed crime as a result of some dire financial need. When you think about what's done with them here, it's awful actually. 'What is the minimum kind of space a person needs, what kind of architecture?' I reckon architecture isn't important, and… At least, I don't how to answer that. I need a place where I feel at home."

CONSTRUCTION SITE

"Normally a cell of this size is a one man-cell — it's eight square metres — and you're entitled to it alone. It's your lawful right anyway, but it's actually not the square metres but the cubic metres — I mean space, air or whatever, but since there wasn't enough room, or isn't…"

"How many square metres is that?"

"Square metres? Eight — you can see for yourself, it's two metres wide and four metres long. And with all the furniture it's naturally pretty cramped. Yeah, there's not much room left. In a new building like, for example, in Dresden it's fastidious, exposed, screwed down, there the tables screwed down, the bed's screwed down, wardrobes, shelves, everything, you can't move anything anywhere. You can't hang a picture on the wall like here, instead there's a bar for pictures, and pictures have to be attached to this bar, and they have to be attached in such a way that you can look behind them and they have to be loose.

Then you can only … according to regulations you can only have ten letters in the cell, yeah … if you get more mail you have to bring it to your property in storage. You can only have twenty pieces of music in the cell — cassettes, CDs or computer game cassettes, um … CDs. And you can only possess three plants and these plants can't be more than 30 cm. The outside wall must be completely clear the whole time, there can't be anything on the windowsills. Yes … and that's against the law actually — according to the law the cell is your, your, your … how should I say … not your property, but there you can be alone, yeah and only when there's reasonable suspicion then they can search the cell. But in reality it's totally different; there are arbitrary inspections of the cells, and essentially almost every day. Yeah, in Bautzen, for example, the prison director regularly makes inspections personally and when he sees a plant that's over 30 cm high then he gets a pair of scissors and cuts it off. And when you have four plants, then one of them is gone when you come back to the cell from work."

F

The prison guards keep their distance and decline to be interviewed. Too difficult to reconcile their existence on the outside with the more concentrated one inside, where you are forced to play a role. They observe us, like they do the prisoners, from a distance, strangely. They give us knowing tips on how to deal with the prisoners; who they believe they can see right through. In truth they understand them as little as we do. They oversee lives, which they themselves don't understand. We are constantly being observed. Are there any moments — when are we not under observation? Later, we become aware of furtive attempts at nearer contact.

Inside the institution we have an exceptional status. The relationship both to the prisoners and to the administration deviates from the norm, in that there is little communication with the so-called free world. We have total freedom of movement. We are blocking one of the main driveways to the prison, while destroying the house and the car. We are creating a situation which is unaccustomed and which changes nothing. Everything would have to be rethought from the beginning, but we are unable to. We grant ourselves and the prisoners a week of sunshine and in return are exploited by the administration: For the director and those responsible at the Ministry of Justice, this project can mean an increase in sovereignty: If the director can enter into contact with the outside and at the same time sustain the functioning of the prison within, then he acquires the right to make decisions in exceptional circumstances and is thus especially empowered under normal circumstances.

Director of the prison: "Regarding the decision to permit you, as an exception, to carry out this work, a contributing factor was that we hoped to be able to busy the prisoners in a sensible and mentally stimulating way; so we can do something in this way for public relations and so the security concerns, that one naturally always has when someone from outside enters the prison and does something that deviates from the normal routine, that these security reservations were not so significant and could be ignored."

G
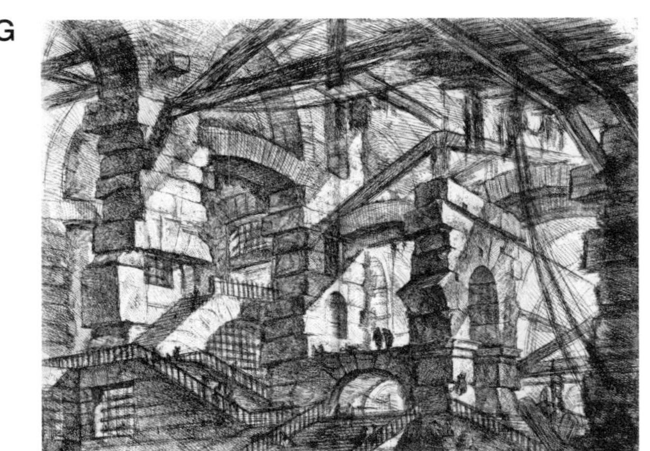

The prison is an experiment. Additionally, the prisoners are responsible for commenting on this experiment and their experiences in their cells as soon as they have left them. The prison drifts into the field of imagination.

When the employees leave the institution, they separate—in the old way—their lives inside the prison, their profession, from their own private world. This chasm is as significant as the importance they attach to their profession. There are certainly employees who smuggle things into the prison, thus helping to maintain a culture of trade. The prisoners are their trading partners and this relationship between retailers and consumers is a compensation for the lack of other forms of communication. Everyone preserves their fears. There are two fears; the fear of the prison and the fear of the outside.

Why not? Society wants to preserve its prison as a type of "black box", as a place for the suppression of trivial problems, as the idea of another life. But all films about prison are false, and this film is no exception. The film is also a mishmash of preconceptions. Perhaps it is about the consolation that nothing can be said that doesn't equate to itself. Cinema and the prison function in a similar way. However, in the cinema ideas are transformed into images and characters, whereas the people in prison and their interrelations are transformed into ideas. Although, this place is no less an imprisonment.

A Prisoner reads: "Everything burned. The pale morning sun on the late summer day was like glowing lime. A burnt face raised the protruding chin, with two hollows in the gaunt cheeks and a watery gaze and spoke: Scuccia, the world is about to end. Let me look at you all. I've never seen you during the day, only in the dark. What's up, your women are on strike? And laughed a toothless grin.

Who had he spoken to? A band of strizzi who were roasting in the sun in front of a small bar in Marinella. Among them was also Momoletto. The scuccia replied to him: Momoletto, man, are you still alive? I always hear that work is suicide. Momoletto was small and short with a contemptuous gaze, always laughing like a jumping jack. Next to him, another person was having someone pour mineral water into his hand and washing his face. That was Alfredino, a long beanpole, black haired with the flat-pressed nose of a Moroccan, and Vicietto, a teddyboy, elegant, a suit with polka-dots, a big tie with a big knot, and a tiepin, with still no beard on him. Alfredino's whole face, rubbed over with his hands, gleamed with mineral water.

Alfredino, you martyr, listen to a friend, throw in the work, the Metro Goldwyn Mayer Club calls you too. And he tore open his mouth like a drain and roared, like the lion from Metro-Goldwyn-Mayer roars. Twice, three times, the empty gaze cast into the void." He laughs. "That was a whole page."

A   Waldheim is now Germany's oldest prison. A historical rendition of new prisoners being admitted to the prison in the first half of the 18th century.

B   Willey Reveley: "Plan for Jeremy Bentham's Panopticon", 1791. Bentham solves the problem of surveillance in the modern world. The tower in the centre of the circular prison reduces the number of guards needed.

C   The picture shows the construction of the prison on the foundation of a former monastery. The German author Karl May was imprisoned at Waldheim from 1870 to 1874. The "Waldheim Trials" were held here in 1950.

D   Nicolas Philippe Harou-Romain: "Plan for a Prison", 1840. "A prisoner prays in his cell in front of the centrally located guard tower."

E   "Correctioners at work", view of the Waldheim "almshouse, orphanhouse, house of correction and workhouse" with the former Augustinian monastery and present-day St. Otto Lutheran Church and Prison Chapel, 1809.

F   Anonymous (collection Michel Hennin): "While lying on an iron bed, Robert-François Damiens submits to interrogation by two judges, March 28, 1757". After his death the body was removed from the penal system as the main object of punitive repression. A short time later Léon Faucher drew up a list of regulations for the "House of Young Prisoners in Paris": "The prisoners' day begins at six o'clock in the morning…"

G   Hopeless visions of dungeons. Giovanni Battista Piranesi: "The Gothic Arch", first draft (1751–1754), Plate XIV from the series "Le Carceri d'Invenzione".

BACKSTAGE

INDEX

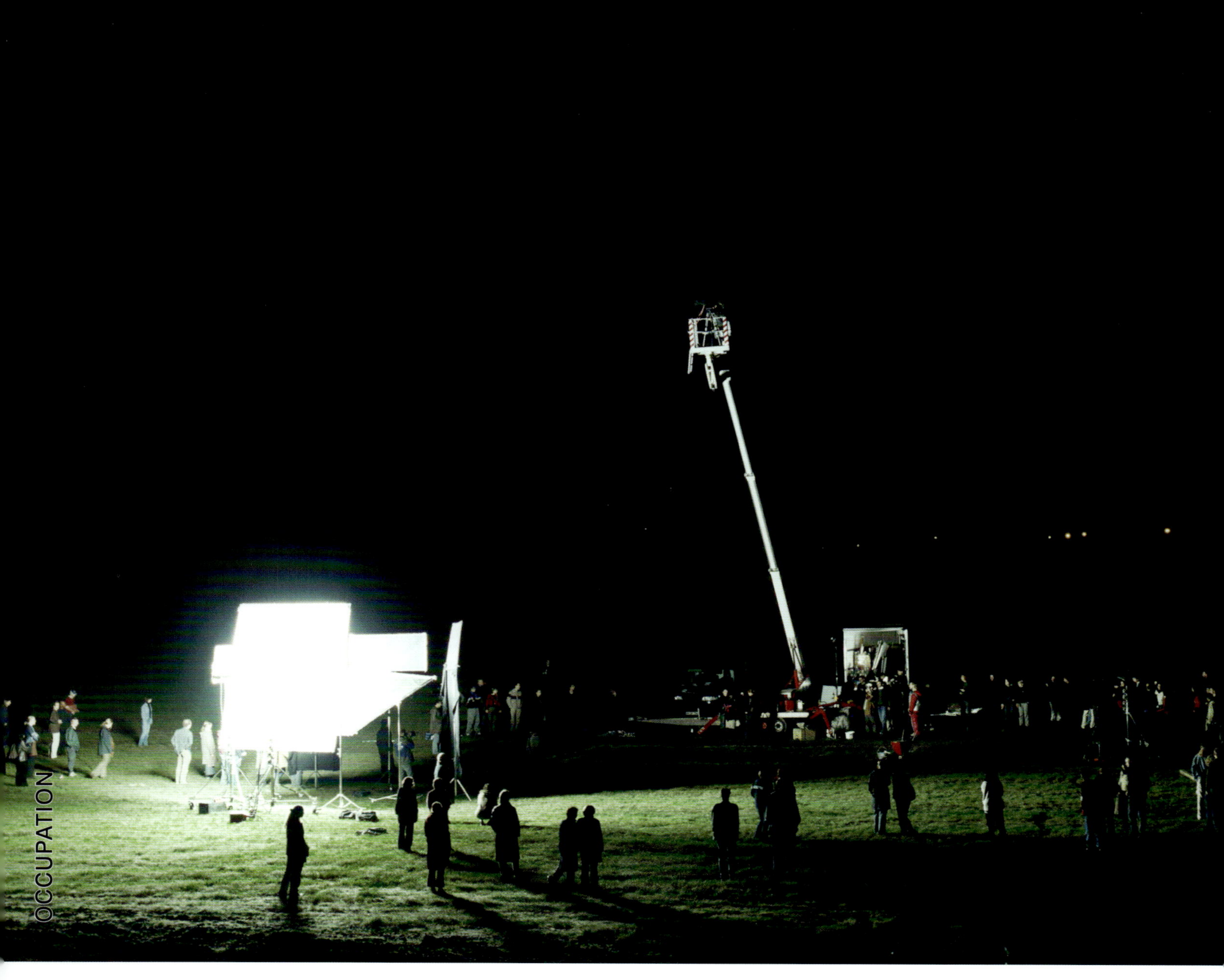
OCCUPATION

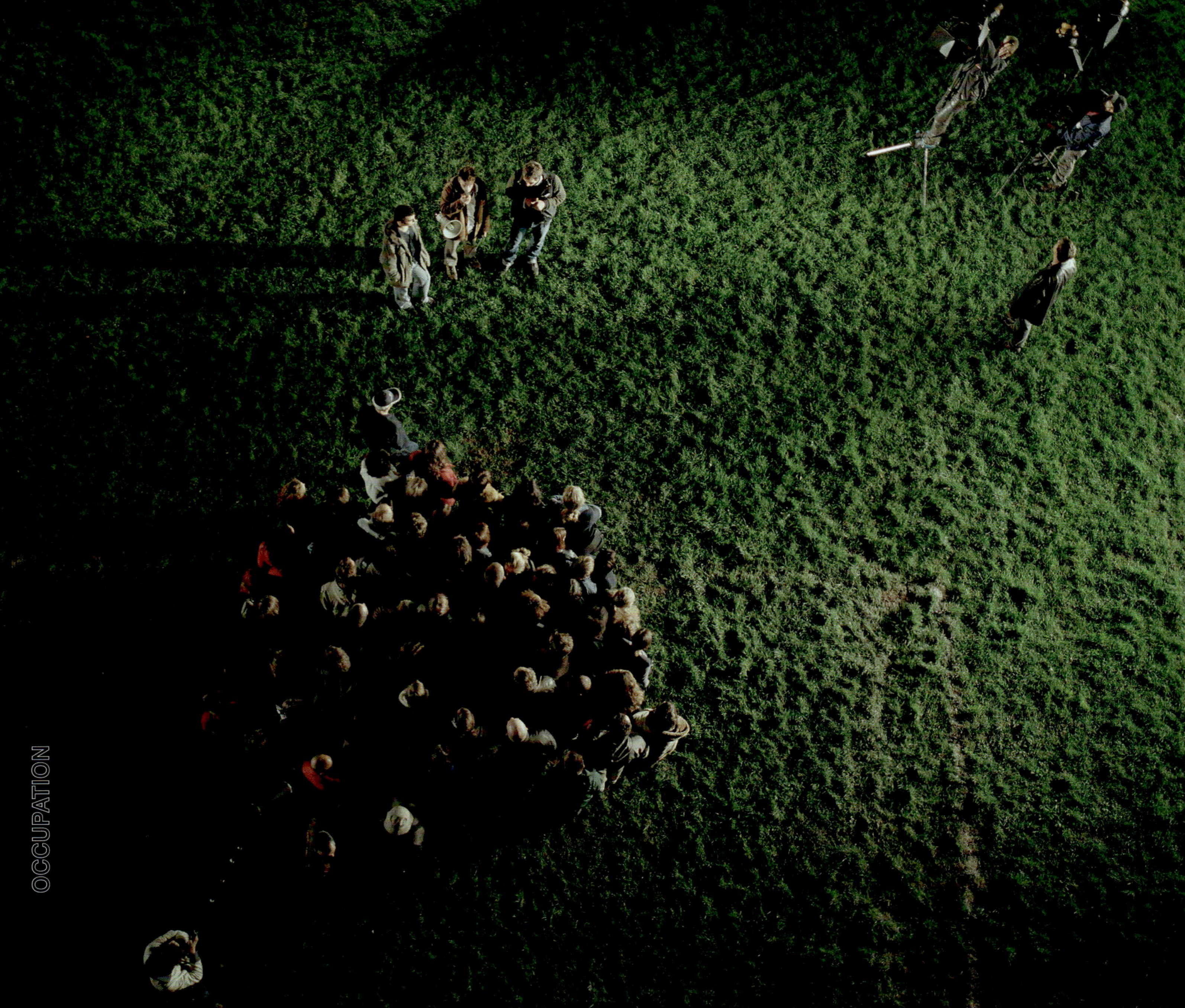

Statisten willigten in einen Filmdreh ein, der ihre eigene
Lage beschrieb: Ein Filmteam, das von Schauspielern des
Leipziger Schauspielhauses gespielt wurde, inszenierte
eine Massenszene. Die Menge stand auf einem markierten
Rechteck in der Größe einer Kinoleinwand und erhielt
uneindeutige Anweisungen.

Extras agreed to participate in the shooting of a scene whose
motive was the very situation in which they found themselves. A film crew, played by actors from Leipzig's Municipal
Theatre, is filming a crowd scene. Standing in a marked-
off rectangle the size of a movie screen, the crowd of extras
is being given contradictory orders.

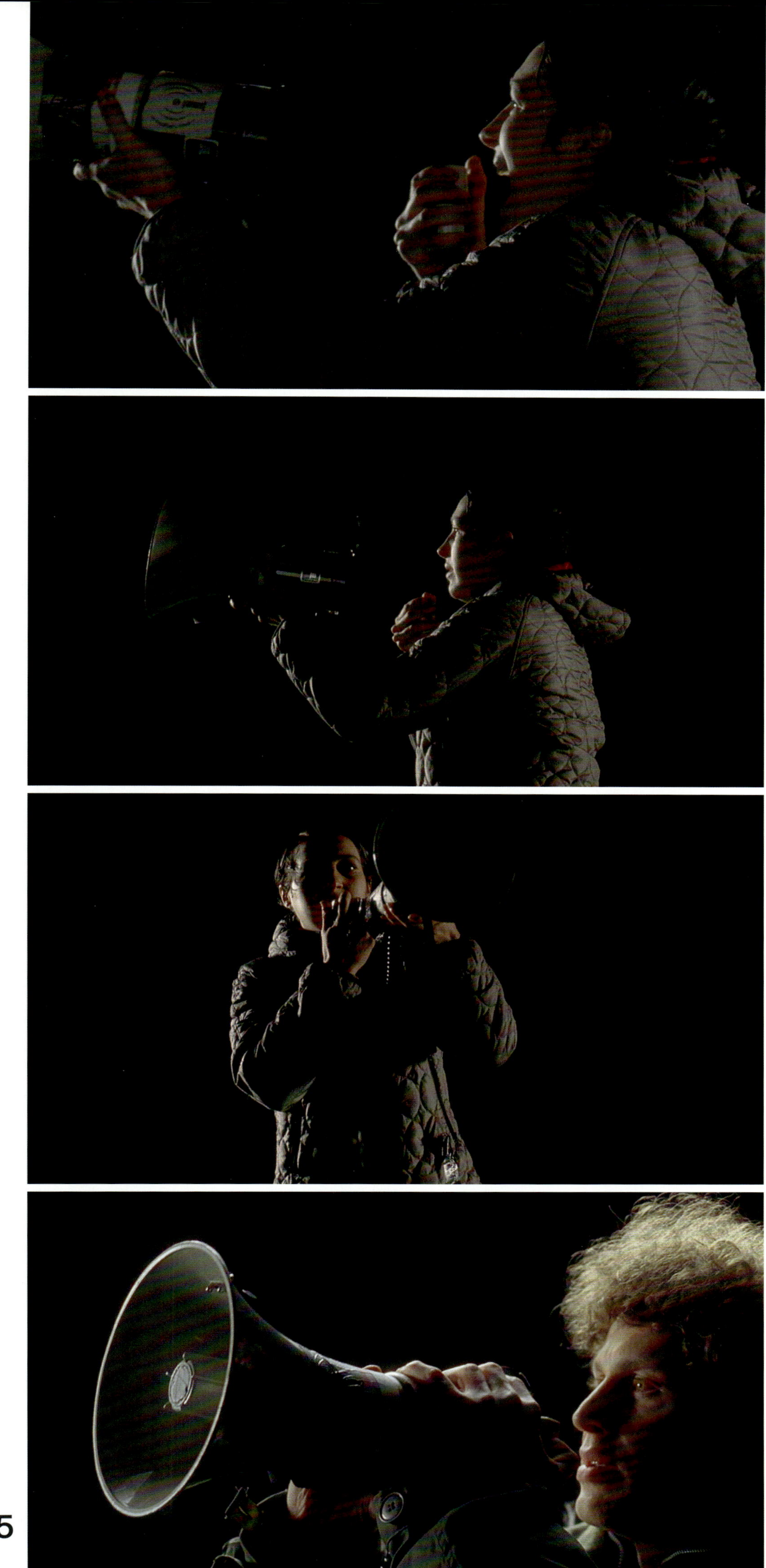

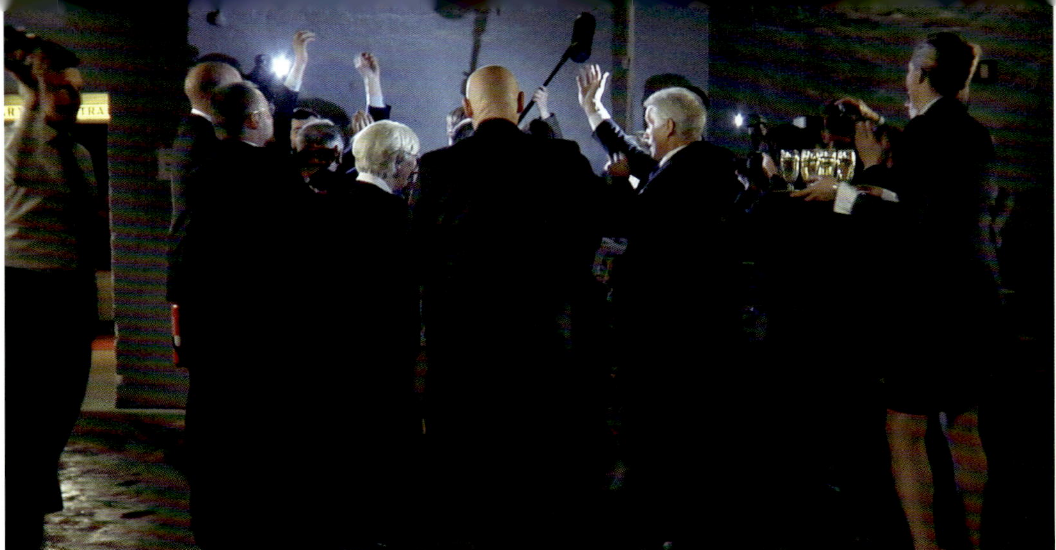

All that doesn't matter any more. Left and right. This is no time to be carping! You do understand that, don't you?

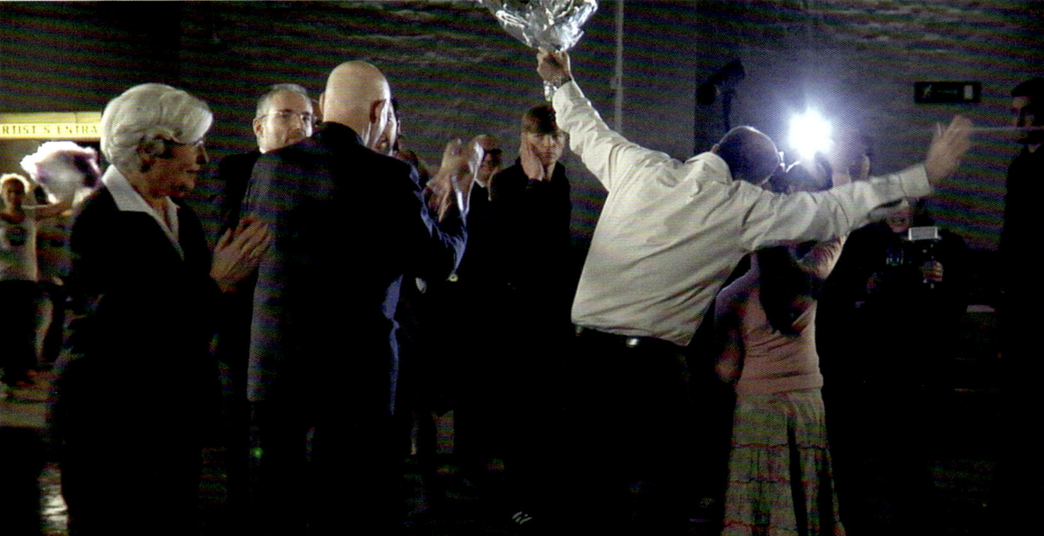

What does that mean in terms of external relations? What is going to be different now?

Everything will be different! Just wait. We're going to start again from scratch.

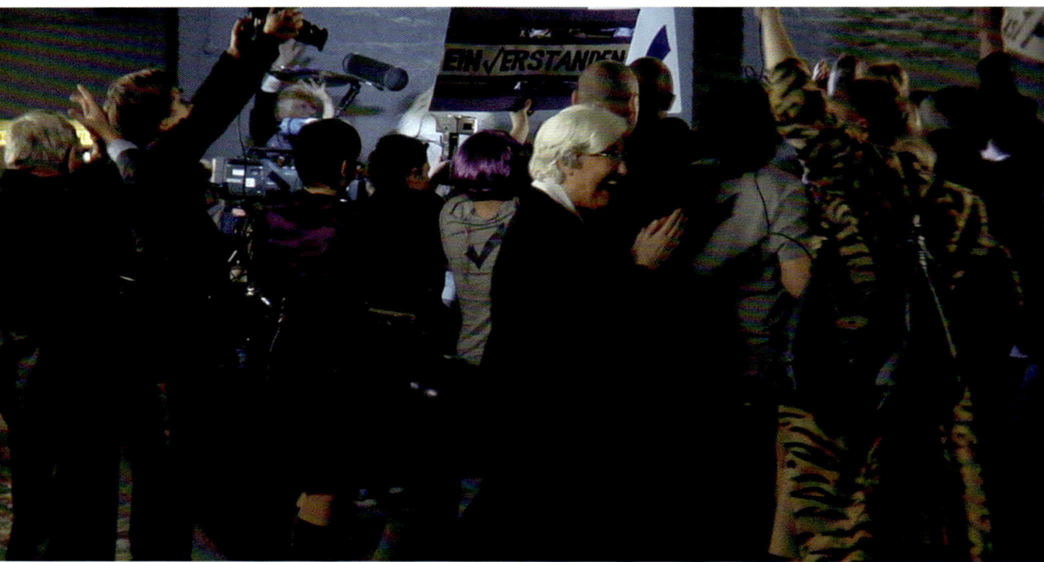

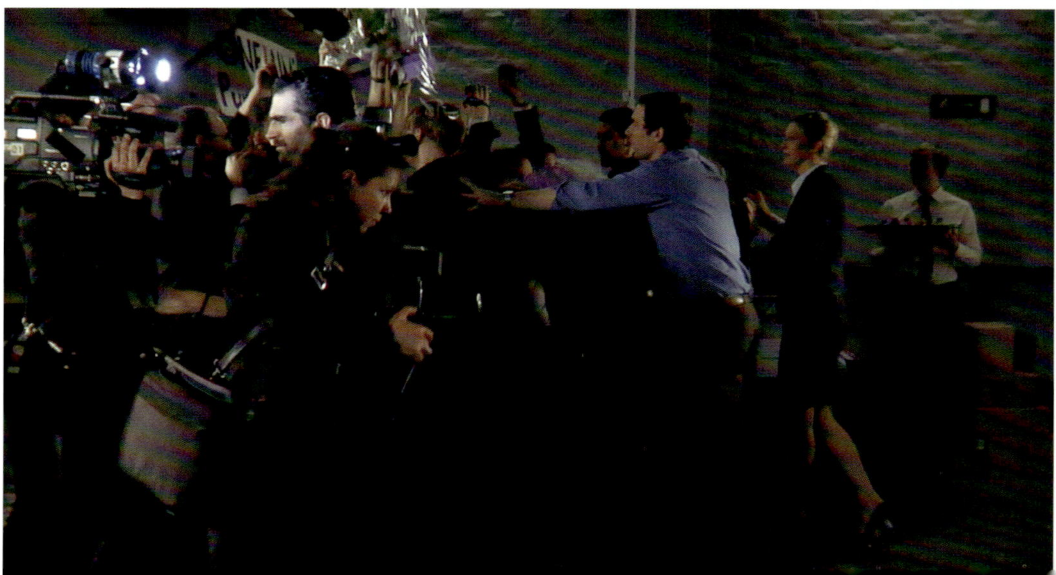

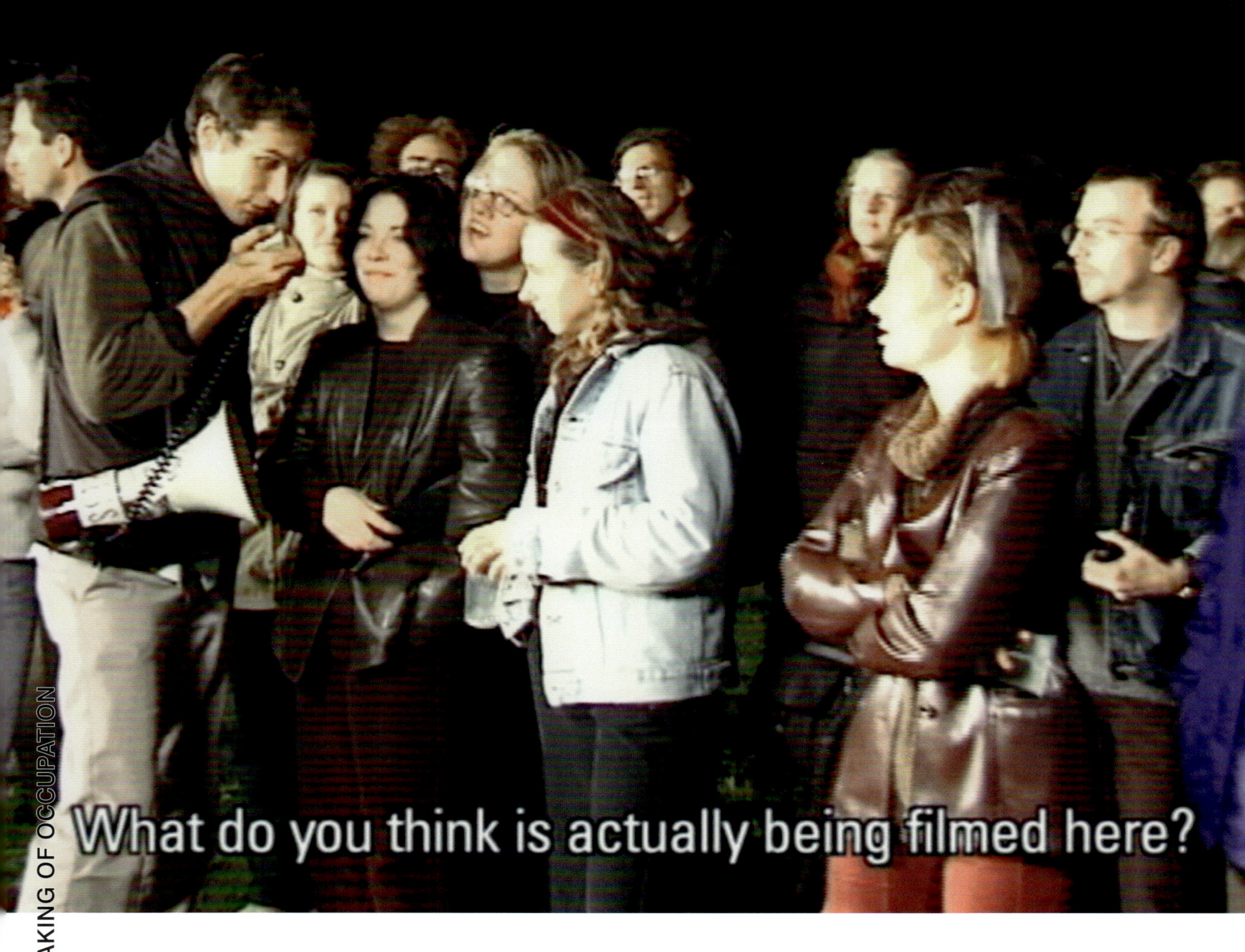
What do you think is actually being filmed here?

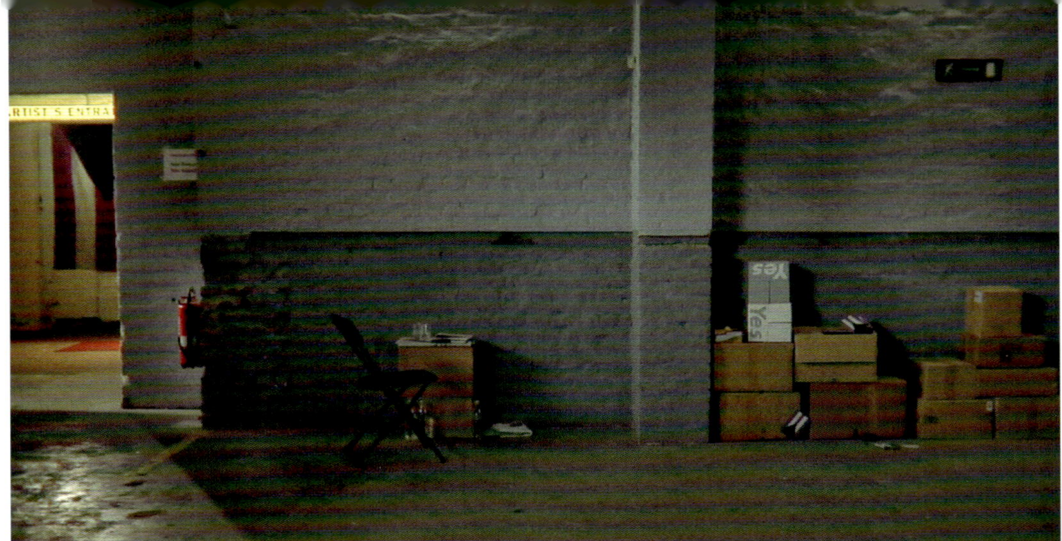

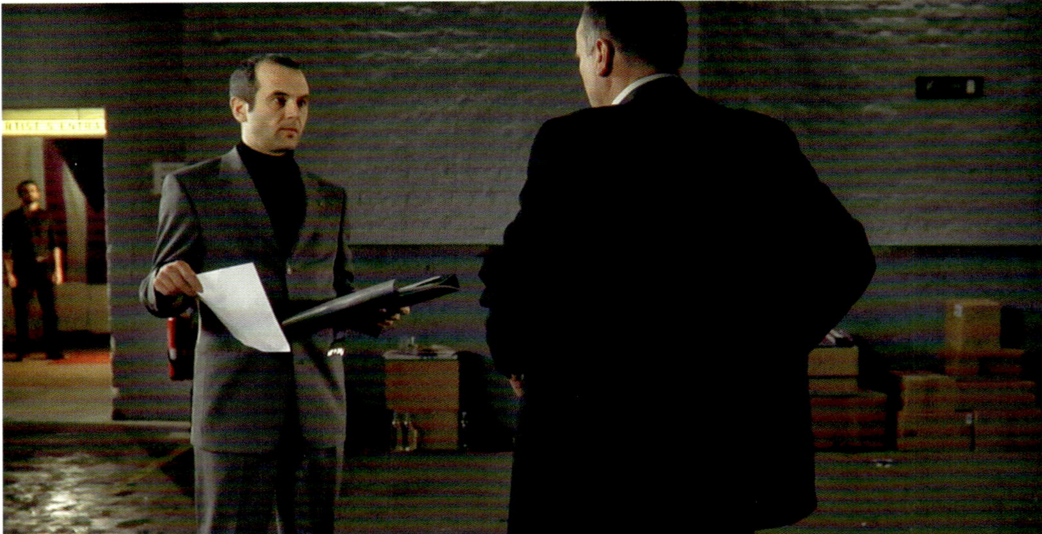

I am not going to do either of them. One has to refuse. Why? Why me, and why only after the election? I do not intend to reveal all my reasons for the public at large.

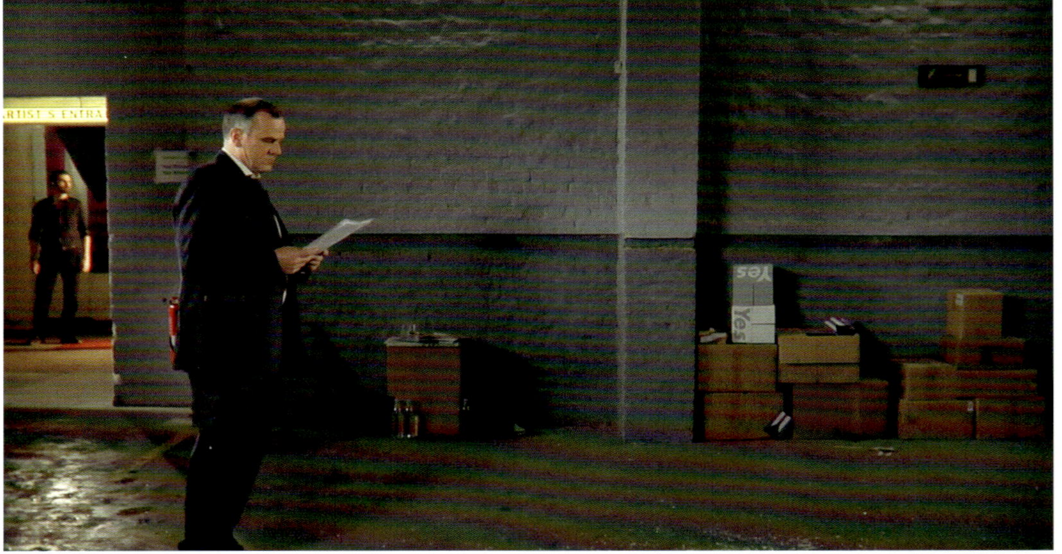

It is perfectly clear to me that the only possible step I can take is to decline to accept the power that lies within my reach … That is my decision!

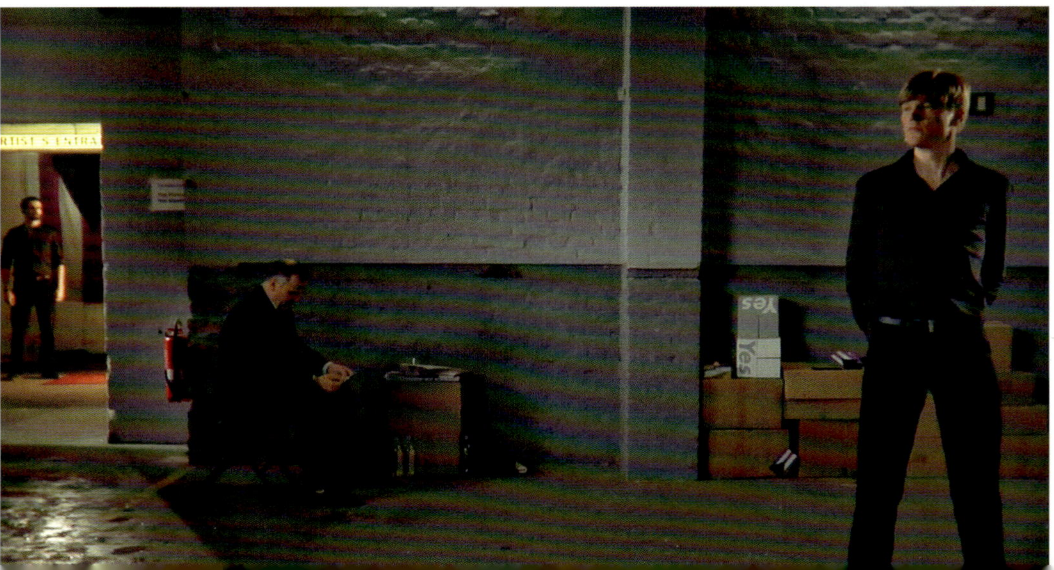

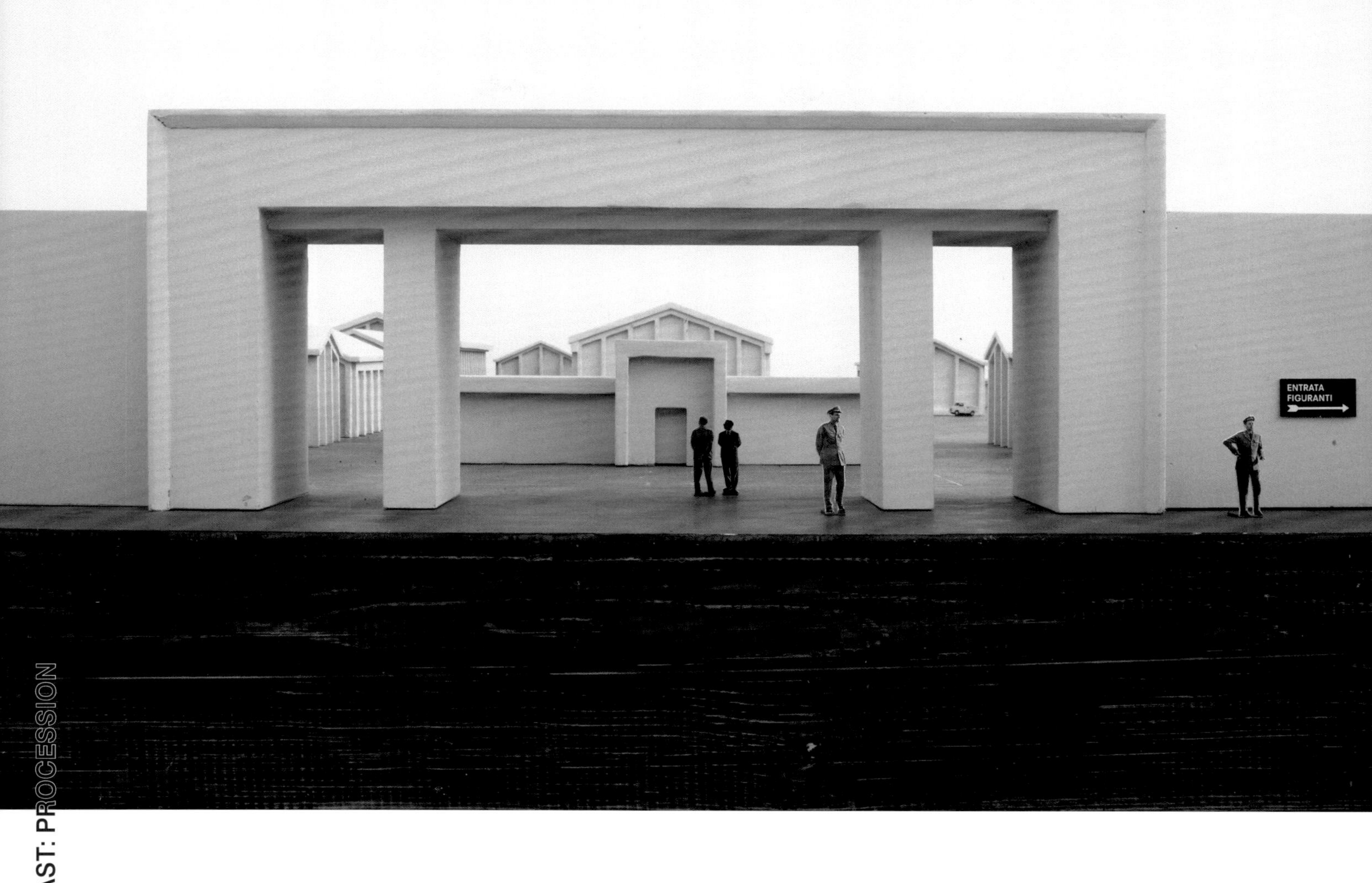ENTRATA
FIGURANTI

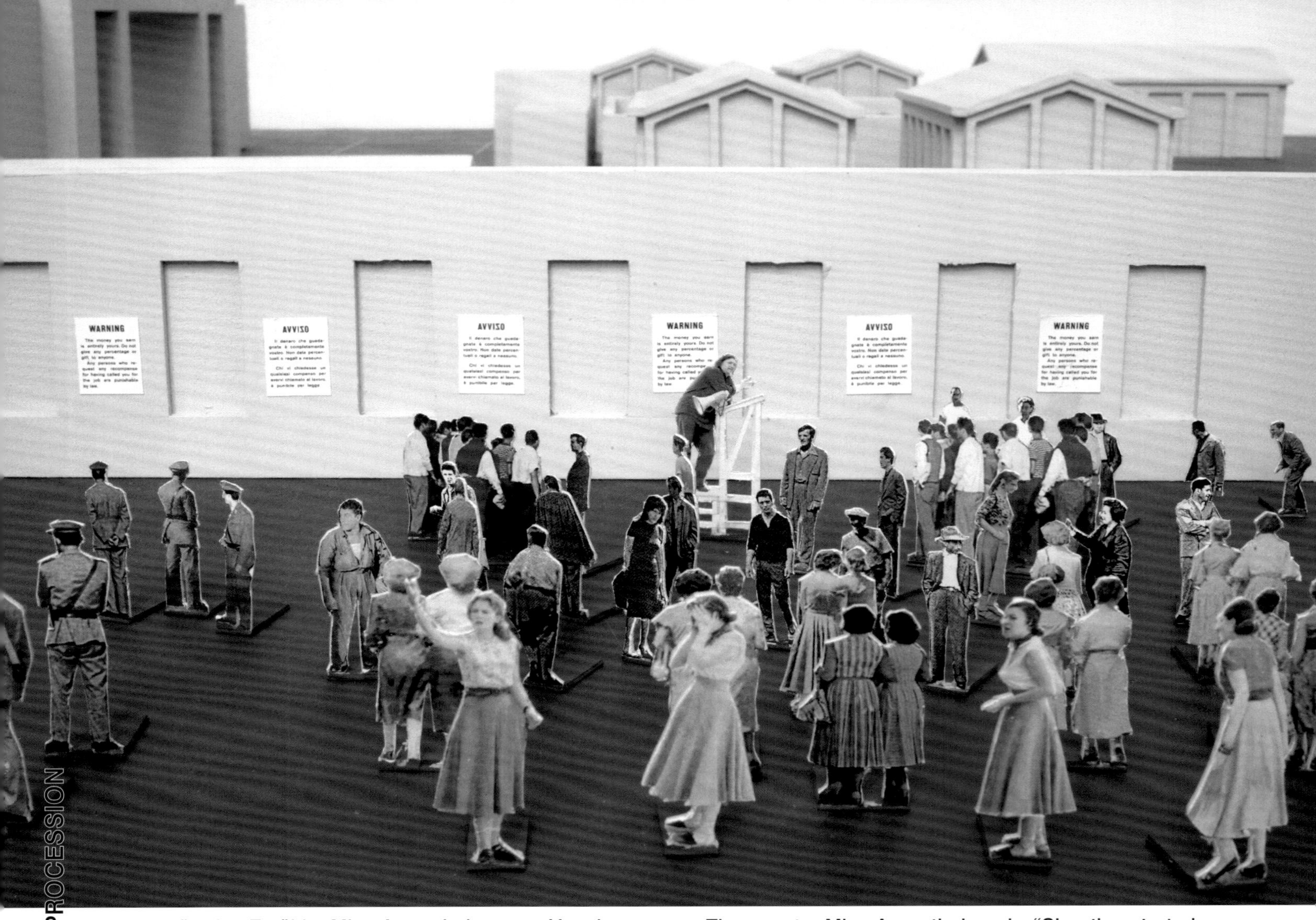

Man hört den Erzähler Mino Argentieri sagen: „Vor ein paar Tagen begannen die Dreharbeiten für einen Monumentalfilm und die Art dieses Films legte nahe, dass die Anzahl der Statisten sich auf etwa 6.000 belaufen würde. Eine riesige Menschenmenge wurde von dem Gerücht angezogen, dass zu Beginn der Dreharbeiten eine große Anzahl von Statisten benötigt würde. Entgegen der Erwartung fast aller Anwesenden wurden am Ende nur 1.500 Personen nach Cinecittà eingelassen. Diejenigen, die draußen bleiben mussten, waren bitter enttäuscht und begannen gegen die Organisatoren zu protestieren."

The narrator Mino Argentieri reads: "Shooting started a few days ago for a monumental film, and the nature of this movie suggested that the number of extras would come to about 6,000. The huge crowd was attracted by rumours they had heard about a massive recruitment drive for a large number of extras as shooting was about to begin. Contrary to the expectations of almost all those who showed up, only 1,500 were allowed inside the Cinecittà. Those who had to remain outside were bitterly disappointed and started railing against the organisers."

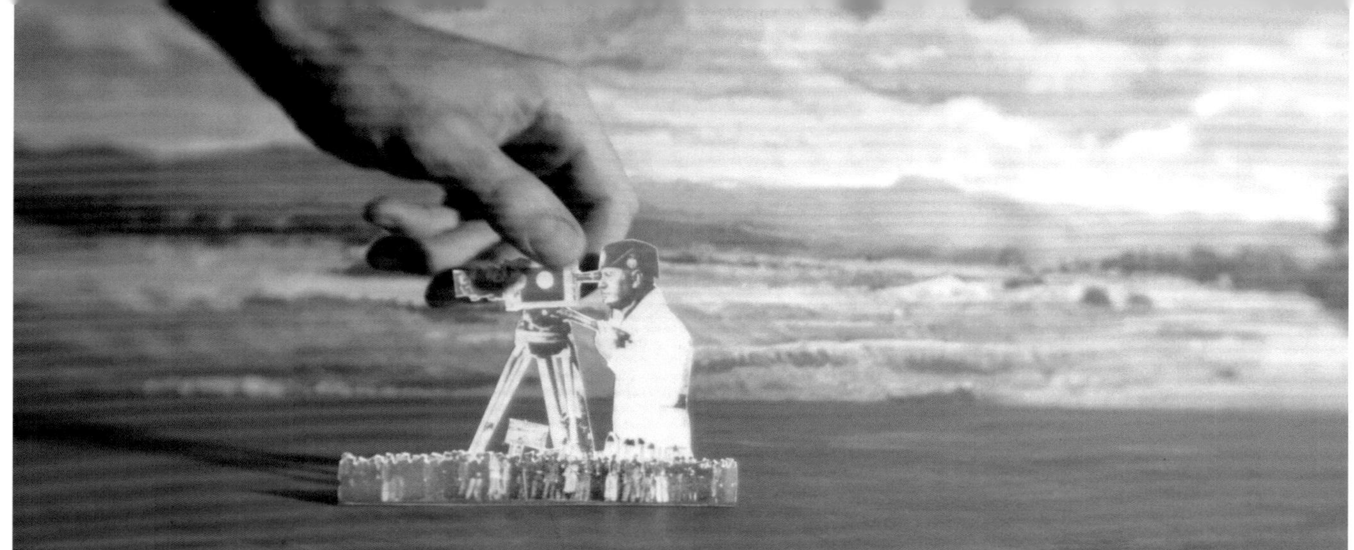

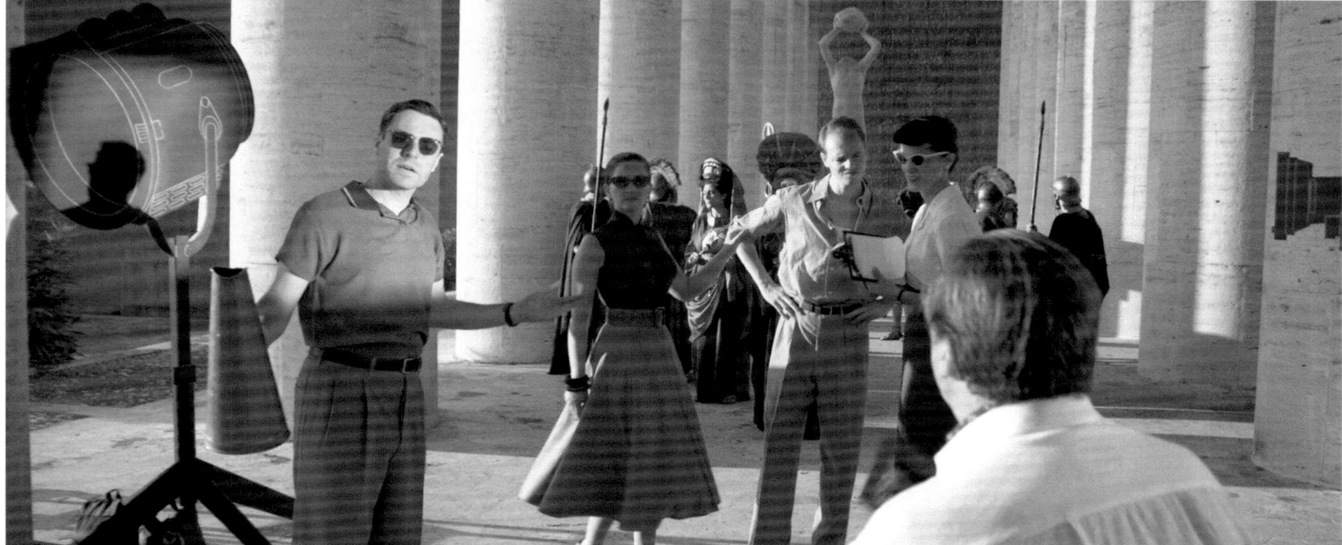

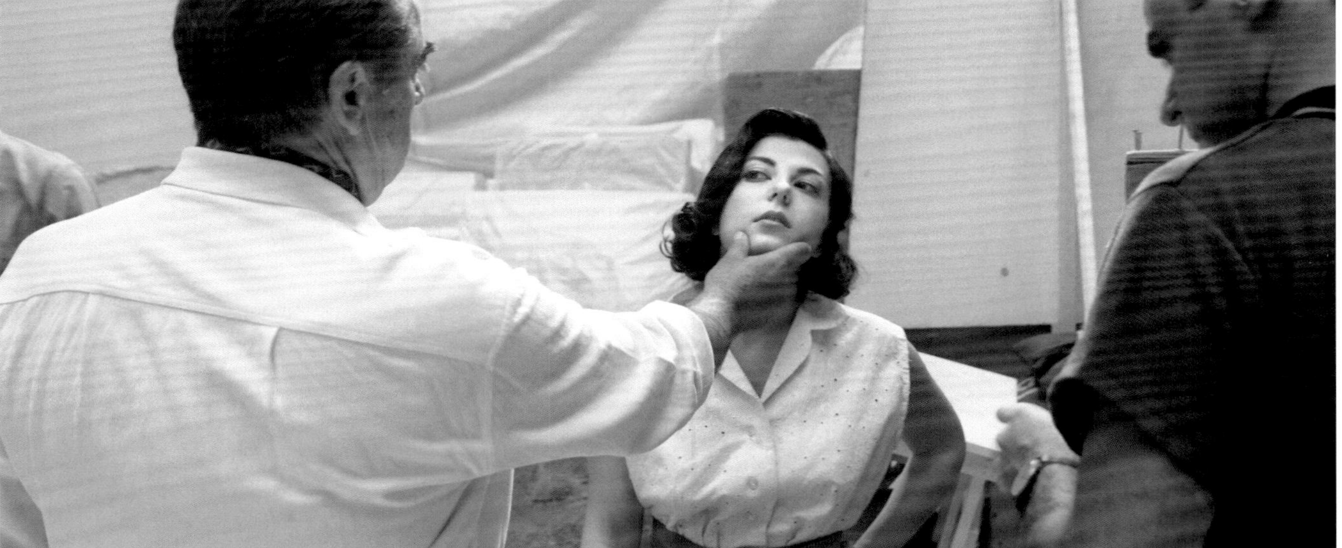

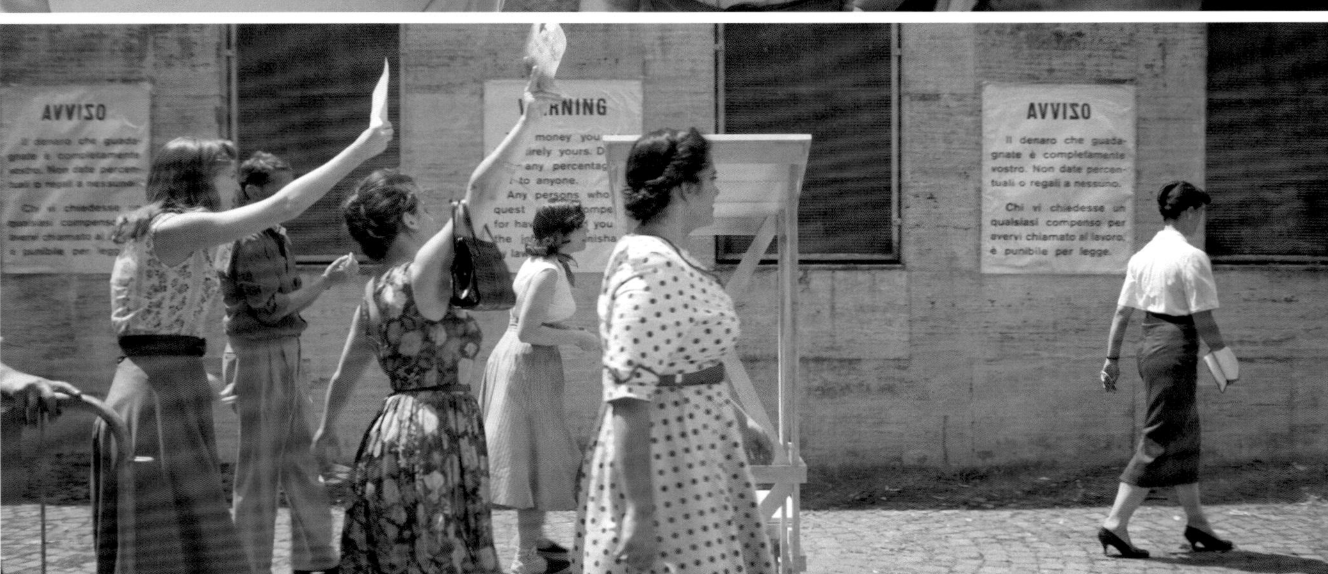
AVVISO
WARNING
AVVISO
Il denaro che guada-
gnate è completamente
vostro. Non date percen-
tuali o regali a nessuno.

Chi vi chiedesse un
qualsiasi compenso per
avervi chiamato al lavoro,
è punibile per legge.

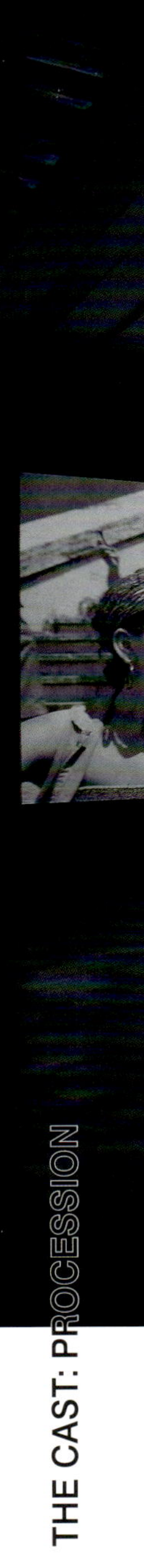

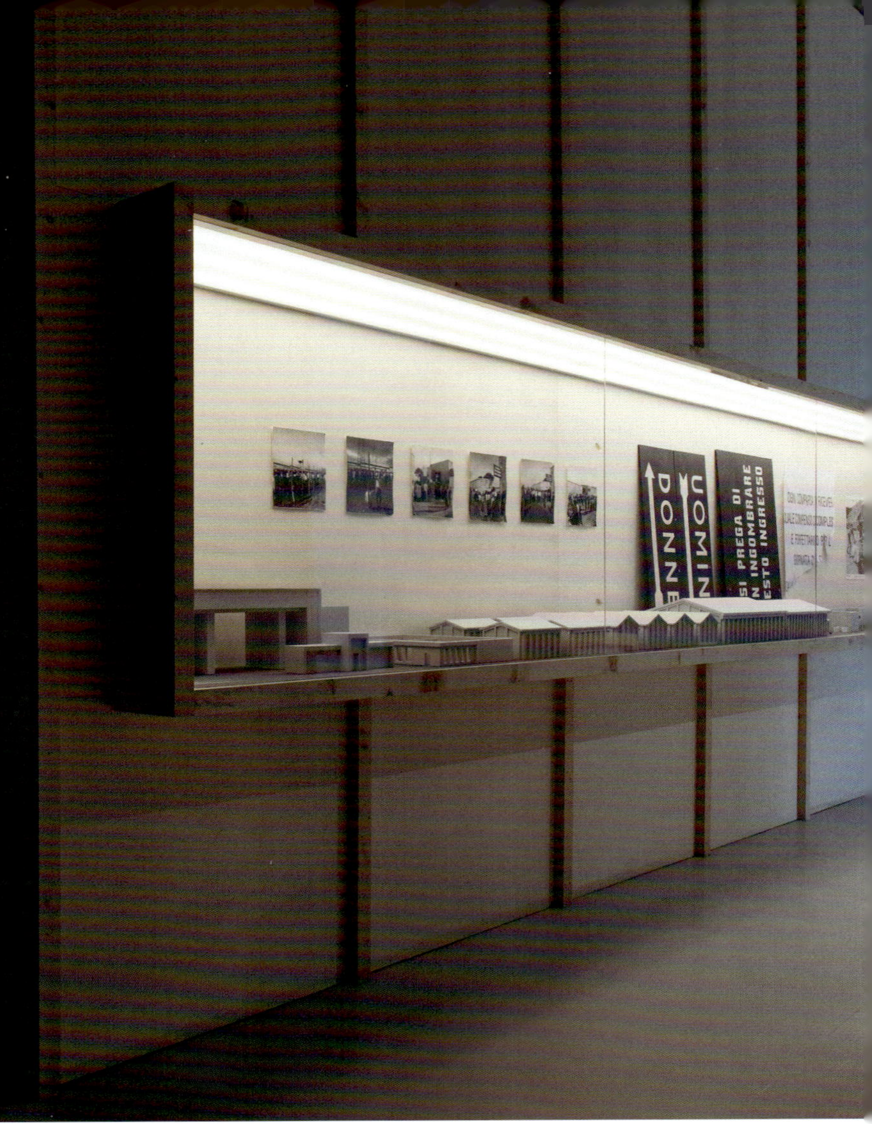

THE CAST: PROCESSION

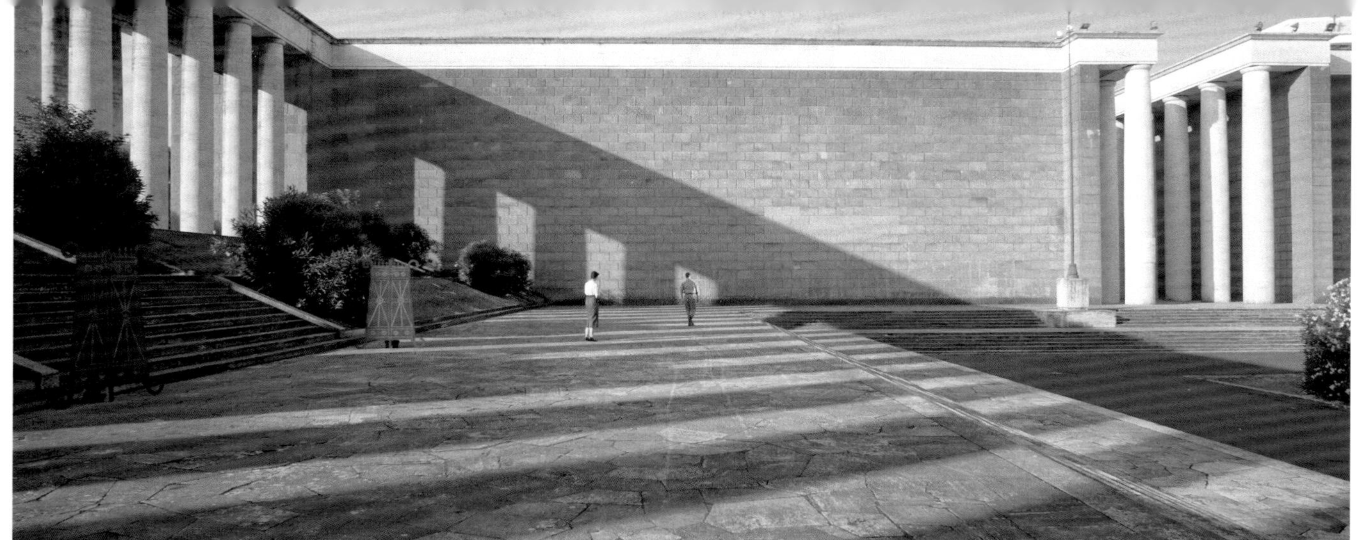

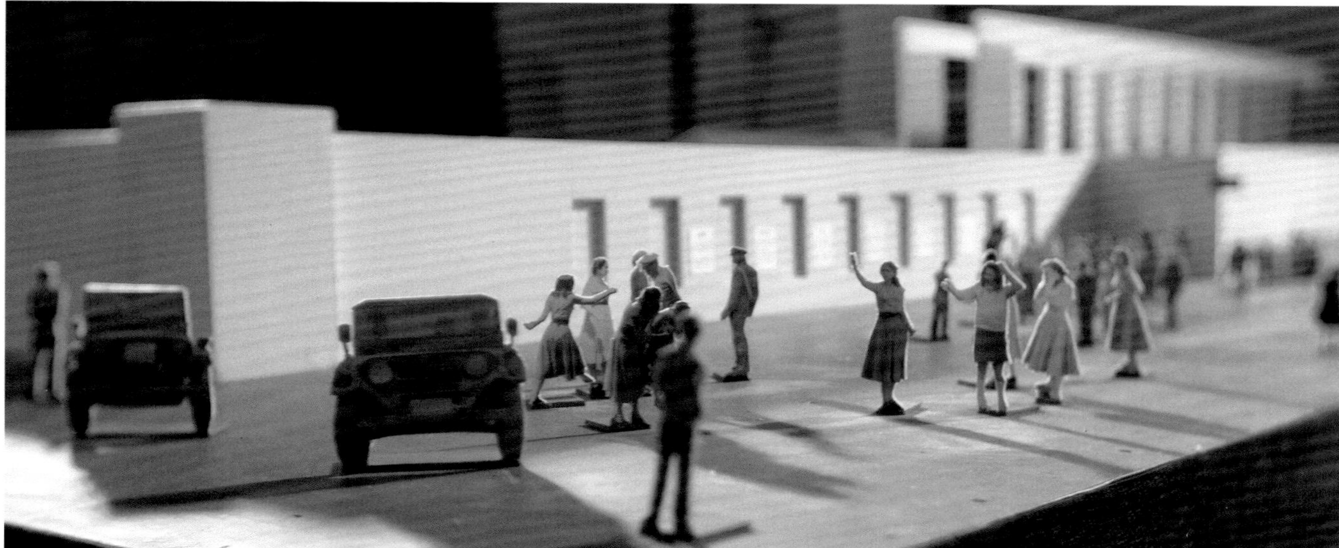

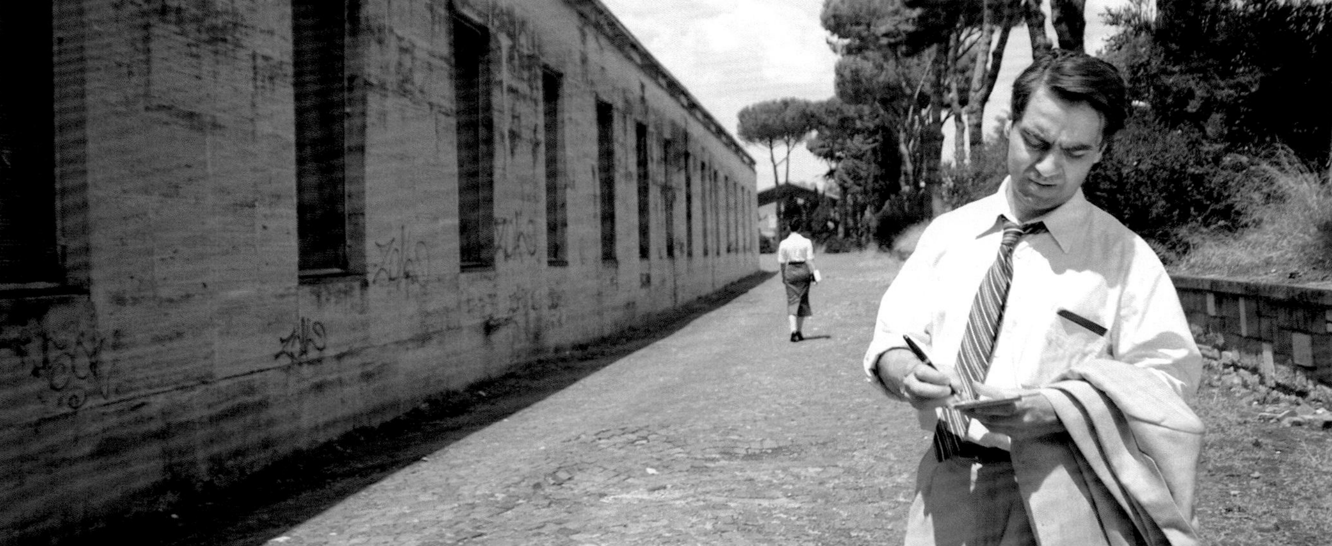

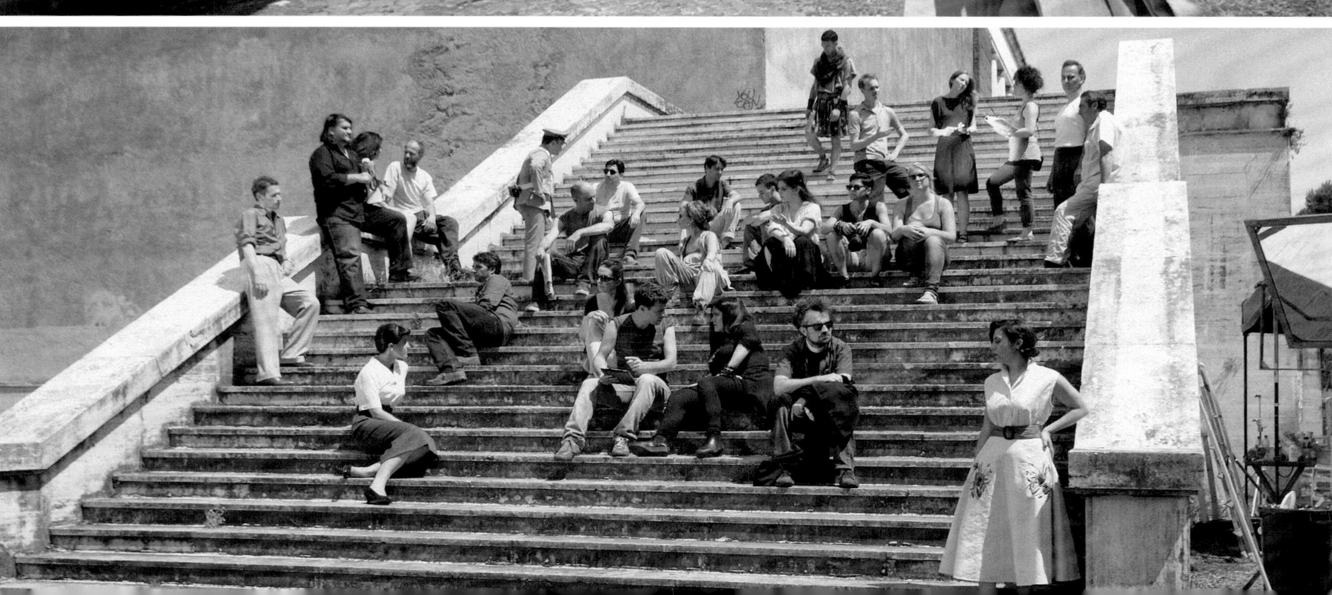

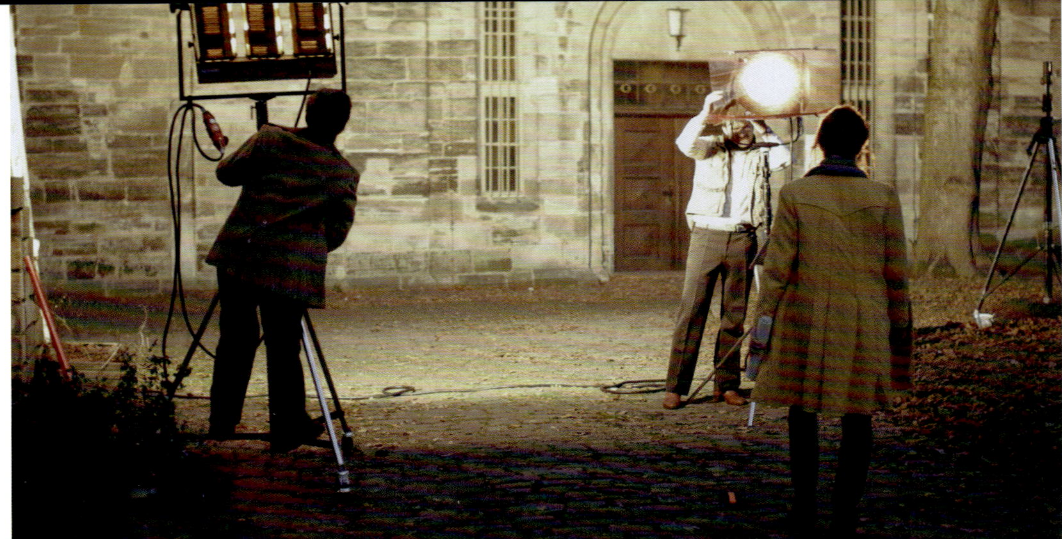

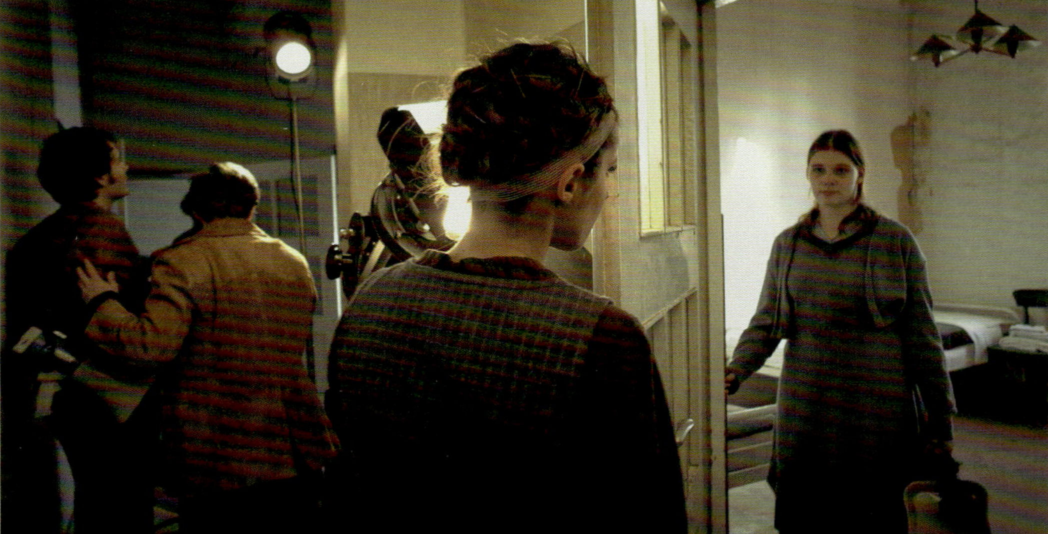

I thought the film aims
to tell people outside about
conditions in here.

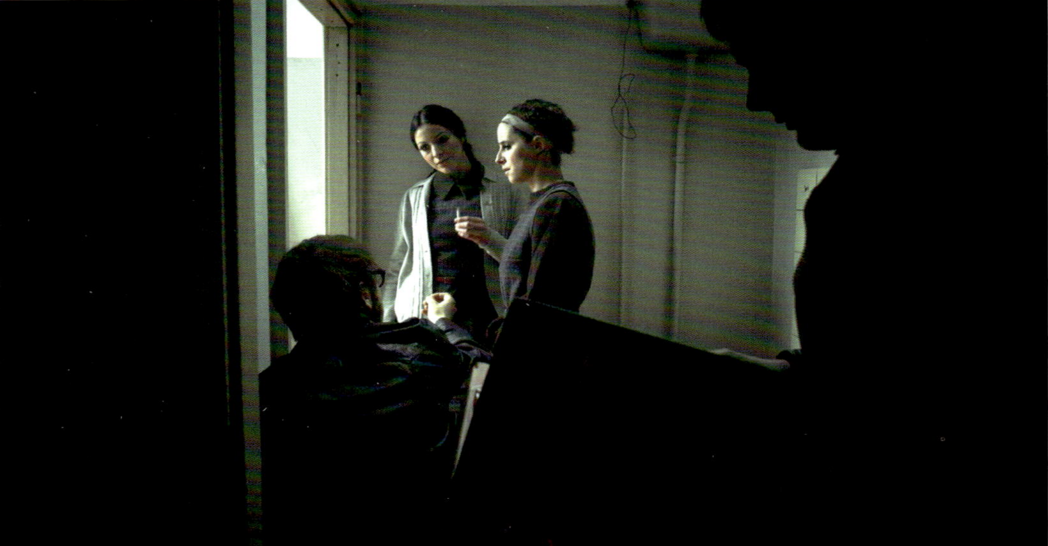

Right, but film lags behind
current political debate.

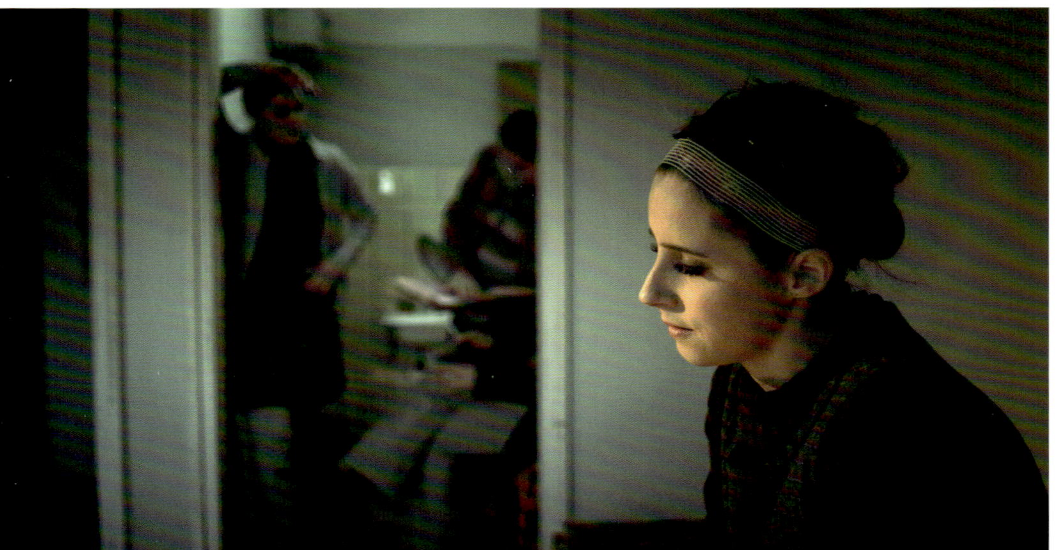

So you just have to be more
radical!

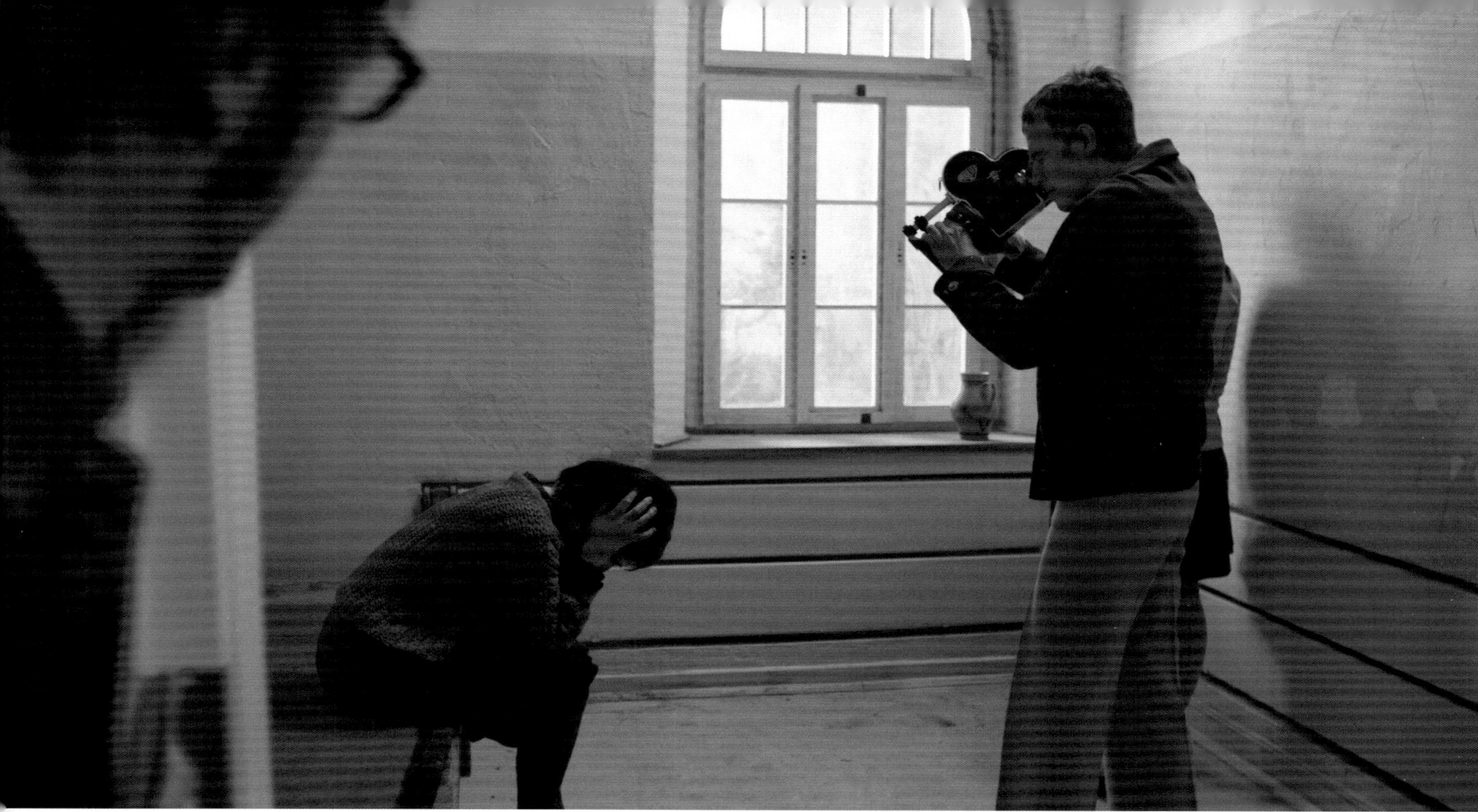

Eberhard Itzenplitz, Regisseur des Films *Bambule*, plädierte während der Dreharbeiten 1970 dafür, die Insassinnen im Mädchenerziehungsheim durch Schauspielerinnen zu ersetzen. Er erzählte später: „Wehe, wenn man mit ihnen beim Mittagstisch grundsätzliche theoretische Erörterungen über Heimzöglinge im Allgemeinen oder über Verwahrung oder über grundsätzlich Politisches führen wollte, dann war man geliefert. Das konnten sie nicht." Der Film beruht auf Ulrike Meinhofs Recherchen, unter anderem in Breitenau, wurde aber in Berlin gedreht. Meinhof, die auch das Drehbuch schrieb, war von dem Ansatz der Regie mehr und mehr enttäuscht, bis sie das Set verließ. 1970 schrieb sie, kurz bevor sie in den Untergrund ging: „Ein Fernsehspiel, das die Mädchen verschaukelt, man darf sagen: ein Scheißspiel … Ändern wird sich nur etwas, wenn die Unterdrückten selbst handeln."

While shooting *Bambule* in 1970, the director Eberhard Itzenplitz argued that the inmates of the girls reformatory should be replaced by actresses. As he later put it: "Woe, if you were trying to have a political conversation with them at the lunch table and discussed matters of custody or upbringing in children's homes and reformatories, it would be pointless." The film is based on Ulrike Meinhof's research, among others in Breitenau, but was filmed in Berlin. Meinhof, who also wrote the screenplay for the film, became increasingly frustrated with the director's approach and left the set. In 1970, shortly before having gone underground, she wrote: "A television play that tricked the girls who took part is a fucking game … Things will only change when the underdogs are allowed to play themselves."

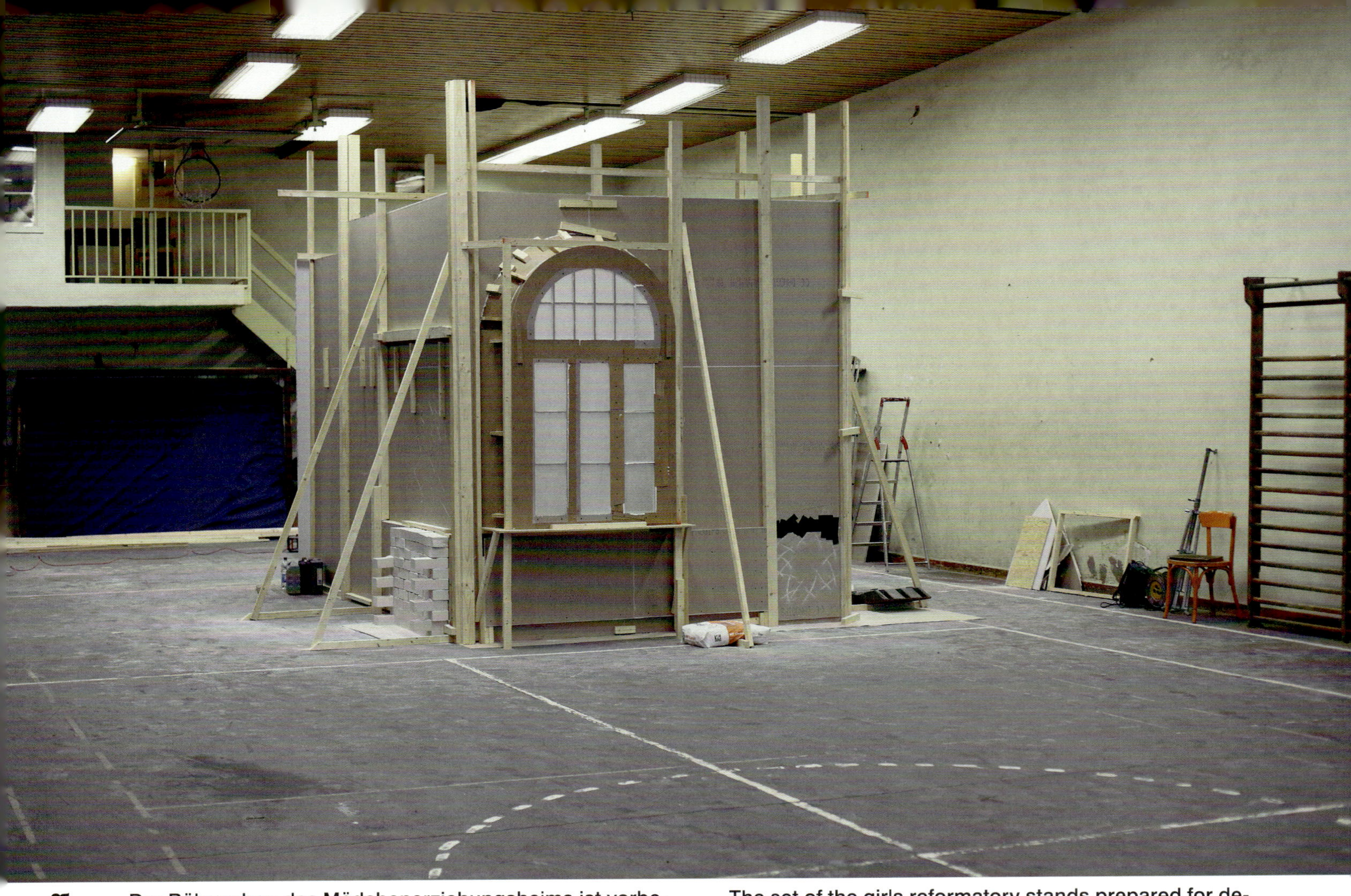

Der Bühnenbau des Mädchenerziehungsheims ist vorbe-reitet, um zerstört zu werden. Die Schauspielerinnen brechen durch die Kulisse nach außen.

The set of the girls reformatory stands prepared for de-struction. The actresses break through the fake walls to free themselves.

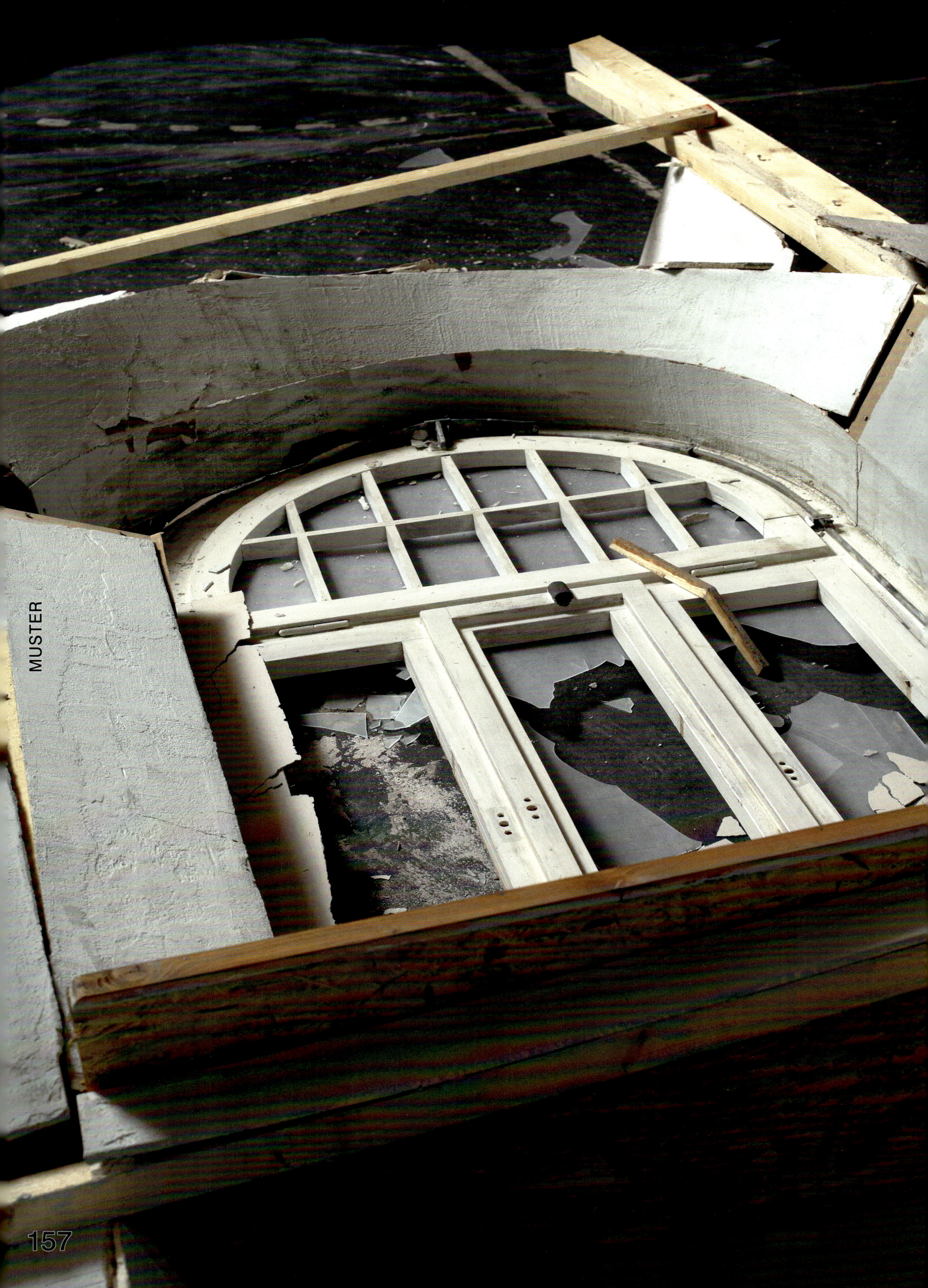
MUSTER

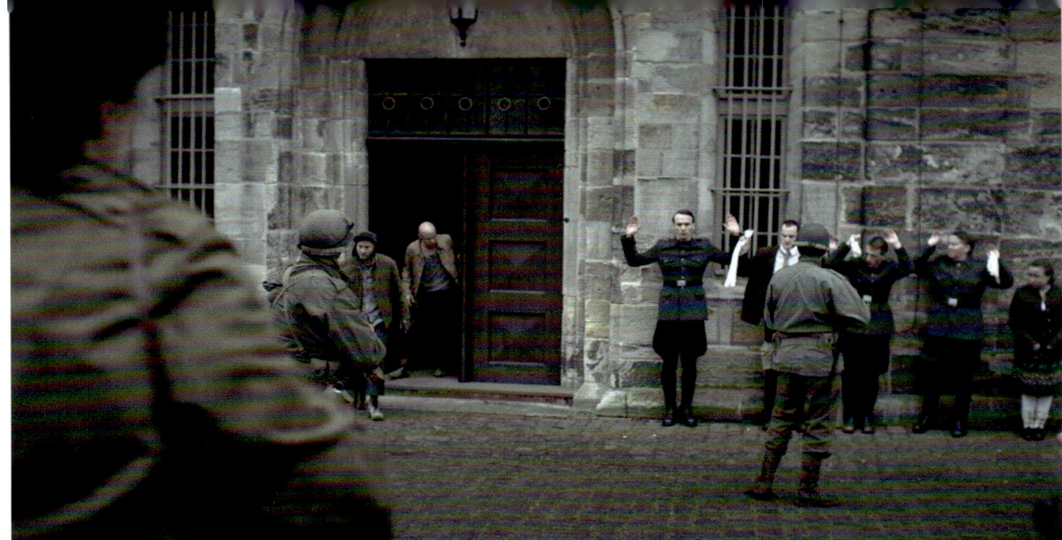

We are scouts from the
86th Cavalry Reconnaissance
Squadron, 6th Armored
Division. This is the U.S.
3rd Army. You are free!

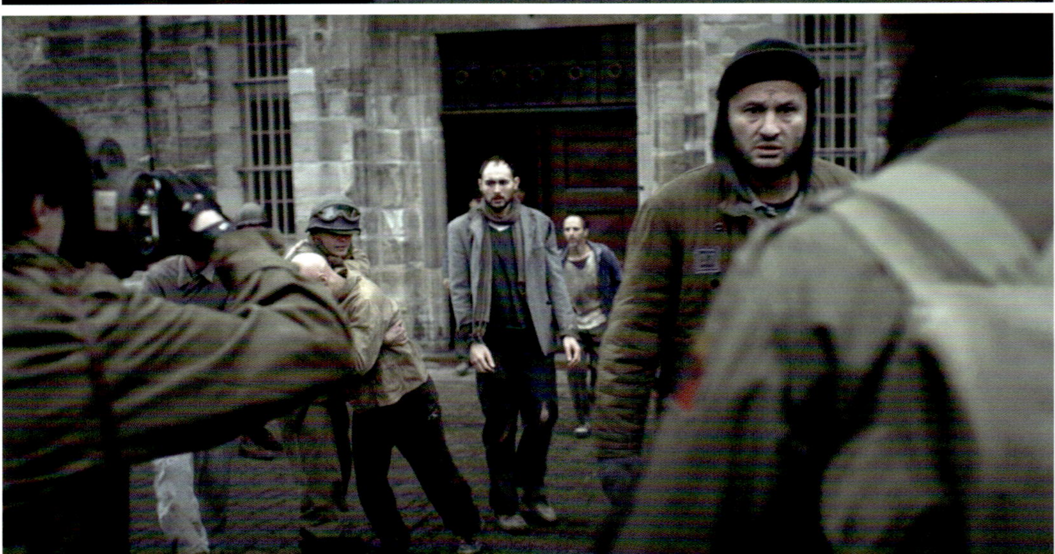

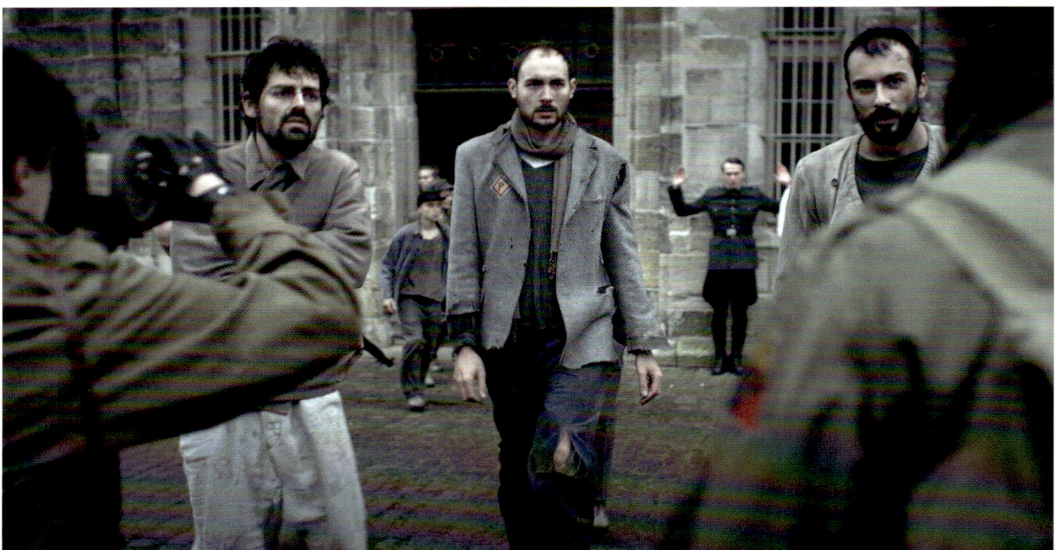

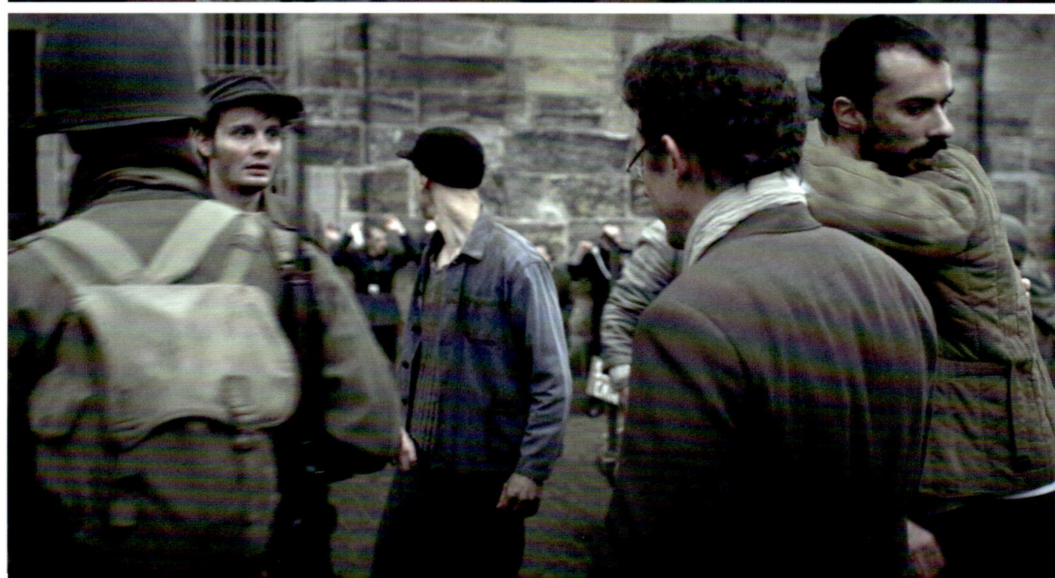

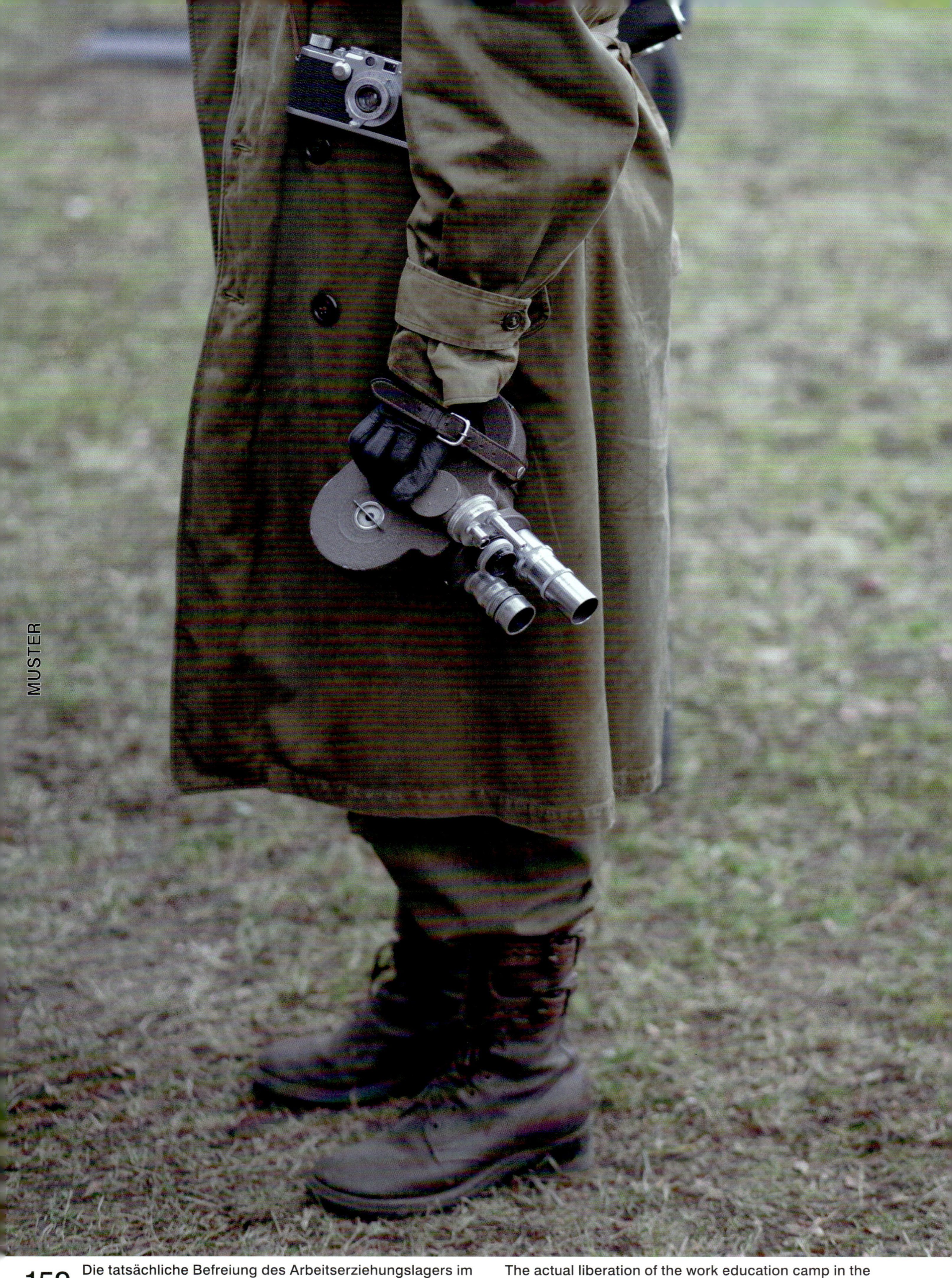

159 Die tatsächliche Befreiung des Arbeitserziehungslagers im Frühjahr 1945 wurde nicht dokumentiert.

The actual liberation of the work education camp in the spring of 1945 was not documented.

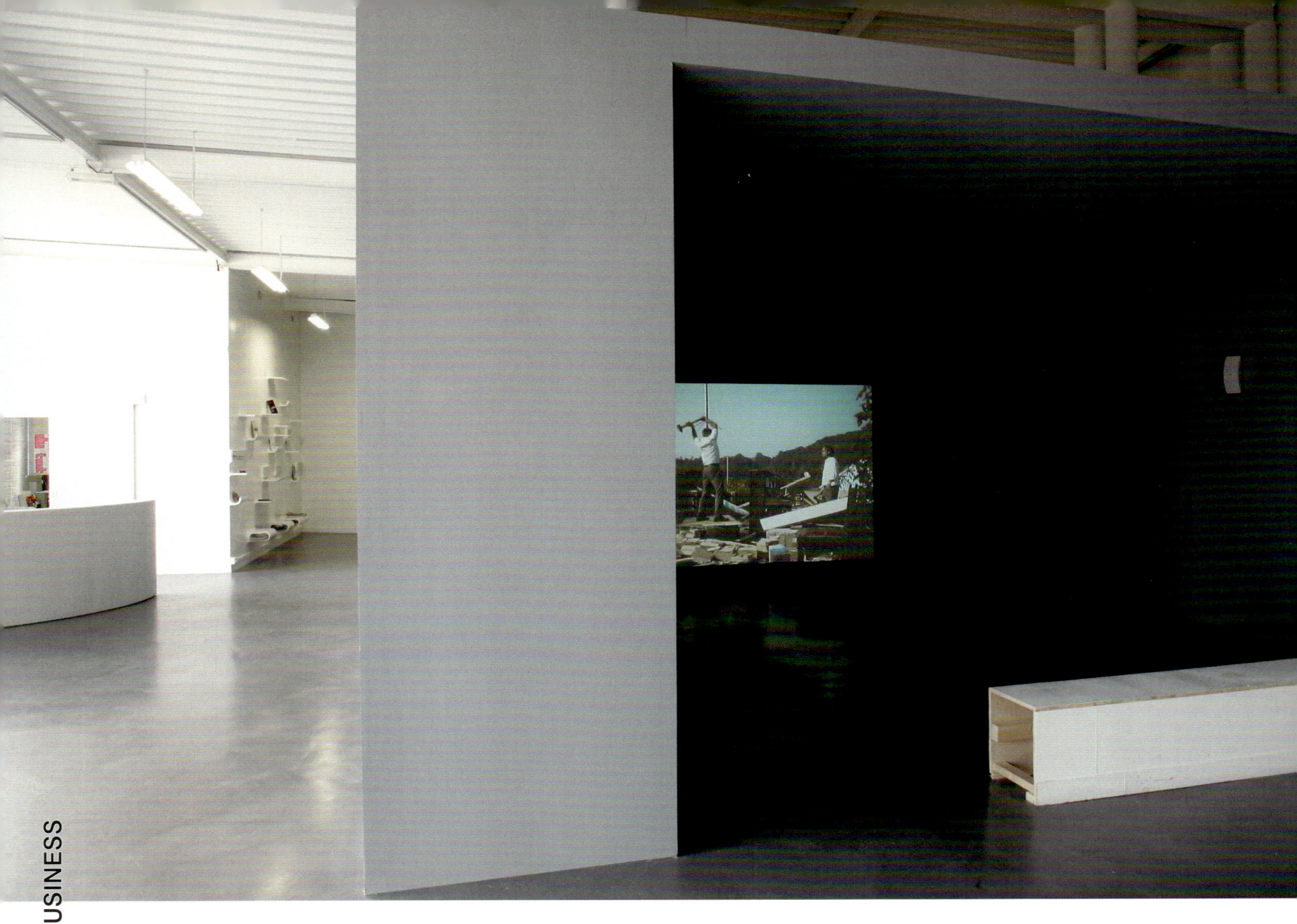

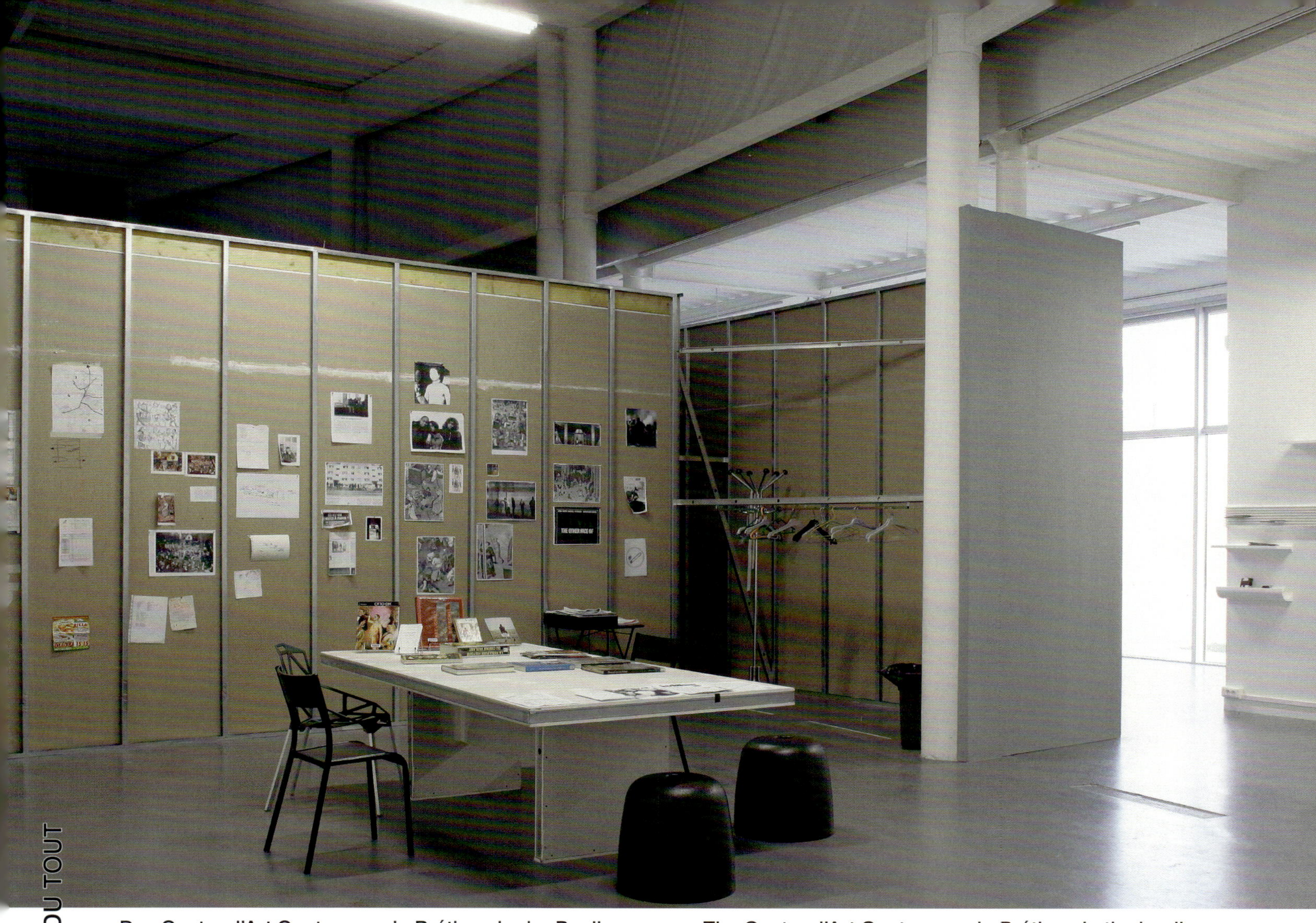

Das Centre d'Art Contemporain Brétigny in der Banlieue von Paris wurde durch die Architektur in zwei Bereiche geteilt: vorn die Ausstellung, hinten Räume für die Produktion eines ortsspezifischen Films.

The Centre d'Art Contemporain Brétigny in the banlieue of Paris was divided into two parts by the architecture: in front, the exhibition; in back, the rooms for the production of a site-specific film.

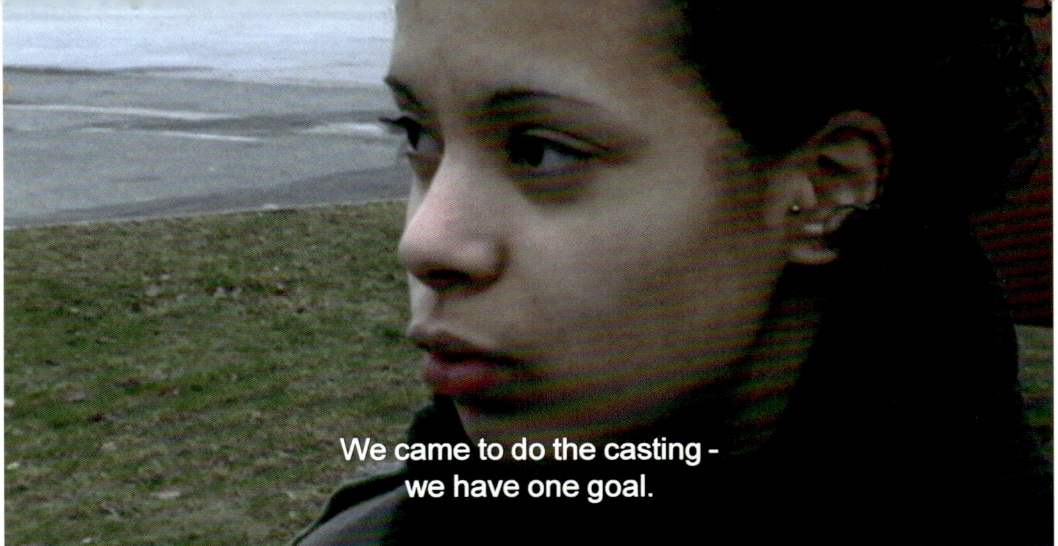
We came to do the casting -
we have one goal.

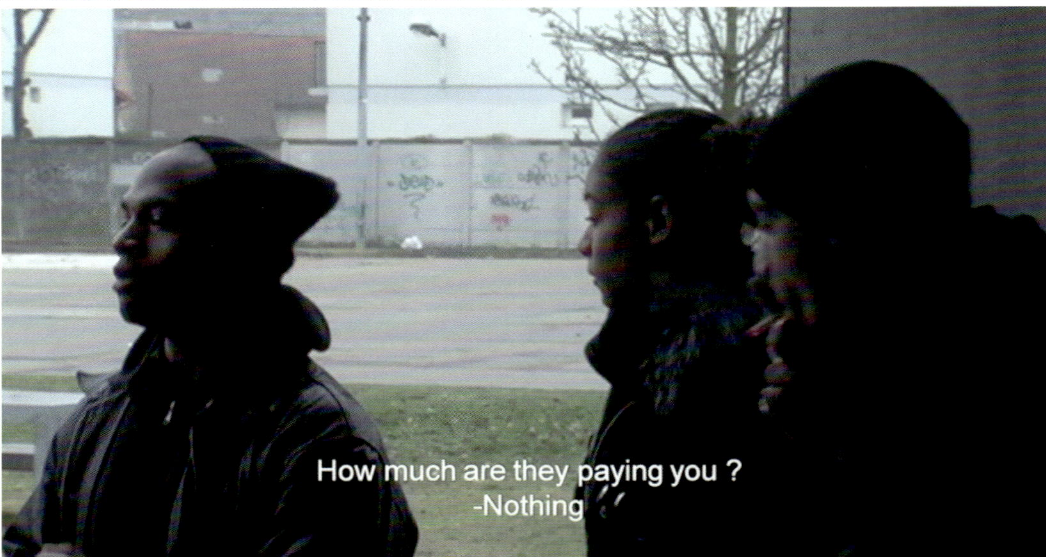
How much are they paying you ?
-Nothing

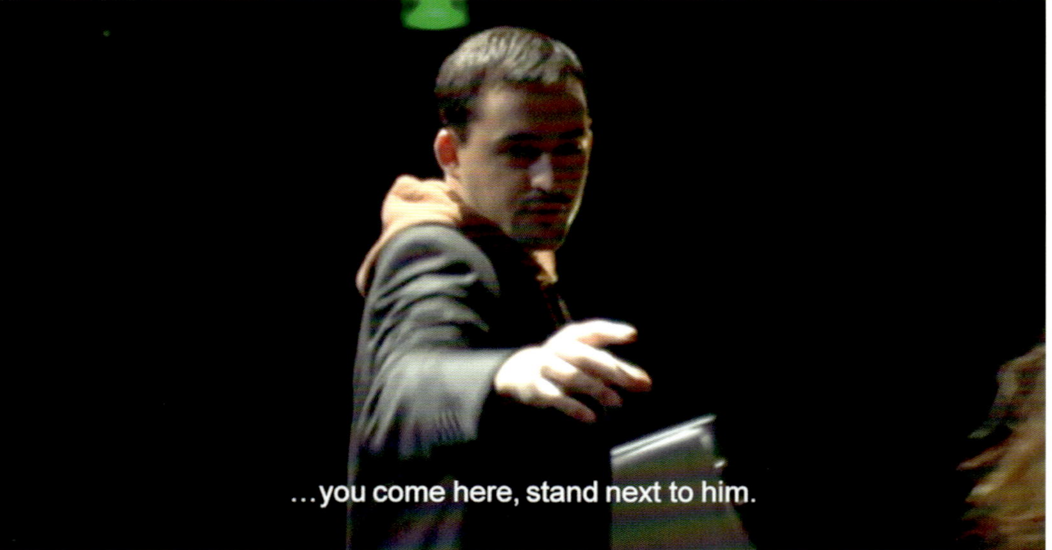
...you come here, stand next to him.

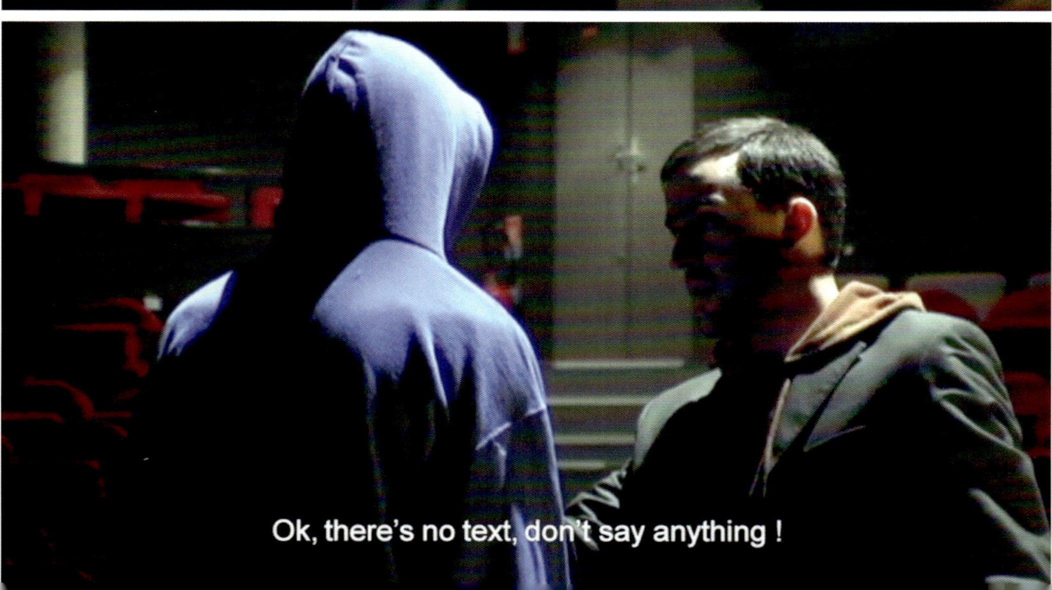
Ok, there's no text, don't say anything !

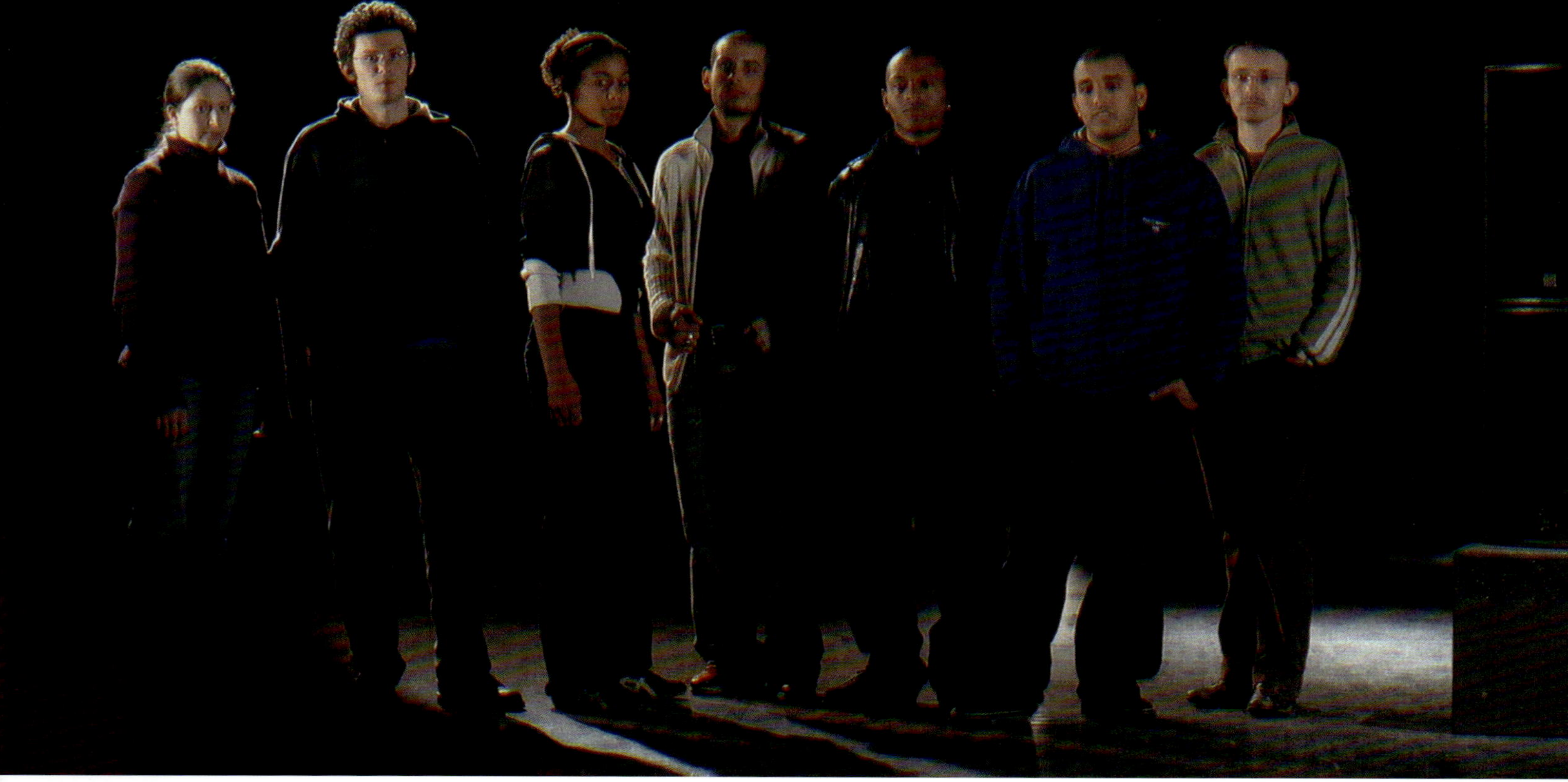

Die jungen Statisten haben an einem Casting teilgenommen und wurden alle aufgenommen. Es gab keine Auswahl, sie müssen sich nicht selbst spielen. Sie erhalten eine Rolle im Film.

The young extras took part in an audition and were all accepted. There was no selection process, they don't have to play themselves. They get a role in the film.

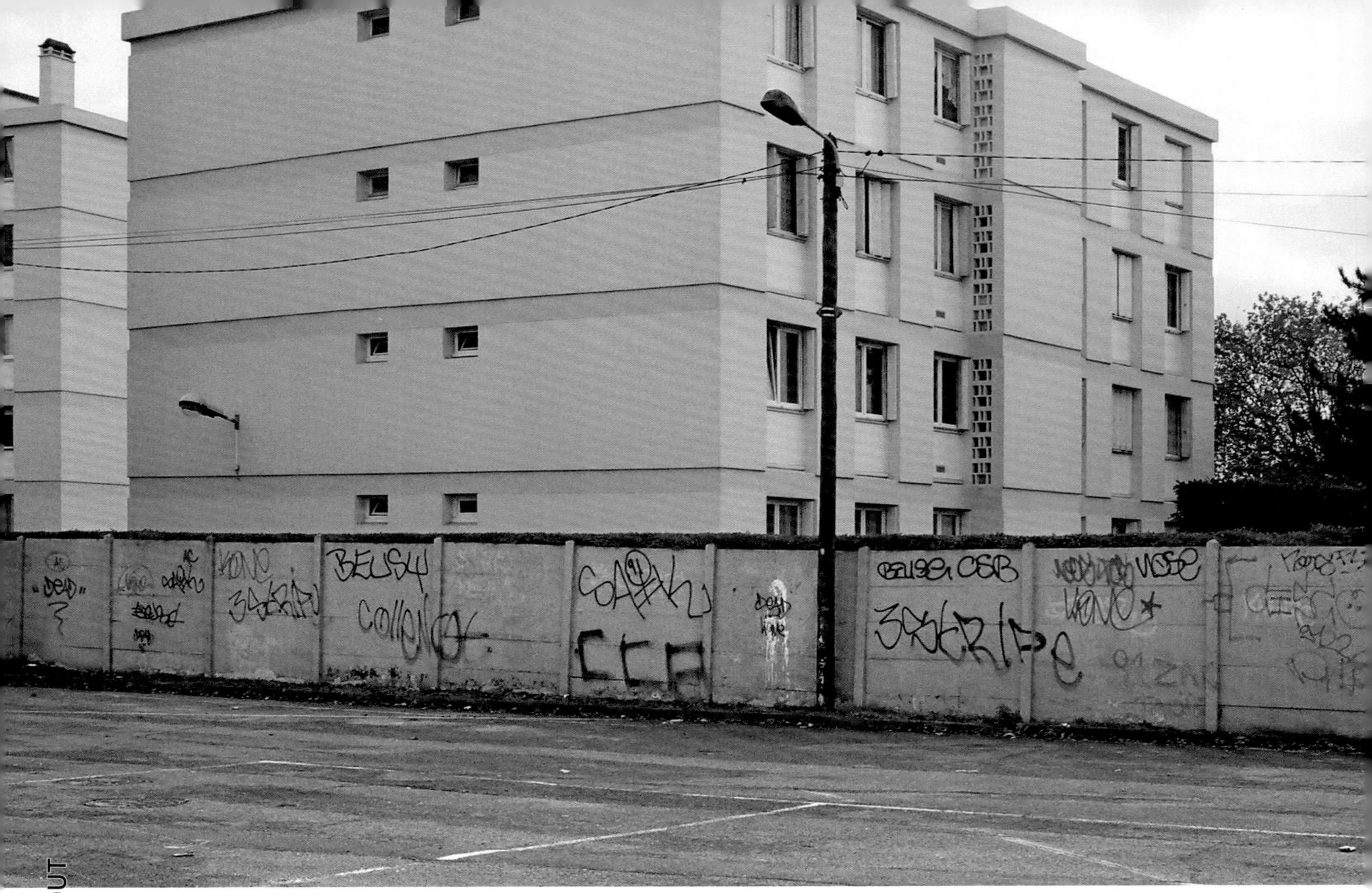

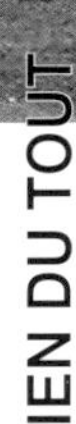

RIEN DU TOUT

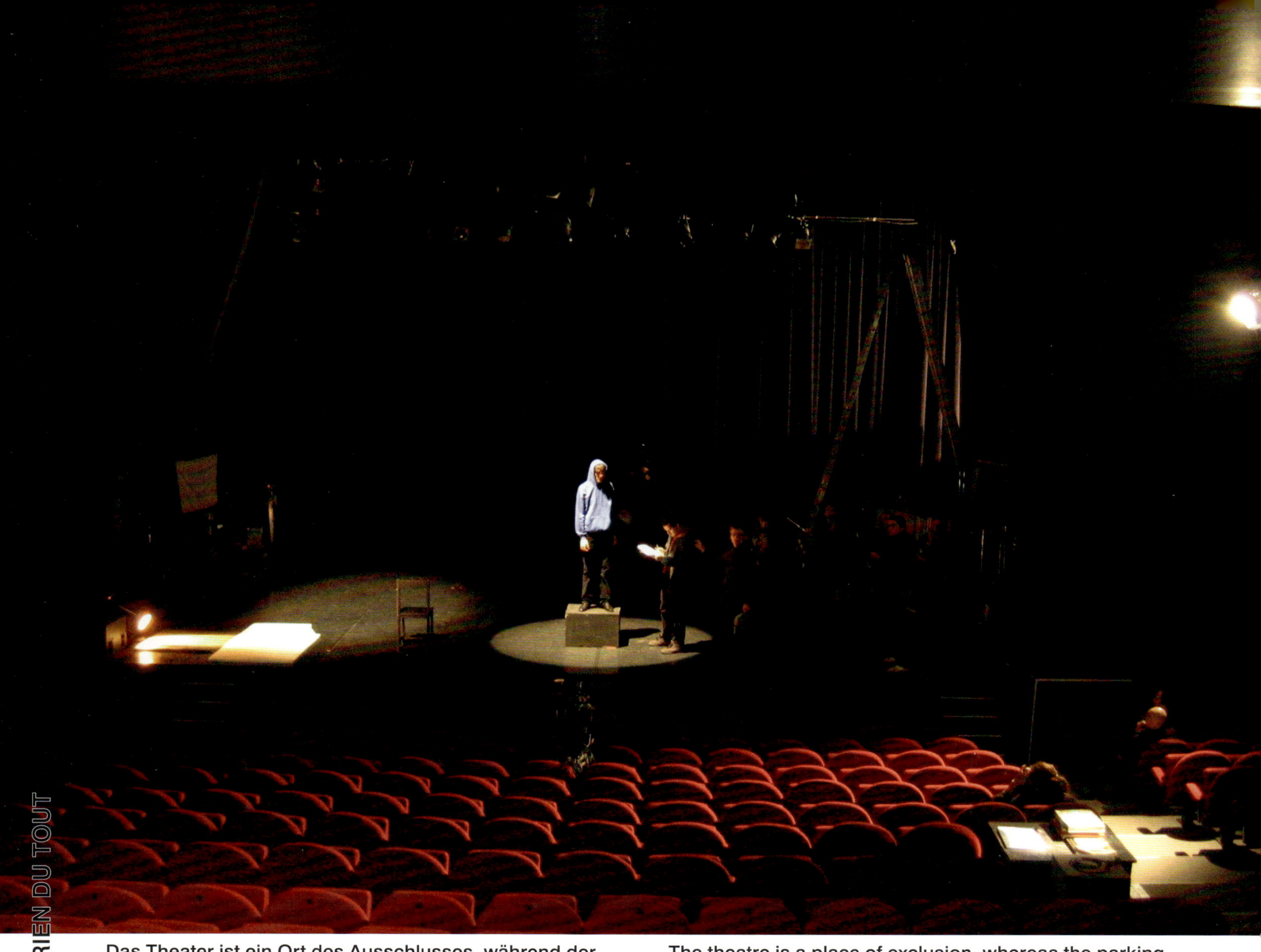

Das Theater ist ein Ort des Ausschlusses, während der Parkplatz vor dem Gebäude zur Bühne wird.

The theatre is a place of exclusion, whereas the parking area in front of the building becomes the stage.

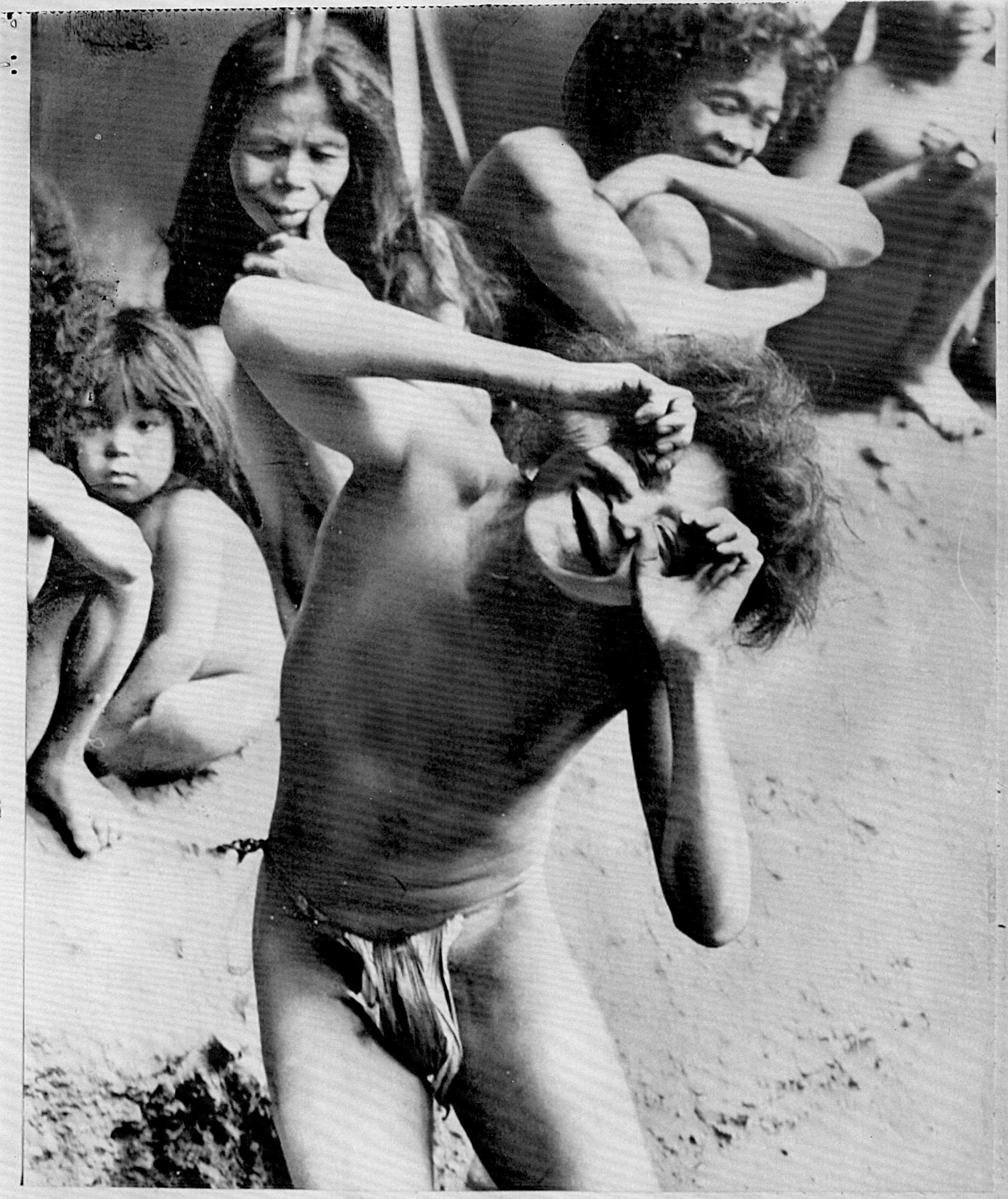

In den 1970er Jahren wurden auf den Philippinen die Tasaday entdeckt, die wie in der Steinzeit lebten. In den 1980er Jahren bezweifelte ein Schweizer Journalist ihre Identität und warf ihnen vor, sich nur verkleidet zu haben.

In the 1970s, the Tasaday, who lived like Stone Age dwellers, were discovered in the Philippines. In the 1980s, a Swiss journalist questioned their identity and accused them of just wearing costumes.

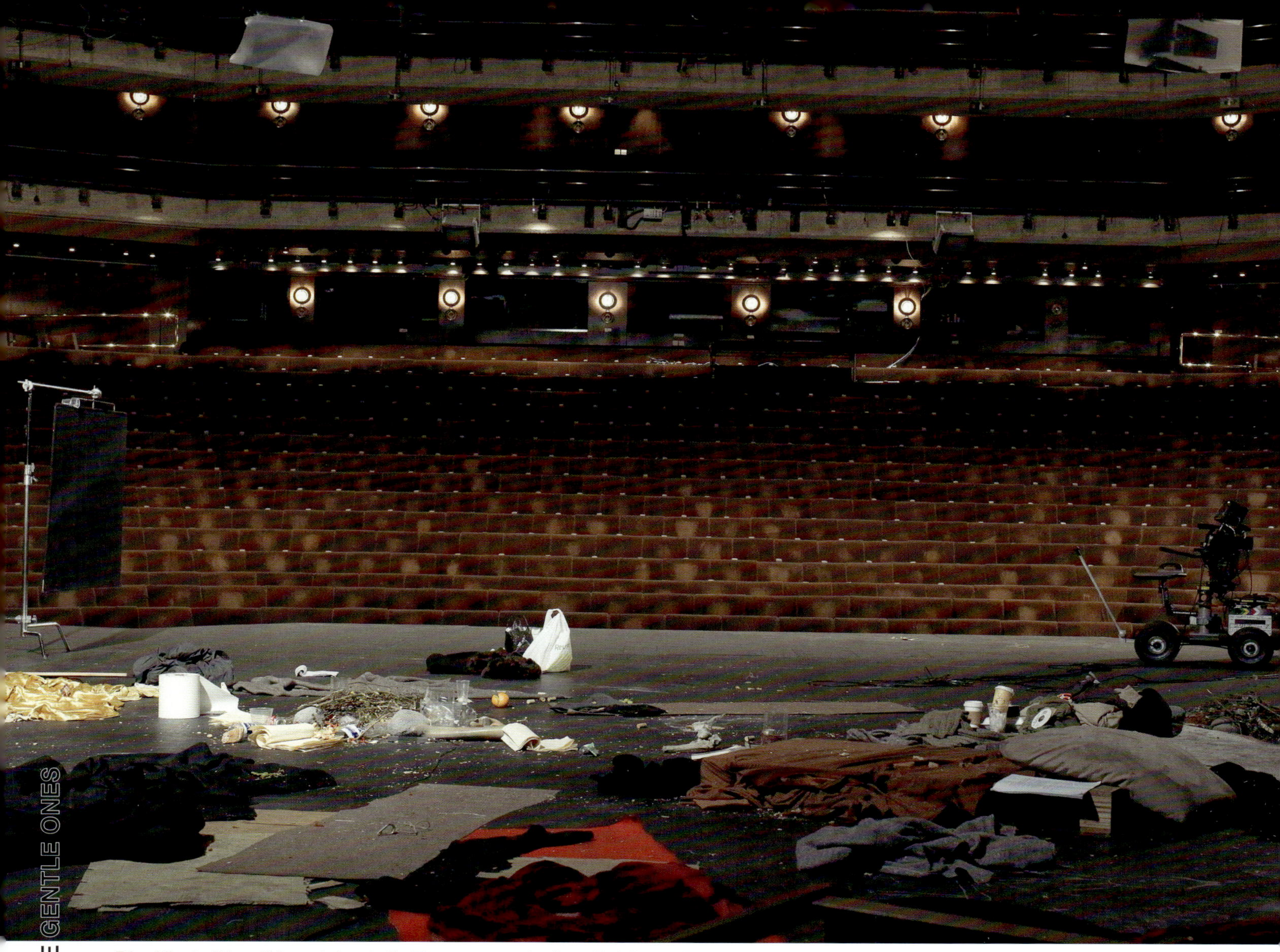

Die „Vierte Wand" bezeichnet die Trennung zwischen Publikum und Bühne.

The fourth wall signifies the division between the audience and the stage.

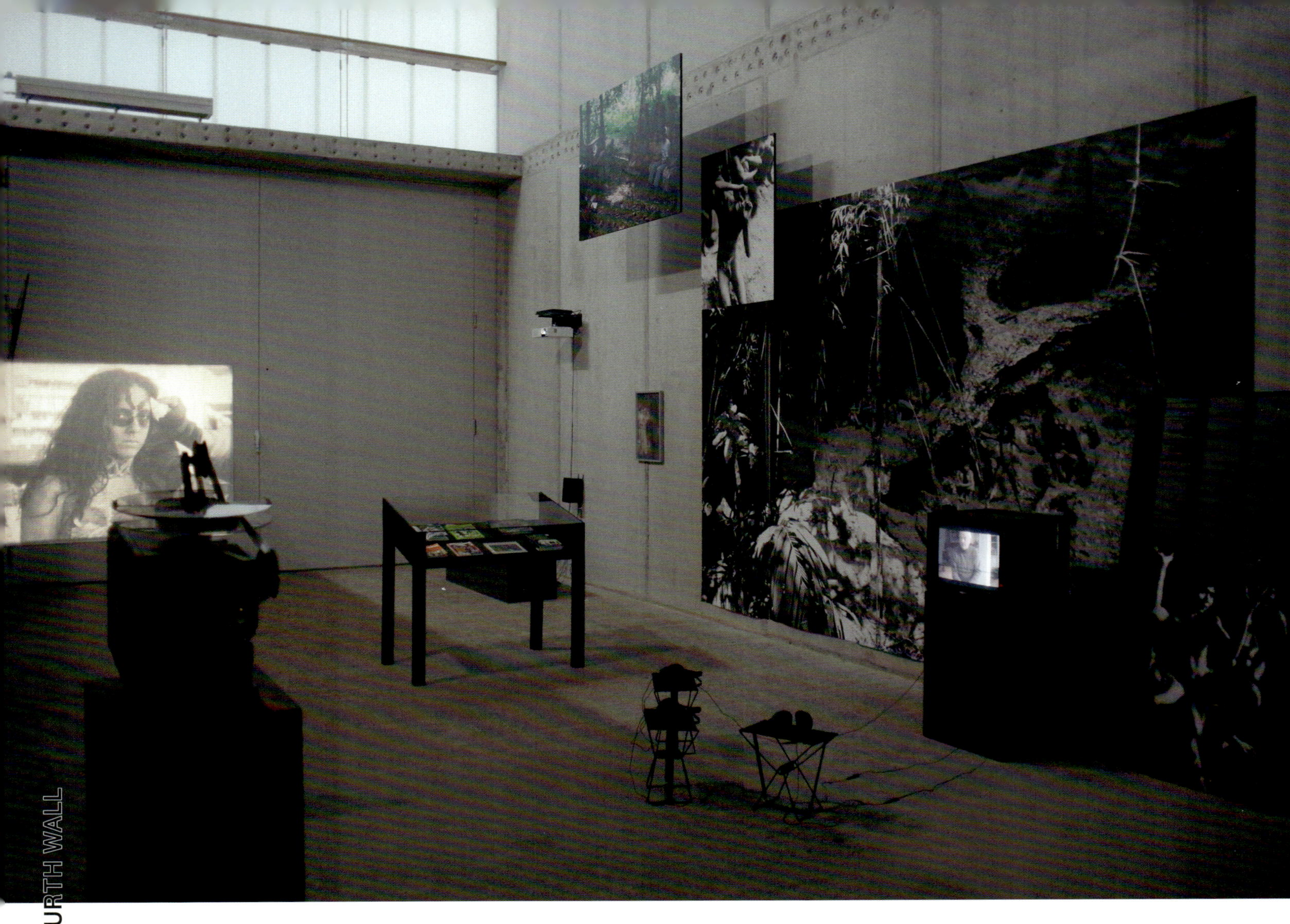

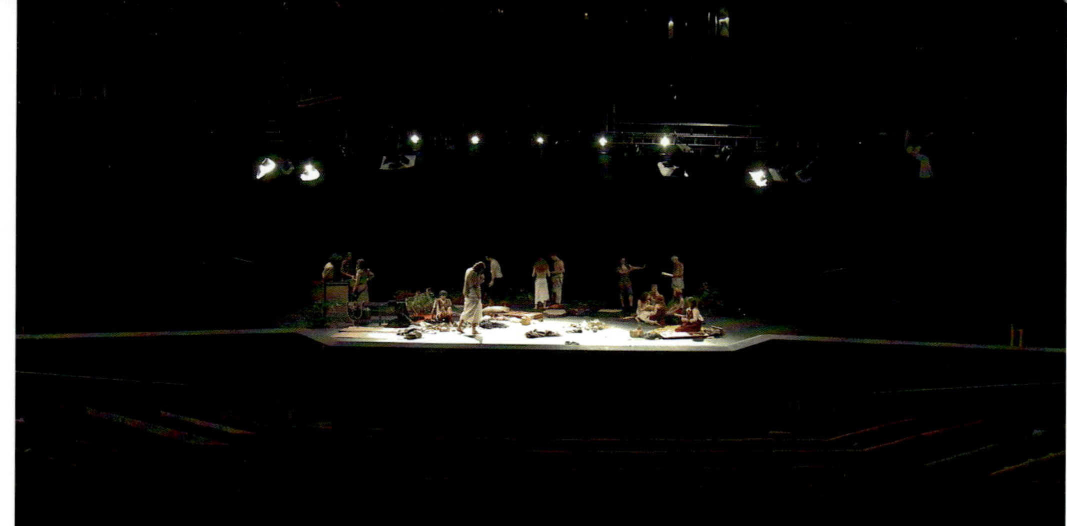

We.

We speak a language.

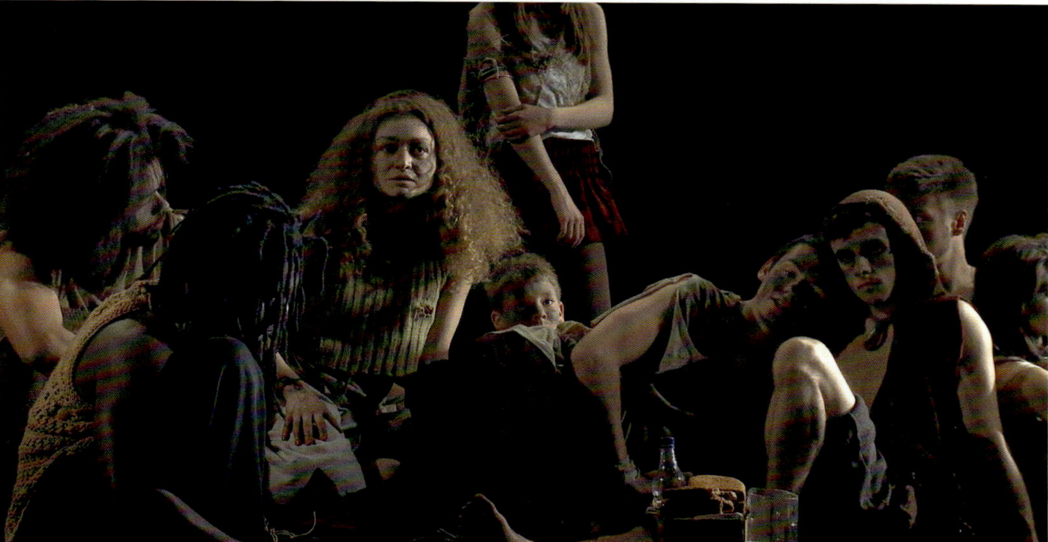

Have a.

We have a name.

Horrible.

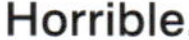
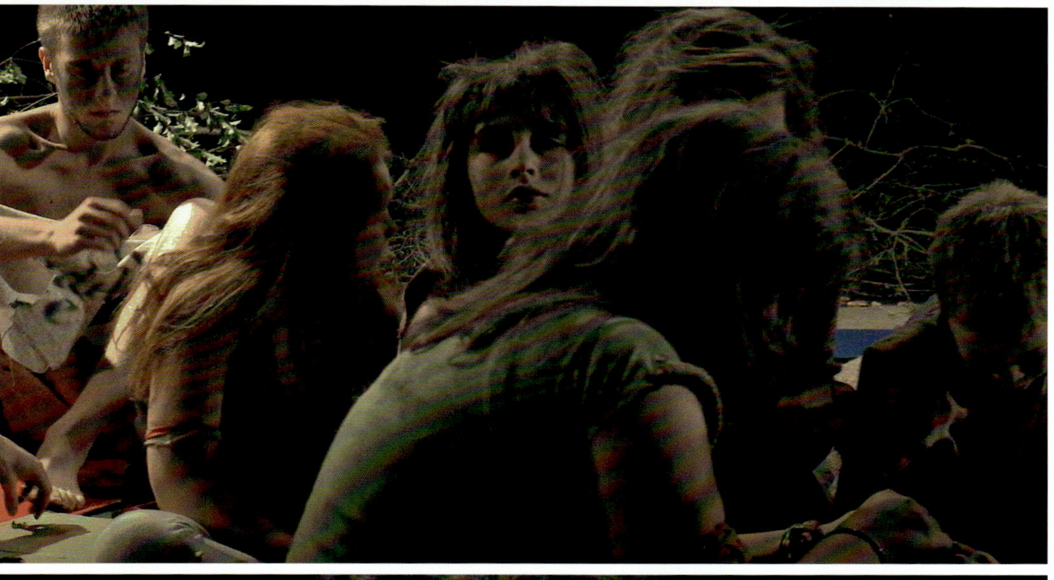

We speak a language that nobody understands.

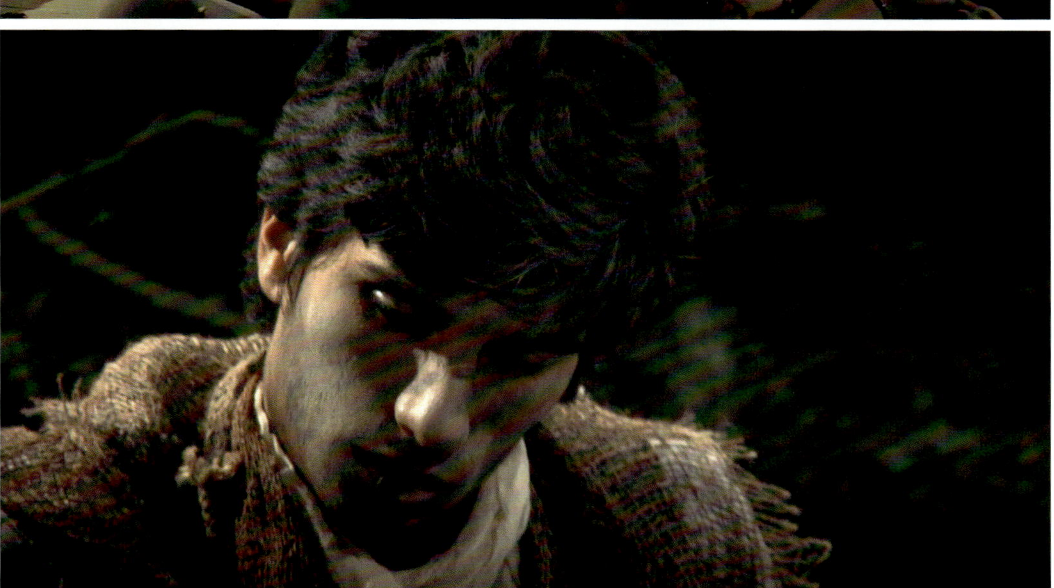

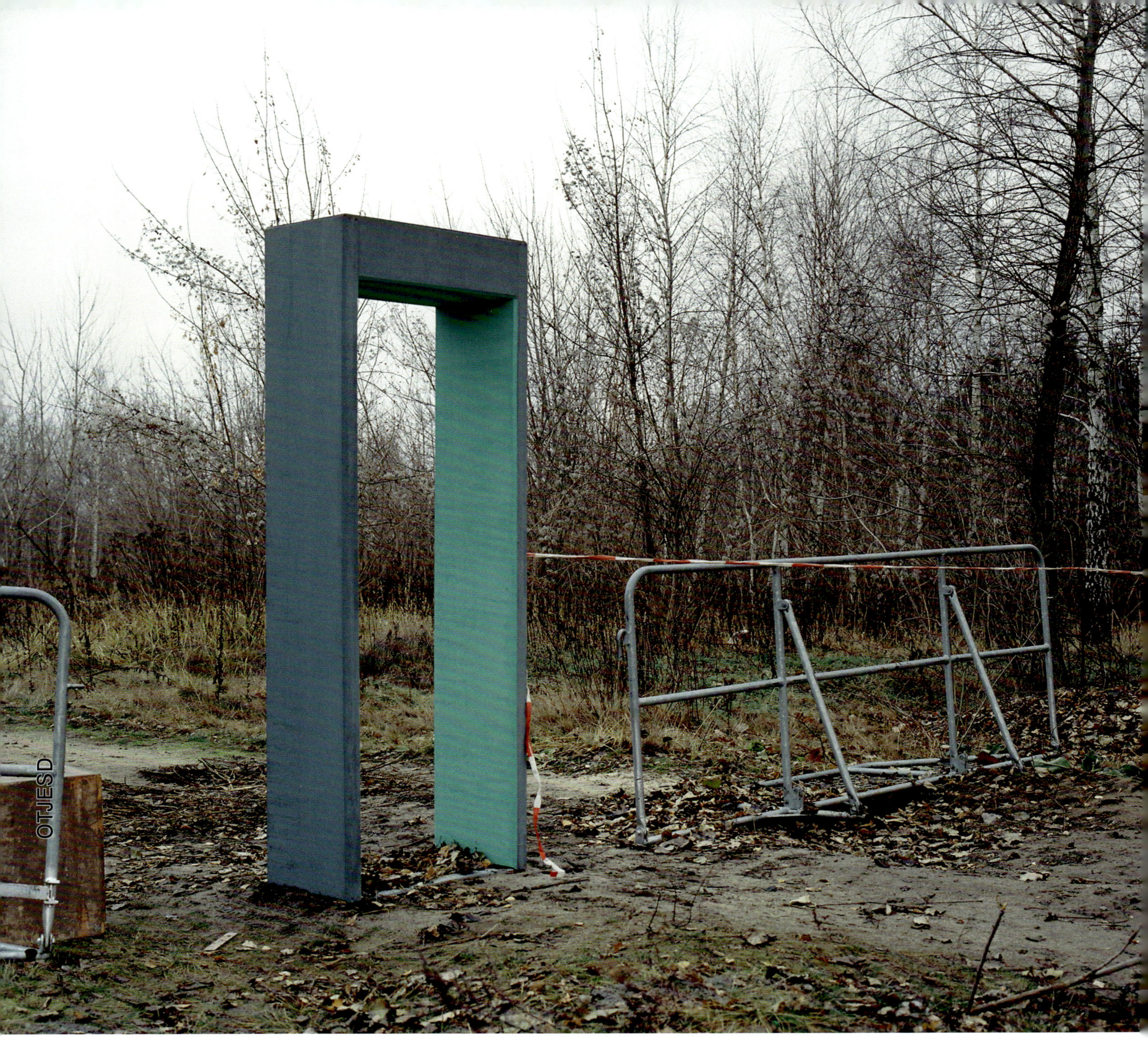
OTJESD

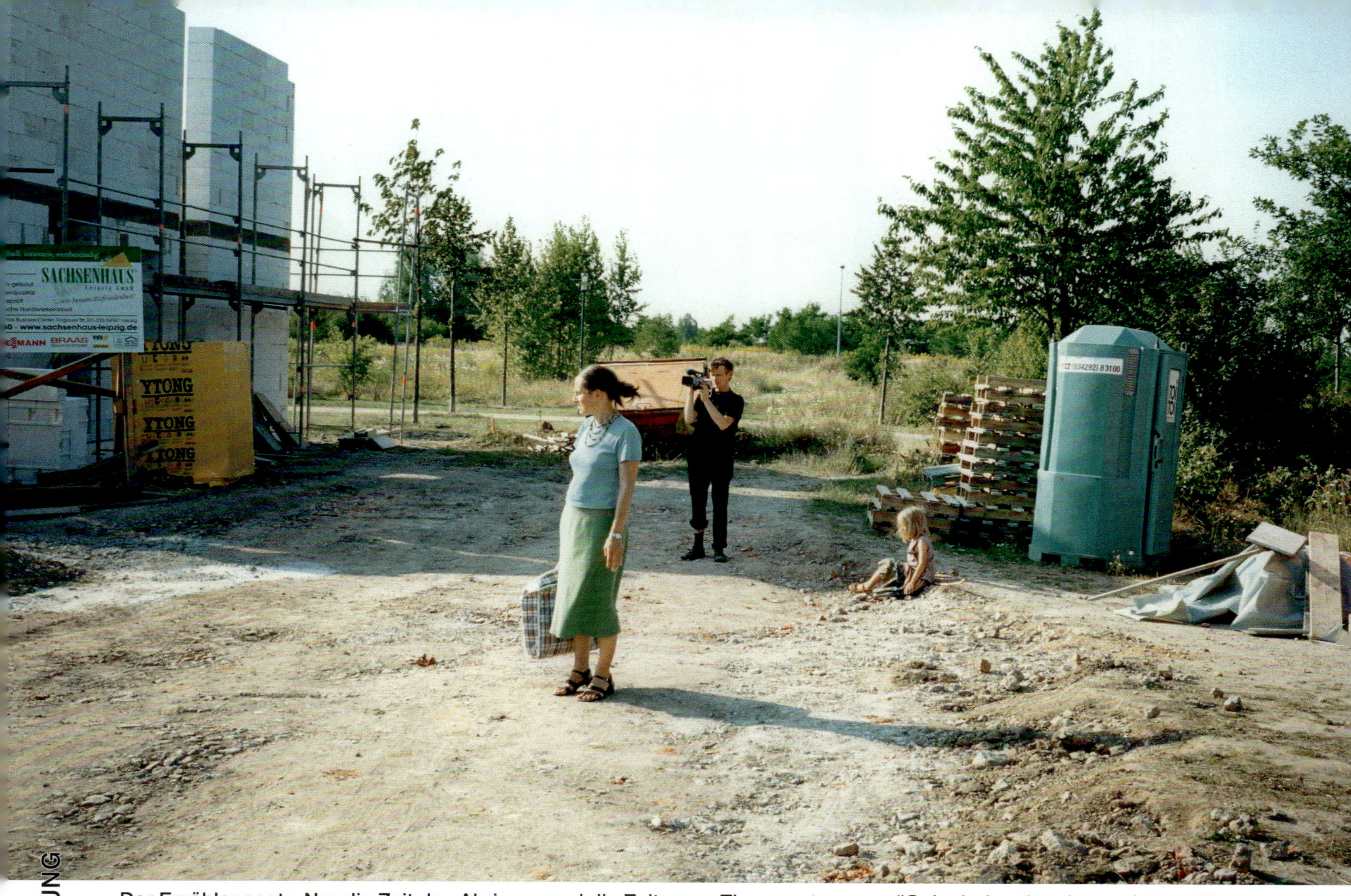

Der Erzähler sagt: „Nur die Zeit des Abrisses und die Zeit des Aufbaus bieten einen Blick hinter die Oberfläche, die sich langsam in diese Bilder einschreibt. Die gegenwärtige Ansammlung von verschiedenen Bauten um eine definierte Fläche ist genauso widersprüchlich wie die Geschichte seines Ortes selber. Sobald die Oberfläche entstanden ist, kann man sagen, dass der Film gescheitert ist, genauso wie das Areal, das der Gegenstand seiner Betrachtung war."

The narrator says: "Only during the phase of demolition and construction does one get a glimpse under the surface, a surface that inscribes itself onto these images. The present collage of different buildings around a predefined area is as contradictory as the history of the place itself. As soon as the surface is in place, you could say that the film has failed, just like the area that was its subject."

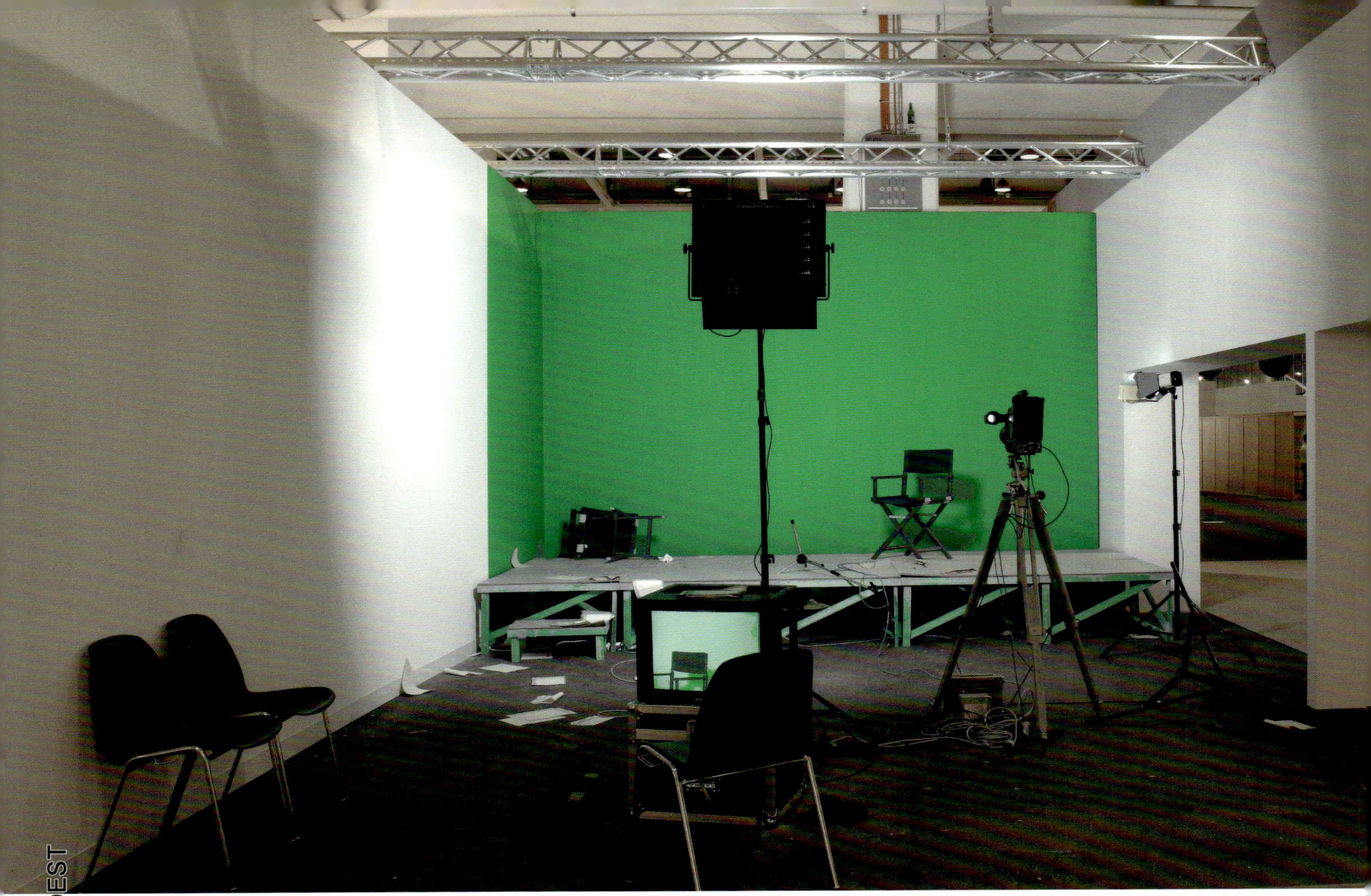

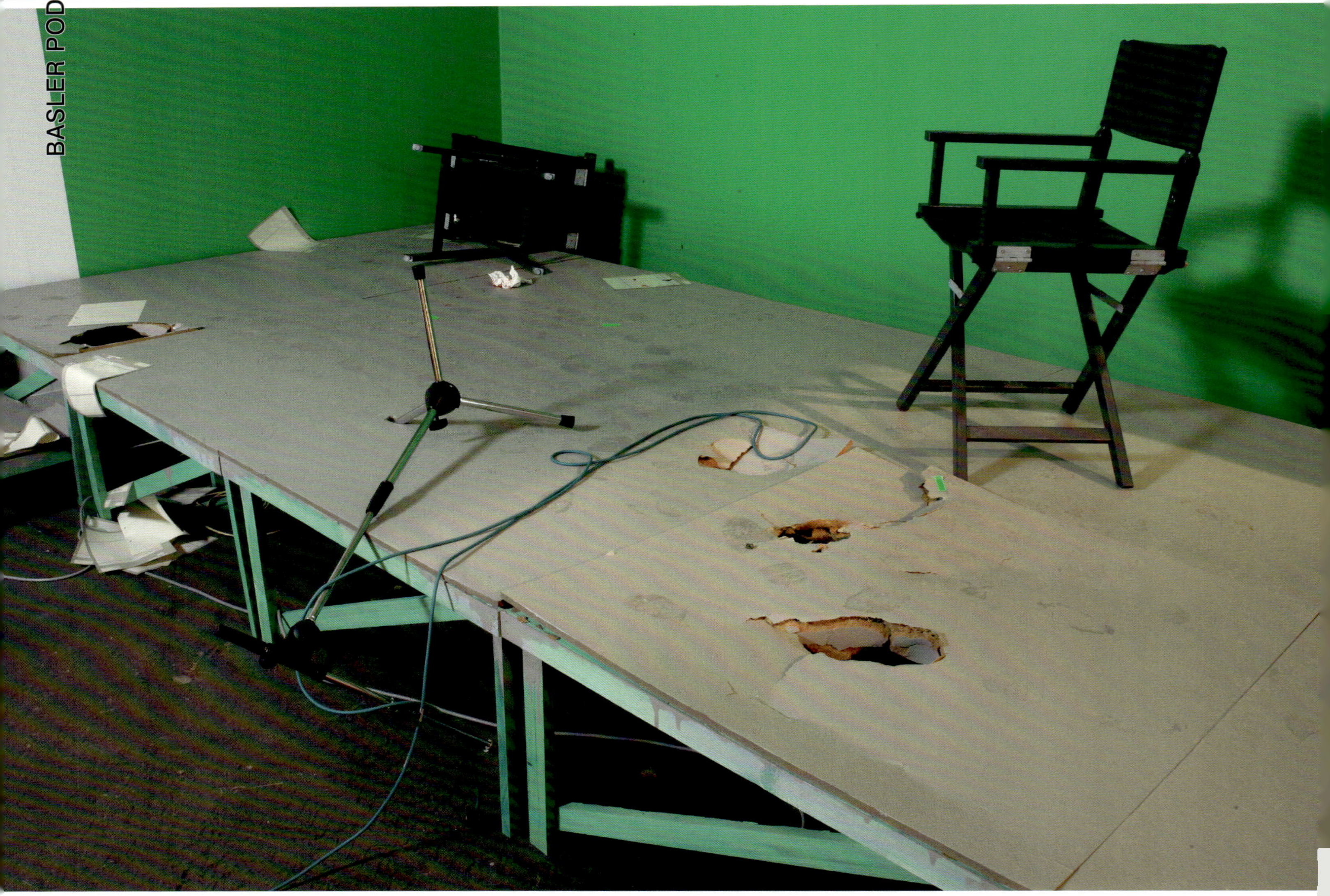

BASLER PODEST

IM DIESSEITS DES BLICKS HINTER DIE KULISSEN

Sabeth Buchmann

Wenn es etwas gibt, das die Filme Clemens von Wedemeyers wie ein roter Faden durchzieht, dann ist es das Sujet der Probe. Der hiermit assoziierte Blick hinter die Kulissen ist ein Blick, dem sich (scheinbar) zeigt, was üblicher Weise unsichtbar bleibt und der zugleich die Skripte zu seinen „Backstagedramen" liefert: wartende Statisten, improvisierende Darsteller, autoritäre Regisseure, rebellierende Mitarbeiter, ungeplante Dialoge, nebensächliche Ereignisse. Stellt die Probe im Theater oder Film ein gängiges, der Metareflexion dienendes Darstellungsmittel dar, ist sie im Kontext der bildenden Kunst keineswegs selbstverständlich. Gemäß der vorherrschenden Vorstellung experimentieren Künstler oder probieren allenfalls etwas aus. Doch nicht nur Clemens von Wedemeyer, sondern eine ganze Reihe seiner Kollegen, so seine (Kooperations-) Partnerin Maya Schweizer oder auch Pauline Baudry / Renate Lorenz, Gerard Byrne, Keren Cytter, Harun Farocki, Omer Fast, Ana Hoffner, Eva Meyer / Eran Schaerf, Constanze Ruhm, Katarina Zdjelar u.a. rekurrieren auf das Format der Probe als einer signifikanten Nahtstelle zwischen performativen und visuellen Künsten. Als erweiterte Version des Making-of bestehen ihre künstlerischen Appropriationen aus häufig ineinander verwobenen double plot lines aus Fiktion und Dokumentation. Im Unterschied zum klassischen Making-of stellt die semidokumentarische / semifiktionale Probe kein supplementäres Genre im Sinne einer Rekonstruktion der Werkgenese dar; hingegen liegt die Betonung auf dem „in the making" von Rollen und Darstellungsregeln, von Mono- und Dialogen, von Aktionen und Szenen, von Kamera-, Ton-, Beleuchtungs- und Schnitttechnik.

Wie von Wedemeyers Film *Die Probe* (2008) auf buchstäbliche Weise verdeutlicht, wird damit kein experimentelles oder unvollständiges künstlerisches Produktionsstadium insinuiert: Die Probe *ist* vielmehr das Werk – indes eines, das als modus operandi seiner selbst zur Aufführung kommt. So besteht *Die Probe* aus der (scheinbar) ungeschnittenen Sequenz einer im Backstagebereich eines Auditoriums angesiedelten Szene. Ein eben gewählter Präsident, der – für die Zuschauer indes nur hörbar – auf der Bühne bejubelt wird, probt hier mit einem Berater seine Antrittsrede, in der er entgegen aller Erwartungen seinen Amtsverzicht erklären wird. Sobald er den Backstagebereich verlassen hat, beginnt der Loop von Neuem.

Die Probe bringt somit die Quintessenz des modernen Dramas, sprich den Akt und Moment der Entscheidung auf den buchstäblichen Punkt: Im klassischen Drama Ausdruck eines souverän handelnden, weil zwischen zwei oder mehreren Optionen wählenden Subjekts[1], besteht die „alles entscheidende" Entscheidung in *Die Probe* ironischerweise darin, gerade jene mit größtmöglicher Handlungsautorität, mithin mit Regierungsmacht ausgestattete Rolle abzulehnen. Angesichts der damit aufgeworfenen Frage, ob und auf welche Weise die Öffentlichkeit ab Sekunde 1 nach der Wahl weiterhin am politischen Prozess beteiligt ist, mag es kein Zufall sein, dass die gezeigte Szene an einem Ort stattfindet, von dem das Publikum üblicherweise ausgeschlossen ist. Damit ist die Sphäre der Hinterbühne respektive des Offs gemeint, die – wie die Medien- und Theaterwissenschaftlerin Stefanie Diekmann in ihrem Buch *Backstage. Konstellationen von Theater und Kino* zeigt – konstitutiv sowohl für avantgardistische „Konzepte zu einer Re-Organisation des Theaterraumes"[2] als auch für populäre Theater- und Kinofiktionen ist. Die Verkehrung von Bühne und Hinterbühne habe dabei klassischerweise die Funktion, „bekannte Raumordnung(en) in andere Topologien (aufzulösen)"[3]. Solche „Ortswechsel und Entgrenzungsbewegungen"[4] sind Diekmann zufolge dazu angetan, bestehende „Demarkationslinien"[5] zwischen dem Realen und Fiktiven, mithin dem Sozialen und Ästhetischen – und das heißt schließlich auch zwischen dem Dokumentarischen und Fiktiven – gleichsam auf die Probe zu stellen.

Die Probe stellt demnach genau diesen zwischen Passage und Grenze oszillierenden, d.h. einen der Darstellung räumlich und zeitlich vorausgehenden Ort und Vorgang dar, der erst in der Fiktion als Bestandteil topologischer Blickordnungen ansichtig wird. Von Wedemeyers Film impliziert genau das: Eine Verschaltung von „Zuschauerraum und Hinterbühne"[6], die uns jene Szene, die wir sehen, als fiktive Probe einer Inszenierung präsentiert, welche zugleich unserem Blick entzogen bleibt. Wir sehen demnach nicht, was wir sehen, sondern wir sehen, was wir üblicherweise nicht sehen. Dieses auf Raum- als Blickumkehr beruhende Wechselspiel zwischen Sichtbarmachung und Sichtbarkeits-entzug weist die Probe – und hier zeigt sich eine ihrer grundlegenden Bedeutungen für die bil-dende Kunst – als Strategie aus, der Faktizität des Bildes die Möglichkeit seiner Alterität ent-gegenzuhalten: In *Die Probe* ist es das in letzter Sekunde umgeschriebene Skript. Wie im „wirk-lichen" Drama kommt die unerwartete Wendung (fast zu) spät, aber nicht, wenn alle Würfel schon gefallen sind.

Eine solche, für den Topos der Probe charakte-ristische, auch in anderen Arbeiten von Wede-meyers charakteristische Zuspitzung auf die inne-ren Konflikte seiner Protagonisten weist selbst-redend einen metareflexiven Kern auf. Denn die Möglichkeit der Umschrift eines vorgegebe-nen Skripts betrifft, so die Botschaft, zugleich die Möglichkeit, jene für die „Demarkationslinien" zwischen Realität und Fiktion konstitutiven Rollen- und Handlungsmuster zu verändern. Begreift man *Die Probe* in dem zuvor skizzierten Sinn als Quintessenz des modernen Dramas, d.h. als Möglichkeits- und Ausdrucksbedingung von Entscheidungsfreiheit, die, sobald die In-szenierung einmal steht bzw. das Werk vollendet ist, nicht mehr gegeben ist, tritt zugleich seine eminent politische Bedeutung zutage. Denn da der eben gewählte Präsidentschaftskandidat bei der Erprobung eines anderen als des ihm zugedachten Skripts gezeigt wird, lässt die aus-geschlagene Position der Macht zugleich als Rolle erscheinen, die prinzipiell auch von anderen „gespielt" werden könnte.

In diesem Licht betrachtet impliziert der fiktive Einblick in den Backstagebereich als einen Raum, in dem sich die „eigentliche" Produktion vollzieht, einen Nexus von Aktualität und Virtualität (Gilles Deleuze): Das heißt, dass die Kategorie des Bildes sich als Manifestation einer möglichen, durch ein zugrunde liegendes Skript prinzipiell variierbaren (und aussetzbaren) Handlung erweist. Ein solches sowohl an (post-)konzeptuelle als auch an das postdramatische Verfahren erinnern-des Modell, demzufolge eine Instruktion oder ein Drehbuch in einem aktiven, weil je nach Aus- und Aufführung sich verändernden Dialog mit den jeweiligen Werken steht, lässt weitere Rück-schlüsse auf *Die Probe* zu. So erkennen wir auch hier einen direkten Konnex zwischen Skript und Film – ein Moment, der die geloopte Narration selbst als Bedingung und Effekt ihres Dargestellt-

und Gefilmtwerdens ansichtig werden lässt. Die für das Verfahren der Probe charakteristische Spannung zwischen mimetischer und reflexi-ver Rolleninszenierung integriert dabei Brechts Strategie der Verfremdung als eine Fiktion, die der topologischen Umkehr von Blick- und Raum-ordnung immanent ist.

Dieser reflexive Nexus spielt auch in anderen Arbeiten von Wedemeyers eine zentrale Rolle – so in der mit Maya Schweizer ursprünglich für das CAC Brétigny entwickelten Film- und Video-installation *Rien du tout* (2006). Auch der auf HD-Format übertragene 35 mm- und Video-Film weist eine Verkehrung klassischer Raum- und Blickordnung in dem Sinn auf, als Film- und Video-kameras das Dies- und Jenseits institutioneller „Demarkationslinien" miteinander in Beziehung setzen: In diesem Fall die Theaterbühne mit einem außerhalb des Theatergebäudes gelegenen Parkplatz. Die Hinterbühne ist gleichsam aus dem Theater ausgezogen und befindet sich nun in einem vermeintlich „realen", dem geschlos-senen Raum der Institution entgegensetzten Off. Auch hier korrelieren Figuren der Umkehr mit der Transformation institutioneller Rollenhie-rarchien: Während die Szene zunächst von einer tyrannischen Regisseurin beherrscht wird, die eine zunehmend ins Stocken geratende Probe eines Stücks über die Banlieues im Paris des Mittel-alters orchestriert, treten sukzessive die im Off wartenden Statisten in den Vordergrund. Hierbei handelt es sich um Schüler einer Schule, die in einer heutigen, als soziales Problemgebiet gelten-den Banlieue liegt. Ihre Dialoge, die den Anschein „schlechter", weil allzu absichtsvoller Improvi-sation erwecken, basieren dabei auf Gesprächen, die von Wedemeyer und Schweizer beim voraus-gegangenen Casting mit ihnen geführt hatten.[7] Vergleichbar mit Verfahren Cytters, Fasts oder Ruhms erweist sich auch hier die filmische Narra-tion als eine Montage aus Drehbuch und Proto-kollen, welche die „Demarkationslinie" zwischen fiktiven und sozialen Rollen- und Handlungs-mustern programmatisch verwischt. Dem entspricht auf formalästhetischer Ebene die Juxtaposition von 35 mm Film und Video: Während die Theater-probe im Gestus von Plansequenzen gedreht ist, sind die mit Video gefilmten Außenszenen im Gestus von TV-Dokumentationen gehalten. Stilis-tisch erinnern sie an die nur wenige Monate vor den Dreharbeiten zu *Rien du tout* in den Medien verbreiteten Bilder randalierender Jugendlicher in den Pariser Banlieues: Zumeist mit sogenann-tem migrantischem Hintergrund waren ihre Re-volten eine Antwort auf rassistische Ausgrenzung und Diskriminierung, so in Gestalt massiver Poli-zeigewalt vor allem gegenüber jungen, männlichen Migranten. Doch die auf Interviews beruhenden Dialoge stellten weniger einen Versuch der Authen-tifizierung der dargestellten Rollen als vielmehr eine Ironisierung jener Rollenbilder dar, die von den Jugendlichen seitens der Medien und der Politik konstruiert wurden. So drehen sich ihre Gespräche um alles Mögliche, um Jobs bei McDonald's ebenso wie um Zukunftsträume.

Die Weise nun, in der *Rien du tout* soziale Skripte zu heterogenen Rollenporträts montiert, erinnert nicht von ungefähr an Jacques Rancières Gedanken zum Drama des Volkstheaters des frühen 19. Jahrhunderts: Dieses, als Ort und Medium der „Vermischung von all dem, was im Leben vermischt ist" charakterisierend, verdankt es sich der Gleichzeitigkeit multipler Momente und Ereignisse – nach Rancière von „ein[em] Aufstand hier und ein[em] Gespräch über Liebe da"[8]. Das Neben- und Miteinander von Protagonisten und Statisten, von Höhepunkten und Nebensächlichkeiten, von geplanten und zufälligen Darstellungsmomenten, macht auch in *Rien du tout* die Hinterbühne, die „Backstage", zu einem Ort, an dem die Schnittstellen der je spezifischen Artikulationsbedingungen sozialer und medialer Akteure dazu angetan sind, auf aktiver Mitgestaltung der Darsteller beruhende Rollenmuster hervorzubringen.

Der Nexus aus mimetischen und reflexiven Darstellungsregistern lässt uns somit fragen, ob in *Rien du tout* das Soziale *als* Fiktion und das Soziale *der* Fiktion zum Thema wird. Auch in dieser Hinsicht scheint der Topos der Probe insofern von Bedeutung, als es sich hierbei nicht um das Format des in den 2000er Jahren hochpopulären Reenactments handelt – mit anderen Worten nicht um ein nachträgliches „Remake" einer historischen Gegebenheit, sondern um eine „in actu" zur Aufführung kommende Gemengelage aus künstlerischer Recherche und kollaborativer Produktion.

Die Probe erscheint somit in zweifacher Hinsicht als modus operandi: Als reales, d.h. produktionstechnisches *und* als fiktives, d.h. inszeniertes „in the making" von Darstellungsstrategien, die sich im Akt der Darstellung gleichsam selbst dokumentieren. Der somit thematisch werdende Nexus aus Technik / Verfahren und Sujet / Inhalt beruht dabei wesentlich auf einer kollaborativen Interaktion zwischen Regie, Darstellern und Produktionsteam. Eine Bedingung, an der die Theaterregisseurin in *Rien du tout* augenscheinlich scheitert und die sich – so die Botschaft des Films – erst im (handlungsentscheidenden) Akt der kollektiven Aneignung des „Drehbuchs" durch die Statisten erfüllt.

Nun wäre es im Kontext der Gegenwartskunst nicht das erste Mal, dass Repräsentanten marginalisierter Gruppen zu Protagonisten „institutionskritischer" Partizipationsmodelle avancieren. Doch *Rien du tout* ist weit entfernt davon, Partizipation zum Sozialen der Kunst zu verklären. So geriert sich die de- und reterritorialisierende Suchbewegung der Videokamera nicht als bruch- und reibungslose Überschreitung des Symbolischen ins Reale, sondern als inversiver Vorgang. Wenn die Regisseurin am Ende den Parkplatz

betritt, wird sie zur Nebendarstellerin jener im Stil eines Mittelalterspektakels gehaltenen Performance der Statisten, die damit die Theaterprobe zur „Geschichte" machen. Diese Inversion vollzieht sich auch in den theaterhistorischen Referenzen: So rekurriert die Figur der tyrannischen Regisseurin und des von ihr drangsalierten Assistenten auf das 1982 erschienene Stück *Katastrophe* von Samuel Beckett, jedoch mit umgekehrten, „klassischen" Geschlechterverhältnissen. Becketts ausgesprochen dystopischer Blick auf die Möglichkeit gesellschaftlichen Fortschritts hallt in *Rien du tout* insofern wider, als bestehende Hierarchien augenscheinlich nicht allein schon durch die Ersetzung strukturell männlicher durch weibliche Machtpositionen aufgebrochen werden; erst in der Erprobung kollektiver Partizipation, so der Plot, werden strukturelle Veränderungen zu einer realistischen Option. Das für die Probe kennzeichnende Motiv der Umschrift bestehender „Skripte" erweist seine Bedeutung demzufolge sowohl auf ästhetischer als auch auf gesellschaftlicher Ebene: Welche Rollenbilder und Darstellungsregister sind hinfällig und verbraucht, welche müssen überarbeitet oder neu erfunden werden?

Die damit einhergehende Frage danach, wer unter welchen Bedingungen an symbolischen und realen Bild- und Raumordnungen partizipiert, stellt sich auf beispielhafte Weise auch in der dreikanaligen, anamorphotisch anmutenden Videoinstallation *Muster* (2012) – von Wedemeyers Beitrag zur dOCUMENTA (13) –, in dessen Zentrum das ehemalige Benediktinerkloster Breitenau in der Nähe von Kassel steht. Jede der in einem Dreieck angeordneten Leinwände repräsentiert ein signifikantes Datum deutscher Geschichte: 1945 als Jahr der Befreiung des zu diesem Zeitpunkt als Konzentrationslager dienenden Klostergebäudes durch die US-amerikanische Armee, 1970 als Jahr, in dem der mit dem Namen Ulrike Meinhof verbundene Film *Bambule* über die Missstände in einem Mädchenerziehungsheim entstand, als welches Breitenau zwischenzeitlich diente sowie 1994, vier Jahre nach der deutschen Wiedervereinigung, das in *Muster* durch die Führung einer Schulklasse durch das zum damaligen Zeitpunkt als psychiatrische Klinik und heute als Bildungsstätte genutzten Gebäude repräsentiert ist. Den drei Zeitebenen entsprechen dabei genau jene von Michel Foucault untersuchten Raumtypen, die auf den disziplinargesellschaftlichen, mithin auf Ein- und Aussperrung beruhenden Zusammenhang von Kloster- / Kirchen, Militär- / Gefängnis- / Lager-, Klinik- und Internatsarchitektur verweisen. Somit ist es auch in dieser Arbeit einmal mehr der Topos der Probe, in dem sich Sozial- und Mediengeschichte auf der Darstellungs-, d.h. auf fiktionaler Ebene, miteinander verknüpfen.

Insofern Meinhofs Drehbuch zu *Bambule* den Dreh- und Angelpunkt von *Muster* bildet, ist es auch hier wieder ein „Skript", das zu einer im Probenmodus inszenierten Schnittstelle zwischen den unterschiedlichen, zugleich ineinanderfließenden Darstellungs- und Zeitebenen gerät: So sind die (scheinbaren) Probenarbeiten dazu angetan, die von autoritärer Unterwerfung zeugende Situation der Mädchen in dem zum Erziehungsheim umgewandelten ehemaligen Konzentrations- und Arbeitslager nicht nur darzustellen, sondern Möglichkeiten der Veränderung – etwa durch Beteiligung der Betroffenen – zu ersinnen. Da der Regisseur den Mädchen diese Möglichkeit ausschlägt, da er den Mädchen Rollenbewusstsein abspricht, fragt eine der jugendlichen Darstellerinnen, „warum der Film gut ist, wenn er nichts verändern kann." Der Probenmodus spitzt also das klassische „Film-im-Film"-Sujet im Sinne einer respräsentationskritischen (Selbst-)Transformation zu. Das doppelte Spiel aus Rollendarstellung bei gleichzeitiger Gestaltung der Darstellerin als einer Figur, die sich darin übt, aus ihrer Rolle auszusteigen, lässt uns im Fall der eben beschriebenen Szene programmatisch im Unklaren darüber, ob es sich dabei um ein reales oder fiktives Reenactment von *Bambule* handelt – ein Moment, das an eine Bemerkung Brees, der an Jane Fondas Figur in *Klute* (1971) angelehnten Protagonistin in *X Characters RE(hers)AL* (2004) von Constanze Ruhm erinnert: „Ich meine, man probt, eine andere zu sein, und dann, wenn man eine andere geworden ist, probt man wieder diejenige zu werden, die ursprünglich anders werden wollte."[9]

Die in der (fiktiven) Duplizierung der Probe aufscheinende Reflexion auf pädagogische Formate bildet mit Einschränkung die Schnittstelle der drei Filmteile. Wie bereits in *Rien du tout* stellt sich auch hier die Hierarchie aus Anweisung und Ausführung als Kern institutionalisierter Machtverhältnisse dar – im Rahmen von Fernsehproduktionen genauso wie im Rahmen von Vermittlungsprogrammen, die auch für Institutionen wie die der documenta charakteristisch sind. Sie zeugen, wie einst Bazon Brocks *Besucherschule*, von dem Anspruch, elitäre Kunstbegriffe durch Partizipation breiter Zielgruppen aufzubrechen. Aus dieser Perspektive betrachtet stellt sich *Muster* demzufolge weniger als Beitrag zu deutscher Erinnerungskultur, denn als ortsspezifischer Diskurs über die historisch und politisch hochkodierten Verbindungslinien zwischen Kunst, Medien und Museumspädagogik dar. So klingen in den Methoden der Heimerziehung nicht nur die in *Bambule* thematischen Kontinuitäten zu den Zwangsarbeiterlagern der Nazis nach; sie klingen auch, wenn auch auf gebrochene Weise, im autoritären Umgang des Regisseurs mit seinen Darstellern und der Figur des „Schulmeisters" an, der eine desinteressierte Schulklasse durch das nun als Gedenkstätte fungierende Kloster Breitenau führt. Insofern in dieser Szene Darsteller aus den beiden ersten Teilen – so die Künst-

lerin Angela Melitopoulos in ihrer zur politisch reflektierten Vermittlerin gewandelten Rolle als Kriegsreporterin und Protagonistin der Film-Proben – wiederauftauchen, inszeniert *Muster* das „Film-im-Film"-Motiv als zugleich diachrones und synchrones Darstellungsverfahren: Die jeweiligen Sequenzen erscheinen somit nicht als lineare Narrationen, sondern als alterierbare Versionen eines zugrunde liegenden Narrativs.[10] Da dieses auf dem Modell der Probe in seiner Funktion als Schnittstelle zwischen Produktion und Rezeption beruht, rückt hier – wie auch schon in *Die Probe* und *Rien du tout* – die Frage nach den Möglichkeiten alternativer Darstellungs- respektive Vermittlungsformate in den Vordergrund. Insofern in der ersten, 1945 spielenden Szene populäre Formate der (Re-)Education, so TV-History-Shows à la Guido Knopp unterschwellig parodiert werden, stellt sich die retro-fiktive, an Meinhofs Drehbuch angelehnte Probe als ein Wiederanknüpfen an verdrängte Beispiele radikaler Medienpraxis dar. So durfte das Fernsehspiel erst 1994, also 24 Jahre nach seiner Fertigstellung, gezeigt werden. Auf diese Weise die nachhaltige Zensur einer Produktion zum Thema machend, die dazu angetan war, einem Massenpublikum die Kontinuitäten der Naziideologie am Beispiel einer exemplarischen pädagogischen Institution der Nachkriegs-BRD vor Augen zu führen, verweist *Muster* zugleich auf die unausgesetzte Verdrängung linksradikaler Auseinandersetzung mit der deutschen Vergangenheit. Wenn vor diesem Hintergrund der Regisseur den jugendlichen Darstellern einzutrichtern versucht, dass nicht sie, sondern nur die Zuschauer fühlen sollen, so ist unter dem Stichwort der „Wirkungsästhetik" schließlich auch der Zusammenhang zwischen autoritärer Pädagogik und (massen-)medialen Rezeptionsstrategien angesprochen. Es ist demnach kein Zufall, dass die in den *Bambule*-Proben auftretenden „Beleuchter" nicht nur als Mittler zwischen hierarchischem Autoritätsprinzip und kollektiver Aktion, sondern auch als Mittler zwischen Produktions- und Rezeptionssphäre agieren. Sie bilden gleichsam die „Demarkationslinien", welche die unterschiedlichen Raum-, Darstellungs- und Zeitebenen (Arbeitslager, Erziehungsheim, Gedenkstätte und Filmstudio) miteinander verbinden. Ihre Solidarität mit den gedemütigten Darstellern resultiert schließlich in der von Postpunk à la Einstürzende Neubauten untermalten Zerstörung der Filmkulisse, welche als Spuren respektive Vorboten vergangenen respektive künftigen Widerstands in der dritten, 1994 spielenden Sequenz wieder auftauchen.

Zweifelsohne erscheint die Probe in *Muster* nicht nur als Sujet, sondern seinerseits als ein (anti-)pädagogisches Format, das die Position der Betrachter auf direkte Weise adressiert. Entsprechend stellt sich die Frage, ob und auf welche Weise sich auch ihnen jene Möglichkeit der Desidentifikation eröffnet, die in dem Aufstand der Darsteller gegen die ihnen zugedachte Rolle(n) angedeutet ist. Das Einreißen der Kulisse – Inbegriff hierarchischer Blick- und Raumordnung – legt dies zumindest auf symbolischer Ebene nahe.

Die für institutionskritische Verfahren der 1990er charakteristische Ortsspezifik erfährt hier eine dem postdramatischen Theater vergleichbare Fiktionalisierung insofern als die Filminstallation den Raum der Darstellung in den Raum der Rezeption übersetzt. Dem szenografischen Charakter der 2- und 3-Kanal-Projektionen von Wedemeyers entsprechend, stehen wir – die Betrachter – stets zugleich an den Vorder- und Rückseiten jener Bilder, die wir als Demarkationslinie zwischen Illusions- und Realraum erkennen. Indem die (fiktive) Probe weniger als ein von singulären Produktionen her gedachtes Making-of, denn stärker als ein modulares „in-the-making" von Rollen und Szenen ins Blickfeld tritt, präsentiert sie sich uns als Reflexionsmedium jener Parameter, die zeitgenössischer Praxis an den Schnittstellen von Kunst, Film und Theater heute zugrunde liegen. Diese lassen die Leistungserwartung an Produktionsformen wie jene von Wedemeyers steigen: Die Kunstöffentlichkeit muss ebenso mitgedacht werden wie ein mediales Massenpublikum.[11] Hierzu passt die Rolle heutiger Künstler als flexible Multitask-Produzenten, die von Wedemeyers Filmpraxis als ein doppeltes Sehen von Kunst (vermittelter) Arbeit *am* und *als* Werk freilegen. Das Sujet der Probe weist, wie die im vorliegenden Essay exemplarisch zur Sprache gekommenen Arbeiten des Künstlers vielschichtig zeigen, Veränderungspotenzial in dem Sinn auf, als es sich selbst auf die Probe stellt.

1 Siehe hierzu Ivan Nagel: *Gemälde und Drama. Giotto Masaccio Leonardo*, Frankfurt am Main: Suhrkamp, 2009 und meinen sich hierauf beziehenden Aufsatz „Autonomie auf Probe", in: Leonhard Emmerling, Ines Kleesattel (Hg.): *Politik der Kunst*, Bielefeld: transcript Verlag, 2016 (im Erscheinen).

2 Stefanie Diekmann: *Backstage. Konstellationen von Theater und Kino*, Berlin: Kulturverlag Kadmos, 2013, S.19.

3 Ebd.

4 Ebd.

5 Ebd., S.38 ff.

6 Ebd., S.50.

7 Diese und andere Informationen zur Produktion von *Rien du tout* basieren auf Gesprächen mit den beiden Künstlern.

8 Jacques Rancière: „Das Theater der Gedanken", in: Ders.: *Der verlorene Faden. Essays zur modernen Fiktion*, Wien: Passagen Verlag, 2015, S.115–136, hier: S.117.

9 Ich verdanke dieses Zitat Constanze Ruhm.

10 Ein Moment, das sich auch in den zwei Präsentationsmodi von *Muster*, zum einen als Filminstallations- und zum anderen als Fernsehfilm manifestiert.

11 Siehe hierzu meinen Aufsatz „Shared Production(-Values)", in: Sabeth Buchmann, Ilse Lafer, Constanze Ruhm (Hg.): *Putting Rehearsals to the Test. Practices of Rehearsal in Fine Arts, Film, Theater, Theory, and Politics*, Berlin: Sternberg Press, 2013, S.32–45.

ON THIS SIDE OF THE LOOK BEHIND THE SCENES

Sabeth Buchmann

If there's anything Clemens von Wedemeyer's films have in common, it's the subject of the rehearsal. The look behind the scenes associated with the rehearsal is a look that is (seemingly) allowed to see what usually remains invisible, while at the same time supplying the scripts for its "backstage dramas": waiting extras, improvising actors and actresses, authoritarian directors, rebellious employees, unplanned dialogues, events of peripheral importance. Whereas in theatre and film the rehearsal represents a common performative medium in the service of meta-reflection, it is by no means par for the course in the context of the visual arts. According to prevailing notions, artists experiment, or at most try something out. Yet not only Clemens von Wedemeyer but also a considerable number of his colleagues, for instance his (cooperation) partner Maya Schweizer, but also Pauline Baudry / Renate Lorenz, Gerard Byrne, Keren Cytter, Harun Farocki, Omer Fast, Ana Hoffner, Eva Meyer / Eran Schaerf, Constanze Ruhm, Katarina Zdjelar and others, draw on the rehearsal format as a significant interface between the performing and the visual arts. As an expanded version of the making-of, their artistic appropriations consist of frequently interwoven double story lines, one fictional, the other documentary. Unlike the classical making-of, however, the semi-documentary / semi-fictional rehearsal does not represent a supplementary genre in the sense of a reconstruction of the work's emergence. On the contrary, the emphasis lies on the "in-the-making" status of roles and performance rules, monologues and dialogues, actions and scenes, camera, sound, lighting and editing techniques.

As demonstrated in very literal terms by von Wedemeyer's film *The Test* (2008), this does not suggest an experimental or incomplete stage of artistic production. Rather, the rehearsal *is* the work—if one that is performed as a modus operandi of itself. *The Test*, for example, consists of the (seemingly) unedited sequence of a scene taking place in the backstage area of an auditorium. As heard but not seen by the viewer, the audience is cheering the candidate who

has just won the presidential election; backstage, with the aid of an adviser, he is rehearsing his speech, in which, contrary to all expectations, he will announce his renunciation of the office. As soon as he leaves the backstage area, the loop starts over again.

The Test thus literally cuts to the chase of the modern drama—that is, the act and moment of decision. Whereas in classical drama it is an expression of a subject proceeding confidently because he is capable of choosing between two or more options,[1] the "all-decisive" decision in *The Test* ironically lies in the rejection of precisely that role with the greatest possible decision-making authority—the role furnished with governmental power. In view of the question thus raised as to whether the public is still involved in the political process starting with Second 1 of the film, and if so how, it is perhaps no coincidence that the given scene is performed in a place to which the public is usually denied access— the sphere of the backstage or offstage. As shown by the media and theatre theorist Stefanie Diekmann in her book *Backstage. Konstellationen von Theater und Kino*, this sphere is constitutive both for avant-garde "concepts on the re-organisation of the theatre space"[2] as well as for popular theatre and movie fictions. Within this context, the reversal of stage and backstage classically has the function of dissolving "well-known spatial order[s] into other topologies".[3] According to Diekmann, these "changes of location and boundary dissolution movements"[4] are apt to put existing "demarcation lines"[5] between the real and the fictive—and therefore between the social and the aesthetic, which ultimately also means between the documentary and the fictive—to the test, as it were.

The Test thus represents precisely this place / process oscillating between passage and boundary—i.e. a place / process spatially and temporally preceding the representation—which only becomes visible in the fiction as an element of topological visual orders. Von Wedemeyer's film implies precisely that: a linking of "auditorium and backstage"[6] that presents the scene we see as a fictional rehearsal of a performance that remains hidden from our view. In other words, we don't see what we see; we see what we usually don't see. This interplay between visualisation and invisibility is based on an inversion of space as an inversion of view. And it demarcates the rehearsal as a strategy for countering the facticity of the image with the possibility of its alterity — and that is one of its fundamental meanings for the visual arts. In *The Test*, it is the script rewritten at the last minute. As in a "real" drama, the unexpected turn of events takes place (almost too) late, but not after the die is cast.

It goes without saying that this concentration on the inner conflicts of the protagonists — an aspect characteristic of the rehearsal topos but also of other works by von Wedemeyer — exhibits a meta-reflective core. Because — according to the message conveyed by *The Test* — the possibility of rewriting a pre-established script means the possibility of changing the role and action model constitutive for the "demarcation lines" between reality and fiction. If we conceive of *The Test* in the afore-outlined sense as a quintessence of the modern drama, i.e. as a condition for the possibility and expression of freedom of decision that is no longer given once the production exists or the work has been consummated, its eminent political significance comes to light: because the fact that the just-elected presidential candidate is shown rehearsing a script other than the one meant for him makes the rejected position of power appear as a role that, essentially, could also be "played" by someone else.

Seen in this light, the fictive insight into the backstage area as a space where the "actual" production is realised implies a nexus of actuality and virtuality (Gilles Deleuze). This means that the category of the image proves to be a manifestation of a possible action that can essentially be varied (or omitted) by an underlying script. A model such as this, reminiscent of both (post-) conceptual as well as post-dramatic methods, according to which an instruction or a screenplay engages in active dialogue with the respective work — active because it changes from one execution or performance to the next — permits us to draw further inferences about *The Test*. Here as well, we recognise a connection between the script and the film — an element that reveals the looped narration itself as a condition and effect of its being performed and filmed. The tension between mimetic and reflective role-staging characteristic of the rehearsal process integrates Brecht's strategy of alienation as a fiction inherent to the topological inversion of the visual and spatial orders.

This reflective nexus also plays a key role in other works by von Wedemeyer — for example the film and video installation *Rien du tout* (2006) he developed with Maya Schweizer, originally for CAC Brétigny. The 35 mm and video film converted to HD format likewise exhibits an inversion of the classical spatial and visual orders in the sense that film and video cameras are used to juxtapose the realms on this and the other side of institutional "demarcation lines" — in this case the theatre stage on the one hand and a car-park located outside the theatre building on the other. It is as if the backstage had moved out of the theatre and is now located in a supposedly "real" offstage in contrast to the closed space of the institution. Here again, figures of inversion correlate with the transformation of institutional role hierarchies. Whereas initially a tyrannical woman stage director dominates the scene, orchestrating an increasingly bogged-down rehearsal of a play about the banlieues of medieval Paris, the extras waiting offstage step up to the fore one by one. They are pupils of a school located in a present-day banlieue considered a social hotspot. Their dialogues, which arouse the impression of "bad" (because all-too-intentional) improvisation, are based on conversations von Wedemeyer and Schweizer had conducted with them during the casting session.[7]

Here as well, in a manner comparable to the methods used by Cytter, Fast and Ruhm, the filmic narration proves to be a montage of screenplay and minutes that programmatically blur the "demarcation line" between fictive and social role and action models. On the formal aesthetic level, this is mirrored in the juxtaposition of 35 mm film and video. Whereas the theatre rehearsal has been shot in sequence-shot style, the video-filmed outdoor scenes wear the guise of TV documentaries. Stylistically, they are reminiscent of the images of rowdy youth in the Paris banlieues that had been all over the media just a few months before the shooting of *Rien du tout*. The young people of so-called migrant backgrounds had carried out their revolts as a response to racist ostracism and discrimination, for example in the form of massive police violence, above all towards young male migrants. The interview-based dialogues, however, were less an attempt to authenticate the roles presented than a parody of the role models assigned the teenagers by the media and politics. Their conversations accordingly revolve around all kinds of things, from jobs at McDonald's to their dreams for the future.

If the manner in which social scripts are assembled as heterogeneous role portraits in *Rien du tout* calls to mind Jacques Rancière's thoughts on the early nineteenth-century folk theatre drama, it is no coincidence. Characterising the latter as a place and medium of the "mixture of everything that is mixed in life", Rancière observes that it owes its unique quality to the simultaneity of multiple moments and events — in his words "an uprising here and a conversation about love there".[8] In *Rien du tout* as well, the juxtaposition and blend of protagonists and extras, of climaxes and trivia of planned performance elements and coincidental ones, makes the backstage a place where the interfaces of the respective specific articulation conditions of social and media players are apt to yield role patterns based on the active involvement of the performers in creating them.

The nexus of mimetic and reflective levels of performance thus raises the question of whether the theme of *Rien du tout* is the social situation *as a* fiction or the social aspect *of the* fiction. In this regard as well, the rehearsal topos appears significant to the extent that this is not a case of the re-enactment format so popular in the 2000s — in other words not a retrospective "remake" of a historical situation — but a melange of artistic research and collaborative production performed "in actu".

The rehearsal serves here as a modus operandi in two respects — as a real, i.e. technical, *and* as a fictive, i.e. staged, "in-the-making" of performance strategies that virtually document themselves in the act of their performance. The nexus of technique / method and subject / content that thus takes on thematic status is fundamentally based on collaborative interaction between the director, actors and production team. This is a condition over which the stage director in *Rien du tout* evidently stumbles, and which — according to the message conveyed by the film — is only met by the extras' all-decisive act of collectively appropriating the "screenplay".

This wouldn't be the first time in the context of contemporary art that representatives of marginalised groups advance to become protagonists in "anti-institutional" participation models. *Rien du tout*, however, is certainly not out to idealise participation as the social aspect of art. The deterritorialising / reterritorialising searching motion of the video camera, for instance, does not act as a fluent traversal of the symbolic to the real, but as an inversive process. When, at the end, the stage director enters the car-park, she becomes a supporting actress to the performance by the extras in the style of a medieval spectacle, who thus turn the theatre rehearsal into a "story".

This inversion also takes place in the references to theatre history. The figure of the tyrannical director with an assistant she bullies around, for example, harks back to Samuel Beckett's *Catastrophe*, published in 1982, but with a reversed, "classical" relationship between the sexes. Beckett's markedly dystopian take on the possibility of societal progress echoes in *Rien du tout* in the sense that existing hierarchies are evidently not abolished solely by replacing structurally male power positions with female ones. According to the plot, it is only by rehearsing collective participation that structural changes become a realistic option. The motif of rewriting existing "scripts" — the distinguishing feature of the rehearsal — accordingly proves its significance on the aesthetic as well as the societal

level: which role models and performance registers are obsolete and worn out; which should be revised or invented anew?

The associated question as to who participates in symbolic and real pictorial and spatial orders, and under what conditions, also poses itself in exemplary manner in a 3-channel anamorphicstyle video installation entitled *Rushes* (2012), von Wedemeyer's contribution to the dOCUMENTA (13) revolving around the former Breitenau Benedictine monastery near Kassel. Each of the three screens — which are set up in such a way as to form a triangle — represents a significant date in Germany history: 1945 as the year of the liberation of the monastery building — which had been serving as a concentration camp — by the U.S. Army, 1970 as the year in which *Bambule* was made, a film associated with the name Ulrike Meinhof about the grievous state of affairs in the correctional home for girls housed in Breitenau, and 1994, year four after the German reunification, represented in *Rushes* by the guided tour of a school class through the building, then in use as a psychiatric clinic, and today as an educational institution. The three time levels correspond precisely to the spatial types investigated by Michel Foucault, which point to what monasteries and churches have in common with military and prison camps as well as clinic and boarding school architecture: that which Foucault referred to as the "disciplinary society" and its inherent functions of locking in and locking out. Thus in this work, once again, it is the topos of the rehearsal in which social and media history intermesh on the level of performance, i.e. on the fictional level.

Inasmuch as Meinhof's screenplay for *Bambule* is the key element of *Rushes*, it is here once again a "script" that, staged in rehearsal mode, gets caught up between the different — and at the same time interpenetrating — levels of performance and time. The (ostensible) rehearsal work, for example, tends not only to convey the situation of the girls in the former concentration and work camp that has meanwhile transformed into a correctional institution — a situation testifying to authoritarian subjugation —, but also to devise means of change, for example through the involvement of the persons affected. Owing to the fact that the director, because he denies the girls role consciousness, deprives them of this possibility, he asks the young performers "why the film is good if it isn't capable of changing anything". The rehearsal mode thus takes the classical "film-within-a-film" subject to an extreme in the sense of a representationalcritical (self-) transformation. In the case of the scene just described, the dual game of a role performance in which the performer is simultaneously shown as a figure practising her abandonment of the role programmatically leaves us in the dark regarding what we have here: Is it a real or a fictive re-enactment of *Bambule*?—an aspect reminiscent of a remark by Bree, the character played by Jane Fonda in *Klute* (1971), a role the female protagonist in *X Characters RE(hers)AL* (2004) by Constanze Ruhm was based on: "I mean, you rehearse how to be someone else, and then you try to rehearse being the one who was first learning how to be someone else."[9]

In a sense, the reflection on educational formats mirrored in the (fictive) duplication of the rehearsal forms the interface between the three parts of the film. As was already the case in *Rien du tout*, the hierarchy between instruction and execution makes itself out to be the core of institutionalised power structures—as much within the framework of TV productions as within the context of mediation programmes also characteristic of institutions such as the documenta. As in Bazon Brock's *Visitors' School*, they testify to the claim to dismantle elitist concepts of art through the participation of broad-based target groups. Regarded from this perspective, *Rushes* is accordingly less a contribution to German remembrance culture than a site-specific discourse on the historically and politically heavily encrypted lines interconnecting art, the media and museum of education. The continuities of the Nazi forced-labour camps addressed by *Bambule* thus echo not only in the methods of correctional home education, but also—if in inconsistent manner—in the director's authoritarian treatment of his performers and in the figure of the "schoolmaster" who takes a disinterested school class through Breitenau Monastery, now in its guise as a memorial. Inasmuch as performers from the first two parts—for example the artist Angela Melitopoulos in her role as war correspondent and then protagonist of the film rehearsals, i.e. a role that transforms into that of a politically reflective mediator—turn up again in the third part, *Rushes* plays out the "film-within-a-film" motif as a performance method both diachronic and synchronous in nature. The respective sequences thus appear not as linear narrations, but as alterable versions of a single underlying narrative.[10] Because of the fact that this narrative is based on the model of the rehearsal in its function as interface between production and reception, the question as to means of alternative depiction or mediation formats, respectively, poses itself—as was already the case in *The Test* and *Rien du tout*. Whereas the first scene, re-enacting the situation in 1945, subtly parodies popular (re-)educational formats such as TV history shows à la Guido Knopp, the retro-fictive rehearsal based on Meinhof's screenplay comes across as a recourse to suppressed examples of radical media praxis: the television film was not broadcast until 1994, i.e. twenty-four years after its completion. *Rushes* thus addresses the long-term censorship of a production designed to demonstrate to a mass public the continuities of Nazi ideology as illus-

trated by an exemplary educational institution of the post-war Federal Republic of Germany. And by doing so, it simultaneously points to the ongoing repression of left-wing radical assessments of the German past. If, against this background, the director tries to force down the young performers' throats that not they but the audience are supposed to feel something, the film ultimately also addresses—under the heading of "effect aesthetics"—the relationship between authoritarian teaching methods and (mass-)media reception strategies. It is thus no coincidence that the "lighting technicians" appearing in the *Bambule* rehearsals act not only as agents between hierarchical authority principle and collective action, but also as mediators between the spheres of production and reception. They virtually form the "demarcation lines" connecting the various levels of space, performance and time (work camp, correctional home, memorial and film studio). Their solidarity with the humiliated performers ultimately results in the destruction of the film set to post-Punk music à la the German industrial band Einstürzende Neubauten. As a trace / harbinger of past / future resistance, the film set turns up again in the third sequence, playing in 1994.

In *Rushes* the rehearsal unmistakably serves not just as a subject, but in turn as an (anti-)pedagogical format that directly addresses the viewers' position. The question accordingly arises as to whether, and in what way, the latter are also granted the option of "disidentification" alluded to in the performers' rebellion against their intended role(s): the demolition of the film set—the epitome of hierarchical visual and spatial orders—implies this, at least on the symbolic level.

To the extent that the film installation translates the performance space into the reception space, the site specificity characteristic of institution-critical methods of the 1990s here undergoes a fictionalisation comparable to post-dramatic theatre. In keeping with the scenographic character of von Wedemeyer's 2- and 3-channel video projects, we—the viewers—always stand simultaneously at the front and back of those images we recognise as demarcation lines between illusionary and real space. In that the (fictive) rehearsal comes into focus less as a making-of conceived on the basis of singular productions than as a modular "in-the-making" of roles and scenes, it presents itself to us as a medium for the reflection of those parameters that today underlie contemporary praxis at the interfaces between art, film and theatre. These parameters raise our expectations concerning what production forms such as von Wedemeyer's should achieve: the art public must be taken as much into account as the mass media audience.[11] This corresponds to the role of present-day artists as flexible multitasking producers who expose von Wedemeyer's film praxis as a double perception of art (-mediated) work *in front of* and *as* the artwork. As demonstrated on many levels by the works discussed in this essay as representative examples of the artist's œuvre, the subject of the rehearsal shows potential for change in the sense that it puts itself to the test.

1   On this aspect, see Ivan Nagel: *Gemälde und Drama. Giotto Masaccio Leonardo*, Frankfurt am Main: Suhrkamp, 2009. And my related essay "Autonomie auf Probe", in: Leonhard Emmerling and Ines Kleesattel (eds.): *Politik der Kunst*, Bielefeld: transcript Verlag, 2016. (forthcoming).
2   Stefanie Diekmann: *Backstage. Konstellationen von Theater und Kino*, Berlin: Kulturverlag Kadmos, 2013, p.19. (here translated by JR)
3   Ibid.
4   Ibid.
5   Ibid., pp.38 ff.
6   Ibid., p.50.
7   This and other information on the production of *Rien du tout* is based on conversations with the two artists.
8   Jacques Rancière: "The Theatre of Thoughts", in: idem: *The Lost Thread: The Democracy of Modern Fiction*, London: Bloomsbury Academic, 2016. Quoted from idem: "Das Theater der Gedanken", in: idem: *Der verlorene Faden. Essays zur modernen Fiktion*, Vienna: Passagen Verlag, 2015, pp.115–136, here p.117. (here translated by JR)
9   I am indebted to Constanze Ruhm for this quotation.
10 An element also manifest in the two presentation modes of *Rushes* —as a film installation and as a television film.
11 On this subject, see my essay "Shared Production(-Values)", idem: Ilse Lafer, Constanze Ruhm (eds.): *Putting Rehearsals to the Test: Practices of Rehearsal in Fine Arts, Film, Theater, Theory, and Politics*, Berlin: Sternberg Press, 2013, pp.32–45.

AUFSTAND DES HINTERGRUNDS

Thomas D. Trummer im Gespräch
mit Clemens von Wedemeyer
Berlin, 2009

CLEMENS VON WEDEMEYER: Meine Arbeit *Basler Podest* (2006) habe ich speziell für die Art Basel entwickelt. Als mir die Galerie Jocelyn Wolff vorschlug, für die „Statements" eine Präsentation einzurichten, wollte ich keinen Film zeigen, da mir der Raum zu eng schien und ich dachte, dass sich die Besucher an diesem Ort kaum auf ein längeres Video konzentrieren können. Die Messe erschien mir eher als ein Ort, an dem man etwas über eine Messe und ihre Präsentationsform machen müsste. Ich habe schließlich ein kleines Studio gebaut, das in Form einer Installation eine Geschichte erzählt, dabei aber offen bleibt.

THOMAS D. TRUMMER: Kannst du das kurz beschreiben?

VON WEDEMEYER: Man sieht ein Podest und eine Kamera, die auf das Podest gerichtet ist. Auf dem Podest steht ein Stuhl, daneben ein weiterer, der umgefallen ist. Ein paar Blutstropfen sind auf dem Boden zu sehen, zudem Fußabdrücke, die von einer chaotischen Situation zeugen. Dazwischen liegen Blätter, die durcheinander gewirbelt sind, eine Lampe ist umgefallen. Das heißt, irgendetwas ist passiert, aber man weiß nicht genau, was. Man muss die Spuren lesen. Auf den Papieren lässt sich ein Skript erkennen, das aus Sätzen besteht, die sich immer widersprechen und davon handeln, wie sich zwei Personen grundsätzlich nicht verstehen. Es gibt außerdem einen Monitor, der einen leicht verschobenen Ausschnitt zeigt, sodass die eine Person wahrscheinlich nicht mehr richtig im Bild sitzen würde. Im Hintergrund ist ein Greenscreen, in den man jedes mögliche Bild einblenden könnte, sodass man sich jeden Ort vorstellen könnte, der dort eingespielt wird.

TRUMMER: Es ist eine skulpturale Installation und gleichzeitig wird auch eine Geschichte erzählt.

VON WEDEMEYER: Die Arbeit fügte sich in die Messeästhetik ein, denn es gab tatsächlich in der Nähe einen kleinen Raum, in dem Interviews zwischen Kuratoren und Künstlern geführt wurden, sodass man sich bei meiner Installation zwischen den Galerien und dem Messeservice fragte: „Was ist hier passiert?" Mein Galerist musste für das Publikum eine Geschichte erfinden. Die Besucher haben die Installation oft nicht als Galerierepräsentation erkannt. Manche gingen also einfach in den Raum mit dem Podest hinein, sie wollten direkt nachsehen, was hier los war. Sobald sie allerdings versuchten, sich darauf zu stellen oder sich auf den Stuhl zu setzen, krachten sie ein, weil das Podest nur aus ganz dünnen Pappplatten bestand. Alles war nur auf die Pappe aufgemalt. Am Ende musste der Galerist das Podest absperren lassen, da es die Messeleitung verlangte. Zwei Personen hatten sich leicht am Fuß verletzt.

TRUMMER: Auf den ersten Blick erinnert das *Basler Podest* an ein Fernsehstudio. Bei der Bühne allein denkt man aber auch an eine Performance, die vielleicht dort stattgefunden hat, und man ist nur zu spät gekommen.

VON WEDEMEYER: Es war ein Versuch des Eingriffs in die Gesamtperformance von Messe: ein Versuch, Kunst möglichst so anzupassen, dass sie nicht mehr unterscheidbar ist von dem, was dort den Rahmen ausmacht. Ein Trompel'œil.

TRUMMER: Was passiert dort tatsächlich?

VON WEDEMEYER: Meinst du die Kunstmesse? Das weiß ich auch nicht genau. Aber sie ist Teil der Fiktion. Ohne den Kontext der Messe wären die Dinge nicht so aufgeladen. In der Installation ist wie gesagt gar nichts passiert, es ist nur das Arrangement von kleinen Details beziehungsweise eines Sets, wo plötzlich ein Bühnenbild eine Geschichte erzählt. Es erzählt etwas über einen Konflikt zwischen zwei Personen in einem Fernsehstudio. Das heißt, eigentlich geht es eher um die Frage des Performens oder Repräsentierens als um Extras oder Schauspieler, es geht vielleicht um die Grenze, wo man als Zuschauer anfängt mitzumachen, wo die Interpretation und das eigene Verhalten das Werk definieren.

TRUMMER: Würdest du jemanden, der in ein Fernsehstudio geladen ist, zum Beispiel in eine Talkshow, als Statisten bezeichnen?

VON WEDEMEYER: Nicht unbedingt. Das ist eher eine „eingeladene Person". Auch wenn die Leute geschminkt werden, um im Fernsehen besser rüberzukommen. Die Leute werden zu solchen Shows eingeladen, weil sie etwas von sich selbst und keine Geschichten erzählen sollen. Die Grenze ist aber möglicherweise fließend. Die realen Erfahrungen werden dann schnell zur Fiktion. Etwas Ähnliches habe ich in Münster ausprobiert, als in einem Kino eine Szene gezeigt wurde, die vor dem Kino inszeniert worden war. Im Film *Von Gegenüber* (2007) selber gibt es 80 Statisten, die Passanten spielen. Von daher wird es hier auch ununterscheidbar, wer wirklich spielt und wer nicht. Und als Besucher fängt der wahre Film erst an, wenn man aus dem Kino kommt und selbst im Drehort steht. Die Realität sieht plötzlich aus „wie im Film". Das interessierte mich gerade zu jener Zeit, nicht nur bei *Basler Podest*, sondern auch mehr noch in den Filmen, die zu dieser Zeit entstanden sind. Es fing mit *Occupation* an, dem Film, den ich 2001, 2002 gedreht habe. Hierbei war die Grundidee, dass man Besucher aus dem Kinosaal nimmt und sie in der Nacht auf ein Feld bringt. Ringsherum steht ein Filmteam, das mit ihnen eine Szene inszeniert. Die Besucher werden zu Statisten, sind also nicht mehr passive Betrachter im Kinosaal, die reflexartig auf die vorgegebene Filmhandlung reagieren, sondern sie sind eingebunden in den Prozess, einen Film herzustellen. Die Idee war, dass bei der Premiere genau die Menschen, die im Film zu sehen sind, auch im Zuschauerraum sitzen und sich gewissermaßen in der Leinwand spiegeln. Das Filmteam, das mit den Statisten eine Szene gedreht hat, wurde von Schauspielern gespielt.

TRUMMER: Was hatten die Zuschauer respektive die Statisten zu tun?

VON WEDEMEYER: Sie hatten einerseits auf Anweisungen zu reagieren, die die Schauspieler beziehungsweise das Filmteam ihnen gaben, andererseits haben sie sich nach dem Drehbuch, das ich geschrieben hatte, bewegt. Am Ende stand eine Art Auflösung, bei der die Statisten das Filmteam überrennen. Die Filmlampen fallen um und die Statisten, als Hauptelement der Filmhandlung, verlassen den Film. Damit ist der Film zu Ende. Es gibt quasi eine Revolte gegen die Figuren, die den Rahmen des Werks definieren.

TRUMMER: Und gegen das Drehbuch.

VON WEDEMEYER: Naja, gut, es war ja schon im Drehbuch angelegt. Eine fiktive Revolte also. Am Ende eines Drehbuchs steht ja meist die dramaturgische „Auflösung". In diesem Fall eine sichtbare, symbolische Auflösung der Filmhandlung.

TRUMMER: Der oberste Boss ist also immer der Autor des Skripts?

VON WEDEMEYER: Ja, es scheint so. Man kann sich auch selber überrennen lassen, wenn man es so anlegt. In diesem Fall war es so. Ähnlichkeit dazu hat auch der Film *Rien du tout* (2006), den ich mit Maya Schweizer in Paris gedreht habe: Eine Regisseurin und ein Assistent, sie werden von Schauspielern gespielt, casten Jugendliche aus der Pariser Banlieue für einen Mittelalterfilm. In einer Castingszene, bei der die Auswahl der Statisten wie ein Ritual auf der Bühne in einem Theater inszeniert ist, braucht die Regisseurin aber nur eine Person und schickt alle anderen raus. Diese fangen nun an, die Filmhandlung zu übernehmen. Sie beginnen auf dem Parkplatz die Kostüme anzuziehen und ihre eigene Geschichte zu konstruieren. Die Regisseurin wird von ihrer Filmhandlung und von ihrem Casting enteignet.

A

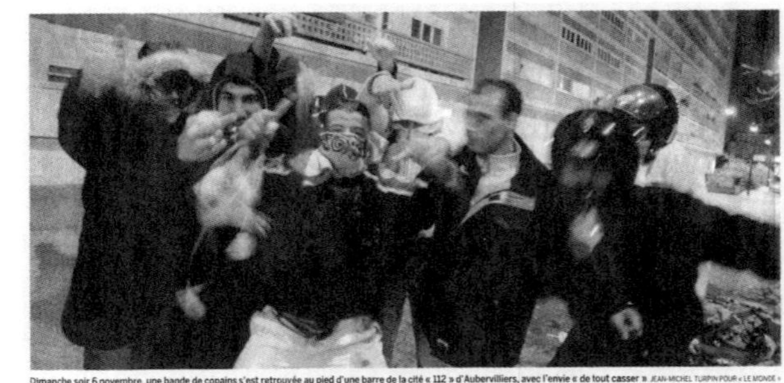

TRUMMER: Ist das auch bei der Installation *Basler Podest* so?

VON WEDEMEYER: Nein, da geht es im Grunde um den Zuschauer, der sich die Situation aneignet und so selber zum Teil der Arbeit wird.

TRUMMER: Der Unterschied zwischen den Filmen und *Basler Podest* besteht darin, dass der Film selber ein Aufzeichnungsmedium ist und man das Geschehen wiedersieht. Bei *Basler Podest* hat man den Eindruck, das Geschehen sei, sobald man den Raum betritt, noch im Gange.

VON WEDEMEYER: Ja, die Kamera und Lampen sind noch eingeschaltet, es ist noch etwas auf dem Monitor sichtbar. Vorn sieht man eine Anordnung, hinten die Kamera. Aber gleichzeitig ist das Ganze eine Falle, um die Besucher mit ihrer Fiktion, welche sie beim Betrachten entwickeln, in eine bestimmte Realität einbrechen zu lassen…

Du hattest nach Statisten gefragt: Bei Wikipedia steht zum Begriff des „Statisten", dass viele große Schauspieler auch als Statisten anfangen, es also eine Hierarchie gibt von background actors, die dann, wenn sie wirklich gut sind, zu richtigen Schauspielern aufsteigen und in die Vordergrundhandlung einsteigen können.

B 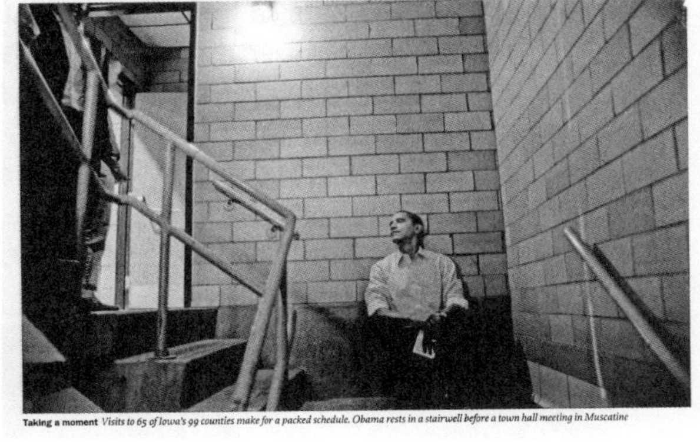

Taking a moment *Visits to 65 of Iowa's 99 counties make for a packed schedule. Obama rests in a stairwell before a town hall meeting in Muscatine*

TRUMMER: Spielen sie dann mehr oder weniger als Schauspieler?

VON WEDEMEYER: Das kommt darauf an, welches Schauspiel man lieber mag. Von Statisten wird nicht verlangt, dass sie sich verstellen, sie müssen nur etwas anziehen und sich alltäglich bewegen. Man sagt, Statisten könnten sich nicht so verstellen – was dafür sorgt, dass es manchmal im Filmhintergrund viel echter aussieht als das, was die Schauspieler im Vordergrund tun. Letztens habe ich einen Film gesehen, bei dem zwei Personen im Vordergrund reden und im Hintergrund sieht man Leute an einer Reling stehen. Man schaut eigentlich nur noch auf diese Statisten, weil sie wirklich gut aussehen und ganz toll arrangiert sind, weshalb die Vordergrundhandlung unwichtig wird.

TRUMMER: Weil du von Vordergrund und Hintergrund sprichst: So besehen wäre der Film eher wie ein Bild zu lesen. Wird diese Wahrnehmung durch die Statisten verstärkt und worin unterscheidet sich ein Statist von einem Requisit?

VON WEDEMEYER: Im Grunde ist der Schauspieler ja auch nur ein Requisit für den Film genauso wie ein Statist. Ein Film ist aus Drehorten, Personen und Requisiten arrangiert. Für manche ist aber wichtiger, welche Geschichte der Ort hat, an dem gedreht wird. Verschiedene Filme legen auf die verschiedenen Elemente des Films unterschiedlich Wert. Der eine Regisseur legt überhaupt keinen Wert darauf, dass die Schauspieler gut sind, der andere will gerade mit Laien drehen. Manchmal ist es auch nicht wichtig, wie es dort im Einzelnen aussieht, wo gedreht wird, aber es ist vielleicht wichtig, dass genau dort ein Teil der Handlung – bei Pasolinis *Medea* zum Beispiel im Baptisterium von Pisa – spielt. Das hat dann natürlich immer noch einen tieferen und nicht nur rein visuellen Grund. Pasolini stellt so etwa einen politischen Vergleich an, in dem er die Struktur der Kirche mit über- und untergeordneten Kulten in Griechenland vergleicht.

TRUMMER: Was ist dir wichtig am Film?

VON WEDEMEYER: Das wandelt sich. Meistens nehme ich Bezug auf die Umstände der Entstehung. Ich versuche also, Werke mit realen Bedingungen zu vermischen. Als ich beispielsweise eingeladen wurde, einen Film zu produzieren, der bei der ersten Moskau Biennale Premiere haben sollte, habe ich den Kurzfilm *Otjesd* (2005) in Berlin gedreht, allerdings mit russischen Einwanderern. Sie spielen Menschen, die vor der Deutschen Botschaft in Moskau anstehen, um ein Visum zu bekommen. Mich interessierte der Versuch, mit den Elementen des Films, den Schauspielern, Drehorten etc., konzeptuell vorzugehen und dann zu sehen, was sich daraus für eine Geschichte entwickelt. Als der Film in Moskau gezeigt wurde, wurde gemutmaßt, er sei von einem russischen Regisseur und an einem Drehort in Russland entstanden. Erst das Wissen um die Schauspieler als russische Emigranten hat dann die Besucher beschäftigt. Die meisten Regisseure arbeiten umgekehrt: Sie haben erst eine Geschichte, die sie unbedingt erzählen wollen, und dann sieht man, wo diese gedreht werden kann. Bei mir entwickeln sich Geschichten um eine vorgefundene Situation und einen Ort. Was mich daneben interessiert, ist, Tautologien, Strukturen und Systeme zu untersuchen und umzudrehen durch Schauspiel oder Performances, wie etwa bei *Occupation*. Es geht darum, die Grenzen oder Trennungen aufzuzeigen, die zwischen Dingen liegen, diese Schnittstellen offenzulegen.

TRUMMER: Mir scheint, dass du Elemente aus der Struktur des Films – seien es Zuschauer, Set, Ort, Kamera und so fort – nimmst, um sie in eine Art wechselseitiges Spiel zu bringen. Die Kamera filmt sich selbst, es entsteht eine Kurzschlusssituation, was in der Praxis der Videokunst der 70er Jahre oft vorkam oder wenn die Zuschauer zu Statisten respektive Schauspielern werden.

VON WEDEMEYER: Genau, es ist ein Feedback oder Kurzschluss. In der Mitte wird dann das Objekt unwichtig.

TRUMMER: Die Closed-Circuit-Installationen der 70er Jahre sind im Gegensatz zu deinen Arbeiten immer ohne Erzählung. Dan Graham hat wirklich nur die Struktur des Mediums im Sinn.

VON WEDEMEYER: Ja. Dan Graham, auf dessen Arbeit ich mich bei meinem Projekt *Von Gegenüber* im Rahmen der skulptur projekte münster 07 bezogen habe, verwendet Spiegel und Fenster für sein Kinomodell, sodass sich Außen und Innen vermischen. Die Arbeit von Graham hat eine skulpturale Klarheit und logische Stringenz. Aber mich interessiert auch die Benutzung des Mediums. Das System „Kino" besteht ja nicht nur aus einem Kinosaal.

TRUMMER: Wie ist es, im öffentlichen Raum zu handeln statt im Studio?

VON WEDEMEYER: In Münster hatte ich das Interesse, wirklich einmal eine gesamte Straße absperren und zu sehen, wie funktioniert das, kann man das einfach machen und wie reagieren dann die Passanten? Wir haben eine Woche in und um einen Bahnhof gedreht, zwischen den Passanten. Ich erinnerte mich an einen Text von Dziga Vertov zu *Der Mann mit der Kamera*: Weil er immer auf der Straße gedreht hat, überlegte er, wie man es schaffen kann, dass Passanten nicht immer in die Kamera blicken. Er kam darauf, dass es am besten ist, man würde so tun, als sei ein Unfall passiert oder jemand wäre hingefallen, weil dann automatisch Leute kommen, um sich die Szene anzusehen, sodass man schon die Gruppe hätte, um zu filmen, und die Passanten auch nicht mehr in die Kamera schauen würden. Man kann das quasi umkehren, wenn du jetzt an Statisten und Schauspieler denkst: Man macht mit Schauspielern eine gewisse Szene, sodass alle anderen auf der Straße zu Statisten werden.

C

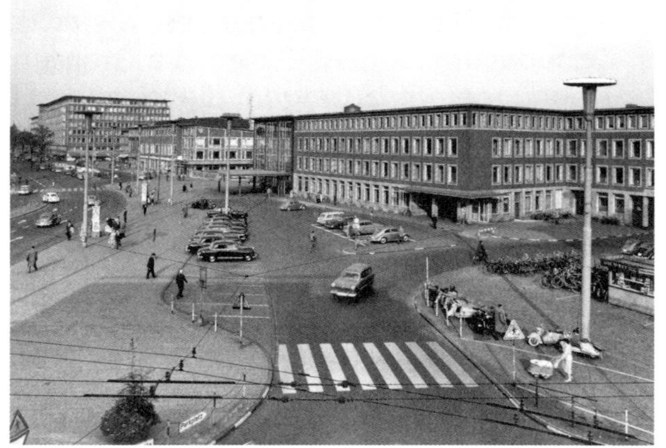

TRUMMER: Aber die Kamera ist sozusagen immer der Voyeur.

VON WEDEMEYER: Eigentlich ist ja noch vielmehr der Zuschauer der Voyeur und die Kamera ist nur ein Mittler. Manchmal weiß der Kameramann auch gar nicht genau, ob es echt oder unecht ist, was er gerade filmt, und erst der Zuschauer weiß es, wenn überhaupt, später. Für die Ausstellung *The Fourth Wall* (2009), die ich im Barbican Centre in London gemacht habe, habe ich über einen Fall auf den Philippinen in den 70er Jahren recherchiert, bei dem eine Gruppe von Personen, die Tasaday, wie in der Steinzeit in Höhlen im Urwald gelebt haben soll. Innerhalb

von zwei Jahren waren immer wieder Journalisten und mit ihnen Kameras dort. Was damals von National Geographic und anderen berichtet wurde, hatte man für wahr gehalten. Fünfzehn Jahre später, nachdem die Gruppe in Vergessenheit geraten war, kam ein Schweizer Journalist wieder auf die Philippinen und behauptete, dass die Tasaday nur Bauern aus der Umgebung waren, die ihre Kleidung ausgezogen und dort Steinzeit gespielt hätten. Bis heute ist eigentlich unklar, ob oder wieviel gespielt wurde. Es kann sein, dass die „Aufdeckung", dass alles nur gespielt war, die eigentliche Falschmeldung war. Die Faszination einer Aufklärung ist größer, wenn man zu wissen glaubt, dass man betrogen wurde, als wenn man an etwas nur glaubt, ob Betrug oder nicht.

D

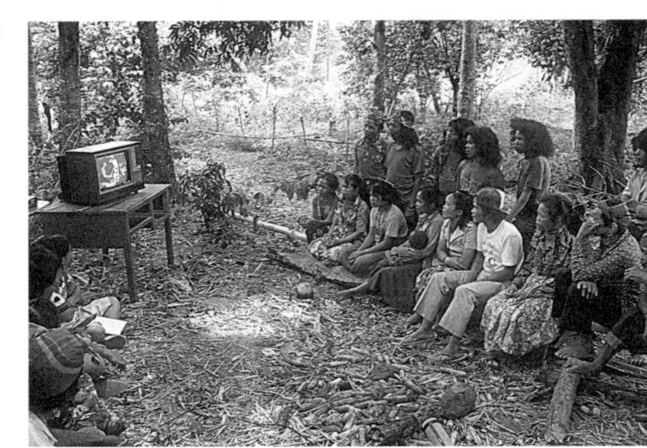

TRUMMER: Die Ent-täuschung ist nicht enttäuschend.

VON WEDEMEYER: Ja, genau. Die Enttäuschung ist notwendiger Teil der Täuschung.

A   Recherchematerial zu *Rien du tout* (2006):
In den Pariser Vororten proben Jugendliche 2005 den Aufstand.
B   Recherchematerial zu *Die Probe* (2008):
Der Präsidentschaftskandidat Obama wartet hinter der Bühne auf seinen Auftritt bei einer Wahlkampfveranstaltung.
C   Recherchematerial zu *Von Gegenüber* (2007):
Der Nachkriegsbau des Bahnhofs von Münster im Jahr 1959, endgültig fertiggestellt wurde er 1960.
D   Recherchematerial zu *The Fourth Wall* (2009):
Die Tasaday schauen das Fernsehprogramm 20/20 (ABC News), in dem sie beschuldigt werden, Fremden ein Steinzeitleben nur vorzutäuschen.
E   Recherchematerial zu *Rien du tout* (2006):
Unruhen in den Pariser Banlieues 2005. Jugendliche spielen aktuelle Fernsehnachrichten nach: Sie proben den Aufstand. Sie haben im Jugendkulturhaus bereits Molières *Der Bürger als Edelmann* aufgeführt.
F   Recherchematerial zu *Die Probe* (2008):
Obama gibt während des Wahlkampfs ein Telefoninterview.
G   Recherchematerial zu *Otjesd* (2005):
Reisende stehen für ein Visum vor der deutschen Botschaft in Kiew an.
H   Recherchematerial zu *The Fourth Wall* (2009):
Besucher beobachten den vermeintlichen Steinzeitstamm der Tasaday aus einem Hubschrauber.

BACKGROUND REBELLION

Thomas D. Trummer in conversation with Clemens von Wedemeyer
Berlin, 2009

CLEMENS VON WEDEMEYER: My work *Basler Podest* (Basel platform, 2006) was made especially for the Art Basel. When the Gallery Jocelyn Wolff asked me to come up with a documentation for the "Statements", I did not want to show a film; the space seemed too small, and I thought that the visitors would not be able to concentrate on a longer video here. In my eyes, the fair was rather more a place where something should be done about an art fair and its form of presentation. I ended up building a small studio that narrates a story in the form of an installation yet remains open-ended.

THOMAS D. TRUMMER: Could you briefly describe it?

VON WEDEMEYER: You see a platform and a camera facing the platform. On the platform, there is a chair; next to it, a second one has fallen over. A few drops of blood can be seen on the floor as well as footprints, indicating a chaotic situation. There are also pieces of paper lying around and a lamp that has fallen over. All this means that something has happened, but what exactly is not clear. You have to read the traces. On the pieces of paper, a script can be deciphered consisting of sentences, all of them completely contradictory, about two people who simply do not understand each other. There is also a monitor showing a slightly displaced detailed view, so that one of the two persons cannot most likely be seen properly. In the background, there is a green screen into which any picture might be faded, making it easy to imagine any possible location there.

TRUMMER: It is a sculptural installation and, at the same time, it tells a story.

VON WEDEMEYER: The work was able to fit in well with the aesthetics of the art fair, as there was a small room nearby where interviews could be held between curators and artists. When people saw my installation amidst the galleries and the regular activity of the fair, they asked themselves: "What has happened here?" So my gallery owner had to invent a story. Often visitors did not see the installation as a gallery exhibit, so some of them simply went into the room with the platform to see for themselves what had happened here. But when they tried to step onto it or sit down on the chair, they fell down, because the platform was only made of very thin sheets of cardboard. Everything was only painted onto the cardboard. In the end and on demand of the fair authorities, the gallery owner had to close off the platform. Two people had slightly injured their foot.

TRUMMER: At first sight, *Basler Podest* is reminiscent of a television studio. The platform alone makes you think of a performance which might have taken place there and which you have simply missed.

VON WEDEMEYER: It was an attempt to interfere with the overall performance of the art fair: an attempt to adjust art as much as possible and in such a way that it can no longer be distinguished from the parameters of the fair as such — a case of trompe-l'œil.

TRUMMER: What actually takes place there?

VON WEDEMEYER: You mean at the art fair? I don't really know either. But it is part of the fiction. Without the context of the fair, things would not be so laden with meaning. As I said, nothing as such took place in the installation; it is only the arrangement of small details and a stage set, in which a story is unexpectedly narrated. It tells of a conflict between two people in a TV studio. In other words, it is actually more a question of performing or representing than about actors or extras; it is, perhaps, a question of the fine line at which the audience begins to participate, and where interpretation and your own reaction define the work.

TRUMMER: Do you regard someone who is invited to a television studio — to a talk show, for example — as an extra?

VON WEDEMEYER: Not necessarily. They are simply "an invited person", even if the people are styled and given make-up to look better on TV. The people are invited to such shows because they have to talk about themselves and not tell stories, although the boundary between the two is probably quite fluid. Real experiences quickly become fictional. I tried out something similar in Munster, where, in a cinema, a scene was shown that had actually been staged in front of the cinema. In the film *Von Gegenüber* (*From the Opposite Side*, 2007), there are 80 extras acting as passers-by. Here, too, it is impossible to distinguish between who is actually acting and who is not. And as a visitor, the real film only begins when you leave the cinema and find yourself at the film's very location. Reality suddenly looks "like in the film". At the time, I was interested in all this, not only with regard to *Basler Podest*, but even more so in the films I made back then. It started with *Occupation*, which I shot in 2001, 2002. The basic concept of the film was to take the audience out of the cinema hall and lead them onto a field at night. A film team was then positioned around them, and together they staged a scene. The audience became the extras. They were no longer passive viewers inside the cinema, reacting reflexively to the film action shown, but were rather wound up in the process of producing a film. The idea was that, at the premiere, exactly those people who were to be seen in the film were also seated in the auditorium, essentially reflected onto the screen. The film team was made up of actors that shot a scene with the extras.

E

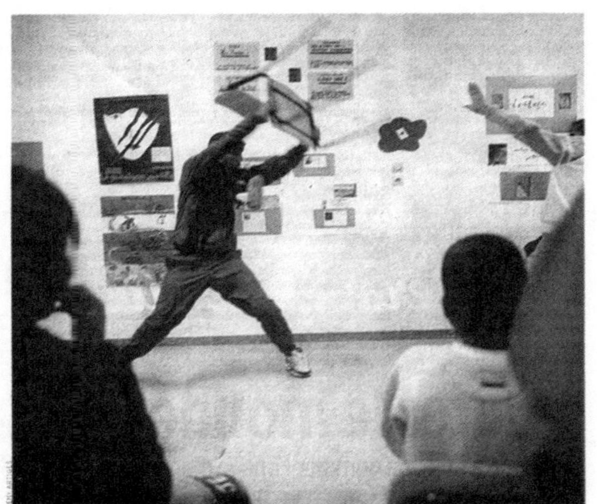

Séance d'improvisation sur les programmes télé au collège Léopold-Sédar-Senghor à Corbeil-Essonnes. En octobre, des élèves ont joué *Le Bourgeois gentilhomme* à la MJC de la ville.

TRUMMER: What did the audience or the extras have to do?

VON WEDEMEYER: On the one hand, they had to respond to instructions that the actors or the film team gave them. On the other hand, they played according to the script that I had written. In the end, there was a kind of dissolution in which the extras overrun the film team. The film

spotlights tip over, and the extras—the main element of the film's action—leave the film. So the film is over. There is a kind of rebellion against the figures who define the frame of the work.

TRUMMER: And against the script.

VON WEDEMEYER: Well, this was already dictated by the script. A fictional revolt, as it were. In general, there is always a dramaturgical "dissolution" at the end of a film script—in this case, a visible, symbolic dissolution of the film plot.

TRUMMER: So the big boss is always the author of the script?

F

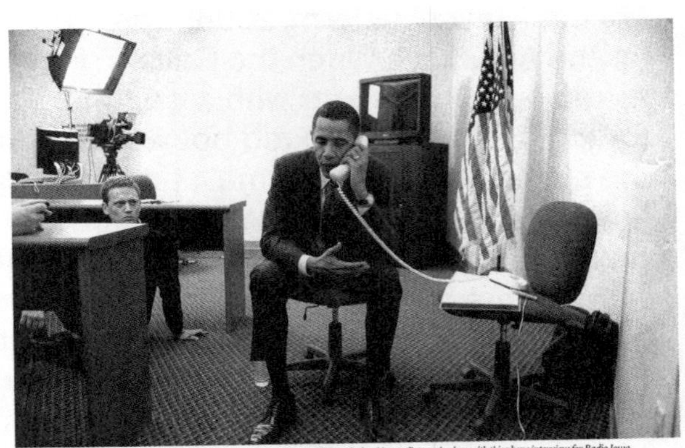

On call Iowa press secretary Tommy Vietor, left, makes sure his boss sets aside time for local journalists, as he does with this phone interview for Radio Iowa

VON WEDEMEYER: Yes, it looks like it. You can let yourself be overrun, if that's what you want. And that was the case here. The film *Rien du tout* (Nothing at all, 2006) which I shot with Maya Schweizer in Paris is similar: a female director and an assistant—actors play the parts—cast teenagers from the Paris banlieues for a medieval film. When choosing the extras in a casting scene, arranged like a ritual on a theatre stage, the director only requires one person and all the others are ordered out. They, in turn, begin to take over the narrative of the film. Already in the parking lot, they start putting on their costumes and slowly construct their own story. The director is ousted from the story of the film and her casting.

TRUMMER: What about the installation *Basler Podest*? Is it similar?

VON WEDEMEYER: No, in that work, it is essentially about the viewer who takes over the situation and thus becomes a part of the work.

TRUMMER: The difference between the films and *Basler Podest* is such that film is a recording medium and that you are watching past action. With *Basler Podest*, you get the impression that the action is still taking place the moment you enter the room.

VON WEDEMEYER: Yes, the camera and the lamps have not been switched off, and there is still something visible on the monitor screen. In the foreground, you see an arrangement, and in the background the camera. Yet, at the same time, all of it is a ploy in order to let the visitors access a certain reality—through the fiction that they are creating as they view the scene. In response to your query about the extras: the entry for "extra" in Wikipedia explains that many famous actors began their careers as extras, meaning that there is a hierarchy of background actors who, provided they are very good, move up to become genuine actors filling in the foreground action.

TRUMMER: Under these circumstances, do they act more or less as actors?

VON WEDEMEYER: That depends on which kind of performance you prefer. Extras are not asked to act in a certain way; they just have to put on something and move about normally. It is said that extras are not as good at pretending so that the background action sometimes looks more genuine than what is being played by the actors in the foreground. I recently saw a film in which two people are seen talking in the foreground, and in the background there are these people posing by a railing. All you focus on are the extras, because they look really attractive and are perfectly arranged, making the foreground action become unimportant.

TRUMMER: As you speak of foreground and background, it seems that we should perhaps read the film as a picture instead. Is this emphasised by the extras, and what is the difference between an extra and stage props?

VON WEDEMEYER: An actor is ultimately nothing but a stage prop for the film—as much as an extra is. A film is made up of locations, persons and props. For some, however, the history of the location where the film is shot is more significant. Various films put different emphasis on the varied elements of the film. One director may not be concerned about the quality of an actor at all, while another one only wants to shoot with extras. Sometimes the visual nature of the film's location is not important, but perhaps it is much more relevant that precisely a part of the action takes place there—as, for example, the baptistery in Pasolini's *Medea*. There is, of course, a much deeper—and not just visual—reason for this. By contrasting the structure of the church with super- and subordinate cults in Greece, Pasolini is thus also drawing a political comparison.

TRUMMER: What do you consider important in film?

VON WEDEMEYER: That changes. Most of the time, I refer to the circumstances of its making,

so I try to make works that merge with real conditions. When I was invited to produce a film to be premiered at the first Moscow Biennale, for example, I shot the short movie *Otjesd* (2005) in Berlin—using Russian immigrants. They play people who are queuing to apply for a visa in front of the German Embassy in Moscow. I was interested in using the elements of the film, the actors, the locations, etc. conceptually, in order to see what kind of a story that would lead to. When the film was shown in Moscow, people thought that a Russian director had shot it in Russia. Only when they later found out that the actors were Russian emigrants did they show an interest in them. Most directors work the opposite way: first they have a story that they want to tell at all costs, and then they look into where it can be made. In my case, stories develop around a given situation and location. What I am likewise interested in is investigating tautologies, structures and systems and inverting them by means of drama or performances, as in *Occupation*. It is a question of exposing the boundaries or divisions that lie between things, and to reveal these interfaces.

G

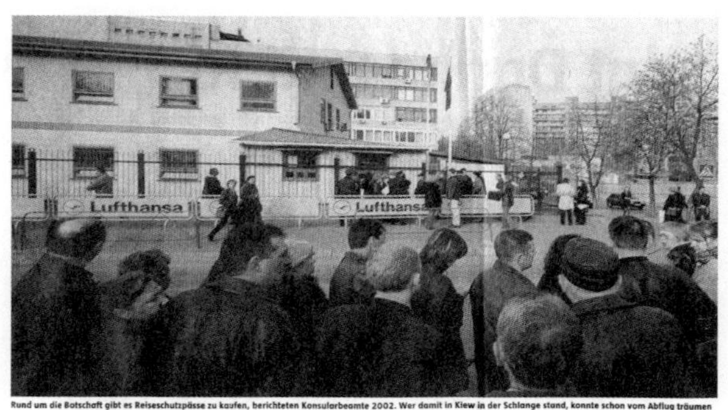

Rund um die Botschaft gibt es Reiseschutzpässe zu kaufen, berichteten Konsularbeamte 2002. Wer damit in Kiew in der Schlange stand, konnte schon vom Abflug träumen

TRUMMER: You seem to be taking elements from the structure of films—such as audience, set, location, camera and so forth—to involve them in a kind of interplay. The camera films itself, resulting in a short-circuit situation prevalent in video art of the 1970s or when spectators became extras or actors.

VON WEDEMEYER: Exactly, it is a feedback or short circuit. The central object is no longer significant.

TRUMMER: In contrast to your works, the closed-circuit installations of the 1970s never have a story. Dan Graham, for instance, is only interested in the structure of the medium.

VON WEDEMEYER: Yes. Dan Graham, whose work I referred to in my project *Von Gegenüber* in the context of the skulptur projekte münster 07 (sculpture projects munster 07), used mirrors and windows for his cinematic model so as to merge the outside and the inside. Graham's work has a sculptural clarity and a logical rigour. But I personally like to make use of the medium as well.

189

"Cinema", as a system, does not only consist of a cinema hall.

TRUMMER: What does it mean to be active in the public space instead of in the studio?

VON WEDEMEYER: In Munster, I really wanted to close off the entire length of one street to see how this would work, whether it could simply be done, and how passers-by would react. For one whole week, we shot in and around the station, between the passers-by. I remembered a text by Dziga Vertov concerning *Man with the Movie Camera*: because he was always filming in the street, he wondered how he could prevent passers-by from not always looking directly into the camera. It occurred to him that it would be best for him to pretended an accident had happened or someone had fallen down, because then people would automatically come to the scene and he would already have a group to shoot, yet the passers-by would no longer be looking at the camera. In terms of extras and actors, you could essentially invert this: you stage a certain scene with actors so that all the other ones in the street turn into extras.

TRUMMER: But the camera is always the voyeur, so to speak.

H

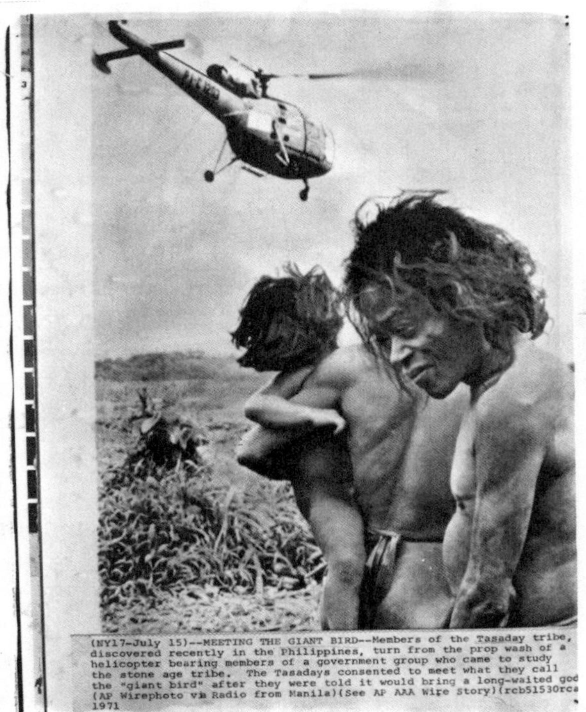

(NY17--July 15)--MEETING THE GIANT BIRD--Members of the Tasaday tribe, discovered recently in the Philippines, turn from the prop wash of a helicopter bearing members of a government group who came to study the stone age tribe. The Tasadays consented to meet what they call the "giant bird" after they were told it would bring a long-waited god (AP Wirephoto via Radio from Manila)(See AP AAA Wire Story)(rcb51530rca 1971

VON WEDEMEYER: To be honest, the viewer is actually more of a voyeur, and the camera merely the intermediary. Sometimes even the cameraman himself is not sure whether what is being filmed is real or unreal; only the viewer will later find out, if at all. For the exhibition *The Fourth Wall* (2009) that I held at the Barbican Centre in London, I researched about a case in the Philippines in the 1970s, in which a group of people, the Tasaday, apparently lived in caves in the jungle like in the

Stone Age. Over a period of two years, journalists kept going there with their cameras. Everything that the reportages by National Geographic and the like had shown was considered real. Fifteen years later, after the group had fallen into oblivion, a Swiss journalist returned to the Philippines claiming that the Tasaday had simply been peasants from the region who had taken off their clothes and enacted life in the Stone Age. Up to the present day, it is still unclear if and how much was acted out. It could very well be that the "disclosure", that all of it was merely performed is the actual hoax. The fascination of a certain disclosure is greater if you think you know that you have been cheated than if you only believe in something, whether it is a lie or not.

TRUMMER: Illusion is not disillusioning then.

VON WEDEMEYER: Exactly. Disillusionment is a necessary part of illusion.

A   Research materials on *Rien du tout* (2006):
Juveniles simulate a rebellion in the suburbs of Paris in 2005.
B   Research materials on *The Test* (2008):
The presidential candidate Obama is waiting backstage for his appearance at a campaign event.
C   Research materials on *From the Opposite Side* (2007):
The post-war Munster train station built in 1959 and completed in 1960.
D   Research materials on *The Fourth Wall* (2009):
The Tasaday watch the television programme *20/20* (ABC News) where the accusation is made that they are impostors just faking a Stone Age existence.
E   Research materials on *Rien du tout* (2006):
Riots in the banlieues of Paris 2005. Juveniles re-enact contemporary TV news reports: They simulate a rebellion. They have already performed *The Bourgeois Gentleman* at the Youth Cultural Centre.
F   Research materials on *The Test* (2008):
Obama is interviewed on the phone during the election campaign.
G   Research materials on *Otjesd* (2005):
Travellers are queuing for a visa at the German Embassy in Kiev.
H   Research materials on *The Fourth Wall* (2009):
Visitors view the alleged Stone Age tribe of the Tasaday from a helicopter.

APPENDIX

AUTOREN / AUTHORS

SABETH BUCHMANN

„Im Diesseits des Blicks hinter die Kulissen" (übersetzt von Judith Rosenthal, Deutsch–Englisch)

"On this Side of the Look Behind the Scenes" (translated by Judith Rosenthal, German–English)

Kunsthistorikerin und -kritikerin. Professorin für Kunstgeschichte der Moderne und Nachmoderne an der Akademie der bildenden Künste Wien. Zusammen mit Helmut Draxler, Clemens Krümmel und Susanne Leeb gibt sie *PoLYpeN*, eine bei b_books Berlin erscheinende Reihe zu Kunstkritik und politischer Theorie, heraus. Regelmäßige Beiträge für Monografien, Kunstzeitschriften und Ausstellungskataloge. Zuletzt erschienene Publikation: Hg. mit Ilse Lafer und Constanze Ruhm: *Putting Rehearsals to the Test. Practices of Rehearsal in Fine Arts, Film, Theater, Theory, and Politics*, Berlin: Sternberg Press / Akademie der bildenden Künste Wien, 2016.

Art historian and critic. Professor of art history of modernism and post-modernism at the Academy of Fine Arts Vienna. Together with Helmut Draxler, Clemens Krümmel and Susanne Leeb she is the editor of *PoLYpeN*, a series published by b_books Berlin on art criticism and political theory. Regular contributions to monographs, art magazines and exhibition catalogues. Recently published: co-ed. with Ilse Lafer and Constanze Ruhm: *Putting Rehearsals to the Test. Practices of Rehearsal in Fine Arts, Film, Theater, Theory, and Politics*, Berlin: Sternberg Press / Academy of Fine Arts Vienna, 2016.

LILIAN HABERER

„Screens in Transition: Zur Diffusion im Kinoraum" (übersetzt von Brian Currid, Deutsch–Englisch)

"Screens in Transition: On Diffusion in the Cinema" (translated by Brian Currid, German–English)

Kunstwissenschaftlerin und Kuratorin. Seit April 2016 Vertretungsprofessur für Kunst im medialen Kontext an der Kunsthochschule für Medien in Köln. Wissenschaftliche Mitarbeiterin am Kunsthistorischen Institut der Universität zu Köln 2011–2016. Projektkoordinatorin des DFG-Forschungsprojekts „Reflexionsräume kinematographischer Ästhetik" 2007–2014.

Art historian and curator. Since April 2016 she has been a visiting professor for Art History in the context of Media at the Academy of Media Arts Cologne. Research assistant at the Art History Institute at the University of Cologne 2011–2016. Project coordinator of the DFG research project "Spaces of reflection of cinematographic aesthetics" 2007–2014.

ZOLTÁN KÉKESI

„Jenseits der Vereinnahmung" (übersetzt von Herwig Engelmann, Englisch–Deutsch)

"Beyond Occupation" (translated by Herwig Engelmann, English–German)

Autor und Kulturwissenschaftler. Gaststipendium am Geisteswissenschaftlichen Zentrum Geschichte und Kultur Mitteleuropas (GWZO) an der Universität Leipzig 2016. Senior Research Fellow am Zentrum für Jüdische Geschichte, New York 2014–2015. Fakultätsmitglied am Institut für Kunsttheorie und Curatorial Studies an der Ungarischen Universität der Bildenden Künste, Budapest seit 2009. Gastdozent an der Humboldt-Universität zu Berlin. Zuletzt erschienene Publikation: *Agents of Liberation, Holocaust Memory in Contemporary Art and Documentary Film*, Budapest / New York: CEU Press, 2015.

Writer and cultural researcher. Visiting fellow at the Centre for the History and Culture of East Central Europe (GWZO) at the University of Leipzig 2016. Senior research fellow at the Center for Jewish History, New York 2014–2015. Faculty member at the Department of Art Theory and Curatorial Studies at the University of Fine Arts, Budapest since 2009. Guest lecturer at Humboldt University, Berlin. Recently published: *Agents of Liberation, Holocaust Memory in Contemporary Art and Documentary Film*, Budapest / New York: CEU Press, 2015.

MATTEO PASQUINELLI

„Die Stimme der Finanzsingularität" (übersetzt von Herwig Engelmann, Englisch–Deutsch)

"The Voice of Financial Singularity" (translated by Herwig Engelmann, English–German)

Gastprofessor für Medientheorie an der Staatlichen Hochschule für Gestaltung Karlsruhe und Herausgeber des Sammelbands *Alleys of Your Mind, Augmented Intelligence and its Traumas*, Lüneburg: Meson Press, 2015.

Visiting professor in Media Theory at the Karlsruhe University of Arts and Design and editor of the anthology *Alleys of Your Mind: Augmented Intelligence and its Traumas*, Lunenburg: Meson Press, 2015.

MARIE-FRANCE RAFAEL

„Die Zukunft holt uns ein", Gespräch mit Clemens von Wedemeyer (übersetzt von Ariane Kossack, Deutsch–Englisch)

"The Future Is Catching up on Us", conversation with Clemens von Wedemeyer (translated by Ariane Kossack, German–English)

Promovierte Kunsthistorikerin und wissenschaftliche Mitarbeiterin an der Muthesius Kunsthochschule in Kiel. Lehrt regelmäßig an der Universität der Künste Berlin, an der Kunstakademie Münster sowie an der Freien Universität Berlin.

Art historian and researcher at the Muthesius University of Fine Arts and Design in Kiel. Guest lecturer at the Berlin University of the Arts, at the Academy of Fine Arts Munster, and at the Freie Universität Berlin.

THOMAS D. TRUMMER

„Aufstand des Hintergrunds", Gespräch mit Clemens von Wedemeyer (übersetzt von Ariane Kossack, Deutsch–Englisch)

"Background Rebellion", conversation with Clemens von Wedemeyer (translated by Ariane Kossack, German–English)

Kurator und Kunsthistoriker. Seit 2015 Direktor des Kunsthaus Bregenz.

Curator and art historian. Since 2015 director of the Kunsthaus Bregenz.

CLEMENS VON WEDEMEYER

„Sun Cinema, Mardin, Türkei, 2010" (übersetzt von Ariane Kossack, Deutsch–Englisch); „The Making of Big Business" (übersetzt von Steven Black, Deutsch–Englisch)

"Sun Cinema, Mardin, Turkey, 2010" (translated by Ariane Kossack, German–English); "The Making of Big Business" (translated by Steven Black, German–English)

Künstler und Filmemacher. Einzelausstellungen (Auswahl): *P.O.V.*, Neuer Berliner Kunstverein 2016; *Muster*, MCA Chicago 2015; *The Cast*, MAXXI, Museo nazionale delle arti del XXI secolo, Rom 2013; *The Fourth Wall*, Barbican Centre London 2009. Teilnahme an der dOCUMENTA(13), Kassel 2012. Seit 2013 Professor für Medienkunst (Klasse Expanded Cinema) an der Hochschule für Grafik und Buchkunst Leipzig.

Artist and filmmaker. Solo exhibitions (selection): *P.O.V.*, Neuer Berliner Kunstverein 2016; *Muster*, MCA Chicago 2015; *The Cast*, MAXXI, Museo nazionale delle arti del XXI secolo, Rome 2013; *The Fourth Wall*, Barbican Centre London 2009. Participation at the dOCUMENTA(13), Kassel 2012. Since 2013 Professor of Media Arts (class Expanded Cinema) at the Academy of Fine Arts Leipzig.

WERKINDEX (AUSWAHL) / INDEX OF WORKS (SELECTION)

SQUARE

Video übertragen auf 35mm, 3min, 1,66:1, 2016

video transferred to 35mm, 3min, 1.66:1, 2016

Der Platz vor der Hamburger Kunsthalle aus großer Entfernung von oben gefilmt: Die Bewegungen der Passanten werden zu interpretierbaren Mustern.

The square in front of the Hamburger Kunsthalle filmed from high above: The movements of passers-by become interpretable patterns.

P.O.V.

Installation mit 7 Projektionen, 2015–2016

installation with 7 projections, 2015–2016

In dem mehrteiligen Projekt *P.O.V.* (Point Of View) werden Bildräume und Grenzen der subjektiven Kamera auf Grundlage von Amateurfilmaufnahmen des Rittmeisters Frhr. Harald von Vietinghoff-Riesch untersucht, die er im Zweiten Weltkrieg gedreht hat. In *Against the Point of View* wird eine Szene aus dem historischen Filmmaterial als Computerspiel-Umgebung in der Art eines „Virtual Battlefields" rekonstruiert, um so nach divergenten Blickwinkeln und alternativen Verläufen der Ereignisses zu suchen. In *Die Pferde des Rittmeisters* werden die Pferde der Wehrmacht und die vor ihr flüchtenden Zivilisten zu einem Bild des Kriegs neu montiert. Mit dem Kulturhistoriker Klaus Theweleit und dem Direktor des Neuen Berliner Kunstvereins Marius Babias werden in *Was man nicht sieht* Themen wie Soldaten als Touristen und Ethnografen hinter der Kamera besprochen. *P.O.V.* ist in Zusammenarbeit mit Eiko Grimberg verwirklicht worden.

In the multi-part project *P.O.V.* (Point Of View) pictorial spaces and boundaries of the subjective camera are examined based on the amateur footage from the Second World War shot by cavalry captain Frhr. Harald von Vietinghoff-Riesch. In *Against the Point of View* a scene from the historic footage is reconstructed as a computer game environment in the way of a "virtual battlefield" with an alternative course of events. In *Die Pferde des Rittmeisters* (The horses of the cavalry captain) the horses of the Wehrmacht and the civilians fleeing from it are reassembled in a picture of the war. The cultural historian Klaus Theweleit and the director of the Neuer Berliner Kunstverein Marius Babias discuss subjects in *Was man nicht sieht* (What you can't see) —like soldiers behind the camera as tourists and ethno-graphers. *P.O.V.* has been realized in collaboration with Eiko Grimberg.

Bestehend aus / composed of

OHNE TITEL (ALLES)

16mm, 4min, Farbe, stumm, 1,33:1, 2016

16mm, 4min, colour, mute. 1.33:1, 2016

IM ANGESICHT

16mm übertragen auf Video, 7min, Farbe, stumm, 1,33:1, 2016

16mm transferred to video, 7min, colour, mute. 1.33:1, 2016

WAS MAN NICHT SIEHT

Video, 42min, Farbe, Ton, 1,33:1, 2016

video, 42min, colour, sound, 1.33:1, 2016

ARTEMOWSK 1941

16mm übertragen auf Video, 8min, s/w, stumm, 1,33:1, 2016

16mm transferred to video, 8min, b/w, mute, 1.33:1, 2016

ANDENKEN

Video, 5min, Farbe, stumm, 1,78:1, 2016

video, 5min, colour, mute, 1.78:1, 2016

DIE PFERDE DES RITTMEISTERS

16mm übertragen auf Video, 10min, Farbe, Ton, 1,33:1, 2015

16mm transferred to video, 10min, colour, sound, 1.33:1, 2015

AGAINST THE POINT OF VIEW

Video, 18min, Farbe, Ton, 1,78:1, 2016

video, 18min, colour, sound, 1.78:1, 2016

ESIOD 2015

Video, 38min, Farbe, Ton, 1,78:1, 2016

video, 38min, colour, sound, 1.78:1, 2016

2051: Eine Frau kehrt nach Wien zurück, um ihr Bankkonto zu schließen, auf dem nicht nur Geld, sondern auch Erinnerungen gespeichert sind. Aber die Kundin wird vom Computersystem nicht erkannt und muss sich einem „Memory Check" unterziehen. Der Film entstand im Zusammenhang eines Kunst am Bau Projekts der Erste Group Bank AG, Wien.

2051: A woman returns to Vienna to close a bank account in which not only money, but also her memories are stored. Only, the customer is not recognised by the computer system and therefore has to undergo a "Memory Check". The film was made in the context of the art for architecture project of Vienna's Erste Group Bank AG.

A RECOVERED BONE

3D-Print, 55 × 13 × 9cm, Videoschleife, 2015

3D print, 55 × 13 × 9cm, video loop, 2015

Ein Akt digitalen Diebstahls. In Stanley Kubricks *2001: A Space Odyssey* (1968) wird ein Knochen – erstes Werkzeug und erste Waffe – in einer Geste des Triumphes in den Himmel geschleudert. Mit Hilfe von 3D Scanning und Modeling Technologie wurde das Objekt aus der berühmten Szene digital ausgelesen und seine Form physisch rekonstruiert.

An act of digital theft. In Stanley Kubrick's *2001: A Space Odyssey* (1968) a bone —first tool and first weapon—is flung toward the heaven in a gesture of triumph. The object is excised from the famous scene and reconstructed in its shape by using 3D modeling technology.

EVERY WORD YOU SAY

Verschiedene Medien, Installation, Ton, Skulpturen, Video, 2014

mixed media installation, sound, sculptures, video, 2014

In der Villa Salve Hospes – zeitweise Sitz des Deutschen Spracharchivs und heutiges Domizil des Kunstvereins Braunschweig – wurden historische, wissenschaftliche und fiktive Erzählungen zusammen gebracht. Ein Hörspiel-Parcours durch das Haus erforscht die Stimme als akustisches Phänomen. Interaktive Stücke verhandeln die Zukunft von Sprache als Kommunikationsmittel und Identitätsspender. Historische Audio-Dokumente und Sound-Installationen mit computerbasierter Soundsynthese skizzieren in der Vermischung von Fakten und Fiktionen Geschichten aus dem Archiv des Gründers Rudolf Zwirner. Sprache und Geräusche konstruieren so einen filmischen Raum ohne traditionelle Bilder. In dem Film *Automatisierte Sprachanalyse zu psychologischen Zwecken* werden zwei historische Patientengespräche vor und nach einer Lobotomie von Psychologen und Linguisten computergestützt untersucht.

In the Villa Salve Hospes—temporary headquarters of the German Languages Archives and today domicile of the Kunstverein Braunschweig—historical, scientific, and fictional narratives were brought together. A radio play-tour through the house explores the voice as an acoustic phenomenon. Interactive pieces negotiate the future of language as a means of communication and defining identity. Historical audio documents and sound installations with computer-based sound synthesis outlined in the blending of fact and fiction stories from the archives of the founder Rudolf Zwirner. That way, language and sounds construct a cinematic space without traditional images. In the video *Automatisierte Sprachanalyse zu psychologischen Zwecken* (Automated speech analysis for psychological purposes) two patient interviews before and after brain surgery undergo a computer supported analysis by psychologists and linguists.

Bestehend unter anderem aus / composed among others of

AUTOMATISIERTE SPRACHANALYSE ZU PSYCHOLOGISCHEN ZWECKEN

Video, 30min, Farbe, Ton, 1,78:1, 2014

video, 30min, colour, sound, 1.78:1, 2014

THE CAST

Installation, Video, Skulpturen, 2013

installation, video, sculptures, 2013

Das Projekt, erstmals ausgestellt im Museum MAXXI in Rom, ist die Untersuchung eines Ortes der Kulturproduktion, insbesondere des Studios Cinecittà und seiner Geschichte. Dabei wurde gleichzeitig das Verhältnis von Bildhauerei und Kino in Szene gesetzt. Hunderte von Skulpturen, die in der Geschichte des italienischen Kinos Verwendung gefunden hatten, sind in einer Werkstatt der Cinecittà Filmstudios (Rom) versammelt.

Für *Afterimage* wurde mit Hilfe von Laser-Technologie dieser Raum gescannt, um mittels der gewonnenen Daten in der Postproduktion einen Animationsfilm zu kreieren, der als Panorama installiert eine immersive Erfahrung ermöglicht.

The Beginning. Living Figures Dying zeigt die Beziehung zwischen Mensch und Skulpturen in der Kinogeschichte. Das Video besteht aus Fragmenten von Filmen, die die Erstellung, Verehrung und Zerstörung von humanoiden Skulpturen im Kino zeigen.

The Cast: Procession erinnert an einen Vorfall 1958 in Cinecittà während der Dreharbeiten an dem Film *Ben-Hur* (1959). Tausende von Statisten versuchten, die Tore zu durchbrechen, um Arbeit und angemessene Bezahlung zu bekommen. Skulpturen, die auf die Geschichte von Deukalion und Pyrrha (Ovid) verweisen, erweitern die Ausstellung.

The project, first exhibited at MAXXI Rome, is the investigation of a cultural production site, especially the studio Cinecittà and its history. At the same time, the relationship between sculpture and cinema is staged. Hundreds of sculptures that have been used in Italian films are stored in a workshop at the film studio Cinecittà.

For *Afterimage*, the original space was scanned by laser technology and then during post-production an animated film was made from this, creating an immersive experience.

The Beginning. Living Figures Dying depicts the relationship between humans and sculptures throughout cinema history. It is made up of film fragments that deal with the phases of the creation, adoration and destruction of humanoid sculptures in cinema.

The Cast: Procession recalls an incident that took place in 1958 in Cinecittà (Rome) during the shooting of the movie *Ben-Hur* (1959), when thousands of extras tried to force open the gates and enter the studios demanding work and appropriate wages. Sculptures that refer to the story of Deucalion and Pyrrha (Ovid) broaden the exhibition.

Bestehend aus / composed of

AFTERIMAGE

halbkreisförmige Videoinstallation, 6 min, Farbe, Ton, 6 × 2,1 m, 2013	semi-circular video installation, 6 min, colour, sound, 6 × 2.1 m, 2013

THE BEGINNING. LIVING FIGURES DYING

Multi-Kanal-Videoinstallation, 18 min, Farbe, Ton, 1,78:1, 2013	multi-channel video installation, 18 min, colour, sound, 1.78:1, 2013

THE CAST: PROCESSION

Video, 14 min, s/w, Ton, 2,35:1, 2013	video, 14 min, b/w, sound, 2.35:1, 2013

REMAINS: THE MYTH OF DEUCALION AND PYRRHA

Glasfaser-Harz-Skulpturen, 2013	fiberglass resin sculptures, 2013

CAST BEHIND YOU THE BONES OF YOUR MOTHER

3D-Druck-Skulpturen, Ton, Lautsprecher, 2015	3D-print sculptures, sound, loudspeakers, 2015

MUSTER / RUSHES

3-Kanal-Videoinstallation, 3 × 27 min und 79 min (lineare Version), Farbe, Ton, 1,78:1, 2012	3-channel video installation, 3 × 27 min and 79 min (linear version), colour, sound, 1.78:1, 2012

Ein Kloster, einst ein Gefängnis, dann ein Konzentrations- und Arbeitslager, in den 1970er Jahren Mädchenerziehungsheim und heute eine psychiatrische Klinik, seit den 1980er Jahren auch Gedenkstätte. Hier sieht man wiederkehrende Muster an einem Ort im Laufe der Zeit. Die drei Zeiten laufen synchronisiert auf drei Leinwänden. In der linearen Spielfilmversion sind die Passagen so ineinander geschnitten, dass es immer wieder zu Erinnerungen und Zeitverschiebungen kommt.

A convent, once a prison, then a concentration and labor camp, later a girls reformatory in the seventies and today a psychiatric clinic that has also been the Breitenau memorial since the 1980s. Here, in that one place, one can see recurring patterns over time. In the linear feature film version, the three individual passages are woven together so that memories and shifts in time are produced, all of which revolve around the same location.

SUN CINEMA

zweiseitige Leinwand, 2010	double-sided screen, 2010

SUN CINEMA LOCATION

Video, 59 min, Farbe, Ton, 1,78:1, 2010	video, 59 min, colour, sound, 1.78:1, 2010

Im Rahmen des Projekts „My City" des British Council wurde ein skulpturales Open-Air-Kino mit Blick auf die mesopotamische Ebene an der Stadtgrenze der türkischen Stadt Mardin entwickelt. Während das Kino in der Nacht zu Filmvorführungen dient, hat die Rückseite der Leinwand die Funktion eines Spiegels, der die Abendsonne hinunter ins Tal spiegelt. *Sun Cinema Location* dokumentiert das Projekt aus einer subjektiven Kameraposition und zeigt, während das Open-Air-Kino gebaut wird, den Alltag und die im öffentlichen Raum stattfindenden Rituale.

In the context of the project "My City" by the British Council, a sculptural open-air cinema was developed at the border of the Turkish city of Mardin, overlooking the Mesopotamian plain. Whereas the cinema serves for film pro-jections at night, the back of the screen functions as a mirror, reflecting the evening sun down to valley. *Sun Cinema Location* documents the project from a subjective camera position, filmed during the realisation of the open-air cinema while depicting everyday life in the city of Mardin and its rituals in public space.

THE FOURTH WALL

Installation, Videos, 16 mm, Fotoabzüge, 2009	installation, videos, 16 mm, prints, 2009

Historisches Sujet des Projekts ist eine Gruppe moderner Höhlenbewohner: die Tasaday, ein Stamm, der offenbar im Jahr 1971 noch wie in der Steinzeit lebte. Ihre Echtheit wurde allerdings später bezweifelt und als Schwindel erklärt. Die Arbeit *The Fourth Wall*, entstanden für die Londoner Barbican Art Gallery, diskutiert genau diese Illusion des Authentischen. Der Titel bezeichnet die imaginierte Trennung zwischen Bühnen- und Zuschauerraum.

In *Against Death* erzählt ein Forscher seinem Freund, einem Anthropologen, von einem Ritual, dem er sich unterzogen hat und das ihm Unsterblichkeit verleihen würde. Der Film endet mit einer Demonstration der erworbenen Unsterblichkeit des Forschers, um dann nahtlos an den Beginn des Films wieder anzuschließen.

The Gentle Ones entstand aus der Idee, Schauspielstudierende mögen auf der Theaterbühne des Barbican Centre eine isolierte Gruppe spielen, die nichts anderes außerhalb des Theaters kennt und einzig vom Publikum lebt.

The centre of the work is a historical incident around a group of contemporary cavemen: the Tasaday, a tribe that in 1971 apparently was still living in the Stone Age. Soon, doubt arose as to the authenticity and swindle was suspected. *The Fourth Wall*, made for London's Barbican Art Gallery, debates the illusionistic nature of the authentic. The title refers to an imaginary divide between stage and audience.

In *Against Death* an explorer is seen telling his anthropologist friend about a ritual he undertook which granted him immortality. The scene concludes with the explorer demonstrating his inability to die, and then seamlessly loops back to the beginning.

The Gentle Ones originates from the idea of asking drama students to play an isolated group on the stage of the Barbican Centre that knows nothing outside the theatre and is only kept alive by the audience.

Bestehend aus / composed of

INTRO

16 mm, 3 min, s/w, stumm, 1,33:1, 2009	16 mm, 3 min, b/w, mute, 1.33:1, 2009

WOOD

2-Kanal-Videoinstallation, 7 min, Farbe, stumm, 1,78:1, 2009	2-channel video installation, 7 min, colour, mute, 1.78:1, 2009

HOW TO RE-ESTABLISH
THE TRUTH ABOUT
THE TASADAY? – INTERVIEW
WITH JOHN NANCE

Video, 55 min, 1,78:1,
2009

video, 55 min, 1.78:1,
2009

RECEPTION

3-Kanal-Videoinstallation,
13 min, Farbe,
Ton, 1,33:1, 2009

3-channel video installa-
tion, 13 min, colour,
sound, 1.33:1, 2009

HOW TO DEAL WITH THE
UNCONTACTED? – INTERVIEW
WITH GEOFFREY FRAND

Video, 35 min, 1,78:1,
2009

video, 35 min, 1.78:1,
2009

HOW TO CREATE AN UNBELIEVABLE
FICTION? – INTERVIEW
WITH RUGGERO DEODATO

Video, 30 min, 1,78:1,
2009

video, 30 min, 1.78:1,
2009

THE GENTLE ONES

Video, 28 min, 1,78:1,
2009

video, 28 min, 1.78:1,
2009

AGAINST DEATH

35 mm übertragen
auf Video, 9 min, Farbe,
Ton, 1,85:1, 2009

35 mm transferred
to video, 9 min, colour,
sound, 1.85:1, 2009

FOUND FOOTAGE

Video, 31 min, Farbe,
Ton, 1,33:1, 2008–2009

video, 31 min,
colour, sound, 1.33:1,
2008–2009

THE INNER CAMPUS

2-Kanal-Videoinstallation,
55 min, Farbe,
Ton, 1,78:1, 2008

2-channel video installa-
tion, 55 min, colour,
sound, 1.78:1, 2008

Diese Reihe von zehn Interviews entstand an der Universität von Santa
Barbara, Kalifornien. Sie beschäftigen
sich mit den Beziehungen zwischen
den Studierenden und dem geografi-
schen, sowie dem psycho-histori-
schen Raum des Universitätscampus.

This series of 10 interviews was realised
at the University of Santa Barbara,
California. It addresses the relations
between the students and the geographic as well as the psycho-historic
space of the university campus.

DIE PROBE / THE TEST

Video, 12 min, Farbe,
Ton, 1,78:1, 2008

video, 12 min, colour,
sound, 1.78:1, 2008

In einem Backstage-Bereich probt der
neu gewählte Präsident die Rede zu
seiner Wahl, in der er das Amt ablehnt.

In a backstage area, the newly elected
president rehearses the speech
with which he will refuse the power.

GETRENNTER
MONOLOG /
DIVIDED MONOLOGUE

Diaprojektion,
80 Diabilder, 2007

slideshow,
80 slides, 2007

Zwischen die Bilder, angeordnet im
Schuss-Gegenschuss-Verfahren, sind

wie in einem Stummfilm Texttafeln ein-
geschoben, die über den Dialog zu
informieren scheinen. Nach einer Weile
erkennt man jedoch, dass die beiden
Personen nicht miteinander reden,
sondern getrennt voneinander einen
selbstreflexiven Monolog führen.

As in a silent movie, the images,
arranged in a shot / reverse shot style
are interposed by slides with text of
what appears to be their dialogue.
After a while one becomes aware that
the two characters are not in fact talking to each other but to themselves
in a self-reflexive, divided monologue.

VON GEGENÜBER /
FROM THE
OPPOSITE SIDE

35 mm, 39 min, Farbe,
Ton, 1,66:1, 2007

35 mm, 39 min, colour,
sound, 1.66:1, 2007

Passanten laufen durch den Bahnhof, Polizisten stehen vor einem Kino,
eine latente Bedrohung liegt in der
Luft. Wer ist Passant, wer ist Statist?
Das rastlose Bild auf der Leinwand zeigt
einen subjektiven Blick, man hört
Atmen und laufende Schritte. Physisch
in der Bewegung der Kinokamera
gefangen, findet der Betrachter langsam
heraus, durch wessen prekäres Auge
man schaut.

Passers-by running through the station,
police officers standing in front of
a cinema, a latent threat is in the air.
Who's a passer-by, who is an extra?
The restless image on screen shows
a subjective view, one can hear
breathing and ongoing steps. Physically caught in the movement of the
movie camera, the viewer finds out slowly through whose precarious eye one
looks.

METROPOLIS,
REPORT FROM CHINA

in Zusammenarbeit
mit Maya Schweizer,
Video, 42 min, Farbe,
Ton, 1,33:1, 2004–2006

in collaboration with
Maya Schweizer, video,
42 min, colour, sound,
1.33:1, 2004–2006

Ein Film, der Recherchematerial für
ein Remake von Fritz Langs Klassiker
Metropolis (1927) sammelt und zugleich die urbanen Utopien und ihre
soziale Realität in China in Frage stellt.
Eine Fiktion trifft eine andere.

A film that gathers research material for
a remake of Fritz Lang's classic *Metropolis* (1927) and that questions urban
utopias and their social reality in China.
One fiction meets another.

RIEN DU TOUT

in Zusammenarbeit
mit Maya Schweizer,
Video, 35 mm,
30 min, Farbe, Ton,
1,78:1, 2006

in collaboration with
Maya Schweizer,
video, 35 mm, 30 min,
colour, sound,
1.78:1, 2006

Ein Casting in einem Theater in der
Pariser Banlieue. Eine Regisseurin
und ihr Assistent entfremden sich zunehmend, die überflüssigen Laien-
Schauspieler beginnen währenddessen
auf dem Parkplatz zu tanzen und
feiern.

A casting in a theatre in the banlieue of
Paris. The director and her assistant
grow increasingly estranged, the super-
fluous amateur actors and actresses
in the car park outside begin to celebrate
and dance.

BASLER PODEST

Installation, Monitor,
Kamera, Stühle, Holz-
plattform, Scheinwerfer,
Stromkabel, Transport-
koffer, Papiere, 2006

installation, monitor,
camera, chairs, wooden
platform, spotlight,
electric cables, flight-
case, papers, 2006

Die Installation *Basler Podest* – entstanden für die Art Basel 37 – zeigt die
Überreste einer vermeintlich gescheiterten Podiumsdiskussion: eine erhöhte
Plattform; Stühle, die teilweise um-
gekippt sind; ein umgefallener Mikrofon-
ständer; Beleuchtung; eine Kamera,
die auf das Podium gerichtet ist; ein
Monitor, der das Kamerabild überträgt;
und Skript-Seiten, lose über den
Boden verteilt. In dem Raum sind die
Ereignisse zum Stillstand gekommen.
Der Besucher tritt als Statist in die
Szenerie; seine Beobachtung und Imagination wird zum Schlüsselelement
und zur Voraussetzung der Arbeit, die
letztlich auf die unklare Grenze zwischen
Realität und Fiktion verweist.

The installation *Basler Podest*, created
for the Art Basel 37, shows the remains of a supposedly failed panel discussion: an elevated platform; chairs,
some of which have been tipped over;
a microphone dropped to the ground;
lighting; a camera directed at the stage;
and a monitor showing the image
the camera transmits; and script pages
loosely scattered over the ground.
In this space the events have come to
a standstill. The viewer appears, as
an extra in the scene; his observations
and imagination is the key element,
as well as the prerequisite for the
work, which ultimately refers to the unclear boundary between reality and
fiction.

OHNE TITEL
(REKONSTRUKTION)

16 mm übertragen
auf Video, 3 min,
Farbe, Ton, 1,33:1,
2005

16 mm transferred
to video, 3 min,
colour, sound, 1.33:1,
2005

Ein Tänzer verlässt immer wieder
den unbestimmten Bildraum – er scheint
mit dem Blick der Kamera bis zur Er-
schöpfung zu streiten. Dazwischen
wartet er still mit dem Gesicht zur Wand.
Die Aufnahmen zum Film entstanden
während der Proben zu einem Solo-
stück des Tänzers und Choreografen
Alexandre Roccoli.

Over and over again, a dancer vanishes from the vaguely defined visual space —he seems to be clashing, to the point of exhaustion, with the camera's point of view. In the intervals, he waits quietly, his face to the wall. The footage in the film was shot during rehearsals for a solo piece by dancer and choreographer Alexandre Roccoli.

OTJESD

16 mm übertragen auf Video, 15 min, Loop, Farbe, Ton, 1,5:1, 2005

16 mm transferred to video, 15 min, loop, colour, sound, 1.5:1, 2005

THE MAKING OF OTJESD
Video, 10 min, Farbe, Ton, 1,33:1, 2005

video, 10 min, colour, sound, 1.33:1, 2005

In einer fünfzehnminütigen Einstellung zeigt der Film eine nachgestellte Szene in der wirkliche russische Einwanderer vor dem fiktiven deutschen Konsulat in Moskau auf ihr Visum warten. *The Making of Otjesd* zeigt das Set in einem Berliner Wald sowie Rechercheaufnahmen. Die beteiligten Schauspieler erzählen von ihren realen Erfahrungen.

In a single fifteen minute shot, the film captures an imaginary scene of actual Russian immigrants waiting for visas in front of the fictitious German consulate in Moscow. *The Making of Otjesd* shows the set in a Berlin forest as well as research material. The actors involved talk about their real experiences of migration.

DIE SIEDLUNG

Video, 20 min, Farbe, Ton, 1,78:1, 2004

video, 20 min, colour, sound, 1.78:1, 2004

Eine Recherche zu einem Film: Schauplatz ist ein Leipziger Plattenbaugebiet, an dessen Rändern sich verlassene Militärbaracken sowie seit den 1990er Jahren Einfamilien- und Reihenhaussiedlungen finden. Die Kamera trifft auf Personen, deren Erzählungen von Stagnation und gescheiterten Utopien zeugen.

Location research on a film: The setting is an area of pre-fab blocks of flats surrounded by abandoned military barracks and by settlements of detached homes and terraced houses built in Leipzig in the 1990s. The camera captures people whose stories bear witness to stagnation and failed utopias.

DAS BILDERMUSEUM BRENNT

3-Kanal-Videoinstallation, 27 min, Farbe, Ton, 1,78:1, 2004–2005

3-channel video installation, 27 min, colour, sound, 1.78:1, 2004–2005

Ein Schauspieler in verschiedenen Rollen: Als Besucher, Bewacher und illegaler Bewohner läuft er durch ein leeres Museum. Die einzelnen Charaktere bemerken, aber begegnen sich nicht. Die Aufnahmen entstanden

2004 im unfertigen Neubau des Museums der bildenden Künste Leipzig.

An actor in a series of roles: As a visitor, a guard and an illegal tenant, he walks through an empty museum. The individual characters are aware of one another but never meet. The footage was shot in 2004 in the unfinished new building of Leipzig Museum of Fine Arts.

SILBERHÖHE

35 mm übertragen auf Video, 10 min, Farbe, Ton, 1,66:1, 2003

35 mm transferred to video, 10 min, colour, sound, 1.66:1, 2003

In Halle-Silberhöhe, einer Plattenbausiedlung in Ostdeutschland, werden Wohnblocks abgerissen. Die Montage fügt die einzelnen Kameraeinstellungen zu einer trostlosen, dystopischen Szenerie zusammen und referiert dabei auf eine Technik, die Michelangelo Antonioni in seinem Film *L'eclisse* (1962) anwandte.

In Halle-Silberhöhe, an area in East Germany with pre-fab blocks of flats where the buildings are being torn down. The montage collects the separate camera shots to create a bleak, dystopian setting, at the same time a comment on a technique used by Michelangelo Antonioni in his 1962 film *L'eclisse*.

BIG BUSINESS

Video, 25 min, Farbe, Ton, 1,33:1, 2002

video, 25 min, colour, sound, 1.33:1, 2002

THE MAKING OF BIG BUSINESS
Video, 27 min, Farbe, Ton, 1,33:1, 2002

video, 27 min, colour, sound, 1.33:1, 2002

Der Film ist ein Remake des gleichnamigen Slapstick-Klassikers von Stan Laurel und Oliver Hardy (1929). Ein Streit entbrennt, in dessen Verlauf sowohl Finlaysons Haus, sein Klavier wie auch Stan und Ollies Auto zerstört werden. Der Film wurde in der Justizvollzugsanstalt Waldheim in Sachsen gemeinsam mit den Insassen realisiert. *The Making of Big Business* kommentiert die Dreharbeiten des Films in dem ältesten Gefängnis Deutschlands. Neben Interviews mit Gefangenen und dem Gefängnisdirektor werden auch die Geschichte des Orts und die Rahmenbedingungen der Produktion gezeigt.

The film is a remake of the slapstick Laurel and Hardy classic (1929) of the same name. An argument breaks out in the course of which Finlayson's house, his piano and Stan and Ollie's car are demolished. The film was shot on location with inmates of Waldheim Prison, in Saxonia. *The Making of Big Business* comments on the shooting of the film in Germany's oldest prison. Along with interviews of inmates and the prison warden, the video also relates the history of the place and the conditions of production.

OCCUPATION

35 mm, 8 min, Farbe, Ton, 1,85:1, 2001–2002

35 mm, 8 min, colour, sound, 1.85:1, 2001–2002

THE MAKING OF OCCUPATION
Video, 10 min, Farbe, Ton, 1.33:1, 2002

video, 10 min, colour, sound, 1,33:1, 2002

Eine nächtliche Massenszene soll gedreht werden. Eine Markierung auf dem Boden hält die 200 wartenden Statisten zusammen. Regie und Aufnahmeleitung sind sich uneinig. Die unruhige Menge entwickelt ein Eigenleben, und das Filmteam verliert die Kontrolle.

A nighttime scene is to be filmed. Held together by a mark on the ground, 200 extras await their cues, and yet the direction and production staffs are in conflict with one another. The restless crowd develops a life of its own as the film team loses control of the situation.

MASS

Video, 3 min, Farbe, Ton, 1,78:1, 1998

video, 3 min, colour, sound, 1.78:1, 1998

Überblendungen von Found Footage Bildern von Massenaufläufen und politischen Demonstrationen aus den 1920er Jahren verdichten sich zu einer grauen Fläche.

Found footage sequences of mass assemblies and political demonstrations from the 1920s are superimposed and blur to a grey surface.

BETEILIGTE / CONTRIBUTORS

HAUPTDARSTELLER / LEADING ACTORS

Julia Berke (*Occupation*), Rita Breitkreiz (*Otjesd*), Mirko Böttcher (*Die Probe*), Jeff Burrell (*Muster*), Geoffrey Burton (*Against Death*), Yann Chermat (*Rien du tout*), Ekaterina Choulman (*Otjesd*), Victor Choulman (*Otjesd*), Stephanie Cumming (*Esiod 2015*), Sven Dolinski (*Esiod 2015*), Tarik Goetzke (*Muster*), Jörn Knebel (*Occupation*), Tómas Lemarquis (*Muster*), Angela Melitopoulos (*Muster*), Mario Mentrup (*Das Bildermuseum brennt*), Inge Offermann (*Rien du tout*), James Rochfort (*Against Death*), Bernhard Schütz (*Die Probe*), Arndt Schwering-Sohnrey (*Muster*), Berndt Stübner (*Occupation*), Oona von Maydell (*Muster*), Sabine Wackernagel (*Muster*)

KAMERA / CINEMATOGRAPHY

Moritz Fehr (*Automatisierte Sprachanalyse zu psychologischen Zwecken*), Frank Meyer (*Big Business, Das Bildermuseum brennt, Die Probe, Die Siedlung, Esiod 2015, Muster, Occupation, Otjesd, Rien du tout, Silberhöhe, The Cast: Procession, The Fourth Wall, Von Gegenüber*), Rosario Romagnosi (*Rien du tout*), Arthur Zalewski (*The Making of Occupation*)

MONTAGE / EDITING

Eiko Grimberg (*Andenken*), Janina Herhoffer (*Against the Point of View, Esiod 2015, Muster, The Beginning. Living Figures Dying, The Fourth Wall*)

PRODUKTIONSLEITER / PRODUCTION MANAGER

Florence Alexandre (*Rien du tout*), Florian Brüning (*Esiod 2015*), Mark Gibbons (*The Fourth Wall*), Caroline Kirberg (*Muster*), Patrick Lambertz (*Die Probe*), Sylvia Loinjak (*Otjesd, Von Gegenüber*), Ernek Reder (*The Cast: Procession*), Holm Taddiken (*Big Business, Das Bildermuseum brennt, Occupation, Silberhöhe*)

PRODUZENTEN / PRODUCERS

Tracy Bass (*The Fourth Wall*), Florian Brüning (*Esiod 2015*), Pinky Ghundale (*The Fourth Wall*), Thomas Herberth (*Esiod 2015*), Gaëlle Jones (*Rien du tout*), Caroline Kirberg (*Muster*), Ute Leonhardt (*The Cast: Procession*), Christina Schachtschabel (*Otjesd*), Holm Taddiken (*Big Business, Das Bildermuseum brennt, Occupation, Silberhöhe*), Joachim von Vietinghoff (*Otjesd*)

DREHBUCH / SCRIPTWRITER

Leis Bagdach (*Reception, The Gentle Ones*), Maya Schweizer (*Metropolis, Report from China, Rien du tout*)

DRAMATURGIE / DRAMATURGY

Paolo Caffoni (*The Cast*), Berardo Carboni (*The Cast: Procession*), Eiko Grimberg (*Muster, P.O.V.*)

REGIEASSISTENZ / ASSISTANT DIRECTOR

Leis Bagdach (*Occupation, Sun Cinema Location*), Aurélio Cardenas (*Rien du tout*), David Dickson (*The Fourth Wall*), Rita Glória-Curvo (*Von Gegenüber*), Eiko Grimberg (*Sun Cinema Location*), Sabine Huzikiewiz (*Von Gegenüber*), Gesa Knolle (*Die Probe*), Alexandra Neuss (*Muster*), Lotte Schreiber (*Esiod 2015*), Dirk Waldeck (*Das Bildermuseum brennt*)

TON / SOUND

Nigel Batting (*The Fourth Wall*), René Blümel (*Big Business, Das Bildermuseum brennt*), Tobias Böhm (*Muster*), Brendan Crehan (*The Fourth Wall*), Moritz Fehr (*Automatisierte Sprachanalyse zu psychologischen Zwecken*), Reiner Gerlach (*Die Probe*), Alexander Heinze (*Von Gegenüber*), Dirk Sommer (*Silberhöhe*), Karim Soufi (*Rien du tout*), Herbert Verdino (*Esiod 2015*)

TONGESTALTUNG / SOUND DESIGN

Moritz Fehr (*Every Word You Say*), Maximilian Liebich (*Esiod 2015*), Niels Loewenhardt (*Das Bildermuseum brennt, Occupation*), Thomas Wallmann (*Afterimage, Das Bildermuseum brennt, Die Probe, Metropolis, Report from China, Muster, Ohne Titel [Rekonstruktion], Rien du tout, Sun Cinema Location, The Beginning. Living Figures Dying, The Fourth Wall, Von Gegenüber*)

MUSIK / MUSIC

Birke J. Bertelsmeier (*Esiod 2015*), Die Fremden (*Muster*), Matthias Pintscher (*Occupation*)

CHOREOGRAFIE / CHOREOGRAPHY

Alice Chauchat (*Esiod 2015*), Alexandre Roccoli (*Ohne Titel [Rekonstruktion]*)

BESETZUNG / CASTING

Miriam Locker (*Die Probe, Muster*), Lotte Schreiber (*Esiod 2015*)

SZENENBILD / PRODUCTION DESIGN

Carla Ehrlich (*Muster*), Imogen Hammond (*The Fourth Wall*), Anamarie Michnevich (*Die Probe*), Gianpaolo Rifino (*The Cast*), Renate Schmaderer (*Esiod 2015*), Arthur Zalewski (*Das Bildermuseum brennt*)

KOSTÜME / COSTUME DESIGN

Walter Barrotta (*Das Bildermuseum brennt*), Clara Camus (*Rien du tout*), Julia Cepp (*Esiod 2015*), Chat (*Occupation*), Katja Kirn (*Die Probe, Von Gegenüber*), Heather Mac Vean (*The Fourth Wall*), Julia Schiller (*Muster*), Andrea Sorrentino (*The Cast: Procession*)

HAAR UND MASKE / HAIR AND MAKE-UP

Gina Anderson (*The Fourth Wall*), Anja Heineman (*Die Probe*), Danielle Hooker (*The Fourth Wall*), Michael Käpernick (*Muster*), Kim Kemper (*Von Gegenüber*), Kiky von Rebental (*Esiod 2015*), Andrea Sorrentino (*The Cast: Procession*)

ATELIER MITARBEIT / STUDIO ASSISTANCE

Marisa Baptista (*Muster, Sun Cinema, The Fourth Wall*), Hedvig Berglind (*Orte unter Einfluss / Affected Places*), Monika Czyżyk (*P.O.V.*), Köken Ergun (*The Fourth Wall*), Lukas Hoffmann (*A Recovered Bone, Every Word You Say, Orte unter Einfluss / Affected Places, P.O.V.*), Dalibor Knapp (*The Cast*), Anamarie Michnevich (*Basler Podest*)

AUFTRAGGEBER / COMMISSIONS

Hamburger Kunsthalle (*Square*), Neuer Berliner Kunstverein (*P.O.V.*), Erste Group Bank AG – Art in Architecture project (*Esiod 2015*), Braunschweiger Kunstverein (*Every Word You Say*), MAXXI Rome (*The Cast*), dOCUMENTA (13) (*Muster*), British Council Istanbul – My City Project (*Sun Cinema*), Barbican Centre – Curve Commission (*The Fourth Wall*), skulptur projekte münster 07 (*Von Gegenüber*), CAC Brétigny, 4th Berlin Biennial (*Rien du tout*), Galerie Jocelyn Wolff (*Basler Podest*), 1st Moscow Biennial (*Otjesd*), Schrumpfende Städte (*Silberhöhe*), Kunst im Gefängnis e.V. (*Big Business*)

BILDNACHWEIS / IMAGE CREDITS

SCREEN

A   Claude-Nicolas Ledoux: *L'Architecture considerée sous le rapport de l'art, des moeurs et de la legislation, Vol. 1*, Paris: de l'impr. de H. L. Peronneau, 1804, Bibliothèque nationale de France.

B   Archiv Clemens von Wedemeyer / Clemens von Wedemeyer's archives.

C   Alhazen (al-Haitham): *Kitab al-Manazir (Book of Optics)*, ca. 1021, Sulimaniye Library (Fatih Collection), Istanbul, in: Hans Belting: *Florenz und Bagdad. Eine westöstliche Geschichte des Blicks*, München / Munich: C. H. Beck, 2008, S. / p. 112.

D   Vitruvius: *De architectura*, 1521, in: Hans Belting: *Florenz und Bagdad. Eine westöstliche Geschichte des Blicks*, München / Munich: C. H. Beck, 2008, S. / p. 259.

DATA BANK

A   BOA – Büro für offensive Aleatorik (Office for Offensive Aleatory Aesthetics), Auftraggeber / client: Henke und Schreieck Architekten, 2008, www.boanet.at / projekt / erste-campus

B   Rice + Lipka Architects: „The Library of Babel", in: Kate Bernheimer, Andrew Bernheimer: „Fairy-Tale Architecture", *Design Observer*, 2013, www.designobserver.com / feature / fairy-tale-architecture / 38273

C   *American Phrenological Journal*, Nr. / No. 22 (1855), S. / p. 17; auch / also: „Prospectus for the Octagon Settlement Company", 1856, in: *The Octagon Settlement Company, Kanzas, Containing Full Information for Inquirers*, New York: Fowler & Wells, 1856.

D   Archiv Clemens von Wedemeyer / Clemens von Wedemeyer's archives.

E   Archiv Clemens von Wedemeyer / Clemens von Wedemeyer's archives.

F   ZOOM visual project, Auftraggeber / client: Henke und Schreieck Architekten, 2011, www.zoomvp.at / wp-content / gallery / central-station / 02_c2012-zoom-vp_quartier-belvedere-_c26

CHURCH, PRISON, MUSEUM

A   Friedemann Schreiter: *Strafanstalt Waldheim: Geschichten, Personen und Prozesse aus drei Jahrhunderten*, Berlin: Ch. Links, 2014, S. / p. 75.

B   Michel Foucault: *Überwachen und Strafen. Die Geburt des Gefängnisses*, Frankfurt am Main: Suhrkamp, 1981, Abb. / Fig. 17.

C   JVA Waldheim, www.orte-der-repression.de / einrichtung. php?id=79

D   Michel Foucault: *Überwachen und Strafen. Die Geburt des Gefängnisses*, Frankfurt am Main: Suhrkamp, 1981, Abb. / Fig. 21.

E   Friedemann Schreiter: *Strafanstalt Waldheim: Geschichten, Personen und Prozesse aus drei Jahrhunderten*, Berlin: Ch. Links, 2014, S. / p. 39.

F   Sammlung / Collection Michel Hennin: *Estampes relatives à l'Histoire de France. Tome 102, Pièces 8789–8879, période: 1756–1757*, hier Nr. / here no. 8840, Bibliothèque nationale de France, département Estampes et photographie.

G   Hamburger Kunsthalle / bpk, Kupferstichkabinett / Department of Prints and Drawings, Foto / photo: Christoph Irrgang.

BACKSTAGE

A   Zeitungsausriss aus / clipping from *Le Monde*, November 2005, Archiv Clemens von Wedemeyer / Clemens von Wedemeyer's archives.

B   Zeitungsausriss aus / clipping from *TIME Magazine*, Jg. 170 / H. 24 (10. Dezember 2007), Vol. 170 / No. 24 (December 10, 2007), Archiv Clemens von Wedemeyer / Clemens von Wedemeyer's archives.

C   Presseamt Stadt Münster / Munster Press Relation Office.

D   John Nance, 1988, mit freundlicher Genehmigung des Fotografen / by courtesy of the photographer.

E   Zeitungsausriss aus / clipping from *Le Monde*, November 2005, Archiv Clemens von Wedemeyer / Clemens von Wedemeyer's archives.

F   Zeitungsausriss aus / clipping from *TIME Magazine*, Jg. 170 / H. 24 (10. Dezember 2007), Vol. 170 / No. 24 (December 10, 2007), Archiv Clemens von Wedemeyer / Clemens von Wedemeyer's archives.

TEXTNACHWEIS / TEXT CREDITS

SCREEN

„Sun Cinema, Mardin, Türkei, 2010", zuerst erschienen in: Barbara Büscher, Verena Elisabeth Eitel, Beatrix von Pilgrim (Hg.): *Raumverschiebung: Black Box <> White Cube*, Hildesheim: Olms, 2014, S. 155–160.

"Sun Cinema, Mardin, Turkey, 2010", first published in: Barbara Büscher, Verena Elisabeth Eitel, Beatrix von Pilgrim (eds.): *Raumverschiebung: Black Box <> White Cube*, Hildesheim: Olms, 2014, pp. 155–160.

CHURCH, PRISON, MUSEUM

„The Making of Big Business", zuerst erschienen in: Clemens von Wedemeyer: *Seven Films*, Santiago de Compostela / Leipzig: Xunta de Galicia / Spector Books, 2009, S. 91–96.

"The Making of Big Business", first published in: Clemens von Wedemeyer: *Seven Films*, Santiago de Compostela / Leipzig: Xunta de Galicia / Spector Books, 2009, pp. 91–96.

IMPRESSUM / COLOPHON

AUSSTELLUNG / EXHIBITION

Kuratorin / Curator
  Petra Roettig

Konzept / Concept
  Clemens von Wedemeyer,
  Petra Roettig

Wissenschaftliche Mitarbeit /
Curatorial Assistance
  Mechthild Achelwilm

Direktor / Director
  Hubertus Gaßner (bis 30.9.2016)
  Christoph Vogtherr (ab 1.10.2016)

Geschäftsführer / Managing Director
  Stefan Brandt

Assistenz Direktor / Assistance Director
  Daniel Koep

Sekretariat Direktor / Director's Office
  Olga Fallmeier

Assistenz Geschäftsführer /
Assistance Managing Director's Office
  Nora Kathmann

Sekretariat Geschäftsführer /
Managing Director's Office
  Christine Dunemann

Personalwesen / Personnel Office
  Anastasia Panagiotopulu,
  Ruth Neumann

Fundraising und Sponsoring /
Fundraising and Sponsoring
  Anuschka Lichtenhahn, Gesa Huget,
  Saskia Helin, Sonia Mahnkopf

Controlling und Finanzen /
Controlling and Finance
  Marco Smailus

Buchhaltung / Accounting
  Veronika Kossek

Kassenkoordination /
Coordination Cash Registers
  Jörg Reinholz

Sammlung Alte Meister /
Collection Old Masters
  Sandra Pisot

Sammlung 19. Jahrhundert /
Collection 19th Century
  Markus Bertsch

Sammlung Klassische Moderne /
Collection Modern Art
  Karin Schick

Sammlung Kunst der Gegenwart /
Collection Contemporary Art
  Brigitte Kölle, Petra Roettig

Kupferstichkabinett /
Prints and Drawings
  Andreas Stolzenburg

Bibliothek / Library
  Andrea Joosten, Ursula Fischer,
  Henrike Schröder, Monika Wildner

Archiv Kupferstichkabinett /
Archive Prints and Drawings
  Michaela Pens, Michael Schramm,
  Sören Schubert, Ursula Sdunnus

Restaurierung Graphik und
Photographie / Conservation Paper
and Photography
  Sabine Zorn

Buchbinderin / Bookbinding
  Anja Zuschke

Digitalisierungsprojekt /
Digitalisation Project
  David Klemm, Christoph Irrgang

Ausstellungskuratorin /
Exhibition Curator
  Annabelle Görgen-Lammers

Provenienzforschung und Historisches
Archiv / Provenance Research and
Historical Archive
  Ute Haug; Ulrike Saß, Anna Seidel
  (Projekte / Projects)

Wissenschaftliches Volontariat /
Curatorial Assistance
  Mechthild Achelwilm,
  Désirée de Chair, Judith Rauser

Sekretariat Sammlung /
Office Collections
  Ingrid Beckmann, Ursula Trieloff

Restaurierung und Kunsttechnologie /
Conservation and Art Technology
  Silvia Castro (Alte Meister /
  Old Masters), Eva Keochakian
  (19. Jahrhundert / 19th Century),
  Heike Schreiber (Klassische
  Moderne / Modern Art), Barbara
  Sommermeyer (Kunst der
  Gegenwart / Contemporary Art),
  Claartje van Haaften (Projekte /
  Projects)

Bildung und Vermittlung /
Learning and Visitor Experience
  Wybke Wiechell, Alke Vierck,
  Sophie Winckel, Ute Klapschuweit
  und das Team der freien Kunst-
  vermittler / and the team of freelance
  guides

Veranstaltungsmanagement und
Programmkoordination / Management
and Program Coordination
  Susanne Schatz,
  Philine Schomacher

Aufsichtsdienst / Museum Surveillance
  Margarethe Thams, das Team
  der Aufsichten und das Team der
  HRC Sicherheitsdienste / team
  of gallery guards and HRC Sicherheitsdienste GmbH

Kommunikation und Marketing /
Communication and Marketing
  Jan Metzler

Pressearbeit / Press Office
  Mira Forte, Julia Schmid

Öffentlichkeitsarbeit / Public Relations
  Martina Gschwilm

Besucherbüro / Visitor Services
  Anna Schröder-Weisel,
  Vilma Campestrin,
  Ulrike Heuer, Christine Gerdum,
  Anna-Lena Schuhmacher

Registrarabteilung und Ausstellungs-
koordination / Registrar's Department
and Exhibition Coordination
  Meike Wenck

Registrarabteilung /
Registrar's Department
  Konstanze Jäger, Kazusa Haii

Medientechnik / Media Technology
  Tobias Boner

Art Handling
  Jochen Möhle, Ulugbek Ahmedov,
  Sebastian Conrad, Peter
  Hochkamer, Karl-Heinz Schneider,
  Holger Schumacher, Gunther
  Maria Kolck und Team / and team

Gebäude und Technik /
Building and Technology
  Ralf Suerbaum

Haustechnik / Building Technology
  Wolfgang Ernst, Andreas Horn

Hausarbeiter / Assistance Caretaking
  Thomas Schmid

Hausmeisterei / Caretaking
  Volker Ruge und das
  Team der Reinigungskräfte /
  and the cleaning team

PUBLIKATION / PUBLICATION

Diese Publikation erscheint anlässlich der Ausstellung / This publication accompanies the exhibition

*Clemens von Wedemeyer.
Orte unter Einfluss / Affected Places*

Hamburger Kunsthalle,
Galerie der Gegenwart

30. September 2016 – 8. Januar 2017 /
September 30, 2016 – January 8, 2017

Hamburger Kunsthalle
Stiftung Öffentlichen Rechts
Glockengießerwall
20095 Hamburg
Deutschland / Germany
Tel. +49 (0)40 428131-200
Fax +49 (0)40 42854-3409
www.hamburger-kunsthalle.de

**HAMBURGER
KUNSTHALLE**

Mit freundlicher Unterstützung durch /
With the generous support of

STIFTUNG KUNSTFONDS

Hamburg | Kulturbehörde

Herausgegeben von / Edited by
Hubertus Gaßner,
Petra Roettig

Buchkonzeption / Book Concept
Clemens von Wedemeyer,
Christoph Gnädig

Redaktion / Editing
Christoph Gnädig

Gestaltungskonzept und Satz /
Design Concept and Typesetting
Fabian Bremer, Pascal Storz

Bildbearbeitung / Lithography
hausstætter berlin

Lektorat und Korrektorat /
Copyediting and Proofreading
(Deutsch / German)
Christoph Gnädig, Anne König

Lektorat und Korrektorat /
Copyediting and Proofreading
(Englisch / English)
John Middleton, Ames Gerould

Übersetzungen / Translations
Steven Black, Brian Currid,
Herwig Engelmann, Ariane Kossack,
John Middleton, Judith Rosenthal

Gesamtherstellung / Production
druckhaus köthen GmbH & Co. KG

Erschienen bei / Published by
Spector Books
Harkortstraße 10
04107 Leipzig
Deutschland / Germany
www.spectorbooks.com

Auslieferung / Distribution

Deutschland und Österreich /
Germany and Austria
GVA, Gemeinsame Verlagsauslieferung Göttingen GmbH & Co. KG
www.gva-verlage.de

Schweiz / Switzerland
AVA Verlagsauslieferung AG
www.ava.ch

Frankreich und Belgien /
France and Belgium
Interart Paris
www.interart.fr

Großbritannien / UK
Central Books Ltd
www.centralbooks.com

USA und Kanada / U.S. and Canada
RAM Publications + Distribution Inc.
www.rampub.com

Australien und Neuseeland /
Australia and New Zealand
Perimeter Distribution
www.perimeterdistribution.com

Andere Länder / Other countries
Motto Distribution
www.mottodistribution.com

Unter Berücksichtigung einer geschlechtergerechten Sprache – die grundsätzlich nicht möglich ist – und um die Lesbarkeit zu erleichtern, werden in diesem Buch weibliche und männliche Sprachformen verwendet, wobei immer alle (Gender-)Formen mitgemeint sind. / Considering gender-neutral language —which is not possible in principle— and in order to facilitate readability, in this book feminine (female) and masculine (male) forms of speech are used, whereas (but always) all forms are (also) essentially meant.

Erste Auflage / First edition
Printed in Germany

ISBN 978-3-95905-102-6